School-based Research

Education at SAGE

SAGE is a leading international publisher of journals, books, and electronic media for academic, educational, and professional markets.

Our education publishing includes:

- accessible and comprehensive texts for aspiring education professionals and practitioners looking to further their careers through continuing professional development

- inspirational advice and guidance for the classroom

- authoritative state of the art reference from the leading authors in the field

Find out more at: **www.sagepub.co.uk/education**

2nd Edition

School-based Research
A guide for education students

Edited by Elaine Wilson

$SAGE

Los Angeles | London | New Delhi
Singapore | Washington DC

Los Angeles | London | New Delhi
Singapore | Washington DC

SAGE Publications Ltd
1 Oliver's Yard
55 City Road
London EC1Y 1SP

SAGE Publications Inc.
2455 Teller Road
Thousand Oaks, California 91320

SAGE Publications India Pvt Ltd
B 1/I 1 Mohan Cooperative Industrial Area
Mathura Road
New Delhi 110 044

SAGE Publications Asia-Pacific Pte Ltd
3 Church Street
#10-04 Samsung Hub
Singapore 049483

Editor: James Clark
Assistant editor: Monira Begum
Project manager: Jeanette Graham
Assistant production editor: Thea Watson
Copyeditor: Rosemary Campbell
Proofreader: Sharon Cawood
Indexer: Anne Solomito
Marketing manager: Catherine Slinn
Cover design: Wendy Scott
Typeset by: C&M Digitals (p) Ltd, Chennai, India
Printed by MPG Books Group, Bodmin, Cornwall

First published 2013

Library of Congress Control Number: 2012938869

British Library Cataloguing in Publication data

A catalogue record for this book is available from the British Library

MIX
Paper from
responsible sources
FSC
www.fsc.org
FSC® C018575

ISBN 978-1-4462-4748-8
ISBN 978-1-4462-4749-5 (pbk)

CONTENTS

Section 4: Paradigms   285

Entries in **Bold** type in the text denote glossary entries.

FOREWORD

Most teachers, in my experience, want to improve; it is part of the professional self. They differ, of course, in the routes they choose to take towards this goal. In the search for insights into how they can continue to develop, some become critical readers of other people's research and ideas. But, eventually, many conclude that the best way of understanding their own practice, and that of the institutions in which they work, is to engage in some kind of research. This book is intended to help teachers who want to embark on that journey.

Looking back it is hard to believe that, less than 30 years ago, the idea of teachers researching their own practices was seen as controversial. Lawrence Stenhouse, who is widely recognized as the founding parent of teacher research, identified a number of objections to their involvement which were prevalent at that time. First, there were questions about 'the accuracy of teachers' self-reports' – 'teachers', some argued, 'do not know what they do'. Second, they were likely to be 'biased' – they had too much of an interest in the outcomes to be objective. Third, they were 'theoretically innocent'. And fourth, put bluntly, they lacked the time – they 'taught too much' to achieve the kind of intellectual distance research required (reported in Rudduck and Hopkins, 1985: 15–16).

This book is dedicated to the memory of Donald McIntyre and Jean Rudduck. Both were professors of education at Cambridge, and both were convinced that teachers had crucial roles to play in research; indeed they dedicated their lives to this cause. As central architects of the revolution in education which took place here at the turn of the millennium, they sought to harness the full weight of the University to this endeavour. Sadly, both died during 2007 (one of a heart attack and the other of cancer), but not before each, in their different way, had made major contributions to the development of research-based approaches in schools.

For McIntyre the key to educational progress lay in developing teachers' 'craft knowledge' (Brown and McIntyre, 1993). By this he meant the nexus of understandings which link teachers' knowledge of what to teach (their subject(s)), how to teach it (their pedagogical knowledge) and to whom (their understanding of their pupils). Researching these practices, rigorously and systematically, offered a way forward. In a series of action-based projects he explored ways of engaging with teachers and schools around *their* concerns and, crucially, in partnership with them.

Rudduck started in a similar place. Her early work supported teachers in a variety of research endeavours, most notably in relation to understanding how to implement changes to classroom practice (Rudduck, 1991). Over time, however, she began to shift her attention from a teacher-centred view of educational innovation towards a more pupil-centred one. Her last book, written with Donald McIntyre shortly before she died, explored the numerous ways in which pupils and teachers can work together to bring about practical changes in classroom conditions. It is a powerful testimony to the importance both of taking teachers seriously and of giving weight to 'pupil voice' (Rudduck and McIntyre, 2007).

But can the insights of teachers and their pupils count as a contribution to knowledge, the central canon around which universities are organised? Or should teachers just sit back and let others determine how they teach? Stenhouse was adamant that teachers had a central role to play – and that governments and policy-makers neglected them at their peril.

He defined 'research' as 'systematic and sustained enquiry, planned and self-critical, which is subject to public criticism and to empirical tests where these are appropriate' (Rudduck and Hopkins, 1985: 19). After three decades of teacher-led research his definition, and the challenges it implies, still rings true. If schools are to engage with their own futures in a planned and coherent way, they need the quiet but insistent voice of research. They need to invest in their own development by encouraging their members to acquire the basic tools – key ideas, key concepts and key methods.

As we move towards the vision of a research-based profession, there is quite a lot to learn and a great deal to fight for.

John Gray
Cambridge

ABOUT THE EDITOR

Elaine Wilson is a Senior Lecturer in Science Education at the Faculty of Education, and Fellow of Homerton College at the University of Cambridge.

She was a secondary school chemistry teacher in Bath and Cambridge and was awarded a Salters' Medal for Chemistry teaching while working at Parkside Community College in Cambridge.

Elaine teaches undergraduates and secondary science PGCE students, coordinates a 'blended learning' Science Education Masters course and helped set up the new EdD course at the Faculty of Education.

She has received two career awards for teaching in Higher Education, a University of Cambridge Pilkington Teaching Prize and a National Teaching Fellowship.

Elaine is currently working on teacher education reform and development, and is part of an international research project working with educators in Kazakhstan.

NOTES ON CONTRIBUTORS

Roland Chaplain was Senior Lecturer at the University of Cambridge, Faculty of Education. He has published books and papers related to stress and coping in schools (staff, managers and pupils), and their relationship to school effectiveness, particularly in respect of social behaviour. Related areas include stress and psychological distress among teachers, head teachers and pupils, managing pupil behaviour and school improvement. In 2006 he wrote *Challenging Behaviour* in collaboration with Dr Stephen Smith of the University of Florida, which utilized results from research in the USA and England in the application of behavioural and cognitive-behavioural approaches to develop self-regulation and problem solving in pupils. His latest book is *Managing Behaviour in the Primary Classroom*.

Christine Counsell is Senior Lecturer at the University of Cambridge, Faculty of Education, where she has run the history PGCE course for 10 years, and taught on Masters programmes. Christine taught history in state comprehensive schools, holding posts as Head of History, Head of Humanities and finally as a deputy Head in Bristol. As Advisory Teacher for Gloucestershire LEA and later as PGCE tutor for the University of Gloucestershire, she broadened her expertise into primary education. Her best-selling pamphlet, *Analytical and Discursive Writing at Key Stage 3* (1997) enshrined her passion for developing language and literacy through history. She has carried out in-service training and consultancy for primary and secondary teachers in over 80 local authorities and has been invited to address teachers and teacher educators all over the UK and Europe, including Cyprus, Estonia, Ireland, Italy, Malta, the Netherlands and Norway. Christine is editor of the Historical Association's journal, *Teaching History*. She has published widely in history education and teacher education and is currently researching the experience of school-based PGCE mentors.

Helen Demetriou has been a Research Associate at the Faculty of Education of the University of Cambridge since obtaining her PhD in developmental psychology from the Institute of Psychiatry, University of London in 1998. During this time, she has also lectured in developmental psychology at the University. Her research has included *Sustaining pupils' progress at Year 3* (for Ofsted); *Boy's performance in modern foreign languages* (for QCA); *Friendships and performance at transfer and transition* (for DfES); *Consulting pupils about teaching and learning* (ESRC-funded project); and *How young children talk about fairness* (internally funded). Helen is currently working with Elaine Wilson on a Gatsby-funded project: *Supporting opportunities for new teachers' professional growth*.

Michael Evans is Senior Lecturer in Education and Deputy Head of Faculty at the University of Cambridge. He has extensive experience in foreign language teacher education and in the teaching and supervision of doctoral students in language education. He directs the MPhil in Research in Second Language Education. He is currently co-director of a national study of the impact of government initiatives on the provision and practice of language teaching at KS3 in England. He has published on a number of second language education topics, drawing on empirical research conducted in secondary schools. He is co-author of *Modern Foreign Languages: Teaching School Subjects 11–19* (London, RoutledgeFalmer, 2007).

Alison Fox is Senior Lecturer at the University of Leicester. She is an experienced researcher who has worked on a wide range of projects at both the University of Cambridge and at the Open University, including inter-university collaborations, commissioned research, and work funded by a charitable trust.

Ros McLellan taught secondary mathematics and psychology for eight years prior to joining the Faculty of Education at the University of Cambridge in 2000. Since then, she has worked as a researcher on two externally funded research projects based in Faculty: 'Raising Boys' Achievement' (2000 to 2004) and 'Subject Leadership in Creativity in Secondary Design and Technology' (2005 to present). She was recently appointed a Lecturer in Teacher Education & Development/Pedagogical Innovation. Ros enjoys working collaboratively with practitioners to develop and refine strategies that make a real difference to teaching and learning in the classroom. Her research interests include achievement motivation (the focus of her PhD thesis), creativity, gender and achievement, and student attitudes and self-concepts.

Kris Stutchbury is a Senior Lecturer in Education and Director of the PGCE course at the Open University. She has 20 years of experience of teaching in school and was a Head of Science for 12 years. Kris's interests include ethics, assessment and approaches to educational change.

Keith S. Taber is a Reader at the University of Cambridge, Faculty of Education. He qualified as a teacher of chemistry and physics in 1982. He taught science in comprehensive schools, and developed a taste for classroom research when he registered for a diploma course for science teachers. He undertook an action research project on girls' under-representation in physics in a school where he taught for his Masters degree dissertation. After moving into further education as a physics and chemistry lecturer, he registered for part-time doctoral study, exploring how his students' ideas developed during their college course. After completing his doctorate, Keith moved to Cambridge to join the Faculty of Education, where he works with those preparing to be teachers; with experienced teachers enquiring into aspects of teaching and learning; and with research students training to be educational researchers. His book, *Classroom-based Research and Evidence-based Practice: A Guide for Teachers*, is also published by SAGE.

Paul Warwick is a Lecturer in Education at the University of Cambridge. He is a member of the Early Years and Primary Masters PGCE team, focusing on courses in science, ICT, DT and researching practice. He is a convenor of the Teacher Education Special Interest Group at the Faculty and makes contributions to various MEd courses.

Mark Winterbottom is a Lecturer in Science Education in the Faculty of Education, University of Cambridge. He previously taught in secondary schools. He teaches on undergraduate and Masters level programmes, including the Postgraduate Certificate of Education and the science MEd course. His current research interests include teacher education, ICT and the classroom environment. His publications include *The Non-Specialist Handbook: Teaching Biology to Key Stage 4* (Hodder), and *Teaching and Learning Primary Science with ICT* (Open University Press).

INTRODUCTION: WHY SHOULD TEACHERS DO SCHOOL-BASED RESEARCH?

Teachers constantly reflect on classroom interactions and question why students behave and perform in a particular way. However, to understand why things happen in the way they do necessitates standing back and taking time to deliberate more explicitly about practice. This requires the conscious management of thinking and activity through setting aside time to:

- learn about theories or codified explicit knowledge
- engage in activities and make explicit tacit knowledge
- justify and develop new knowledge
- subject new ideas to the critical scrutiny of other practitioners.

Types of knowledge about teaching and learning

Knowledge about teaching and learning is constantly developing and evolving and can be classified into three broad categories.

Firstly, we have explicit knowledge that has been codified formally using a system of symbols and language which can be easily communicated or diffused. This codified academic knowledge may be object-based or rule-based. For example, we have come to understand the nature of the chemical bond and know a fair amount about our own human development, and we were probably introduced to this in secondary school science lessons. This sort of knowledge is found in textbooks. Furthermore, it is related to our ongoing intellectual development and progresses through a hierarchy leading to greater levels of abstraction. In a school context, codified knowledge can also take the form of organization-specific, rule-based information such as records, correspondence and manuals.

There is also a vast educational research literature of well-grounded propositions which, although abstract in nature, have the potential value to be highly applicable in classrooms. The second form of knowledge which is tacit, practical and implicit is used by teachers to perform their job and make sense of classrooms. This knowledge is hard to verbalize because it is expressed through action-based skills, is difficult to make explicit or to represent in a textual form because it is largely acquired informally through participation in teaching situations, and it is often so 'taken for granted' that teachers are unaware of its influence on their behaviour. This knowledge is context-specific and is not easily codified but nonetheless also plays a key role in school-based practices and activities. The third form of knowledge is cultural knowledge which is also context-specific and is associated with the shared assumptions and beliefs that are used to perceive and explain classroom reality and to assign value and significance to new information and ideas. The curriculum is imbued with cultural values and the translation of this into teaching episodes will also be value-laden with the thoughts behind the choice of words, tone, storylines, and other elements which are not explicitly articulated but can be picked up by learners nonetheless.

Donald McIntyre argued that there is a gap between the first type of codified research knowledge and the second type – teachers' everyday practice knowledge. McIntyre suggested that this gap was created because the kind of knowledge that research can offer is of a very different kind from the knowledge that classroom teachers need to use. Such codified research knowledge is not easily translated into practical knowledge because each classroom context is different and what works for one teacher, or in one school, or with one class, or on one occasion, may not translate directly into action in another. This is because each school is unique, each classroom different, hour by hour and each teacher has their own

> individual 'schemata' for recognizing classes or pupils or situations as being similar to others they have dealt with before, each schema incorporating a range of more or less remembered individual cases, and on corresponding repertoires of actions that have seemed to work in some circumstances in the past. (McIntyre, 2005: 359)

In other words, teachers make judgements based on their beliefs and values, and these have developed through a range of experience. The role of the teacher/researcher is to try to bridge the gap between codified research knowledge and the everyday 'craft' knowledge of teachers. So researching practice is about challenging beliefs and values through encountering new ideas from other teachers and codified research knowledge, so that well informed judgements can be made in classrooms which ultimately increases the well-being and attainment of every student in each class. Box I.1 uses Donald McIntyre's (2005) words to summarize the reasons why teachers ought to engage in school-based research. These words are even more pertinent as 'craft knowledge' dominates educational policy 'reform' at the time of writing this second edition.

Box I.1

'A first suggested way of dealing with the gap between codified research knowledge and "craft" knowledge starts from the understanding that the two contrasting kinds of knowledge at the ends of the spectrum both have inevitable limitations but also have considerable and mutually complementary strengths. This first way of dealing with the gap is in my view well conceived but has not received the attention it deserves.

Three elements are necessarily involved in this way of dealing with the gap. First, there has to be a recognition – which we shall assume here – that the characteristics of classroom teachers' craft knowledge and of research-based knowledge, as we have described them, are in no way inappropriate but, on the contrary, are in both cases necessary for their purpose, and also mutually complementary in potentially highly fruitful ways.

Second, realization of the potential value of their complementarity depends upon some movement, in both cases, from the extreme ends of the continuum. Third, time, energy and helpful procedures are needed to foster effective dialogue, exploring relationships between their two kinds of knowledge, including the development of new syntheses of the two kinds of knowledge. When productive, this process of dialogue – which might be either metaphorical or literal – should culminate in classroom teachers themselves investigating the merits of research-based proposals by testing them through action research in their own teaching. This approach is based therefore on the premise that research can be helpful in improving the quality of classroom teaching, but equally on a second premise that research cannot be helpful except through quite complex processes culminating in classroom teachers engaging in dialogue with research-based proposals.' (McIntyre, 2005: 362–3)

Reflecting as learning

Professional learning and teacher knowledge is embodied, contextual and embedded in practice. Teacher learning takes place at several levels of conscious awareness. In day-to-day classroom interactions, teachers draw on their intuitive tacit knowledge gained through previous experience. This 'hot action' is coloured by feelings and reactions and relies on an instant response, building up 'knowledge in action'. More measured reactive or reflective learning takes place through interpretation of the situations accompanied by short reactive reflection which might take place at the end of a teaching episode or in conversation with another teacher.

Changes in practice occur through deliberative learning. This requires a more conscious management of thought and activity through setting aside time to learn about and engage in activities which are directed towards a clear workplace goal. Deliberative action or 'knowledge for action' (Table I.1) is what takes place during systematic classroom-based research (Wilson and Demetriou, 2007).

Table I.1   Teacher judgements (Wilson & Demetriou, 2007)

Implicit/Tacit Judgements	Reactive/Reflective Judgements	Deliberative Judgements
'Hot' action Judgements based on intuition	Judgements linked to actions and the classroom environment	'Cooler' action Judgements based on deep understanding of the dynamics of teacher/student relationships and the contextual features
Mainly emotional responses	Respond to affective and social contexts	Cognitive domains also involved
Knowledge in action	Knowledge of action	Knowledge for action
'Act' like a teacher		'Think like' a teacher
Recognize patterns	Rapid interpretation	Review involving discussion/analysis and deliberative decision making
Instant response	Intuitive response	
Routine action	Routines punctuated by rapid decisions	Planned action with progress reviews
Some awareness of the situation	Implicit monitoring	Conscious monitoring of thought and activity
	Short reactive reflection	Self-management Evaluation

Researching practice

To research classroom practice involves searching for information, and in the process creating new knowledge about particular teaching situations. In this way, teachers' personal tacit knowledge is extended through their daily experiences both inside and outside class-rooms. However, for this tacit knowledge to be made explicit so that it can be shared with other practitioners, it must be articulated through dialogue and reflection and presented in a way that is meaningful to other practitioners and researchers, so that it will contribute to our understanding about how children learn and develop or better understand how schools function. Alternatively, this knowledge might involve the development of new ideas about innovative teaching approaches which might inform what other teachers do.

Making more informed judgements through classroom-based research

Teachers exercise judgements when they choose how to act and decide what to do in their classrooms. These judgements may be intuitive or explicit, often have important consequences and are not only driven by rational thinking but to a large degree by human experiences and emotions. Moreover, this professional judgement is always value-laden and not based simply on technical judgement. Becoming involved in classroom-based research involves standing back and identifying personal values so that these are taken into account when interpreting what is seen in classrooms. In other words, we learn to be teachers through the growing capacity to make appropriate judgements in the changing, and often unique, circumstances that occur in our different classrooms. However, with time, teachers become more familiar with classroom situations and there is a danger that 'habit', rather than thoughtful deliberation can dominate actions. Having the opportunity to stand back and think about an issue or problem can aid sensitivity and wisdom to complex classroom interaction.

Researching practice presents the opportunity to problem-solve more intelligently, through drawing on existing research findings and by using rigorous methods to collect evidence which helps clarify our thinking. Experiences of participating in an informed way offer the teacher for whom teaching has become a routine a sense of freedom, of meaning, of worthiness and consequently increased self-esteem. Therefore, generating practice-based knowledge can often be liberating for the individual teacher while not necessarily being directly transferable to other classrooms. It could be argued that the real value of classroom-based research is in the process of building the capacity to reflect critically on our own practice so that more students learn, and better because teachers understand the process.

Reflection and reflexivity

Reflection-in-action and the term *reflective practitioner* were first used by Donald Schön in 1983. Schön described how reflection-in-action could be used by professionals as a tool to improve their practice. He argued that reflection-in-action involves teachers retrospectively analysing their own actions and attempting to determine how these actions influence classroom events.

The notion of *reflexivity* goes further and requires more deliberative thinking. In other words, reflexivity is an interactive process that takes into consideration the relationship between the teacher, the students and the learning context, and also examines the underlying assumptions and priorities that shape interaction within a given time, place and situation. Furthermore, the process can also be transformative, in that, by definition, it requires a teacher to make a major shift in their understanding of classrooms. It is also integrative in that it involves interrogating taken-for-granted topics such as gender, policy or power. At its heart is the idea that practice is rooted in the same skills of critical thinking and sceptical inquiry that underlie most scientific and critical disciplines. Finally, it is certainly a problematic concept because it is always difficult to think reflexively and to challenge one's own presuppositions in relation to seemingly fundamental topics like assessment and gender.

To sum up, reflection is related to self and improving future practice through a retrospective analysis of action. Even in the reflection-in-action process, reflection is post facto, relating to completed stages and analysing them before taking the next step.

Reflection is future-focused in that it seeks to improve practice through an understanding of the relative successes and failures of previous events. However, it remains connected to the past focusing on completed stages: reflection takes the form of a cumulative body of knowledge that can then be used to improve practice. Although reflection influences the development of reflexive practice, there are profound differences. Being reflexive involves a teacher also being proactive through explicitly requiring the re-evaluation of assumptions and priorities that shape classroom interactions.

Reflexivity can be used to provide insight into priorities before the teacher reacts inappropriately. Reflexive practice in this manner can have an immediate impact in improving practice, as practitioners are able to incorporate new insights into each interaction. Hence, one key difference relates to when the process of introspection takes place. In reflection, it takes place after an interaction, whereas the reflexive process incorporates interactive introspection into each interaction.

Creating new knowledge about teaching and learning

In published educational literature about teaching and learning, the direction taken by professional researchers seems to follow two basic approaches. In simple terms, the first is research on education which is concerned with understanding how children learn and develop. This research is carried out through both empirical and theoretical studies and the outcome of this work is published in educational journals and textbooks.

Secondly, and equally important to the classroom practitioner is classroom-based research which uses ideas often generated via knowledge created through empirical and theoretical work, which is then used to inform what teachers do in their specific classrooms.

Research that contributes to understanding

Professor Neil Mercer, at the University of Cambridge, is a very experienced and prolific educational researcher, and in the following extract from an interview with the author he explains the rationale for a recent research project he undertook, which contributed to our understanding of how children learn through the use of dialogue.

> we realized that we wanted to know whether the kind of claims that were becoming common, based on Vygotsky's research back in the '30s, about the relationship between social interaction and children's cognitive development, were justified. It seemed to us that there wasn't actually any empirical evidence to show that Vygotsky's claim that children's interactions, with adults especially, and other people, shape the way they think. It seemed plausible and sensible, but was there any strong evidence? And we thought, well, we should try and look at whether there is, by setting up some sort of conditions in which we would say, well, children are given a special quality of interaction, a certain quality of interaction. We will then see if that affects what they learn and how well they understand things. And we will compare them systematically with children who are just going about life in a sort of ordinary way. So we had that theoretical interest – was Vygotsky right about the relationship between what he called the intra-mental or psychological, and the intermental or social? (Mercer interview, 2007)

The outcome of this particular research project has been published in a very influential book, *Words and Minds* (Mercer, 2000) – in other words, it has now become explicit, codified knowledge which is considered to be essential subject knowledge for aspiring teachers.

Creating practical knowledge based on an intervention

In a different research project, Professor Mercer and Dr Lyn Dawes worked together on a classroom-based intervention in which teachers introduced group work to investigate what would happen if students were given more opportunity to engage in dialogue. Professor Mercer describes the research rationale for this practical-based, knowledge-generating project:

> We also were motivated by some practical questions, which was that people were concerned about the quality of groupwork in school, when children work together. One lot were saying 'groupwork's great', while another lot of people were saying 'it seems to be a bit of a waste of time. They should be sitting more and listening to teacher and so on, getting a lot more out of it'. And we thought, can we show that if you set up groupwork in a certain

structured, organized way, it achieves certain sorts of goals, that you can say make it worthwhile? (Mercer interview, 2007)

The outcomes of both projects are published in the educational literature and while both projects are very relevant to classroom teaching, the work remains largely inaccessible to most school-based teachers.

Part of the process of teachers accessing this literature is to attempt to bridge the gap between such important codified knowledge and teachers' tacit everyday knowledge.

Teachers creating new knowledge about teaching and learning

Teachers can also create new knowledge which will be invaluable to them personally and to other practitioners in similar educational contexts. In the process of undertaking such research, a teacher will also come to better understand the dynamics of their classroom.

Finally, a further concern is the perceived imprecise nature of research undertaken by teachers. Teachers themselves often believe, together with other critics of small-scale qualitative studies, that the only legitimate research is large-scale and quantitative, seeking clear-cut conclusions and a steer for future strategies and policies.

In summary: Teachers develop criticality as their theoretical knowledge increases, and become more expert as their pedagogical skills increase. Thus it is important for teachers to be able to integrate **theory** and practice as they relate to curriculum, teaching practice, and assessment knowledge in the areas that are the focus for professional learning. Teaching is a complex activity in which moment-by-moment decisions are shaped by teachers' beliefs and theories about what it means to be effective. Theoretical understandings give coherence to these decisions.

How this book will help

Written by members of the PGCE M-level teaching team who cross the boundaries between academic research and classroom teaching as part of their role as teacher educators, each author has been a classroom teacher and so understands the complexity and tensions of being in the classroom from firsthand experience, but also contributes to the generation of academic codified research knowledge.

This book is aimed at beginning teachers involved in classroom research as part of their M-level initial teacher education, as well as serving teachers completing Masters courses. Our aim is to try to demystify the research process so that teachers can systematically research their classrooms in a rigorous way. To this end, we have illustrated the principles by exemplifying each stage using existing M-level and expert researchers' published work set in school contexts.

Section 1: Using existing research to understand and plan school-based research

Chapter 1: Becoming a reflexive teacher

Chapter 2: Refining a research focus and asking questions

Chapter 11: What data is available about the school context?

Chapter 4 : Researching primary school classrooms

Chapter 3: Using and reviewing literature

Section 2: Carrying out and reporting on classroom-based research

Chapter 5: Research design: methodology

Chapter 6: Doing the right things and doing things right: ethical considerations

Chapter 7: Data-collecting methods

Chapters 9 and 10: Analysing textual data

Chapter 8: Handling data

Chapters 11 and 12: Analysing numerical data

Chapter 13: Writing about the research

Section 3: Methodologies

Section 4: Paradigms

Chapter 14: What is action research?

Chapter 15: How to do action research

Chapter 16: The case study

Chapter 17: Building theory from data: grounded theory

Chapter 18: Beyond positivism: 'scientific' research into education

Chapter 19: Interpretivism: meeting our selves in research

Figure 1.1   Book layout

The structure of the book

Section 1 is about critically engaging with the existing research literature and planning classroom-based research. Chapter 1 introduces the idea of becoming a reflexive teacher and guides the novice researcher through the process of critically reading existing literature. Chapter 2 provides examples using PGCE M-level work. Chapter 3 discusses how to review literature so that you can produce a literature review. The new Chapter 4 in this edition includes examples from primary school classrooms.

Section 2 is about carrying out and reporting on classroom-based research. Chapter 5 introduces methodology but from a research design perspective and in terms of finding the best methods to answer your question. Later on, when you come to write a thesis, you can extend your understanding of other possible methodologies through reading Chapters 14–17 in Section 3, which look in depth at action research, using case studies and grounded theory. There is a new ethics chapter (Chapter 6) in this edition. Chapter 7 summarizes the limitations and strengths of each data collection method and Chapter 8 considers how to handle and analyse data. Chapters 9 and 10 deal with qualitative data, which is mainly in the form of words, and Chapters 11 and 12 look at quantitative data which is mainly in the form of numbers. Chapter 14 provides advice on the difficult task of writing about your work. Section 4 builds on the idea of paradigms.

Second edition

In this new edition we have added new chapters, updated certain sections and added new references to illustrate the points being made.

In Section 1, as well as updating Chapters 2 and 3, we have added a new Chapter 4 about researching primary school classrooms. This chapter is written by two primary phase experts, Paul Warwick and Roland Chaplain, and will make the book more useful for primary phase teachers too.

In Section 2 we have split up Chapters 5 and 6 into research methods and ethics. Kris Stutchbury's ethics chapter will strengthen this important area and help teachers to do the right thing at the planning stages as well as doing things right as they collect data in classrooms. Chapters 7 and 8 have been updated and there is a new updated version of Mark Winterbottom's chapter using contextual valued-added data as a background to understanding basic statistics. Chapter 13 has a new section on how to transform a thesis into a research paper.

In Section 3 there is a new chapter (14) which defines precisely what action research is, with Chapter 15 explaining how to do action research in a classroom.

Section 1

USING EXISTING RESEARCH TO UNDERSTAND AND PLAN SCHOOL-BASED RESEARCH

This section is about clarifying the purpose and direction of school-based research. The section starts with Chapter 1 setting out the rationale for why teachers ought to engage in school-based research and then follows in Chapter 2 with a guide to identifying, refining and narrowing a research focus. Chapter 3 helps the reader to find and read literature critically and then explains how to write this up in the form of a literature review. The final chapter is a new chapter about researching primary classrooms.

CHAPTER 1

BECOMING A REFLEXIVE TEACHER

Elaine Wilson

Chapter overview

This chapter will start off by arguing that successful teaching is about positive interaction, but that being an effective teacher is also about engaging critically with ideas and being aware of personal values. This requirement to be critical is illustrated using an often 'taken for granted', common sense and seemingly unproblematic system of labelling children by ability which is highly prevalent in the UK at the time of writing. The notion of being critical is explored using ability as a context and by looking at three seminal papers which discuss this notion.

Becoming a teacher involves more than just being 'told what to do', developing skills or mimicking other teachers. Therefore, reflecting *on* and *in* classrooms is an important part of becoming a teacher and is the essence of researching practice. Through the process of researching classroom practice, teachers come to recognize the depth and quality of their individual and collective expertise. Writing about this research is a way of articulating, sharing and examining practice which will also extend knowledge about teaching.

Teaching is about interaction

Teaching is an action which firstly aims to bring about learning, secondly takes account of where the learner is at, and thirdly has regard for the nature of that which has to be learnt. Therefore, teaching chemistry is different from teaching swimming; teaching how to ride a bicycle is different from teaching how to be virtuous. Each activity requires a different knowledge base on the part of the teacher and a different approach to helping students learn. Indeed, it is difficult to justify an action which disregards either the state of readiness of a learner or the nature of the subject matter as teaching.

> The lecture on a complex scientific topic which pays no regard to the level of understanding of the audience could hardly be called teaching. (Pring, 2000: 23)

Consequently, it seems to be the case that obtaining information about the state of readiness of the learner is as important as having extensive subject-specific knowledge. Furthermore, the three components of teaching are more likely to be realized through reflecting *in* and *on* actual classrooms, by teachers finding out about learners in those classrooms and through the subsequent adoption of appropriate approaches to bridge the knowledge gap between learner and teacher.

Box 1.1

Teaching therefore is the conscious effort to bridge the gap between the state of mind of the learner and the subject matter (the public forms of knowledge and understanding) which is to be learnt, and as such the teacher's expertise lies in understanding both.

It is possible for a teacher to use a wide range of activities, for example instruction, questioning, arranging practical experiences or structuring the classroom in a particular way, as long as students learn what the teacher intended.

Therefore, becoming a teacher initially involves questioning how expert classroom teachers:

1 decide on how to bring about learning
2 ensure that the chosen activities are relevant to the kind of learning to be brought about
3 ensure that these activities are relevant to the state of mind and motivation of the learner.

However, teachers do not act on their own. They are part of a larger enterprise, and their authority derives from their participation in communicating to another generation the public understandings and procedures we have inherited. Consequently, teachers ought to be aware of the origins of their specific area of public understanding and how the procedures in operation have come about.

Educational discourse

To engage in dialogue with other teachers, parents and students involves using educational **discourse**, that is, the way in which we talk about educational practice. However, educational discourse, like other forms of specialist discourse, is constructed by the specialist group and serves the interests of the particular group. In some situations, where such discourse remains unchallenged, it comes to be perceived and experienced by groups as though it offers an explanation of a natural, shared process or common-sense wisdom. An example of this is pupil grouping in secondary schools where the common practice is to group students according to 'ability'. In this case, 'ability' has become a 'common-sense' concept that in the UK is seen as a natural way of talking about children. However, there are those who dispute this – for example, Bourne and Moon (1995) argue that although we have words such as intelligence and ability, this 'does not mean that they exist any more than the unicorn does'. Talking about ability seems a natural way of talking and so people do not normally challenge this idea, although there is considerable scope for confusion. For instance, Hart et al. (2004) pose the following questions:

- When young people are identified as 'more able' or 'less able' than others, are we saying something about innate intelligence or the inherent capacity to learn?
- Are we implying a fixed or stable difference in degree between those deemed more able and those deemed less able?
- Or are we simply saying something about differences in their current ability to perform certain tasks, their observable ability to do certain things – like reading or mathematical calculations – according to agreed criteria?

Furthermore, if it is important that teaching activities are related to the state of mind and readiness of our students to learn, ought we not examine this 'common-sense' idea of 'ability' more closely? To do this may require us to open our minds to new ideas, to become a reflexive teacher.

Becoming a reflexive teacher

Reflexivity is an interactive process which takes into consideration the relationship between the teacher, the students and the learning context, and also examines the underlying assumptions and priorities that shape interaction within a given time, place and situation. In other words, a reflexive teacher can stand back and examine the underlying beliefs and values which are informing decision-making and actions in classroom situations (see Figure 1.1). These 'hidden' beliefs and values influence our interpretation of 'grey, common-sense' areas such as ability labelling, but it is the ability to be reflexive that will enable us to look at situations, ask further questions and find alternate interpretations.

Challenging 'common-sense' ideas

A feature of common sense is its changing content. What is common sense at one time may no longer be so at another; what is not known at one time might become part of the unquestioned folklore later. On the other hand, common-sense understanding also includes beliefs which seem undeniable, particularly in relation to the physical, personal and social worlds that we live in. To differentiate between ideas which might be classified as part of an indispensable framework within which we identify and think about the physical and social world, and the second category in which ideas are part of a shared discourse of unquestioned beliefs about education, we need to test out these ideas. Teacher-led, classroom-based research may provide an authentic way of testing out such ideas. Pring (2000: 84) argues that classroom-based research 'percolates down to the unquestioned assumptions of everyday life' and that the 'education of common sense' lies in the acquisition of a questioning and critical approach to ideas which appear to be accepted uncritically. Moreover, this framework of ordinary language, together with the accompanying beliefs about the world of education, provides both the starting point and the point of application of existing theoretical knowledge about teaching. In other words, to try to address Hart's questions, we must recognize that ideas emerge from different disciplines and that different theoretical accounts help us to arrive at a clearer understanding of the various perspectives held.

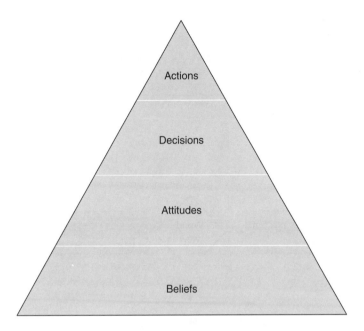

Figure 1.1   Becoming self-aware

Box 1.2   Establishing your world view

How you try to understand the world around you will colour what you consider to be evidence. Searle's big question below brings this point across well:

> How can we square the self-conception of ourselves as mindful, meaning-creating, free, rational, etc., agents with a universe that consists entirely of mindless, meaningless, unfree, non-rational, brute physical particles? (Searle, 2007: 5)

Searle's question confronts us with ideas that we don't usually stop to think about in the rush of everyday life. Nonetheless, these 'hidden' views influence how we think about complex issues and raise further questions. What is your world view? How does your world view influence how you behave in your everyday and professional life? How will you study the world? Are the rules for studying the natural or social world the same?

Knowledge is objective	Knowledge is constructed
• Objects are independent of our perspective. • Knowledge is accumulated through measurement.	• We all see things from different perspectives. • Knowledge is constructed through social interaction.

Figure 1.2   What is your world view?

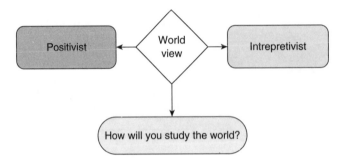

Figure 1.3   Positivist or interpretivist?

Using existing research literature

A trawl of educational literature about teaching will illustrate just how complex class-rooms are and the diverse ways in which research about them is conducted. In some work, people are the 'objects of science' where the researchers attempt to draw generalized and causal explanations. In other work, researchers try to explain what is happening through interpreting the world in their own personal ways. Understanding human beings, and thus researching into what they do and how they behave, calls upon many different methods, each making complex assumptions about what it means to explain behaviours and personal and social activities.

Furthermore, all forms of research are informed by underlying theoretical perspectives. Each of us has a theoretical perspective, even though this may not always be immediately apparent. When we read experts' work, we ought to be aware of the theoretical perspectives informing their viewpoint and appreciate the methods used to collect the evidence, interpret findings and draw conclusions. The various methods used will make claims to generating knowledge about aspects of the area of study, but each method will have a different role, position and purpose. Accordingly, work published from disparate studies will need different types of critical appraisal, should be brought together and interrelated with great care, and will need to be selected and combined in response to the kind of question being asked.

Critical reading activity

In this section, examples of papers representing three different theoretical perspectives to pupil grouping are used to illustrate the points made in the previous section. This chapter will serve as an introduction to theoretical perspectives which will be explored in more detail later in the book. Table 1.1 summarizes the approaches used by the three theoretical perspectives drawn on in the reading activity. This activity will also help you to read educational research critically.

Table 1.1   Comparing three papers from different theoretical perspectives based on ideas about ability grouping

Type	Empirical studies		Theoretical study
Paper	**1. Wiliam and Bartholomew (2004)**	**2. Boaler, Wiliam and Brown (2000)**	**3. Cremin and Thomas (2005)**
Aim	To investigate the influence of ability grouping on student progress	To investigate the experiences of pupils in ability groups	To challenge the idea that comparison of students is a major factor in the alienation and exclusion experienced by students in schools
Stance of the researcher	Analysing the outcomes of teaching so the researcher is distanced from the subject of the research	Observing in classrooms, so involved in and aware of the students' experience	Completely removed from actual schools approaching the issue from a theoretical stance
Type of reasoning	*Deductive:* that is the conclusions are reached by using 'factual' data, such as student examination performance. Therefore, if the premises are true, i.e. test scores, then the conclusions must also be true	*Inductive:* that is the premise of the argument, the students' views, support the inferred conclusions that there is disaffection and polarization among students	*Inductive:* the argument that self-comparison of each student and the endorsement of such a comparison by schools support the conclusion that students are segregated and therefore feel alienated and excluded in schools
Research plan	Longitudinal study over four years following the progress of a large sample of students moving through KS3 testing and through to GCSE examinations	Part of a longer study. This work focuses on the experiences of Y8 students moving into Y9 and beyond	Historical account of contrastive judgements and the presentation of a theoretical model to account for the root of difficulty in schools

(Continued)

Table 1.1   (Continued)

Type	Empirical studies		Theoretical study
Paper	1. Wiliam and Bartholomew (2004)	2. Boaler, Wiliam and Brown (2000)	3. Cremin and Thomas (2005)
Methods used and analysis	Large-scale questionnaire, using 955 students in six schools. Information collected about: socio-economic status of parents, pupil outcome data for KS3 tests and GCSE examinations. Results analysed using statistical methods to investigate correlations	Classroom observation of lessons and questionnaire about student attitudes and beliefs about lessons. Interviews with pairs of students. Data is analysed and ascribed properties related to types identified from observation and students' responses	Review of existing literature to support a theoretical model
Theoretical perspective	The world exists in objectively knowable natural law-abiding reality	The human world is socially constructed	Society organizes itself in oppressive ways and should be transformed
Ideas about the nature of knowledge	Things exist as meaningful entities; they have truth and meaning residing within them and can be measured	Knowledge and therefore meaningful reality are constructed in and out of interaction between humans	Research knowledge serves the interests of particular groups

Activity 1.1   Tips for reading the text

As you read the work, you will find that some parts of the text contain critical, conceptual or causal arguments which should be read very carefully and repeatedly if necessary; others contain illustrative materials and empirical elaborations which can be read more rapidly.

Annotate the text as you read it, marking the progression, twists and turns of the argument as it unfolds. You can devise your own stenographic system (arrows, stars, circling, underlining, etc.) to highlight in a consistent and economical manner the main definitions, logical turning points, conclusions and implications. Don't highlight too much text as this will be unhelpful.

Pay attention to passages that confuse. It may be, as you begin to read educational research literature, that the terms or language used by an author may seem confusing, or that the writing may be impenetrable. With patience and perseverance, you will come to be able to read texts critically, but this will take a bit more time than reading prose that is written to be more accessible. Note down the source of confusion. Is there a key term being used in an unfamiliar or unclear way? If so, revisit the beginning of the text (or any other

(Continued)

Activity 1.1   (Continued)

passages that set up the framework of the argument) to see if there are helpful definitions.

Try untangling complex syntax to see if the writer's meaning becomes clear (and then, having learned a bit about the writer's habits, apply what you know to unravel other difficult passages). Ignoring difficult vocabulary or passages will likely leave you unclear about the author's overall thesis.

Use whatever devices (tables, lists, bullets, diagrams, etc.) give you the best synoptic and synthetic view of the piece you have read. Try to represent the major argument in another form, perhaps as a diagram. Your reading notes will be an invaluable self-teaching and learning aid later.

The first paper by Wiliam and Bartholomew (2004) is an example of work underpinned by what are termed **positivist/objectivist** theoretical perspectives where the methodological approach is based on the scientific method. The knowledge reported in the work is based on an assumption that the world exists in an objectively knowable, singular, natural law-abiding reality. The goal of this method is to predict and control in ways that apply across all contexts. The researcher's perspective is distant and removed from the object of the research.

The second paper by Boaler, Wiliam and Brown (2000) is underpinned by what are termed constructionist/intrepretivist theoretical perspectives where the methodological approach is based on interpreting the views and experiences of students in classrooms. The researcher reduces the complex responses which are not easily quantifiable and interprets these within the contexts of the schools involved in the research.

The third paper by Cremin and Thomas (2005) is informed by critical theory which calls for a radical restructuring of grouping towards the ends of social justice. Whereas critical theory does not dictate a particular methodology, the focus on emancipation is congruent with the same ideas about how we come to know and how ideas come into existence as that which underpins constructionism.

Activity 1.2

Read all three articles and while you are reading the work, consider the following questions:

- What do the authors intend to do in the writing?
- What is the problem the authors are trying to resolve?

(Continued)

Activity 1.2   (Continued)

- What concepts are being used to develop a solution to the problem?
- What evidence do the authors bring to bear on the issue?
- Do the authors argue the points well? Is the work logically consistent and empirically adequate, plausible or convincing and why (not)? What alternative or rival arguments come to mind?
- How does this work fit in with your views of your own education so far?
- How does this work fit in with your views of what you have observed in classrooms so far?
- How does this work fit in with other work that you may have read about the subject so far?
- What are your views about grouping? Have these views altered after reading this work?
- Why do you think that grouping in secondary schools is common practice?

Key ideas

Becoming a teacher involves learning how to bridge the gap between the state of mind of the learner and the subject matter which is to be learnt. This can be done through questioning expert teachers, and through reflecting *on* and *in* classrooms. To teach requires cognizance about how to bring about learning; choose activities that are relevant to the kind of learning to be brought about and ensure that activities are relevant to the state of mind and motivation of the learner.

However, teachers work within larger schools which are bound by procedures and expectations. These procedures and expectations are determined by the wider educational world. Within this educational world, people have a shared discourse which includes common-sense wisdom which may contradict the requirements of the classroom teacher for matching the state of mind and motivation of students, but which nonetheless has become part of the procedures. One example of this is the practice of grouping pupils according to a notion of 'ability'. To fully engage with all the views about this issue requires awareness that we all have theoretical perspectives on which our beliefs are based. Additionally, we need to understand the basis on which these views have been formed. The final section of the chapter explored three different theoretical perspectives on grouping, summarizing the differences in approach and also providing guidance on how to critically read research literature.

Reflective questions

1 In summary, what evidence was provided by each author of the three papers used in the text in arguing their case for or against ability labelling?
2 Did the reasoning of the authors' arguments follow logically to the conclusions that were drawn? Were you able to identify the explicit or implicit indications of the authors' values and assumptions?

CHAPTER 2

REFINING THE FOCUS FOR RESEARCH AND FORMULATING A RESEARCH QUESTION

Elaine Wilson

Chapter overview

This chapter will help the novice researcher to focus on a manageable research area by using a series of questions, activities and strategies to help narrow the area of interest.

When you first embark on a research project you will probably have a definite area of interest in mind. For example, you may be particularly interested in the role of writing to help learning. This is an interesting and important focus, but simply saying you are researching writing to learn is much too broad. The first step then is to narrow the area of interest down and come up with a more manageable narrower scope. Novice researchers tend to find this process fairly daunting: so there are three key questions to answer using the writing example:

- What exactly do you want to find out about writing to learn?
- What has been written about children's writing already?
- What can you realistically manage in the time available to you?

Now try Activity 2.1 which might help to refine the problem area.

Activity 2.1   Generating ideas

Brainstorming is a free-association technique of spontaneously listing all words, concepts, ideas, questions and knowledge about a topic. Start by making a lengthy list about the areas you are interested in researching.

Sorting ideas

Next, sort these ideas into categories. This allows you to sort out your current awareness of the area, decide what perspectives are most interesting and/or relevant, and decide in which direction to steer your research. Create a concept map from the categories you arrived at in the brainstorming stage. Concept maps may be elaborate or simple and are designed to help you organize your thinking about a topic, recognize where you have gaps in your knowledge, and help to generate specific questions that may guide your research. Having done that, decide if you now know enough about the area. Do you need to do further reading? Are you ready to go on to the next stage of 'drilling down' to the core of the problem?

'Drilling down' is a term taken from management literature and simply involves analysing the research area from various perspectives to help narrow the focus. Figure 2.1 provides an example from an educational context where a teacher identified her area of interest as characteristics of successful lessons. This is a huge and complex area so the teacher first considered what a successful lesson might look like from her own perspective as the teacher, then from the school perspective, and finally from the students' perspective. This led on to a series of second-level questions such as: how will I know if the students are learning? As a result of this process, the teacher decided to focus on the students' perspectives of successful lessons. This helped to identify other ideas and raised further questions such as: are the students able to do the work I set? Do they believe they are able to do the work I set? How do students perceive my role? Do students think the work is worthwhile? Do they enjoy the work? In this case, the teacher decided to explore this aspect further through asking a few students for their ideas, talking to colleagues and searching out recent research in the area of student voice and motivation before attempting to formulate her research question. In the next section, I will introduce other strategies that might help you to formulate your questions.

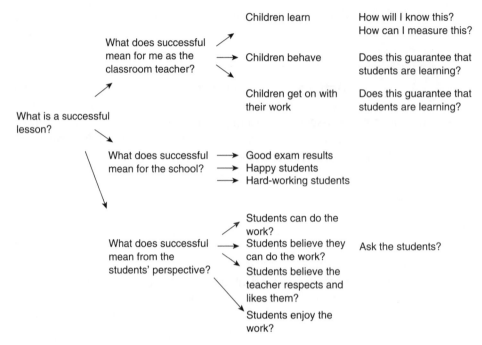

Figure 2.1   Drilling down to the core of the issue

Formulating the research question

Moving from a research topic to a research question

The first stage of moving from a topic to a manageable research question will be informed by your reading, so finding out what is written about your area of interest will not only help you to crystallize your thinking but will also suggest potential methodological approaches for your chosen area of study. Chapter 3 will explain how to search for literature to help you understand the key themes about your chosen topic and how to organize your findings into coherent themes.

Having decided on and refined your research area, it helps if you can hone this into a succinct researchable question. For example, talk to help learning would be a really good area for research, but 'What sort of talk do students engage in during group work in science lessons?' would be a much more helpful starting point for a small-scale school-based research project.

To think about your project, then, ask yourself the following questions:

1   What is known already about this area? What have experts already written about this area and how have they undertaken research? (See Chapter 3 on reviewing literature.)

2   What are my school colleagues' views about this area and what does my higher-degree tutor advise me to do?
3   Why am I doing this research?

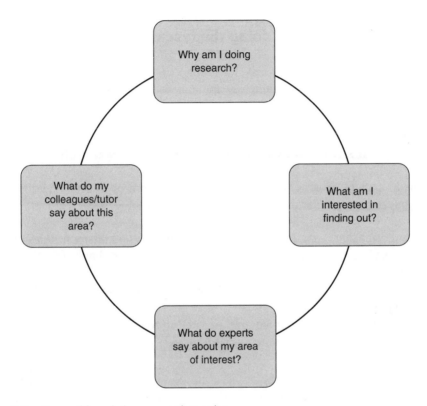

Figure 2.2   Stages of formulating a research question

So you can see that it is unhelpful to start from the premise that you are going to survey the students or carry out interviews or to even think about data collection methods until you have a clear idea of what your precise research question is.

It is important to recognize that undertaking a research enquiry will make extra demands on your time, energy and resources, so your enquiry must be realistically manageable on top of your teaching role, and where possible be seen as no more than extending the activities you are already engaged in within your own classroom or school. The further removed your research is from your usual professional work, the more difficult it will be to undertake. Furthermore, carrying out an enquiry which is not directly related to your own interest or professional work will be less useful to you. Ideas for research will emerge from your own interests and experiences. Sources of inspiration might be a new curriculum development, a recurring difficulty, an idea you encountered on a course or reading a research paper. Moving from a research topic to a research question is an important next step.

Research purpose: why are you doing the research?

Having a clear idea about the rationale for doing your research is important. The main reasons teachers give for undertaking research are listed in Box 2.1.

Box 2.1   Teachers' classroom-based research

Firstly, to explore what is happening in your classroom or to seek new insights into your classrooms. For example:

- How do teachers manage their classes? What are the classroom rules? How are elements such as time, space, pupil behaviour or their own strategies managed?
- How are classroom decisions made: by the teacher, by pupils, or by both through negotiation?
- How is pupils' work monitored and assessed in the classroom?
- How do teachers explain new topics to pupils?

Secondly, to describe or portray an accurate profile of persons, events or situations which will require extensive knowledge of the situation. For example:

- What do teachers and pupils do in the classroom? How do they spend their time?
- What kind of interaction takes place, who talks to whom and about what?
- What do pupils learn, what tasks do they engage in, and with what degree of involvement and success?
- What is a school day or a lesson like from a pupil's point of view? Are any individuals or groups getting a relatively poor deal out of schooling?
- What happens when pupils disrupt lessons or behave in an anti-social manner?

(Continued)

Box 2.1   (Continued)

- What happens when children work in small groups? What sorts of assignments are undertaken? Who decides what? Are the groups collaborative?

Thirdly, to explain a situation or problem, account for patterns relating to the phenomena being researched, or to identify relationships. For example:

- Do teachers and children perceive the same events in different or similar ways?
- Do children read better as a result of a new programme?
- Do children read better in this programme compared with the standard programme?
- Do teachers in the same school or department have similar or different practices, beliefs, expectations, rewards and punishments, and conventions, and how are these understood by the pupils?

Fourthly, to intervene to bring about changes in your classroom. For example:

- Can I raise students' self-esteem in my lessons?
- How can I improve my own teaching?
- What happens in the classroom when there is a change of policy, a new curriculum, work scheme, textbook, course, or new forms of assessment?

For example, a secondary-school English teacher was dissatisfied with the way her students wrote biographical sketches and on 'drilling down' found that her students did not know how to structure or correct their writing. She decided that she would intervene to develop and evaluate a new teaching approach. The teacher's key research question was 'What teaching strategies will help my students recognize the gaps and mistakes in their writing?', and a sub-question was 'How can I help my students write better transitions?'. The new approach involved setting up situations for her students to do peer editing using a new guide designed to help them locate transitions and missing transitions in the text. She monitored the students' work during and following the intervention.

Formulating a clearly stated question will help you to decide on the most useful data to collect to answer your research question. Moreover, having a clear focus will also prevent you stashing away too much information that *may* be vaguely relevant. Having too broad an approach is more likely to cause you angst because of the sheer volume and complexity of information available. In the example given in Figure 2.3 the teacher has narrowed her original very broad approach to a much narrower and manageable question: 'How can I increase students' self-esteem in my lessons?'.

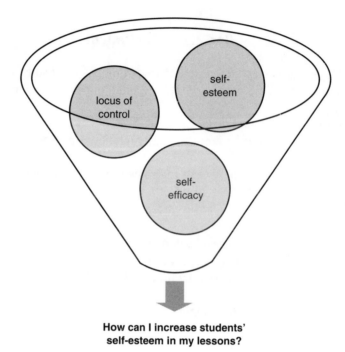

**How can I increase students'
self-esteem in my lessons?**

Figure 2.3   Narrowing your focus

Having a clear open-ended but focussed research question calls for deep thinking and extended literature searching until the same sources re-occur.

Furthermore, it is vital that you focus on a research area that is manageable in the timescale you have available to you, and that what you set out to find is measurable. For instance, it is very difficult to measure understanding directly, as in the case of students' understanding of addition and subtraction. This is because understanding these concepts, facts and skills occurs within the student's head and requires probing more explicitly; therefore a more useful variable to investigate would be to measure student accuracy in applying addition and subtraction by counting the number of times each student answered subtraction and addition problems correctly.

Finally, beware of trying to measure impact or of trying to attribute increased understanding or better pupil test performance directly to your new teaching approach, because there are many variables in each very different classroom. Be cautious in making such causal claims. There is a tendency to want to link pupils' outcomes directly to teaching approaches: however, there are many mediating factors in operation, such as the motivation and aptitude of individual students, the mix of students in your class and the resultant classroom dynamics, which could account for changes.

Looking at expert researchers' questions

Reading more expert researchers' work will help you to learn how to undertake class-room-based research. Identify the authors' research focus and locate their research questions. In the final published paper this will seem like a straightforward linear process, moving effortlessly from identifying a focus through to formulating the question, but as you now know this was probably not the case. The expert researchers will also have spent hours reading relevant literature, and thought long and hard about the purpose of their research before finally framing their research questions. Consider the style of research questions that expert researchers use in their work set out in Box 2.2.

Box 2.2 An example of an expert researcher's school-based research

Paper used: O'Brien, C. (2007) 'Peer devaluation in British secondary schools: young people's comparisons of group-based and individual-based bullying', *Educational Research*, 49(3): 297–324.

O'Brien sets out her research area early in the opening pages; this is to focus on young adolescents' perceptions of two distinguishable bases for being bullied:

1 For group membership, such as one's race or sex as a whole.
2 For individual, unique differences.

At the end of her literature review and before her methods section, she also clearly states her research questions.

'This exploratory study has a threefold aim:

1 Do students evaluate pejorative names differentially?
2 How do students justify their value judgements? On what dimensions are group and individual-based name-calling perceived as similar and different?
3 Are appraisals comparable? Are we comparing "apples and oranges"?'

Activity 2.2

Use the grid in Figure 2.4 below to help you clarify your thoughts about your focus and research question.

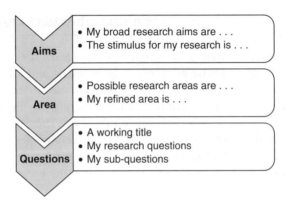

Figure 2.4   Stages of formulating a research question

Further examples of classroom-based research projects

Table 2.1 shows four further examples of classroom-based research. In these examples, the work was undertaken by beginning teachers during their initial teacher education. Two research projects were stimulated by a developing awareness of practice through exposure to new ideas, and the broad research aims were to better understand history teaching and student motivation. The history teacher set out 'primarily to problematize or characterize an aspect of subject learning', while the motivation study was an attempt at understanding why a small group of boys were disaffected in science lessons.

The other two projects took the form of an intervention whereby both teachers tried a new approach and monitored the effect on student learning.

The M-levelness of PGCE work

Each university will have specific criteria for judging M-level work which is used to assess and make judgements about students' work. However, in the introduction we set out generic descriptors for Masters-level work which I will use here to illustrate how PGCE school-based research can meet these requirements.

In essence, these require that Masters-level work demonstrates:

- knowledge and understanding
- the application of knowledge and understanding through problem-solving abilities
- the ability to integrate knowledge and handle complexity by making judgements

- the communication of conclusions and underpinning knowledge and rationale to specialist and non-specialist audiences
- the ability to study in a manner that may be largely self-directed or autonomous.

Table 2.1   Examples of classroom-based research

Research aim	Understanding		Intervention	
Stimulus	Develop new awareness		Dissatisfaction with practice	
Topic area	History teaching	Motivation	Modern languages	Group work
Emerging questions	Elaborate the working conceptual apparatus around moral vs. historical debate, in order to strengthen the analytic power of the definitions/goals history teachers work with. What concerns in my own practice am I seeking to address and illuminate? Justify and define focus on pupil experience?	Why are some pupils disengaged with school work? What prevents students from working? What is work-avoidant behaviour?	Differentiation? Can teachers of MFL differentiate lessons? Is there evidence of impact on FL learning?	Can A-level chemistry teaching be less didactic?
Working title	A critical analysis of commonality and divergence across moral reasoning and causal reasoning, drawing upon a study of four Year 9 pupils' experience of constructing causal explanations of the Holocaust	A case study of Y9 examining pupils' self-perceptions towards learning in a science classroom	A critical analysis of the impact of teaching strategies that cater for differentiation in a class of Y9 pupils of French learning the perfect tense	Does the use of active teaching approaches to encourage independent learning increase students' understanding in Year 12 chemistry lessons?
Research questions	What forms did pupils' reasoning (oral and written) take? How might those forms be classified? What counts as 'reasoning' for me as a history teacher? How adequate is the existing conceptual apparatus for framing these pupils' reasoning experiences?	Why do pupils display work-avoidant behaviour in my Y9 class?	How does the use of different modes of differentiation impact on individual learning? What are the key features of an effective differentiated approach? What are the pupils' perceptions of the differentiated teaching approach?	(1) As far as the pupils themselves are concerned, are lessons dominated by symmetrical dialogue more effective at developing their understanding than lessons without such a bias? (2) Does a topic taught through symmetrical dialogue result in enhanced test performances, compared to a topic taught without such a bias?

Further examples of the sort of research work carried out by PGCE students at the University of Cambridge are published online in the *Journal of Trainee Teacher Educational Research* (http://jotter.educ.cam.ac.uk/).

In the next section, I will use a further example of PGCE M-level work to illustrate how school-based research can meet descriptors of M-'levelness'. The work used was submitted by Owain, a beginning teacher completing a one-year PGCE M-level secondary science course. This work is the final 8500-word report of a classroom-based case study undertaken in the second and third terms of his professional school placement.

The title of his work is: 'A Case Study of Assessment for Learning: A Critical Analysis of the Perceptions and Interactions of Science Students Engaged in Peer-Assessment Exercises in a Year 10 Triple Set *Living and Growing* Teaching Episode'.

This work extends Owain's knowledge and understanding through applying ideas in a research context. It also illustrates how Owain applies knowledge and understanding through problem-solving in a new classroom environment within broader multidisciplinary contexts. Box 2.3 provides Owain's rationale for undertaking this work.

Box 2.3   Introduction

Assessment, the judgement or evaluation of students' learning and understanding [Sadler, 1989], is traditionally associated with testing and examination or a sequence of teacher-led questions. With the inception of league tables, emphasis on summative assessment in schooling has increased. Arguably this is detrimental to learning and understanding, which the summative method, by definition, contributes little to [Black and Wiliam, 1998b]. However, assessment need not exclusively be summative, an assessment *of* learning, but rather may be used to inform and enhance understanding: an assessment *for* learning (AfL). This enables students to become aware of the quality of understanding they demonstrate and how they can improve, a process more efficacious than trial-and-error learning, constituting an evaluative feedback loop [Sadler, 1989]. Using formative assessment effectively could therefore bring learning to learn, rather than learning to be tested to the forefront of education [Black and Wiliam, 1998b; Black, McCormick, James and Pedder, 2006]. Interest in using AfL strategies is evident from the numerous research articles, which examine their effects on students and teachers at all educational levels.

Given the learning benefits that AfL strategies may provide, I undertook a case study investigating the classroom use of peer-assessment in a context under-explored in the existing literature. The participants were members of my Year 10 triple award class, at a Suffolk upper school, studying a GCSE biology module. I first aimed to describe the students' perceptions of peer-assessment and the relationship between how they thought it had affected their learning, and their assessed

(Continued)

Box 2.3   (Continued)

understanding of the material. Secondly, exploring the process, rather than the outcome, I examined the intra-peer-assessment student interactions. This research was carried out in accordance with the ethical guidelines specified by the British Educational Research Association (BERA, 2004: 4), with the participants' informed, voluntary consent. Only students' first names are used in this report.

To help orientate his thinking, Owain read about existing research in his area of interest – assessment for learning – and wrote a literature review (see Chapter 3). The summary of this review is set out in Box 2.4. This review provides evidence of Owain's extended knowledge and understanding of the area of assessment for learning.

Box 2.4   Summary (of the literature review)

This review demonstrates the large extent to which the study of formative assessment is influenced by theoretical perspectives. Peer-assessment has been identified as one method by which formative assessment may be facilitated. Studies of classroom implementation show it to be a practicable option that has met with the approval of teachers. However, relatively little investigation has focused on how peer-assessment in science lessons, or indeed in secondary education, in this country is seen by the individuals most intimately involved in the process. Neither has the nature of the exchanges that occur between the students, which contribute to the theorized effects of peer-assessment, been examined. As Cowie comments: 'Despite the need for active pupil participation, very little is known about pupil perceptions and experiences of assessment for learning' [Cowie, 2005: 138]. These issues will be considered in the establishing of my research focus in the following section.

Owain then identified three research questions which he proposed investigating in his placement schools.

Box 2.5   Research sub-questions

To achieve a more holistic understanding of the peer-assessment, more emphasis on analysing the process from the learners' perspectives is needed. Three research

(Continued)

Box 2.5   (Continued)

sub-questions (RQs) are therefore proposed for investigation in my case study to fulfil this overarching analytical aim:

- RQ1: What are the students' perceptions of peer-assessment?
- RQ2: How do the students interact with each other during peer-assessment exercises?
- RQ3: Is there parity between the students' perceptions of the effectiveness of peer-assessment with regard to their learning and their actual attainment?

In his final report, he discussed how he went about answering his research questions. He set out his research design (see Chapter 5) and explained how he would collect and analyse data.

This report provides evidence of Owain making judgements by demonstrating the ability to integrate knowledge and handle complexity, and formulate judgements with incomplete data.

His written report communicated his conclusions, underpinning knowledge and rationale to other teachers and colleagues in his placement school. Although he worked with a university-based tutor and school-based mentor, he did undertake the study in a manner that was largely self-directed or autonomous. Owain's final summary is set out in Box 2.6.

Box 2.6

This case study found that students' perceptions of peer-assessment encompassed a broad range of positive and negative aspects, depending on the individual, that were largely consistent with those documented in the literature. A key issue for some students was their unfamiliarity with peer-assessment and consequent difficulty in carrying out the protocol, which led them to perceive it as ineffective. To some extent this may explain the findings regarding the students' interactions when engaged in peer-assessment. These were characterized by their briefness and limited exchange of formative verbal feedback. The evidence regarding the relationship between students' perceptions of their understanding and the understanding they demonstrate is limited by the validity of the measures used and the complexities of performing such a comparison.

While these conclusions have validity in the ecological and methodological context of the present study, caution should be taken in generalization, given

(Continued)

Box 2.6   (Continued)

(I) the peer-assessment protocol's specificity and (II) the composition, age and attainment range of the class. There are many different ways of implementing peer-assessment and an even larger suite of AfL strategies. My findings should thus be used as a tentative indicator for how students *might* respond, given a sufficient degree of similarity to the research context described here. Next steps in this research area could be to investigate differences in perceptions and inter-actions between different groups of students, introduce further methods of formative assessment and investigate how they are received, or begin to consider how the protocol employed could be modified to increase its effectiveness, approaching the enquiry as action research.

The aim of this study was to investigate how peer-assessment is viewed and enacted by students, breaking from the tendency of writings on assessment to focus on the teacher's role [Brookhart, 2001]. However, in my own role as a teacher, the experience of teaching a peer-assessment episode has been valuable for informing my practice. I have learned that the exercise *may* be perceived as a positive educa-tional experience and can be successful, provided that necessarily clear instructions and sufficient time are given and that students are familiar with AfL strategies. I would consider using peer-assessment less often and introducing it gradually over an extended time period with simpler methods of self- and peer-assessment, as recommended by both the literature and the participating students. This leads on to my final point, regarding student voice. Some of the comments received from students relating to peer-assessment were remarkably perceptive, demonstrating a good awareness of what helped and hindered their learning and how activities could be modified and improved to further facilitate this. With the caveat of class composition, I will endeavour in the future to provide the opportunity for students to give oral and written feedback on 'the process' of their classroom learning and use this to inform and adapt my teaching to produce improved outcomes for all.

Key ideas

It is likely that your research will solve significant problems in your own classroom and expand your knowledge base of teaching and learning, therefore it is going to be a demanding process. Moreover, such an enquiry will require discipline, stamina and hard work on your part, but as a result of engaging in meaningful activity

(Continued)

(Continued)

of community and scholarship, you will come to understand your practice better. In order that you can do this well, it is really important that you start the research process by refining your initial research concern into precisely formulated research questions. Your research will be more relevant, useful and manageable if it is closely related to an area of interest, does not overly extend your everyday role and can be done within the time constraints. Additionally, when designing the research and defining the data collection methods, try to manage any potential biases/ subjectivities you may have. Furthermore, to be useful, your work ought to make a contribution to teacher knowledge, so to this end seek the support and guidance of a critical friend if you feel you do not have the skills and expertise necessary to carry out the research.

Reflective questions

1 What exactly do you want to find out about your selected area?
2 What has been written about your chosen area of study? Have you done sufficient reading about what has been researched already in your chosen area?
3 Have you thought through and planned how you can realistically manage the research process in the time available?

Further reading

Bell, J. (2010) *Doing your Research Project: a Guide for First-time Researchers in Education and Social Science* (5th edn). Buckingham: Open University Press.

Denscombe, M. (2010) *The Good Research Guide for Small-scale Social Research Projects* (4th edn). Buckingham: Open University Press.

Robert-Holmes, G. (2011) *Doing your Early Years Research Project: a Step by Step Guide* (2nd edn). London: Sage Publications.

Thomas, G. (2009) *How to Do your Research Project: a Guide for Students in Education and Applied Social Sciences*. London: Sage Publications.

CHAPTER 3

REVIEWING THE LITERATURE AND WRITING A LITERATURE REVIEW

Elaine Wilson

Chapter overview

A literature review should meet three criteria: firstly, to present results of similar studies; secondly, to relate your study to the ongoing dialogue in the literature; and thirdly, to provide a framework for comparing the results of a study with other studies. To accomplish this, you will need to: identify suitable search terms; locate appropriate literature; read and check the relevance of the literature; organize the literature you have selected; and, finally, write a literature review. Set out in these five stages, it may look like a straightforward process, however there are many steps involved. Indeed, more experienced researchers often assume that these steps are obvious and straightforward for a novice. This is not the case. Consequently, this chapter is written with the complete novice in mind. The structure of this chapter will follow the five stages mentioned here, although the writing stage will be discussed in Chapter 13. I will start by considering the purpose of reviewing the literature and of writing a literature review.

What is the purpose of reviewing the literature?

Working with literature is an essential part of the research process. Literature is used for disparate purposes throughout the research process, including:

- focusing interests
- defining questions
- arguing a rationale
- theoretically informing your study
- developing appropriate design, or writing a formal literature review.

At every stage of the research process it is vital that you engage critically with published research. If you do this thoroughly the process will help you to generate new ideas and direct your research questions, while also being an integral part of planning your research design. In other words, the actual process of doing a review is an initial important step in carrying out good research, and the outcome of this process, in the form of a written literature review, will provide the evidence that you have been thorough in situating your own work.

Therefore, the purposes of undertaking a literature review are threefold. Firstly, the process will inform your search about what is already known about your area of interest so that you can identify the key ideas in the domain and the important researchers in the field. So that means becoming familiar with the key thinkers in the subject area, along with developing an understanding of the significance of their work. It will be through getting to know who is doing what, and where they are doing this, that you will be able to evaluate the relevance of literature encountered in your search. As you become familiar with specific knowledge areas and vocabulary, it will become apparent where the ideas originated and how they have been developed.

Secondly, during the process of searching existing literature, you will also gain an understanding of the interrelationships between the domain being considered and other subject areas. As you become more knowledgeable about a topic, you might identify other new areas worth studying which will advance your knowledge on that topic.

Thirdly, as you engage with the work and methods of others who are researching the same area you will also come to understand how each researcher has studied the topic. Consequently, the ideas and work of others may also provide you with the framework for your own work, which includes methodological assumptions, data-collection techniques, key concepts and structuring the research into a conventional academic thesis.

Reviewing the literature on a topic can provide an academically enriching experience, but only if it is done properly.

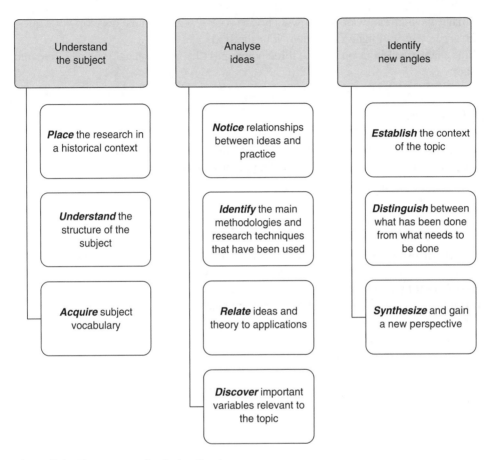

Figure 3.1   The purposes of reviewing literature

Stages of reviewing the literature

The process of reviewing the literature can be broken down into four stages. The first stage is to find the key sources through careful searching and to be discriminating in what you include.

Secondly, setting up a management system to store and catalogue all the sources you find will be invaluable as you start to accumulate a lot of material and especially in helping you to compile the reference list in the final essay or thesis.

Thirdly, you will need to decide which of the many sources you have found are directly relevant to your specific study, be able to read these efficiently and make judgements about which papers you will use and why.

Finally, having read widely, you will choose your research focus, develop your question, argue your rationale and design your method.

This chapter will focus on the first three points and Chapter 5 will help you with research design.

Finding literature

This section will point you towards sources of ideas and describe the type of literature which might be useful, as well as showing you how to search electronic databases.

Searching for literature

There are several ways of identifying potentially useful literature, such as doing hand searches, or using sources recommended in course texts and by personal professional contacts within your field of study. If you are studying for a higher degree, your tutor will probably point you towards the 'classic' material in your area, to get you started. Don't overlook your colleagues and other more immediate contacts. Contact with experts in your chosen field is another recommended method of finding material as they can often help identify work that has yet to be published. This can be done either personally or through an email discussion list. Contact with others working in the same field may lead to literature that you have not uncovered in other ways. In summary then, information can come from many sources, as Table 3.1 illustrates.

Table 3.1 Information sources

Collaborative groups	Publications	The media	Individuals
Chat rooms	Books	TV	Colleagues
Blogs and wikis	Papers	Radio	Librarians
Email lists	Magazines	Videos	Experts/tutors
	Journals	DVDs	Friends
	Reports	Podcasts	
	Pictures		

Using online libraries

The most important databases for education research are listed in Table 3.2.

Table 3.2 Databases of electronic sources

Database	Information
British Education Index	The British Education Index is a specialized database focusing on journals in the field of education published in the UK.
Education-line	Education-line is a database which holds full text journal articles, conference papers, working papers and electronic literature which supports educational research, policy and practice.

(Continued)

Table 3.2   (Continued)

Database	Information
Scopus	Scopus is international in coverage and indexes 16,500 peer-reviewed journals plus book series and conference papers in the fields of Scientific, Technical, Medical and Social Sciences including Arts & Humanities.
Web of Knowledge	WOK provides access to current and retrospective bibliographic information and cited references found in nearly 1,130 of the world's leading arts, humanities and social science journals.
PsycINFO	PsycINFO is an abstract database of psychological literature from the 1800s to the present.
ERIC	Education Resources Information Center (ERIC) is an American English-language database relating to education. ERIC indexes over 650 journals, plus books, research syntheses, conference papers, technical reports and policy papers.

There are also a number of freely available resources including full-text databases, online publications and education journals that can be accessed without the need for a password or any payment:

- Education-line
- Directory of Open Access Journals (DOAJ)
- TLRP (Teaching and Learning Research Programme)
- EEP (Educational Evidence Portal)
- Intute
- Screenonline
- Ontheweb
- CEE: Centre for the Economics of Education
- Digital Education Resource Archive (DERA)

Types of literature

A literature review for the purposes of a dissertation or thesis should be based primarily in the academic literature. This does not mean that there is not a role for sources such as government documents, working papers, conference papers and publications with short print runs. This is often referred to as grey literature. However, you should be clear in your own mind and in the written review about the role of non-academic sources. For example, does a newspaper article or series contribute specific highly relevant information or flag up concerns from the community? You must not use academic journal articles and grey literature as if they are the same kind of reference with equal status. Academic in this context means peer-reviewed work published in scholarly journals. Furthermore, you need to be confident that you have found as much of the available evidence as possible by searching the literature on your chosen topic in a systematic way. Your search must also be open to scrutiny so it can be replicated and updated.

How to search an online database

If you use the British Education Index, your search strategy can often be less closely defined, simply because the BEI is a specialized education database. When using a multi-disciplinary database, such as the International Bibliography of the Social Sciences, more care will be needed to achieve the necessary focus in your search strategy itself.

The British Education Index contains fewer than 100,000 items, whilst ERIC has almost 800,000, so if you search the BEI you can also be more adventurous without the fear of being overwhelmed with results.

In addition, if you access the British Education Index through Dialog DataStar, you will also be able to look at the thesaurus, although this involves a rather cumbersome method to select all the terms of use for your search strategy, whereas the Cambridge Scientific Abstracts, an interface for ERIC, Sociological Abstracts, Linguistics and Language Behaviour Abstracts, etc., present the thesaurus very clearly and in a way which helps you easily select all the appropriate terms to include in your search.

In general, the larger the database, the more abstracts there are and the more important it is to use the thesaurus or set of subject headings, if it is available to you.

Searching databases

To carry out an effective search of an electronic database, you need to understand how these systems work, and how to plan a search to take full advantage of them. The British Education Index (BEI) is based on Boolean logic which uses two main logical operators. It is probably easier to understand this if you have an actual example to look at. For example, Figure 3.2 shows the preliminary stages of a search carried out by Atkinson et al. in their published literature review.

Atkinson, M., Springate, I., Johnson, F. and Halsey, K. (2007) *Inter-school Collaboration: A Literature Review.* Slough: NFER.

In Appendix 6 of the report, the authors tell us that they searched the following sources:

- the NFER Library bibliographical databases
- the current educational research in the UK database (CERUK)
- AEI (Australian Education Index)
- BEI (British Education Index)
- CBCA Fulltext Education (Canadian Business and Current Affairs)
- ERIC (Education Resources Information Center).

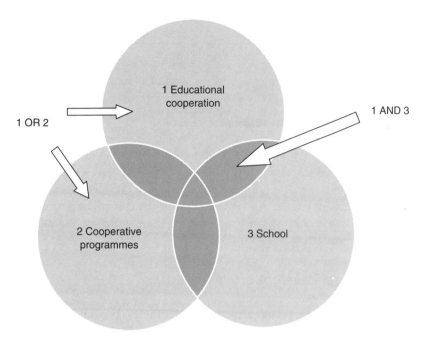

Figure 3.2   Boolean logic and search history

When they searched the BEI, they used a number of terms and Figure 3.2 uses the very first stages of their search to illustrate the difference between Boolean Or/And statements. In the search, the shaded circle with the words 'educational cooperation' represents all the records that contain these words. This search found 1,351 results for these words. The other shaded circles with the words 'cooperative programmes' and 'school' represent all the records that contain 'cooperative programmes' and 'school'. In this case, the database has 373 and 43,786 records respectively. OR logic is most commonly used to search for synonymous terms or concepts and will broaden your search. OR logic collates the results to retrieve all the unique records containing one term, the other, or both. The more terms or concepts we combine in a search with OR logic, the more records we will retrieve. In this search, 1,594 records were located for the search '1 OR 2'.

The authors wanted to retrieve records in which all the search terms are present and this is illustrated by the shaded area overlapping the three circles, representing all the records that contain all three search terms. So they used the AND operator which restricts the numbers of records located by combining each term. The more terms or concepts combined in a search with AND logic, the fewer records we will retrieve.

Setting search parameters

Once you have identified your sources, you also need to decide on the search parameters, such as timescale, geographical scope, age range, types of literature and date of publication.

What is the timescale of your research?

In general, your sources should be recent and if many of your sources are over 10–15 years old, you must explain why this is. You may of course have chosen to use older ideas and theories and, if so, be prepared to explain why. Researchers often use older references when they are 'classic' works or establish a benchmark against which you are comparing things. For example, you may want to trace literature published after an important piece of legislation was introduced.

What is the geographical scope of your review?

It is likely that you will focus on work carried out in the UK, but limiting your review to studies written in English is a recognized source of bias, so this must be clearly stated in your search strategy.

What is the age range or educational level of your study population?

If your research is limited to one educational level, this will help to narrow down the search results.

What types of literature will your review cover?

Decide if you are going to restrict your search to published studies only or if you will also want to use unpublished theses, newspaper articles, opinion pieces, other grey literature and current research too. Including different types of literature in the review will give different viewpoints, but excluding them will narrow your search and make it more focused.

Activity 3.1   Developing your own search strategy

It is much better if you can spend some time thinking about the best keywords and search terms before you start your search. To help you do this, consider the following questions:

(Continued)

Activity 3.1   (Continued)

1 What is your research question? Break this down into its component parts, mapping out all the different subject elements.
2 Compile a list of keywords and phrases that describe these different elements and that you can use as keywords in your search.
3 Are there similar words that describe each of these concepts?
4 Are there any other more specific keywords that could limit your search?
5 How can you combine these keywords together to search? For example, 'Gender AND Science' returns results containing both words. 'Gender OR Science' returns results containing either the word gender or the word science. Use uppercase letters for OR and AND when using search engines.
6 Try using different keywords to find the information you want.

Published meta-analysis literature reviews

Since 1993, the Evidence for Policy and Practice Information and Co-ordinating Centre (EPPI Centre) at the Institute of Education, University of London has coordinated systematic reviews in a range of school-based areas. Review teams based in university departments in the UK conduct extensive searches of literature relevant to particular research questions, and use explicit methods to identify what can be reliably claimed on the basis of the chosen studies. This web-based repository also has a searchable thesaurus and database. Box 3.1 contains a summary report for a recent EPPI review from the online database which reports on learning skills.

Box 3.1   EPPI Review 1501R (Report) and 1501T (Technical Report)

Higgins, S., Baumfield, V. and Hall, E. (2007) 'Learning skills and the development of learning capabilities', in *Research Evidence in Education Library*. London: EPPI Centre, Social Science Research Unit, Institute of Education, University of London.

What do we want to know?

Which teaching approaches that aim to develop pupils' learning capabilities show evidence of the improved learning of pupils?

(Continued)

Box 3.1   (Continued)

Who wants to know and why?

The key aim of this review was to support current policy initiatives: specifically, to support the development of personalized learning by identifying teaching and learning strategies which actively engage and challenge learners, and which develop their ability to focus on their learning skills and their capacity to take ownership of their own progress. A second aim was to identify evidence from research which helps teachers to understand not just what works in terms of specific teaching approaches in specific contexts but why different approaches are successful. This can support teachers in making informed choices about what is likely to be effective in their own context.

What did we find?

There is a tension between approaches to learning skills which emphasize content – in terms of mastery of specific skills – and process – in terms of locating skills within an overall understanding of learning approaches. In the short term, the most effective means to improve performance where the assessment focuses on content knowledge is likely to be direct instruction. In the longer term, or where assessment focuses on conceptual understanding, metacognitive or strategic approaches are likely to be more effective.

Effective approaches are those which explicitly develop the awareness of learning strategies and techniques, particularly when these are targeted at the metacognitive level. The characteristics of these approaches identified by the review include:

- structured tasks which focus on specific and explicit strategies in the subject context
- the capacity in lessons for more effective exchanges between the learner and the teacher concerning the purpose of the activity
- small group interactions promoting articulation about the use of learning strategies
- mechanisms built into learning tasks to promote checking for mutual understanding of learning goals by peers and with the teacher
- enhanced opportunities for the learner to receive diagnostic feedback linked directly to the content of the task.

We can also identify some necessary conditions for these approaches to be successful:

- The teacher needs to have a good understanding of the subject, of different approaches to learning, and be sensitive to the demands of different types of learners.

(Continued)

Box 3.1   (Continued)

- Teachers should have a repertoire of practical tools and strategies to guide the learner and enhance opportunities for feedback about learning.
- Both teachers and learners should have an orientation towards learning characterized by a willingness to engage in dialogue and negotiation regarding the intent and purpose of a particular teaching and learning activity.
- The focus of learning should be on how to succeed through effort rather than ability, and through the selection of appropriate strategies by the learner.

How did we get these results?

From the electronic databases and full-text collections, we identified 1,379 citations. A total of 146 reports were obtained, of which 80 studies were selected for inclusion in the review. The in-depth review focused on a subgroup of 10 studies.

Managing literature

Storing the literature you find

You must be organized and diligent when it comes to keeping references. It is a good idea to set up a system to help you to track and catalogue the sources that you find right from the start of your research project. Retaining and subsequently retrieving the literature will be important at all stages of the process. The system you use will depend on your personal choice. In the past, researchers used handwritten card indexes, but more recently bibliographic software has become more readily available. There are a number of widely used commercial packages that you may want to buy. EndNote® is used widely in university departments and is a powerful database package which enables you to organize, store and search references and abstracts of research literature. It can save you time when writing papers or your thesis, allowing you to input citations directly from EndNote into a Word document, and to create a bibliography without having to type out all the references. You can also use it to access, search and download references directly from online bibliographic databases or library catalogues.

Zotero is a free online package which also allows for the storage of bibliographic information, user notes, and attachments of electronic documents or screen captures, and which integrates with popular academic databases, pooling information related to articles such as citation information and abstracts.

The larger databases, such as the BEI, AEI and ERIC, have a variety of options for saving and transmitting search results to these commercial packages, which may be very useful. Make sure that you can keep track of what you've found and keep your own record of how you completed the searches and the literature that you found. The search terms and combinations of terms that have been used for each individual database should be documented as you may need to make these explicit later. Moreover, this will also be useful if you want to replicate a search you have completed in one database in another. Consequently, when you come to write up your results, you will be able to show the systematic and thorough nature of your search.

Likewise, keep and file copies of relevant books, and, above all, find out what the recommended referencing style is and use it from the start.

Keeping on top of reading

You will probably find lots of sources which will be quite rewarding and the tendency will be to stash these away to be read later. However, this can be daunting and may put you off reading all the material you find, so I would recommend that you sort through all the references as you find them.

Try to develop efficient reading strategies – by this, I mean making good use of your valuable time by avoiding reading irrelevant papers. In addition, try to develop effective reading strategies, which means that when you subsequently set aside the time to read the selected papers you are successful in understanding what you read.

Efficient reading

Read the abstract

The first thing to do is to read the abstract carefully. If the abstract is well constructed, then this will give you a good idea of whether it is worth your while reading the whole article. Reading the abstracts and discarding those that are not appropriate will reduce the number of articles on the pile of things to be read or stored in your bibliographic database.

Sometimes, however, the abstract is not very helpful, so if this is the case, try reading the introduction, key findings or conclusions instead. These sections should give you enough information for you to decide whether it is worth reading the whole article. Box 3.2 provides a simplified description of the basic structure of most empirical research articles.

Box 3.2   The layout of a journal article

Although the exact layout of peer-reviewed journal articles will be determined by the author and the specific journal, most articles reporting on empirical findings will adhere to the following structure:

1 *Introduction/background:* a statement concerning the context of the study, a review of relevant literature and other research in the field, and the identification of some area that has not yet been studied.

(Continued)

> ## Box 3.2   (Continued)
>
> 2 *Purpose:* the main research aims/questions addressed in the article, a statement of what was studied. It can be in the form of a thesis statement which makes a claim of some kind, but this is not always the case.
> 3 *Programme description:* brief details of the programme or intervention under investigation (if relevant).
> 4 *Sample:* sample details, including the number of participants, geographical location/type of setting, age and stage of education and other demographic information pertinent to the study (e.g. gender, ability/attainment, ethnicity, special educational needs).
> 5 *Design and methods:* the study design and methods, including dates of data collection, sampling method, methods of data collection and analysis.
> 6 *Results:* the main findings in relation to the research aims/questions.
> 7 *Discussion:* the interpretation and evaluation of your findings, problems encountered in carrying out the research and implications of the results obtained.
> 8 *Conclusions:* the main conclusions arising from the research, possible applications and further research needed.

Selecting articles for careful study

Don't try to read an academic journal article in the same way as you would a newspaper report or novel. If you just start at the beginning and try to read through to the end, you will get frustrated and may even get the wrong idea that the ideas are too complicated for you to bother with. Most academic articles can't be grasped in a single reading and you may have to engage with them several times, but in different ways.

To quickly gain an overview, familiarize yourself with a chapter or article so that you understand the structure for later note-taking by looking at summaries, headings, sub-headings, tables, diagrams and illustrations. Then read the first sentences of paragraphs to see what they are about and to gauge if the material is useful or interesting, so that you can decide whether just some sections are relevant or whether you need to read it all.

Effective reading

Reading at speed is fine for scanning and skim-reading, but is unlikely to work for reflective, critical reading. The more you read, the faster you will become as you grow more familiar with specialist vocabulary, academic language and reading about theories and ideas.

Nonetheless, even if you have followed the advice given in the previous section, it is likely that you will still have a large number of articles to read, so it would be a good idea to have a systematic strategy for reading these.

1 Sorting papers into categories – sort the articles into piles that are all related to each strand of your research or sub-question. Alternatively, you might want to rank them in order of importance, or even rank each pile.

2   Note-taking – create a table before you start to read the papers, so that you can write down notes as you read. Figure 3.3 gives an example of such a template and is the structure used by Atkinson in the literature review referred to earlier in this chapter. It is worthwhile spending time before you start creating a relevant straightforward table for you to use as you read so that you can go back to these notes at a later time. Make a note of pertinent quotations or extracts as you read, in case you want to use these later. Your literature review ought to be an expression of your own thinking, not a patchwork of borrowed ideas. Therefore it is a good idea to plan therefore to invest your research time in understanding your sources and integrating them into your own thinking. Your note cards or note sheets will record only ideas that are relevant to your focus on the topic; and they will mostly summarize rather than quote. Find your own words for notes on sticky labels. Don't ever write in the book itself.

Title:
Date: Author(s):

REVIEW OF SOURCE
Purpose/focus of literature
Type of collaboration, e.g. no. of schools, etc.
Description of collaboration and its operation/processes
Aims/purpose/intended outcomes (why collaborate?)
Conditions/factors which drive collaboration
Conditions/factors which facilitate collaboration (during)
Recommendations/key factors for best practice
Conditions/factors which inhibit collaboration
Challenges/concerns
Role of LA/government/other organizations in supporting collaboration
Evidence of gains/benefits arising from collaboration

DESCRIPTION OF SOURCE
Sector
Country/area
Participants
Method(s)
When data collected and duration
Source/document type
Key references

REVIEWER'S COMMENTS
Is the reported analysis adequate and correct?
Are the author's interpretations supported by the evidence?
Are there any biases/caveats raised or to be aware of?
Is there a corroboration or triangulation of sources?
Relevance to review (high, medium or low)
Date of review

Figure 3.3   Literature summary template

Source: Atkinson et al. (2007).

Critical reading

When you read papers and books use active reading techniques. Use the note-taking guidelines in Table 3.3 and add your references to your Zotero. This will be a big help when you come to write up your work or if you have to come back to the literature after a break from the research project.

Table 3.3 Organizing note-taking

Citation	RQ	Key findings	Design and methods	Sample	Extracts or quotes	Comments	Rank 1–5
E.g. Author, date, title, journal, volume, issue, pages	Related to your research question	Related to your research question	What kind of research? How was it done?	Who was involved? How many?	Page numbers	Anything else of note	1 = very important 5 = interesting but not important

While you read each paper, ask the following questions.

Purpose of the work

- What is the author's purpose in writing the paper?
- Does this fit in with the area you are interested in? If not, then omit this from your review.
- What is the problem or issue and is this clearly defined?
- Is the significance of the work clearly established?
- Could the problem have been approached more effectively from another perspective?

Structure of the work

Examine the structure of the paper. How does the author structure the argument?

- Identify the main claims the author makes in putting forward their argument.
- Deconstruct the flow of the argument to see whether or where it breaks down logically; see Box 3.3 which uses Fisher's analysis of an argument.

Box 3.3

Extracts from the discussion section from: Pedder, D. (2006) 'Are small classes better? Understanding relationships between class size, classroom processes and pupils' learning', *Oxford Review of Education*, 32(2): 213–34.

The text has been annotated with <u>conclusions underlined</u> (reasons in brackets) and inference indicators *in italics*.

The secondary school study [Pedder, 2001] <u>developed no evidence of simple one-way relationships between class size and optimum conditions for all kinds of teaching and learning. This is a key finding.</u> (Different teachers recognised increased opportunities for promoting and supporting learning in large as well as in small classes; they also recognised constraints in small as well as in large classes). Politicians therefore need to be receptive to *the possibility that benefits to pupils' learning arise in large as well as in small classes* and thus need to promote frameworks within which schools can adopt more flexible approaches to allocating pupils to learning groups of different size for different teaching and learning purposes.

Challenging the claims made by the author

Adopt a sceptical stance towards the authors' claims, checking whether they support convincingly what they assert.

- Does the author have sufficient backing for the **generalizations** they make in a research study?
- How robust are the basic components of the study design (e.g. sample size, intervention and outcome)?
- How accurate and valid are the measurements?
- Is the analysis of the data accurate and relevant to the research question?
- Are the conclusions validly based upon the data and analysis?

Check for biases

Consider whether and how any values guiding the authors' work may affect what they claim. Distinguish between respecting the authors as people and being sceptical about what they write. Keep an open mind, retaining a conditional willingness to be convinced.

- Has the author evaluated the literature relevant to the problem or issue?
- Does the author include literature taking positions she or he does not agree with?

Check for relevance

Check that everything the authors have written is relevant to their purpose in writing the account and the argument they develop.

- In material written for a popular readership, does the author use appeals to emotion, one-sided examples, or rhetorically charged language and tone?
- Is there an objective basis to the reasoning, or is the author merely 'proving' what he or she already believes?

Writing a literature review

Having completed your search and synthesized your ideas, the final outcome of the process will take the form of a written literature review. The purpose of the review is to inform your audience of what is happening in the area. It will also establish you as a credible, well-informed and capable researcher. Additionally, if well constructed, it will help provide a context for your own approach, argue for the relevance and significance of your research question, and justify the appropriateness of your approach.

A good literature review is not just a summary of everything you have read but is rather a well-reasoned purposeful argument which supports your research focus. Therefore, you need to be analytical of the key ideas and then synthesize these into a coherent section of your essay or thesis. In other words, you not only need to know what research has been done in the area but you will also need to demonstrate that you understand how all the ideas relate to each other. For example – political journalists don't simply write down everything that is said in Parliament they analyse how one statement relates to other; they remember what was said last month and note whether it is consistent with this; they look for the vested interest that might be held by those making the judgements.

When you synthesize, you bring things together, relating one to the other to form something new. So writing a good review requires that you:

- read a few good reviews
- write critical annotations
- develop a structure
- write purposefully
- use the literature to back up your arguments
- review and write throughout the research process
- get feedback
- are prepared to redraft.

There are nine errors in synthesizing ideas in a literature review (Dunkin, 1996) that ought to be avoided.

The first two are what Dunkin describes as primary errors of finding and using literature yourself. First, not including all the important work in the area of study will diminish the relevance of your study. This might occur because you have not done sufficient reading or perhaps that you have not set appropriate search boundaries. The second error takes place if you assume that all sources are of equal quality or importance. For example, this might happen if you try to use a reference from an unofficial report to argue against the empirical evidence presented in an international peer- reviewed paper.

Dunkin classifies errors three to seven as secondary errors which are caused when you use literature in an uncritical way. Error three occurs if you present inaccurate information about sampling, methods, design procedures and contexts of the studies written about in the sources you use. Error four happens if you double count references by the original author; for example, if you list different reports from the same project as providing additional confirmation of the same finding. Error five occurs if the author of the original report has not represented their findings fully in their statements of conclusions. The error is compounded if you accept the statements uncritically and actually continue the original authors' misrepresentation of data. Error six consists of claiming that studies yield findings or reach conclusions that they do not. Error seven is a question of ethics and is about suppressing contrary findings. Original reports sometimes contain findings that are actually contradictory to the generalizations which you claim to support.

The final two errors occur when primary and secondary errors are included in generalizations made in your final review. These are error eight, consequential errors where generalizations are made based on flawed errors made earlier in the review, and finally, error nine, when you don't marshal all the evidence relevant to a generalization. These last errors occur in the process of formulating the final conclusion and are a result of a lack of criticality earlier in the review process. This is why it is vital that you read sources very carefully and work closely with your supervisor from an early stage of the research project.

Table 3.4 Common errors in writing a literature review

Primary errors

These are errors made by an author when writing a review

1   Not including seminal work or failing to define the scope of the review appropriately
2   Lack of discrimination; not all the research cited is of equal validity or quality

Secondary errors

These are errors made when the author uses literature in an uncritical way

3   Presenting inaccurate information about sampling, methods, design procedures and contexts of study
4   Double counting of references by original author
5   Non-recognition of faulty conclusions by original author
6   Unwarranted attributions, the original author making claims not justified by the data
7   Suppression of contrary findings

Tertiary errors

These areas are when primary and secondary errors are included in generalizations made in the final review written by
    the author

8   Consequential errors/flawed generalizations as a consequence of earlier lack of criticality
9   Failure to marshal all evidence relevant to a generalization

In summary, the purpose of the review is to critically analyse a segment of a published body of knowledge through summary, classification, and comparison of prior research studies, reviews of literature, and theoretical articles. See Chapter 13 for more guidance on what to include in your literature review.

 ## Key ideas

Setting your own research in the context of other literature on the same or a similar subject adds credibility to your work. It broadens your awareness of other research in the area and provides background information and data that corroborate what you've found. It also ensures that you are not duplicating research that has already been done by someone else. Searching the literature may also challenge your assumptions – you may find that the literature contradicts commonly held points of view or says exactly the opposite to what you were hoping to find. Sometimes, researchers decide to revise their original line of enquiry to take account of new information that has been found during the literature search.

Reflective questions

1 Has your literature search brought up the same names and are you finding the same sources in more than one database? Then you have either done sufficient reading or you might have used very narrow search terms. Ask your tutor for advice.
2 Are you adopting a 'Jeremy Paxman' critical approach to the papers you are reading?
3 Are you being disciplined in storing references in a literature management system?
4 Have you avoided the errors pointed out by Dunkin in constructing your review?

Further reading

Harlen, W. and Schlapp, U. (1998) Literature reviews, Scottish Council for Research in Education. dspace.gla.ac.uk/bitstream/1905/214/1/107.pdf (accessed January 2012).

Hart, C. (1998) *Doing a Literature Review*. London: Sage.

Jesson, J., Matheson, L. and Lacey, F. (2012) *Doing your Literature Review: Traditional and Systematic Techniques*. London: Sage.

Ridley, D. (2012) *The Literature Review: A Step-by-Step Guide for Students* (2nd edn). London: Sage.

CHAPTER 4

RESEARCH WITH YOUNGER CHILDREN: ISSUES AND APPROACHES

Paul Warwick and Roland Chaplain

Chapter overview

This chapter will examine ways to systematically research young children's perceptions of their schooling, focusing primarily on the collection and interpretation of research data. Various chapters in this book address a range of other issues inherent when carrying out and reporting classroom-based research, including, for example, a chapter on collecting data. So why is this chapter necessary?

Despite the shift in recent years to considering children's perspectives in educational research, there has been less emphasis on the practical challenges inherent in conducting research with Early Years and Primary age children. Researching the lives of younger children shares many of the issues which are also pertinent to researching the lives of older pupils. However, there are a number of specific issues that the teacher-researcher should attend to, during the planning and data collection stages, with young children.

These include such practical matters as specific data collection techniques, pupil engagement and social desirability bias, together with wider considerations such as the question of consensual participation in the research process.

In explaining and exemplifying such considerations and issues, we will be drawing on research carried out by Early Years and Primary teacher trainees as a part of a research course jointly taught by the authors at Cambridge University Faculty of Education. Trainees are required to engage in a classroom-based research project as part of their Masters-level Post-Graduate Certificate of Education (PGCE), focusing their studies on pupils' perspectives on issues related to learning. The choice of research topic is left to the individual trainee and, as a result, the projects are extremely varied. A short list of some recent projects is shown in Table 4.1.

Table 4.1 Some representative research projects carried out by Cambridge University Primary PGCE trainees

Project	Methods	Sample details
1. Autism and subject preference: an investigation into whether children with more autistic tendencies prefer folk-physics to folk-psychology subjects	(a) Social Responsiveness Scale (SRS) questionnaire (b) one-to-one semi-structured interviews	(a) 24 pupils aged 7–11 – 'opportunity sample' (b) 6 pupils, selected as representative of groups from questionnaire responses
2. Looking clever or learning: a small-scale exploration of Dweck's mindsets in Year 4 pupils	(a) '3-scale' questionnaire – Dweck (b) one-to-one semi-structured interviews	(a) 18 pupils (b) 7 pupils, selected as representative of groups from questionnaire responses
3. Respecting yourself and respecting others: a study into self-esteem and pupil behaviour in a Year 5 class	(a) Rosenberg Self-Esteem Scale questionnaire (transcription for pupils as necessary) (b) one-to-one semi-structured interviews (c) observations of behaviour (over 3 lessons)	(a) 20 pupils who had returned consent forms (b) 4 pupils, scoring very high or low on RS-ES (c) 9 pupils, range of behaviour profiles
4. The use of sign language with hearing children as a means to communicate and manage behaviour. A study into the perspectives of children in a Year 2 classroom	(a) structured classroom observations, linked to intervention (b) one-to-one semi-structured interviews with TA, pre- and post-intervention	(a) whole class (b) 8 pupils, spread of ability, chosen by class teacher
5. Beyond the classroom walls: a study of Year 4/5 pupils' perspectives on learning in alternative settings	(a) questionnaire (b) semi-structured group interviews, supplemented by individual 'draw and explain' task (c) observations in setting (d) setting evaluation sheet	(a) whole class (b) 2 x groups of 4 pupils, balanced in terms of gender, age and ability (c) & (d) whole class

(Continued)

Table 4.1   (Continued)

Project	Methods	Sample details
6. A study of bilingualism in Year 1: children's perspectives on using their home language	(a) ethnographic observations – event sampling (b) discussions	(a) & (b) 1 class, all EAL; as appropriate across all 30 pupils
7. Level of social development and pupil attitudes towards working together: a study of children's attitudes to collaborative group work	(a) Spence behaviour rating scales (b) social skills performance testing (Spence); results from (i) naturalistic group observations; and (ii) one-to-one semi-structured interviews	(a) completed by class teacher about pupils (b) 6 x Year 2 pupils; different developmental levels (as identified by class teacher)
8. Researching pupil self-concept construction in relation to teacher perception of ability: does an entity theory of intelligence predicate learned helplessness?	(a) ethnographic observations (b) one-to-one semi-structured interviews (c) pre- and post- 'Talking Partners' intervention confidence questionnaire	(a) 3 pupils and 1 adult, when working together (b) 3 pupils and 1 adult (c) 3 pupils
9. Pupils' perspectives of the purpose and value of collective worship: a case study of 10–11-year-olds in a faith school context	(a) focus group discussions (b) collective worship observations	(a) 2 x groups of 6 pupils (b) 3 pupils, representing different faith groups
10. Pupil perspectives on spaces of learning: how Year 6 children perceive the physical environment of the classroom	(a) semi-structured group interviews, based on preparatory photographing activity (b) design task discussions	(a) 42 pupils took 1 photograph each (a) & (b) 7 children, representing coded photograph groups
11. Working on your own, working together: researching Year 3 pupils' perspectives on working as individuals and working as groups in the classroom	(a) statement sorting – individual, leading to whole class discussion (b) statement sorting – groups (c) 'photo elicitation' group interviews	(a)–(c) 12 pupils (b)–(c) mixed ability groups of 4 children
12. Barriers to learning: exploring the relationship between Year 5/6 pupils' attitudes towards intelligence and how they cope with challenge	(a) Dweck questionnaire – short & longer versions (b) self-evaluation tasks	(a) whole class (b) 6 pupils, on basis of questionnaire responses
13. A study into intrinsic and extrinsic motivation: pupil perspectives on reading across the curriculum	(a) modified MRQ questionnaire – puppet stimulus (b) one-to-one semi-structured interviews	(a) & (b) 20 x Year 1 pupils (all who had returned consent forms)
14. Children's views about display in the classroom and its purpose: a study of Year 1 pupils	(a) responses to classroom display (b) observations of interactions with display (c) structured interviews (pilot for (d) & (e)) (d) 'photo elicitation' questionnaire (e) one-to-one semi-structured interviews	(a) whole class (24) (b) whole class (c)–(e) 3 pupils, higher to lower ability

(Continued)

Table 4.1   (Continued)

Project	Methods	Sample details
15. 'How does the way I feel affect my ability to learn?' A study of four Year 3 pupils' views about the relationship between emotions and learning success	(a) role play scenarios and discussion (b) emotion scale linked to 'feelings photographs'	(a) & (b) four pupils, selected by class teacher on basis of social competence with strangers
16. Learning for the future – pupils' perspectives on six areas of learning in upper Key Stage 2	(a) informal classroom observations (b) questionnaire using Senteo voting technology (c) discussion of responses	(a) Year 5 class (b) Year 5 children who had returned consent forms (c) 6 x Year 5 pupils (and 4 x Year 6 pupils)

Irrespective of the selected topic, projects are required to have three common elements: they should address a research question of interest to the trainee; they should focus on pupil perspectives on issues related to learning that are not subject-specific; and the data collection methods should both serve the research intentions and be appropriate to the age and level of development of the group selected for the project.

Researching pupil perspectives

Pupil perspectives were selected as a unifying theme for our trainees' research projects, a decision linked to the history of research into pupils' views of schooling by researchers at the Cambridge Faculty (Chaplain and Freeman, 1994; Flutter and Rudduck, 2004; MacBeath and McGlynn, 2002; MacBeath et al., 2003; Pedder and McIntyre, 2006; Rudduck and McIntyre, 2007; Rudduck et al., 1995).

Writers on pupil voice emphasize the value of pupil agency; they link opportunities for such consultation to the school improvement agenda, emphasizing the importance of pupils being 'able to contribute something to the school' (Rudduck, 2005: 2). Research in this area may relate to such topics as school routines and support mechanisms for pupils (Chaplain and Freeman, 1994), or to any one of a myriad of issues of direct concern to pupils. Yet whilst we recognize that pupils' views should be taken into account when making decisions on school practices which directly affect them, for the purposes of our trainees' research an explicit distinction is made between pupil perspectives and pupil voice. Pupil voice has become a rallying call for some writers to encourage socio-political change and increased democratization in school. But given their limited time and novice status within their placement schools, it would be overly optimistic to expect our trainees to implement even classroom, let alone whole-school, interventions based on any of their research findings. The 'next step' fundamental to student voice research is not within their gift.

Pupil perspectives research, then, has some specific intended outcomes when carried out by any teacher:

- understanding that there are a range of interacting and complex factors which may influence pupil learning and that such factors extend beyond the confines of the planning, teaching and assessment
- understanding that pupils may have views on these factors, which might differ significantly from the views that might be held by the teacher, other adults and other pupils in their school
- focusing on collecting empirical data about issues for pupils in context, using appropriate methods
- reflecting upon the potential significance that their research findings may have for their personal development.

The point is that engagement in such research provides teachers, at all stages of their careers, with an evidence base for the development of reflective teaching.

Getting started

The starting point for any research should be establishing a rationale – put another way, a reason for the investigating of a problem or the qualifying of a casual observation in a systematic and rigorous way. Reasons may emerge from a chance or prolonged observation of classroom behaviour (e.g. the nature of social interaction in different groups), challenging a popular belief (e.g. all pupils enjoy carpet time), replicating an existing study to 'test' its conclusions in a different environment (e.g. phase of schooling), or testing a theory (e.g. pupils' self-concept is related to academic performance).

We do not limit our trainees to a particular research paradigm, methodology, method or topic. They are required to select a project which is achievable (given time, sample and access limitations), and to justify their research design and the methods they will use to collect and analyse data. They may adopt a more qualitative or quantitative approach; but, in practice, most opt for a pragmatic design using ' ... whatever philosophical or methodological approach works best for a particular research problem at issue' (Robson, 2002: 43), and employing qualitative and quantitative methods for data collection and analysis as appropriate. This approach is in keeping with that adopted by many experienced teachers engaged in classroom- and school-based research to support teaching and learning.

Pragmatism emphasizes 'common sense and practical thinking ... to determine the best approach ... depending on the purpose of the study and contextual factors' (McMillan and Schumacher, 2009: 6). Having identified a problem, adopting a pragmatic approach gives the researcher more flexibility in choosing and selecting the most appropriate research methods to solve problems or investigate phenomena of interest as they arise. Pragmatism does not pigeon-hole the research method; since it 'is not a recipe for educational research, it does not offer prescriptions' (Biesta and Burbles, 2003: 114). This makes the approach unlike other paradigms such as positivism and constructivism, which are more prescriptive towards quantitative and qualitative methods respectively. Pragmatism places a high value on choosing a research design that is most *appropriate,* or least inappropriate, to the particular problem at hand. It provides a theoretical basis for conducting mixed methods studies, where qualitative and quantitative approaches are used within a single study (McMillan and Schumacher, 2009; Robson, 2002).

In mixed-methods, quantitative and qualitative methods are often used alongside each other or sequentially (as in a repeated measures design, where you compare data at two different times). In some cases projects will begin with collection of data from an entire class from which a sub-sample is identified to examine in more detail using interviews or role play (e.g. Table 4.1, projects 10, 14 & 16). In others, open discussion or interviews with a small group (perhaps ability group) will reveal differential outcomes, which can then be compared with other ability groups or the whole class (e.g. Table 4.1, projects 5, 6, 8, 9, & 11). A third approach might be to categorize pupils based on a standardized instrument from which extreme examples are identified and a sample of pupils selected for further qualitative investigation (e.g. Table 4.1, projects 1, 2, 3 & 12). Determining which combination is selected – or whether there are other combinations better suited to your purpose (e.g. Table 4.1, projects 4, 13 & 15) – depends on the nature of the problem or question, along with considerations of context, pupils' ages and level of development, and the skills of the researcher. For example, are you interested in how your pupils compare with the wider population or what they feel about an innovative approach adopted exclusively by your school?

Activity 4.1

What popular assumptions of classroom practice might you consider questioning through research?
    For example:

- What do your pupils think about how they are organized for various activities?
- What do they think of the way the classroom is laid out?
- How do their views about the role of rules and routines in your classroom compare with what you intended?

Write a list of your particular areas of interest. Can you convert these into questions that are suitable for classroom research?

The distinct advantage of combining methods is the potential for the ' … confirmation, disconfirmation, cross-validation, or corroboration' of data (Creswell, 2009: 213). This process is known as methodological triangulation (see Chapter 5) – a term borrowed from map reading, where a geographical location is found by reference to the length of one known side and two known angles. A mixed-methods researcher examines the same phenomena from different angles using different methods, in order to obtain a more reliable and authentic view than could be achieved with a single method of collecting data. In deciding on the balance and type of methods, 'ideally, the priority would be equal between the two methods; in practice, priority may be given to one or the other' (Creswell et al., 2010: 229). In the trainees' research the primary focus for data collection is the accounts given, in various ways, by pupils. However, techniques such as classroom observation using informal diaries or rigorous observation schedules may be used to provide triangulated data. For example, Clare's work (Table 4.1, project 7) studying pupils regarded as having behaviour difficulties used a standardized observation tool to verify the specific nature of their difficulties (Spence, 1980), which she then related to their accounts of school life.

Before we move on to considering specific techniques for collecting data, we will discuss the vital importance of the nature of the relationship between the teacher as researcher and young pupils as subjects of the research.

Ethics and consensual participation in the research process

Whether research is constructed and carried out with due regard to ethical considerations is a major determinant of whether it can be thought of as making a serious contribution to educational research (BERA, 2004); and in this regard, consensual participation is a major component of the ethical dimension of the research. In considering the whole notion of consent as it applies to younger children involved in research, we are therefore primarily reviewing some of the consequential/utilitarian and relational/individual ethical questions that are highlighted in Chapter 6 of this book.

Ashlie's outline of ethical considerations for her study of autism and subject preference (project 1, Table 4) – which included a questionnaire and semi-structured interviews – raises a number of issues with respect to consent. She writes:

A clear research plan was formulated for this study and discussed with the school mentor and partnership tutor at the University. Parental consent was sought for every child who participated in the study, through an explanatory letter sent home with a return slip attached, and verbal consent for the study to take place was sought from the head teacher of the school involved. This was essential to ensure that informed consent for every child involved had been received. Details of how to contact [the researcher] were included in the letter sent home and parents were made aware that any questions they had could be answered before they agreed to give their informed consent for their child to take part. Before being interviewed, the selected children were asked for their verbal consent to take part and to be recorded and they were made aware that they could withdraw from the study at any time without giving reasons. At no time during the study were children's own or others' [responses] revealed to participants ... Anonymity was maintained throughout ... as each participant was given a code based on their year group, and this was used to record their [questionnaire] score and any data gathered during interview. No real names of pupils or schools appear in this paper. False names are used during data analysis and discussion.

Activity 4.2

Before reading on, jot down what you see as the most important elements of ensuring the consensual participation of research subjects. Consider carefully whether the fact that the subjects are younger children would make any significant difference to these considerations.

What is abundantly clear from Ashlie's study is that the issue of consent is multi-layered. For younger children, written consent *must* be sought '... of those who act in guardianship (e.g. parents) or as responsible others' (BERA, 2004: 6). What is important here is that the consent must not be by omission, whereby any letter sent home is phrased so that there is an assumption of consent when there is no response from the guardian. Rather, consent must be active, with approval being explicitly given both for the research to be undertaken and for all possible uses of the research data. In particular, it must be clear who will see the research and who will see or have access to the raw data. For example, there is a great difference between providing an eventual paper to a limited audience and sharing data, such as video or audio material, with a wider audience or via the internet. The key thing is that the audience for the research and the eventual use of the data set are made clear.

Techniques for collecting data from younger pupils

MacBeath et al. (2003) helpfully identify three forms of 'consultation' when seeking the perspectives of young children – direct, prompted and mediated; each of these is associated with particular data collection methods. In the present chapter we have categorized methods based on two dimensions – namely, the degree to which the researcher does or does not participate with the group being studied, and, second, whether data is collected directly or indirectly (see Figure 4.1).

	Strongly agree	Agree	Don't know	Disagree	Strongly disagree
I like reading to the class	☐	☐	☐	☐	☐
I like reading to myself	☺	☺	☺	☹	☹

Figure 4.1 Alternative ways of representing a Likert type rating scale

Figure 4.1 gives the impression that the two dimensions are discrete when in fact they are on a continuum. At one extreme the direct participant observer immerses themselves in all aspects of the lives of those being investigated. At the other extreme the indirect non-participant observer remains aloof from those being investigated. Hence researchers pitch themselves at a point along the continuum. The important point is to evaluate exactly where you are on the continuum. In mixed methods you may engage in a form of progressive participation starting with perhaps a screening instrument (e.g. questionnaire), then **immerse** yourself in the activities of a particular group. Making the decision as to where on the continuum you place yourself, along with practical considerations such as time limits and accessibility issues, is a matter for consideration at the methodological and research design phase.

In many studies (e.g. Table 4.1, project 16), methods appropriate to the two dimensions are used in order that a rounded perspective can be obtained; such mixed-methods research – combining approaches that have different degrees of researcher participation and which access pupil perspectives in different ways – can be highly revealing.

So let us now turn to examples of specific data collection techniques and view them using this classification. In each case we limit our focus to issues of particular significance to researching younger children, again reminding the reader that more general guidance appears elsewhere in this book (e.g. **coding** qualitative data in Chapter 10). We also highlight approaches that provide alternatives to children providing extended written responses, as well as those methods that usually feature reading and writing questionnaires; in so doing we suggest ways to make them more accessible for younger children.

Interviews

Interviewing is central to many classroom-based inquiries, particularly those which focus on pupil perspectives (e.g. nine out of 16 studies in Table 4.1 use interviews as one of their data collection methods). In terms of Figure 4.1, interviewing is a prime example of a direct, participatory method of data collection, though it is open to variation. Directly accessing children's views by engaging them directly with critical questions can take several forms, from relatively informal conversations and discussions, through focus group activities to the various forms of structured interview referred to in Chapters 9 and 10 . This continuum means that the researcher has a range of potential direct, participatory tools at their disposal, through which they can enable children to express their thoughts and feelings. But whatever approach is taken to accessing children's ideas directly, researchers need to be aware of: (a) the potential to bias outcomes by asking leading questions, or put simply, putting words into children's mouths; and (b) children's attempts to second guess what they think the researcher wants to hear.

The **semi-structured interview** is a method of data collection that features in many of the projects in Table 4.1, and it is considered elsewhere in this book; here we might consider the semi-structured interview to make some general points related to talking to younger children. The fundamental issue that underlies a successful interview is being clear about the intention behind it, or the research questions that drive it. A clear idea of what you want to ask and how the responses might contribute to your understanding of the topic in question is therefore essential.

Semi-structured interviews are often favoured where the research is small-scale, since this approach allows the data collected to be manageable in analysis. Structuring allows the researcher to consider in advance the themes he or she wishes to develop, and helps to maintain the focus during data collection. More open strategies are particularly important in theory-building approaches; but given the limitations of the projects we are describing, and the nature of the classroom-based research most usually carried out by teachers, semi-structured approaches are often more suitable. The researcher has the option of using a combination of open and closed questions, or the use of structured questions for main themes (e.g. 'Which lessons do you enjoy the most?') and probing subordinate themes through open questions (e.g. 'Why do you like working with your friends the most?' Or 'You say that was a nice lesson. What makes a nice lesson?'). Thus there is flexibility to pursue lines of argument that the researcher or interviewee find interesting.

In most interview situations, but particularly with younger children, there are a plethora of issues to be considered. Generally, the interviewer is an adult, so the practical issues relate to:

- establishing trust
- overcoming reticence
- maintaining informality
- avoiding assuming that children 'know the answers'
- overcoming the problems of inarticulate children
- pitching the question at the right level
- choice of vocabulary
- use of non-verbal cues
- unquestioningly receiving what children think the interviewer wants to hear (adapted from Cohen et al., 2000: 125).

The ability to deal with such issues depends very much on the personal and professional qualities of the interviewer; not least their social competence, such as their listening skills (Chaplain, 2003). Whilst most teachers are expected to be socially competent, effective interviewing often requires at least the honing of such skills. One needs to consider the effect of 'knowing' your respondents personally on their responses. On the one hand this should enable trust, but on the other it can affect the child's response, and you will also be influenced by your existing expectations and experience of working with the child(ren).

Kvale (1996) suggests that an effective interviewer needs to be knowledgeable in the subject matter of the interview; clear in explaining its purpose and procedures; clear in the use of appropriate language; gentle in enabling interviewees to express what they want to say; a sensitive listener and interpreter of non-verbal communication; open to what seems to be important to the interviewee, yet skilled at pursuing the direction of the interview; and with a critical recall that enables earlier interviewee statements to be called upon where necessary. This is quite a list, but what it emphasizes is that such direct, participatory data collection methods are interpersonal encounters. In setting up an interview with younger children, therefore, it is vital to: put them at their ease (including considering where the interview will take place); explain clearly your role as interviewer (remembering that they are probably used to relating to you in your role as a teacher); explain both what the research is about and why their honest involvement is both helpful to you and appreciated; and explain that there are no right or wrong answers. As Ashlie makes clear in the section above on ethics, it is imperative to stress at every encounter that the children may withdraw from the process at any point – parental or carer consent does not mean that the child is obliged to participate.

With younger children it is also important to be aware of the potential for a strong acquiescence response bias (Breakwell, 2006) – children look for what they think the interviewer/teacher wants and often attempt to provide this for them. Rachel (project 2, Table 4.1) provides us with some steps that go some way to countering this; in her interviews she 'aimed to make items clear, non-leading and non-threatening … [and] used a number of open-ended questions, avoiding too many closed and consecutive closed questions'. Recruiting other pupils to carry out the interviews with the children who are the focus of the research is another potential way that acquiescence response bias might be ameliorated. There are issues with this approach, however, such as the time needed for recruitment and training, whether pupils have the required qualities and skills for effective interviewing, the reliability of multiple interviewers, and how the teacher controls the process at a distance. Nevertheless, if such considerations are controlled for, involving pupils in the research process, beyond being respondents, can bring many positives to a school culture of enquiry. And there are ways in which the approach to the interview can better facilitate effective use of pupil interviewers. Prompt statements might be provided that lessen the necessity for these pupils to actively lead the interview; their role is instead to present the statements as a basis for stimulating a response – for example, 'I'm going to present some statements that other children have made about the use of computers in the classroom. I want you to consider each one and tell me what you think about it.' The work carried out for project 4 (Table 4.1) develops this idea of using 'substitute' interviewers. Amy did not include the recruitment of children as interviewers; she wanted to evaluate an intervention that she had implemented, so engaged her Teaching Assistant (TA) as the interviewer to gain an impartial view on its effectiveness.

In interviewing young children, the pros and cons of individual versus group interviews come to the fore. A one-to-one approach ensures that you acquire the un-distilled perspective of a particular individual; yet, as we have indicated above and depending on the nature of the topic, children may be extremely uncomfortable in expressing their uncensored viewpoints to a figure of authority. An alternative is to interview small groups; this facilitates the interplay of perspectives which can enable the interviewer to pursue lines of enquiry with the group that are stimulated by the responses of an individual (see projects 5 and 1, Table 4.1). Thus, the interviewer might find themselves saying such things as 'that's an interesting point of view, what does everyone else think about that?' or 'would anyone like to add anything to what Sam has just said?' Whilst acknowledging that an interview is necessarily an artificial situation, with group interviews the situation is perhaps '… as close as possible to the real-life situations where people discuss, formulate and modify their views and make sense of their experiences' (Barbour and Schostak, 2004: 43). Further, Lewis (1992: 417) has suggested that in group interviews 'when one child is speaking, other children have "thinking time", thus … encouraging greater reflectivity in responses'. Such data can be immensely rich as a result of such interaction, though of course transcription and attribution to particular individuals becomes more complicated.

The researcher also needs to be aware of group dynamics and variation in the social competence of particular groups. In any group there are individuals who will tend to dominate conversations and those who will be reluctant to speak. Some individuals control questions and answers, some only answer, some will only interact with a specific member, and so on (Schmuck and Schmuck, 2000). One way you can better understand this dynamic is by using sociometrics (Rubin et al., 2011), whereby specific coding methods are used to quantify and qualify the verbal and non-verbal behaviour in a group. The researcher can draw upon non-participant indirect methods (e.g. observing interaction and coding 'types of interaction'). Alternatively a non-participant direct approach can be used where children are asked to nominate friends or those they enjoy working and/ or playing with. With the former method results are recorded diagrammatically on a sociogram, which is essentially a series of circles each representing a child, with lines between indicating the nature of the communication or other behaviour. This approach to understanding the social behaviour of members of your class might, of course, be a focus of your study alongside enabling discussion of the substantive topic of your research.

So, in the examples above, the role of the interviewer can be a direct or indirect participant or non-participant, as opposed to individual interviews which are always direct.

Questionnaires and standardized instruments

Questionnaires and standardized instruments (such as behaviour checklists which tend to be rigidly constructed and have age-related norms) are a rapid way of collecting information from larger groups of people. They tend to be less time-consuming than individual or group interviews, both at the data collection and (given computer statistics programs) analysis stages. As Oppenheim (1992: 100) points out, whilst some practitioners limit the term questionnaire to self-administered schedules, others would include interview schedules 'under the general rubric of questionnaires'.

As with all other data collection methods, questionnaires have their drawbacks. For example, like interviews they are self-report measures, meaning that the researcher assumes that a respondent is capable of at least surface introspection (i.e. self-examination of feelings, thoughts and motives). Secondly, unlike open interviews, pursuing a respondent's line of thought is more limited. Thirdly – and especially with young children this is probably the biggest issue in questionnaire construction – avoiding ambiguity in the questions, and using a scoring system which they can relate to (e.g. using smiley faces instead of numbers), is problematic. Nonetheless, questionnaires and standardized instruments are an effective way of collecting quantitative and qualitative data, provided that they are designed in a user-friendly way. This involves taking account of the level of understanding of your respondents, presenting the questionnaire in a way that is likely to attract the interest of younger children, asking questions which are valid (see Chapter 9) and using scoring systems which are suitable for the type of analysis required for the study. The last point may appear to be a truism; however, establishing how you plan to analyse your data *before* you begin designing your questionnaire is essential when collecting quantitative data, since failure to do so can lead to results which are less meaningful or unsuitable for analysis.

One helpful approach is to use existing instruments rather than designing your own, as existing instruments are internally and externally reliable – in other words they have produced similar patterns and ranges of scores in many contexts often over long periods. Using existing instruments will enable you to differentiate between individuals or groups in your class, and will have normative scores for particular age groups, often gathered from thousands of pupils over time. The distinct advantage here is that you do not have to spend inordinate amounts of time designing, piloting and reviewing your own instrument before getting down to collecting your data. Instead you merely administer the instrument following the protocol, analyse the results and compare your group's performance with the existing norms. This enables you to select subgroups (e.g. those who perhaps score high or low on a particular scale) for closer examination using qualitative methods – interviews or observation. A number of instruments and questionnaires have copyright restrictions, and others require you to contact the original author for permission to use them, however a great many are available free of charge. In project 3 (Table 4.1), Rachel used the Rosenberg Self-esteem Scale questionnaire to ascertain levels of self-esteem for the whole class. She analysed the total scores to identify pupils recording high and low self-esteem. Then she conducted interviews with sub-samples representing the highest and lowest scores to determine how pupils with high self-esteem viewed their world compared with those pupils who had low self-esteem.

However, should you decide to construct your own instrument, you should consider the following advice and principles. Questionnaires are one of the *methods* used in surveys (a *methodology* may also use other methods) and can use open or closed questions or a combination of both. Closed questions are often used when you wish to 'test' an existing theory, whereas open questions are more often used to build a theory grounded in the responses of your respondents. People often make the mistake of thinking that constructing a questionnaire is simple – it is not. Producing a set of unambiguous questions, which a group of young children can answer in an authentic way, is a difficult prospect. As with a questionnaire for any age group, to be fit for purpose it must use appropriate language and have a number and types of questions and scoring systems which are within the developmental capabilities of the respondents. When working with younger children, pay attention to the size of the font you use and the size and presentation of the questionnaire. We recommend using a folded A3 format with questions in no less than a 16-point font.

Box 4.1   Questionnaire format

Closed questions usually require respondents to tick a box indicating a status, preference or rating of a statement. Responses are measured at different levels:
   The most basic level is dichotomous:

Are you a boy ☐ or a girl ☐
Do you have a mobile phone? Yes ☐ No ☐

Moving up a level you may wish to offer a multiple-choice question with a number of answers where respondents are required to tick one box (as in question 3 below) or as many boxes as are relevant (as in question 4 below):

3 Are you in year 1 ☐
    year 2 ☐ or
    year 3 ☐

4 Have you ever played any of these games (tick as many as you like):
    Hide and seek   ☐
    Sardines   ☐
    Sleeping lions   ☐
    Jacob's ladder   ☐
    Sqeak piggy squeak   ☐

(Continued)

Box 4.1   (Continued)

Football   ☐
Rugby   ☐
Netball   ☐

You may then supplement this with an additional open question to see what games are most popular with your particular sample.

The next level is ordinal, where respondents are required to rate a particular statement (strongly agree/agree/don't know/disagree/strongly disagree). It is important to remember that such rating scales are arbitrary since the distance between the different levels of agreement are not the same – nor does 'strongly agree', for instance, mean the same to two or more people. Nevertheless it does give some indication of the direction and strength of feeling. Some researchers leave 'Don't know' out of such scales to force a directional choice. However, reducing the number of scores on a rating scale limits the type of analysis that can be used.

Where an instrument exists which has been used with an older age group than the one you plan to study, modifications can be made to the instrument in terms of simplifying the language or coding system. For example, Likert type scales can be replaced by smiley faces or emoticons, which are readily available on the internet and more colourful.

However there is a caveat. Whilst changing the format of the coding or the language level will make the instrument more valid, it may also affect its reliability. You can, however, check whether the changes have affected the strength of the internal reliability of your 'adapted' scale using various measures. As a further safeguard to validity, it may be possible to pilot your changes with a representative sample (pupils of a similar age, but who are not taking part in your study) to see what the language of the questionnaire means to them – you might be surprised!

To overcome younger children's possible reluctance to answer or their fear of strangers (Oppenheim, 1992), one alternative approach is to administer the questionnaire using puppets, as did Sarah (project 13, Table 4.1). Here the researcher used two matched puppets (e.g. Wibbs and Nibs, or similar gender neutral names) similar to those used in the Berkley Puppet Interview (BPI) method (Measelle et al., 1998). In this method some of the pressure is taken off the researcher as the child 'interacts' with the puppet rather than directly with the researcher. The researcher reads out two opposing statements – one for each puppet – and the child is asked which statement is most like them (e.g. Wibbs – 'I like reading my stories to other children'; Nibs – 'I don't like reading my stories to other children'). Such an approach can be extremely useful with very young children. Each item can be scored on an ordinal scale (5 or 7 point), with a low score being very negative and a high score (5 or 7 respectively) being very positive.

Quantitative data is analysed statistically and can have one or two components – firstly, descriptive statistics (describing the data – e.g. the percentage of pupils agreeing with a statement), and secondly, inferential statistics (making inferences about the distribution of a population based on your sample), which allows you to compare the scores of your group/class with the wider population (see Chapter 11). Here is where using an established scale shows its strength, in that you can determine whether or not your sample is truly representative of the wider school population or is skewed.

The important element to keep in mind in utilizing a pragmatic approach is selecting a method which will answer your question, and not limiting yourself to a particular methodology or method. Thus, questionnaires may be just part of your data gathering, which may also include visual methods.

Visual tools and methods

Chapter 7 briefly refers to the use of visual images and goes on to consider techniques of visual mapping that might be used in data collection. Here we consider the use of the visual in terms of a continuum: from the judicious use of photographs, videos or objects used as visual stimuli to supplement questions or lines of enquiry in interviews and discussions (or in questionnaires, as outlined in the previous section), to the exclusive use of visual data. In so doing, we draw a distinction between the use of the visual as a tool (as in the above related to interviews and discussions) and the specific notion of visual methods. So let us first consider the use of visual 'tools' within established methods such as interviewing.

A prime intention in data collection is that children engage with the process, understand what is being asked of them and are given the opportunity to respond fully by whatever means seems appropriate. In interviews, discussions and focus group activities, talking about something concrete can help even adults to clarify and better express their perspectives; with younger children it can make the difference between a luke-warm response and full engagement. Projects 5, 10 and 11 in Table 4.1 all use different visual tools to enhance the discussion or interview process; their use of such tools is highly appropriate both to the foci of their research and to the needs and capabilities of their subject pupils. Employing the idea that when working with young children 'it is important to understand listening to be a process which is not limited to the spoken word' (Clark and Moss, 2001: 5), Catherine (project 5) 'supplemented the discussions with an individual exercise, asking children to draw and explain their favourite alternative setting for learning'. Emma (project 10) 'asked both year six classes … to take one photograph of the thing that they liked best about the classroom … [and then] grouped each data set separately into themes, creating a **coding framework**. I used this framework in order to create a sample of participants who I would interview.' During the interview process 'children could … refer to the photographs they and their peers had taken, all of which I printed to stimulate discussion'. Lastly, Robert (project 11) used 'photo-elicitation' as a preparatory activity to his group interviews. He states:

At the start of each of the group interviews two photos were shown to the interviewees. The first photo was that of children doing group work. The second photo was that of children working on their own. This photo-elicitation was used as a warm-up task to get children thinking about group work and working alone. Photo-elicitation can be an extremely valuable tool when interviewing children because it can quickly build a rapport between the interviewer and the interviewees and dispel any suspicions a child might have about interviews with adults.

These examples, in different ways, exemplify once again the connections between research intentions and approaches, and the necessity of building confidence with the children who are your research subjects. Some use visual stimuli – whether these might be photographs, objects or video – as a stimulus for discussion (as is the case with Catherine and Robert). The idea of 'pupil view templates' takes a similar approach, attempting to elicit what children might say and what they might think in particular circumstances, using a cartoon format with speech and thought bubbles to complete (Wall, 2008; Wall and Higgins, 2006; Wall et al., 2007). Though the language of the children is presented in a written form in this work, the combining of visual prompts with a space to present ideas in language has proved successful in understanding pupil actions and intentions.

Emma's project takes the idea that the visual may constitute data that can be interrogated. The use of visual methods to elicit young children's thinking has been established for many years (Thomson, 2008), sometimes with the intention that their perspectives should have a direct effect on their learning environment (Burke and Grosvenor, 2003). The 'mosaic approach' (Clark and Moss, 2001) advocates the employment of a multiplicity of techniques to stimulate pupil thinking and encourage them to express and challenge their ideas in a genuinely reciprocal research process designed to lead to change. Thus, over time, the children may be involved in creating photo books, model making, map making, engaging in interviews and in observations of their work; such projects also draw upon practitioner and parent viewpoints. Clearly such work, with its triangulation of a myriad of sources of information and its cyclical nature as a project progresses, is beyond the scope of small-scale projects; but it does suggest tools and techniques that might be adopted by those seeking data other than that which can be provided in a spoken or written form.

A central issue with all approaches that employ 'non-standard' data is that of analysis. Where evidence is being gathered using role play, the taking of photographs, the making of videos, drawings and models, or visual mapping techniques (see Chapter 7), the researcher requires a clear basis on which to make an analysis of the data. In a corruption of the intentions of grounded theory (see Chapter 17), there is sometimes a temptation amongst inexperienced researchers to imagine that such data will 'speak' to them, revealing its secrets. In fact, such data requires that the researcher has a clear framework for analysis, drawn from an interpretation of the literature and linked to their research intentions – just as when working with other data. Data will always reveal some surprises, and may even pick holes in a carefully constructed structure for analysis, but the basic rule is that you have to know what you're looking for before you can find evidence that either confirms or denies your hypotheses. This means having some clear perspectives from which you will view the data, whilst being open to surprises. Further, in planning projects that use visual methods it is important to plan in some time whereby the children's intentions about what they have presented can be interrogated; a short discussion about a drawing can often disavow the researcher of their own cherished interpretation of what the children intended when they were drawing.

Key ideas

Though this chapter can only scratch the surface, we hope that it illustrates that research with younger children requires the same systematic approach and regard for rigour that is expected with older pupils and young adults. Whilst methods and approaches intended to engage young children may appear unfamiliar, we hope it is clear that they stem from established research approaches and that their overall intention is the same as for any educational research – to systematically gather and analyse data using methods that are both reliable and valid.

Reflective questions

1   Have you adopted ethical approaches that are appropriate to carrying out work with young pupils?
2   Have you considered your choice of language when interviewing or briefing children? Are responses best written, spoken or visual?
3   How can you encourage children to provide authentic responses, whilst avoiding 'leading' their responses?
4   Can you use existing questionnaires to increase the validity and reliability of your data instruments?
5   Have you considered adapting the level of such data collection instruments to suit the developmental level of young children?
6   Are you using a pragmatic approach to data collection which will allow you to select the most appropriate combination of methods to the problem you have identified?

Further reading

Alderson, P. and Morrow, V. (2011) *The Ethics of Research with Children and Young People*. London: Sage Publications.

Section 2
CARRYING OUT AND REPORTING ON CLASSROOM-BASED RESEARCH

This section will provide both an introduction to some of the philosophical ideas underpinning research and a guide to the more practical side of classroom-based research by introducing methodology and data collection methods. The new chapter on ethics will provide guidance on how to do the right thing and how to do things right when engaging in research. The final chapters will help with the analysis of data and how to write up the research project for examination and publication.

CHAPTER 5

RESEARCH DESIGN

Elaine Wilson

Chapter overview

Chapter 1 introduced the notion that philosophical ideas often remain largely 'hidden', even though such ideas have a profound influence on the actual practice of research. Indeed, the methodology you adopt will be coloured by these 'hidden', beliefs, and at the start of the process it is important that you make these explicit. This chapter will clarify how philosophical ideas inform the premises on which research projects are based. It is by standing back and considering the nature of knowledge and the ways of studying knowledge that your study becomes a research project as opposed to just a classroom evaluation. An important part of planning your research and disseminating your work will involve you making your own theoretical perspective explicit to others reading your work. As classroom teachers we don't often stop to think about the theoretical perspectives informing

(Continued)

(Continued)

our work. However, to be a credible researcher who is truly reflexive will require that you think about **ontology** and **epistemology,** because these underlying beliefs will inform the methodology you choose to use and will provide a context for the research process and a grounding for the logic and criteria you use to make judgements. Chapters 18 and 19 will help to deepen your understanding of the philosophy of educational research.

Theoretical perspectives

Ontology

Ontology is a complex idea. Blaikie (2000: 8) describes ontology as:

> claims and assumptions that are made about the nature of social reality, claims about what exists, what it looks like, what units make it up and how these units interact with each other. In short ontological assumptions are concerned with what we believe constitutes social reality.

The parameters of a study of the natural scientific world can be clearly defined, for example a chemical process can be isolated and studied. However, when social scientists study people, either on their own or together, the interactions can be unpredictable as people can act irrationally, learn and change. The social world is much more complex and defining precisely what the IT is that is to be studied can be difficult. For example, in schools it might be how teachers interact with students or how students learn.

Ontology, is about defining precisely what IT is that you are studying or researching. That is, the nature of the world and reality (from the Greek word ontos, i.e. that which exists), being studied and asks questions like: what is fundamental? What is real, and what is not?

So, a school-focused ontological question might ask, what is engagement? Is it a fundamental thing that can be measured, what is it precisely and can this be defined and measured?

What is epistemology?

If ontology is the study of what there is or what exists in the social world, epistemology is the study of our knowledge of the world. How do we *know* about the world that we have defined ontologically?

Epistemologists ask questions such as:

- What is knowledge and how do we know things?
- Are there different kinds of knowledge?
- Are there good procedures for discovering knowledge?

Epistemology is the study that explores the nature of knowledge (from the Greek word episteme, i.e. that which we know). It answers the questions: how can we come to know things and be certain of what we know?

To illustrate this with the example of engagement used earlier, if we are able to define 'engagement' precisely how then could we 'measure' this in a valid reliable way?

What is methodology?

Methodology consists of overarching ideas about how a research study is designed, and the research design is the strategy which integrates the different components of the research project in a cohesive and coherent way so that your research questions can be answered. Figure 5.1, adapted from Hay (2002), provides a simplified diagram which illustrates where methodology fits within the process.

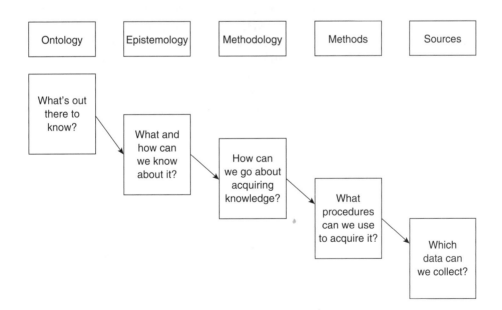

Figure 5.1   Hierachy of philosophical ideas and approaches (adapted from Hay, 2002: 64)

Methodology is the plan of action which informs and links the methods used to collect and analyse data to answer the original research question. Your essay or thesis will include a substantial section about the methodology you have adopted, together with a rationale for the particular methods being used. As you read more about expert work, it will become apparent that some methodological approaches depend heavily on one type of data although increasingly researchers are using a mix of approaches. Research projects, which are largely quantitative in nature, set out to answer 'how many', 'how much', 'who' or 'where' style questions and generate mainly numerical data. Conversely, other more qualitative approaches ask 'what is happening here' type questions which are answered mainly in the form of words.

School-based research tends not to adopt such a polarized stance to methodology and is more likely to take a pragmatic approach and use multiple methods. This approach will be discussed in more detail later in the chapter.

Which research approach will you use?

Once you have decided on a general area of interest and have narrowed your research into a manageable question or **hypothesis**, you will have a clearer idea of the aims and objectives of the research. The next stage will be to decide on an appropriate research approach which is most likely to provide you with evidence to help answer your question or test out your hypothesis. The approach you adopt will be specific to the problem or question you have identified, so it is helpful to think in terms of identifying the best strategy for you, rather than starting with the idea that you are going to do action research. Once you start to plan the process and become clearer about the purpose of your research, it will be easier to identify your methodology and what the most appropriate data collection methods are.

There is however some directionality about this whole process (see Figure 5.2). Research design is not only influenced by the overall research purposes but also by the underpinning ideas driving your research. As you read more about your substantive area of study, you will become more familiar with what is already known about your area of study and also be in a much better position to be able to make decisions about the methods to be used and the sample size to work with.

Unless you are working with a fixed, quantitative design, such as a tightly pre-specified hypothesis-testing process, then it is acceptable to go back and modify your design once you start. It might well be the case that by the end of the research programme, you will have modified your original plan and collected further data. Indeed, some research approaches develop theory during the research process, which means having to be responsive to emerging data to follow up interesting lines, or to look for answers to rather different questions. You may even review the purpose of your study in light of a changed context arising from the way in which the other aspects are developing. Nevertheless, as a novice, it is a good idea to have some ideas at the start of the process about the nature of the data you need to collect and when you should do this.

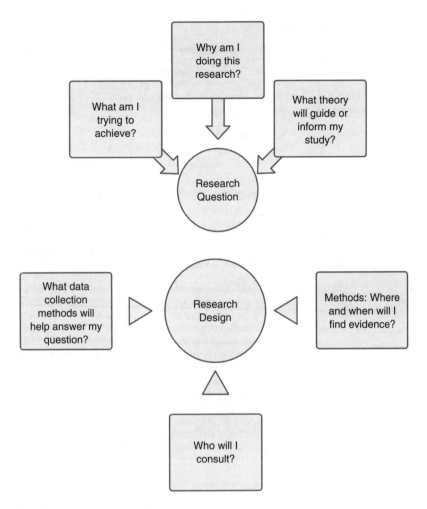

Figure 5.2 Key questions in research design

Research design

When you start out, it is helpful to analyse the research designs used by more experienced researchers. This will not only help you to see what is possible, but will also give you a good insight into the strengths and limitations of the various methodologies and methods being used. To help illustrate this, Tables 5.1 and 5.2 present a summary of the methods and sample sizes used for each research project reported in three exemplar papers.

Table 5.1   Methodology continuum

Qualitative study	Multiple methods study	Quantitative study
Cotton (2006) Teaching controversial environmental issues: neutrality and balance in the reality of the classroom	Donohoe, Topping and Hannah (2012) The impact of an online intervention (Brainology) on the mindset and resiliency of secondary school pupils	Ivens (2007) The development of a happiness measure in school children
Educational Research, 48(2): 223–41	*Educational Psychology*, 32(5): 641–55 http://dx.doi.org/10.1080/01443410.2012 .675646	*Educational Psychology in Practice*, 23(3): 221–39

Table 5.2   Methods and sample sizes

	Ivens (2007) Quantitative study, fixed design	Donohoe, Topping and Hannah (2012) Multiple methods	Cotton (2006) Qualitative study, flexible design
Research Question(s)	Is the School Children's Happiness Inventory (SCHI) a valid and reliable psychometric test?	(1) Will the intervention group move towards a growth mindset after participating in the Brainology program? How will this compare to the comparison group performance over the same time period? (2) Will any significant changes by either group be sustained at follow-up? (3) Does the program impact upon pupils' resiliency, and specifically their sense of mastery? (4) How will the pupils help explain any significant changes in mindset and resiliency?	Do teachers believe that they should take a balanced or neutral view when teaching about controversial issues? What actually happens in their classroom?
Methods What specific techniques were used?	Series of self-report questionnaires for students	Theories of intelligence and resiliency, self-report questionnaires, focus group	Lesson observations, semi-structured interviews with teachers and students
How are the data analysed?	Look for correlation, tested against standardized psychometric test(s)	Statistical analysis and coding of interview transcripts	Themes and issues emerging from close reading of interview transcripts and lesson observations
How are the data shown to be trustworthy?	Large enough sample	Scales validated, constant comparative data analysis	In-depth, rich data collected
Sampling strategy: From whom did the researchers seek data?	One discrete study of 771 8–15-yr-old students, 77 8–11-yr-old students as part of larger study, 41 8–14-yr-old students as an interview transcript	33 secondary school pupils (25 boys and 8 girls), 18 pupils in the intervention group (14 boys and 4 girls) and 15 (11 boys and 4 girls) in the comparison group	Three experienced teachers
Where and when?	In school during a research project	In school over a four-week period	Three schools for a 5–6-week period

Qualitative studies

Cotton's qualitative paper investigated teachers' beliefs about teaching controversial issues and matched these with what was actually happening in their classrooms. She observed three teachers in different schools over a 5–6-week period and also interviewed both teachers and students using a semi-structured interview schedule. She analysed the themes and issues emerging from a close reading of the interview transcripts and lesson observations, and checked the trustworthiness of her data by collecting extensive data and by verifying the accuracy of her interpretation through consulting the teachers concerned.

Quantitative studies

Ivens's quantitative paper investigated the validity and reliability of a modified Subjective Well-Being (SWB) inventory originally used with adults. He modified the psychometric test so that it could be used with school-aged students and renamed the test School Children's Happiness Inventory (SCHI). He subsequently collected data through a series of self-report questionnaires from a large number of students. These data were validated by using statistical correlation.

Multiple methods

The final paper is an example of a mixed-methods approach. This is an exploratory study to investigate the impact of the online interactive programme *Brainology* on the mindset, resiliency and sense of mastery of secondary-school pupils. A quasi experimental pre-, post- and follow-up mixed-methods study was carried out with 33 participants aged 13–14 years. Quantitative data were analysed using analysis of variance. Qualitative data from focus groups were categorized and coded.

Which methodology is useful for school-based research?

The methodological approach adopted will be dependent on the time and resources available to you to undertake school-based research. You are likely to be engaged in a small-scale, short-term, classroom-based project, so using either a case-study or action-research approach is likely to be the most appropriate method.

Case study

Cotton's paper is an example of a case study. Case studies provide detailed knowledge about a single 'case' or small number of cases. In Cotton's paper, the cases are three classroom teachers within the context of different schools. She collected detailed information about each teacher and school through lesson observations and semi-structured interviews with teachers and students, and looked for patterns across the cases. Chapter 16 provides further detailed information about carrying out case studies.

Action research

Donohoe, Topping and Hannahs' paper is an example of researchers directly participating in the process of initiating change, while at the same time researching the effects of such changes on the school, and as such is an example of one cycle of an action research study. Chapters 14 and 15 provide more detailed guidance if you intend to use an action-research approach.

Other methodologies

If you have an extended period of time available to carry out your research, you may be able to use a grounded theory or an ethnographic approach if this is appropriate to meet the aims of your project.

Grounded theory

This approach involves generating theory from data collected during the study and is particularly useful in new, applied areas of research where there is a lack of theory and concepts to describe and explain what is going on. Chapter 17 provides detailed guidance about carrying out a grounded-theory study.

Ethnography

Ethnographic methodology originated in the field of anthropology and describes people and their cultures. In a school context, an ethnographic study would provide a summary of the extensive rich data collected about the participants over an extended, extensive period of observation, while at the same time being culturally immersed in the classrooms. This closeness to the research context is a potential threat to the validity and reliability of the data collection and analysis process; therefore, ethnographers are constantly vigilant of their own interpretation of situations and try to overcome this by verifying and incorporating the perspectives of the participants to validate emerging ideas.

For example, in the paper 'Climbing over the rocks in the road to student engagement and learning in a challenging high school in Australia' (Smyth and Fasoli, 2007), Smyth and Fasoli report on an ethnographic case study of a single secondary school conducted over a five-week continuous period. They used 'embedded interviews' involving observation of in-class teaching prior to extensive one-hour interviews with teachers and student focus groups. All interviews were recorded. Detailed field notes were kept of classroom observations and other activities, including school assemblies, staff meetings and reflections on informal conversations held during teaching breaks in the staffroom. Activity 5.1 uses the criteria set out below to help judge this ethnographic study.

Activity 5.1

Read Smyth and Fasoli's paper. Use the criteria set out below in the form of a series of questions to analyse the ethnographic study and write down what evidence there is that these criteria are met in this paper.

Ethnographic approach

- Does the research avoid disrupting the *natural* setting?
- How does the research focus on *lifestyle* and *meaning?*
- How have the researchers negotiated access to the school?
- How much time have the researchers spent in the classroom?
- How much data have they collected?
- Have the researchers considered both *processes* and *relationships?*
- Do the researchers take account of their own *beliefs, interests, experience* and *expertise* in drawing conclusions?
- Do the researchers describe how their work builds on or contradicts other explanations?
- Do the researchers acknowledge that their findings are their *interpretation* rather than a *literal* description?

Large-scale quantitative studies

When the aim of the research is to seek patterns and the researcher has access to large numbers of participants, perhaps at a whole-school level, then you could use either an experimental or non-experimental fixed research design. Chapters 11 and 12 provide details of these approaches.

1   *Experimental design*: Hidi, Berndorff and Ainley's (2002) paper is an example of an experimental strategy. The central feature of this approach is that the researcher actively and deliberately introduces a change in the situation of the participants with a view to producing and measuring a resultant change in their behaviour. This is an example of a researcher manipulating one variable on another variable – in this case, the detailed design was pre-specified before the main data collection began.

2   *Non-experimental design*: Ivens's paper (2007), on the other hand, uses a non-experimental strategy. Although Ivens draws on a large sample, his approach is different from the experimental approach in that he does not attempt to change the participants' circumstances but rather looks for patterns in the data.

How big should your sample be?

Before starting to collect data for all methodological approaches, you should define the population of your area of interest and determine the size of your sample by using an appropriate sampling strategy. In other words, start by considering who you will include in your research project and why, and be able to justify the selection of this sample.

If you intend to generate big numerical data sets to look for patterns and correlations, you should read Chapter 11 which will explain the different approaches you could take.

If, on the other hand, you are interested in what is going on in a particular setting, then the sampling approach will be different and will be determined by the scope of your study. To this end, your research approach should be either very thorough or confirmed by using multiple methods. Being thorough involves *saturation*, that is continuing to gather information until you reach a point where you are not adding any new data. This is more likely to happen through prolonged engagement with your research, persistent observation, broad representation of the area of study and through dialogue with a critical friend. Chapters 9 and 10 extend these ideas further.

    Key ideas

As an individual classroom practitioner, it is advisable for you to keep your study narrowly bound with a clear manageable focus because the broader the scope, the longer it will take you to collect sufficient data to be confident about the validity and reliability of the claims being made, so that your work will be credible. For example, planning repeated interviews using semi-structured interviews, which produce a small amount of data per interview question, will need a large number of participants, while in-depth interviews producing much richer data can be fewer in number.

Reflective questions

- What is it you want to research?
- How will you measure this?
- How best can you answer your research question?
- Are you trying to study something in depth or make changes and see if they make a difference? So what methodology will you use?
- What are the most useful and appropriate data collection methods to use?

Further reading

Anderson, G. and Arsenault, N. (1998) *Fundamentals of Educational Research.* London: The Falmer Press.

Bridges, D. (2001) 'The ethics of outsider research', *Journal of Philosophy of Education,* 35(3): 371–87.

Busher, H. (2002) 'Ethics of research in education', in M. Coleman and A.R.J. Briggs (eds) *Research Methods in Educational Leadership and Management.* London: Paul Chapman.

Cohen, L., Manion, L. and Morrison, K. (2011) *Research Methods in Education* (7th edn). London: Routledge.

Creswell, J. (2012) *Research Design: Qualitative, Quantitative, and Mixed Methods Approaches* (3rd edn). London: Sage Publications.

Creswell, J. (2012) *Qualitative Inquiry and Research Design: Choosing Among Five Approaches* (3rd edn). London: Sage Publications.

Denscombe, M. (2012) *The Good Research Guide* (3rd edn). Maidenhead: McGraw-Hill (Open University Press).

Pendlebury, S. and Enslin, P. (2001) 'Representation, identification and trust: Towards an ethics of educational research', *Journal of Philosophy of Education,* 35(3): 361–70.

Pring, R. (2004) *Philosophy of Educational Research.* London: Continuum.

Simons, H. and Usher, R. (eds) (2000) *Situated Ethics in Educational Research.* London: RoutledgeFalmer.

Taskakkori, A. and Teddlie, C. (1998) *Mixed Methodology: Combining Qualitative and Quantative Approaches.* Thousand Oaks, CA: Sage Publications.

Thomas, G. (2009) *How to Do Your Research Project: A Guide for Students in Education and Applied Social Sciences.* London: Sage Publications.

CHAPTER 6

ETHICS IN EDUCATIONAL RESEARCH

Kris Stutchbury

Chapter overview

This chapter will introduce the important notion of ethics into the research process. Right at the onset of developing the research design, a researcher must always stick to an ethical code and do the right things whilst also endeavouring to carry out the research in a fair and rigorous way, in other words to do things right.

Introduction

All research involving groups of people interacting with each other has an ethical dimension; educational research is no exception and the ethical issues are often complex. They are likely to emerge and may change as the research proceeds.

On one level, ethics is about obvious things like acting with honesty and integrity, acting within the law and 'doing the right thing'. However, it is also about the integrity of your research. It is about ensuring that you have enough data to draw conclusions, reporting the evidence accurately, and being open about your assumptions and the limitations of your conclusions. It is about 'doing things right'. As researchers, we have a duty to act ethically and to make sure that in reporting our research, the reasoning behind ethical decisions is recoverable by the reader. It is important that the decisions that we make have a defensible moral basis and that the process of making those decisions is transparent.

Many institutions have produced lists of 'ethical guidelines' or principles that should be followed: the British Educational Research Association (BERA) has published a list of such principles (2004). These are underpinned by the ethical respect for

- the person
- knowledge
- democratic values
- the quality of educational research
- academic freedom.

The problem with such lists is that the issues are complex and interconnected; even when you have been through the list it is difficult to be sure that you have covered all the issues. In this chapter we are going to introduce you to a way of thinking about your project that will enable you to identify all the ethical issues. The analysis will help you decide how to behave, but it will also support your whole research design. It will help you to decide how to collect data, how to present your findings and how to choose your participants. Applying the framework will help you to anticipate problems and therefore identify actions that will help to avoid difficulties and improve the quality of your research. We will start with introducing an example, which will be referred to throughout the chapter. If you already have an idea for your own project, you might like to use that alongside the example provided.

Box 6.1   Mary's project

Mary worked in a school that was keen to help their students improve their thinking skills. They had recently developed a whole-school approach to the issue. The approach was introduced on a staff training day, which was followed by a whole day off timetable in which form tutors introduced the approach to their forms. Mary decided to evaluate the use of this approach in a sequence of seven science lessons to see if it helped to make practical work more purposeful. She worked with her Year 8 class. She carried out a questionnaire before and after the teaching

(Continued)

> ### Box 6.1   (Continued)
>
> sequence in order to establish the levels of motivation in practical lessons, and whether or not it had changed. She identified a group of students on which to focus, recording their discussions during the practical sessions and conducting two group interviews, one in the middle of the sequence and one at the end. She also observed the students at work and asked them to keep a reflective log about their learning in the practical sessions.

What is 'an ethical issue'?

In the sorts of projects carried out by teachers in schools, the ethical issues might not seem to be too problematic. The potential for harm is not very great and the sorts of activities that participants are likely to be undertaking are not very different from those that they do every day. Let's consider Mary's case. She is proposing to administer a questionnaire to the whole class; she will be selecting a small group and recording their conversations; she will be asking them to complete a reflective log; and she will be conducting two group interviews (which will be recorded).

Activity 6.1

Think about Mary's project and write a list of the ethical issues that you think Mary should take into consideration. You could consult the BERA guidelines. You might like to do the same for your own project, even if you have not finalized your research design.

The most obvious issue here is 'informed consent'. When children are involved you need to inform the child and the parent that you are asking the child to participate in research, and make it clear that they have the right to withdraw should they want to. Some schools might insist that you send a letter asking for permission for their child to take part and require you to collect reply slips for every child; whereas others would suggest that a letter home informing parents about the research, giving them the chance to ask for more information or opt out is sufficient. Confidentiality is also important. The recordings should be stored on a secure server and only used for the purposes of the research. How to select the sample can present ethical dilemmas as some children might be keen to be involved and some might feel left out. In this case selecting a sample of four from a class of 28 is not too contentious, but it has been known for students to end up using the whole class so that some children did not feel under-valued! How to make the selection requires some careful thought. Mary observed her class during the day off timetable and selected the group that were the most talkative and forthcoming during the exercises designed to introduce the new way of working.

So, obvious ethical issues include:

- informed consent
- confidentiality
- data storage and security – including the use of photographs
- the selection of participants.

Further issues could include:

- When will the children be interviewed? Is it fair to impose on their break time or take them out of lessons?
- How long will the interviews take?
- How long does the questionnaire take?
- Will the research affect the children's ability to finish the work required by the Science Dept?

There aren't any difficult ethical dilemmas here, just some decisions to make about how to collect the data. But you will find that the more you think about a project and consider possible research designs, the more complicated things become, and it is difficult to be sure that you have included everything. The framework that we are going to introduce is based on moral theory and it helps you to identify and consider all the issues by looking at your project from different perspectives. We will demonstrate how, by using the framework, Mary was able to do a much more in-depth analysis of the ethical issues and anticipate some significant difficulties that could have affected the quality and impact of her work.

Introducing an ethical framework

In this section, we describe an ethical tool – a framework for making sense of ethical issues. It takes into account the fact that as you deliberate on the ethical issues associated with a project, you will find that the ideas are connected to each other and that it can be difficult to be logical, consistent and sure that everything has been covered.

The framework that we describe prompts you to think about your situation from different perspectives. By using the framework to analyse a situation, the ethical issues can be tackled *systematically,* within a moral framework. The framework does not provide solutions, but through its use, you are more likely to act ethically and can present the decisions in such a way that the decision-making process is transparent and can be discussed.

The framework has been developed from the work of Seedhouse (1998a) and Flinders (1992). Seedhouse is a philosopher and developed what he calls a 'grid' based on moral theory in order to support the work of healthcare professionals involved in ethical decision-making. Flinders argues that discussion of ethics in qualitative research is often characterized by a lack of models that might help researchers to anticipate and better recognize dilemmas. He proposes four 'ethical frameworks' (based on moral theory) that can be used as a basis for discussion of ethical dilemmas in qualitative research. We have combined the ideas of Seedhouse and Flinders to produce a framework that can be applied to educational research. In this section, we will describe and explain the framework and suggest a methodology for its use in educational research (see Figure 6.1).

The ethical framework

Imagine you are looking down on a pyramid (see Figure 6.1). Each layer represents an area of moral theory that should be taken into consideration when dealing with a situation with an ethical dimension. (A brief introduction to moral theory can be found at www.st-andrews.ac.uk/~ea10/theory.htm.) In the original work, Seedhouse identified a set of boxes within each layer; we have used Flinders's ideas to adapt these boxes to make a framework applicable to educational research.

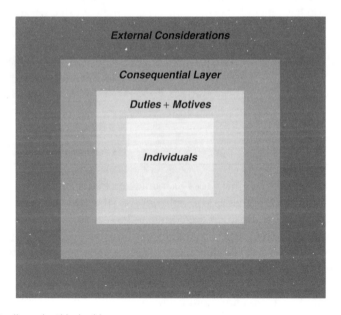

Figure 6.1   Seedhouse's ethical grid

The external or ecological layer

This layer invites us to consider the context of the research and the wishes of people external to the situation, the culture of the institution in which you are working and the relationship between the part of the institution in which you are working and the institution as a whole.

The consequential or utilitarian layer

This layer encourages reflection on the framework: whether 'good' attached to our anticipations for action is increased for humanity as a whole, for a particular group, for the individual or for the researcher personally. We need to consider the effects that the research might have on the participants, the consequences of suggested actions on a school, teachers or students and anyone else who might be affected by the results or the process of carrying out this research.

The deontological layer

This layer considers the duties and motives of the research. Deontologists either decide on a single overriding duty (e.g. never breaking promises), a range of duties, or a hierarchy of duties to guide their actions. It is about avoiding doing wrong. Seedhouse invites us to consider whether our proposed cause of action 'is the right thing to do'. It covers things like not doing harm, beneficence and acting with integrity, truth-telling and promise-keeping. This would include consideration of the way in which the research was carried out, informing participants and interested parties of the outcomes at an appropriate stage, and consideration of how we might deal with sensitive information that emerges. This incorporates the 'situationist' approach to ethics (Oliver, 2003).

Individual layer/relational ethics

 In this layer, we are invited to focus on the 'core rationale' of the project and to consider the needs of the individuals involved. We need to focus on the relationships at the heart of the research. In healthcare, autonomy is an overriding theme; in educational research, Bond (2005) argues that it should be 'trust'.

Using the framework

Seedhouse divides each layer into a set of boxes (Seedhouse, 1998b) which embrace key issues appropriate to that 'layer' of thinking. Using the work of Flinders and Seedhouse together, we have modified these boxes from the original grid to make them more appropriate for educational research. The idea is that the 'boxes' can be used to generate a set of questions that you can use to interrogate your situation. Some possible questions are suggested in Table 6.1, but you might find it more appropriate to focus on the left-hand column and devise your own set of questions that apply to your situation.

Table 6.1   Ethical questions to ask

External/ecological	Questions to consider
Cultural sensitivity	What are the values, norms and roles in the environment in which I am working?
Awareness of all parts of the institution	What is the relationship between the group I am working with and the other parts of the institution as a whole? How does it affect the participants?
Responsive communication – awareness of the wishes of others	How might my work be viewed/interpreted by others in the institution? How will the language I use be interpreted?
Responsibilities to sponsors	What are my responsibilities to the people paying for this research (sponsors, my school, grant awarding bodies)?
BERA codes	Have I stuck to the BERA guidelines?
Efficiency/use of resources	Have I made efficient use of the resources available to me – including people's time?
Quality of evidence on which conclusions are based	Have I got enough evidence to back up my conclusions and recommendations?
The law	What are the implications of what I want to do within the ECM agenda? Do I need written permissions? Is anyone at risk as a result of my research?
Consequential/utilitarian	
Benefits for individuals – informed consent	Have I made sure that all the people involved know what I am doing and why? Are they aware that they can withdraw if they wish? How will I ensure confidentiality?
Benefits for particular groups	What are the benefits of me doing my research to the organization/school/department? Could these be increased in any way? How will I ensure that they know about my findings? Is my work relevant to the school development plan?
Most benefits for society	Is this a worthwhile area to research? Am I contributing to the 'greater good'? Is this something other people working in education might care about?
Benefits for the researcher	Am I going to be able to get enough data to write a good thesis? Is this a topic I really care about? Will this work contribute to my professional development?
Deontological	
Avoidance of wrong – honesty and candour	Have I been open and honest with everyone who might be affected by this research?
Minimization of harm – be fair	Have I treated all participants fairly? Do I have a clear rationale for selecting the participants? Are they willing to be involved?
Reciprocity – do they really understand what I am doing?	What will I do if I find out something that the participants/school/department do not like? How will I report unpopular findings?
Doing the most positive good	Is there any other way I could carry out this research that would bring more benefits to those involved?
Relational/individual	
Genuine collaboration/trust established	Who are the key people involved? How can I build a constructive relationship with them?
Avoiding imposition/ respecting autonomy	Am I making unreasonable demands on any individuals? Do they appreciate that participation is voluntary? Am I acting in a way that might constitute an imposition?
Confirmation of findings	What steps will I take in my methodology to ensure the validity and reliability of my findings?
Respecting persons equally	How will I demonstrate my respect for all participants? Have I treated pupils in the same way as teachers?

In this section, firstly, we will apply the framework as described above to Mary's project. You might like to do it for yourself first – or to think about your own project in terms of the questions above. Secondly, we will draw out some of the features of the framework and highlight the advantages of working in this way.

Applying the framework to Mary's project

We will start with the 'external/ecological' layer. Mary was working in her own school, with her own class, so there were no accessibility issues. The Head had encouraged her to complete her MEd; there is a culture in the school of improving practice by focusing on teaching and learning and Mary is a member of the 'Teaching and Learning Group'. As she focused on the questions, Mary realized that the particular approach to learning that she wanted to investigate was being championed by the Senior Leadership team. There was a risk that she would discover something that would not be welcomed or which would challenge the people prompting this approach. How would they react? She was also concerned about the reaction of the Head of Science because her planned sequence of lessons, including quite a lot of practical work, would take longer than was suggested in the scheme of work.

Moving on to the 'consequential layer', Mary focused on the various groups. There were consequences for the school; if she discovered something negative about the approach that they were adopting, what would the reaction be? On the other hand, she might discover something very helpful that would enable the school to apply the approach more effectively. There would be potential benefits for the pupils in the school, if the project led to the approach being used more effectively, and benefits for the individual participants in that the teacher was taking a personal interest in them. However, if the interviews and reflective log imposed on their social and relaxation time, they might become resentful. There were potential benefits for the teaching and learning group as the work could provide a focus for further activity and obvious benefits to Mary in that she would obtain a higher degree.

The risk of harm (deontological layer) came from the effect on people's morale, confidence or ego, if she discovered something unwelcome about this approach. How to handle the selection of the sample was also an issue that could have upset some of the class. She decided that in order to achieve the benefits identified in the previous section, a policy of openness and collaboration was needed. Mary was anxious not just to produce another study that was considered interesting; she wanted to make a real contribution. As part of her own beliefs about education she realized that she really cares about equipping children with the ability to think for themselves and become independent learners, and that making an impact within the school on this issue was very important to her.

At the heart of the framework is consideration of the key relationships. In Mary's case, it was important that she got on well with the class involved, which is why she used her own form, rather than another group that she taught. The support of the Head of Department, the Teaching and Learning Group and the Senior Leadership team were also important. She needed to build credibility with each group and ensure that she had good, reliable data from a variety of sources.

So where did this analysis lead? As a result of considering these questions the main issue that emerged was around the fact that she was evaluating something that was already in use and that people believed in. The potential difficulties that might arise from discovering something that people did not want to hear emerged at several levels. This often happens when you work through the framework in a systematic manner and serves to highlight the really important issues. As a result of the analysis, she took the following actions:

- She explained her research plan to her colleagues in the Teaching and Learning Group and listened to their suggestions.
- She wrote to the parents of the class, explaining the research and giving them the chance to ask more questions. For the four children in the target group, she asked them to return a slip signed by their parents, agreeing to them taking part in the interviews. This was in accordance with her school's policy.
- She shared her plans with the Head of Science and they jointly worked out a schedule which meant that Mary's class could do the amount of practical work required for the study without falling behind the other classes.
- She arranged to carry out the group interviews in assembly time so that she did not impose on the children's relaxation time. This limited the length of the interviews, but she decided that she would still have enough data.
- On getting some quite negative comments from the children in the second round of interviews, Mary was worried about the potential impact of her research. She shared her emerging findings with the Teaching and Learning Group. Someone suggested that she should carry out a final group interview in which she shared her findings with the children and asked them to confirm her interpretation.

Mary discovered that there were aspects of the approach that the children really enjoyed, but that they found it very repetitive. In fact during the second interview, some were very negative. However, during the final session in which Mary shared her findings with the group, they moderated their comments and explained exactly why they found it repetitive. This resulted in a deeper explanation of the things they did not like about the approach, which was very helpful.

Mary's recommendation to the school was that teachers should try and find ways of varying the approach whilst maintaining the core principle that they should be supporting independent learning. As a result of the way in which she conducted her research, she was able to deliver what could have been interpreted as an unpopular message in a non-threatening manner. She kept people informed throughout; she invited suggestions and welcomed the observer into her classroom; she collected sufficient data to produce credible evidence; and crucially, by sharing her findings with the children, was able to have a dialogue about how the approach might be improved.

Some general observations about using this approach to ethics

It is not intended that you should use all the questions in Table 6.1. They are intended as a guide to support your thinking as you focus on each of the different perspectives.

- In your situation, some of the issues might not apply. Don't feel you have to answer every question at every level.
- As you apply this grid to your own research, there will inevitably be some repetition and overlap. This is not a problem and is inevitable in the complex situations that arise. In fact, this is why linear organizing principles are often difficult to apply. For example, you are invited to focus on the implications for the individuals concerned in the 'consequential layer' and the 'individual layer'. This is entirely appropriate, as on one level you need to consider practical things like 'do they understand my project?' and 'how much time have they got available?', as well as the deeper, emotional implications of what you are asking them to do.
- In his paper, Flinders applies his frameworks to each stage of the research, recognizing that the dilemmas and issues will change as the project progresses. You need to be mindful of the framework and revisit the questions as your focus shifts from gathering data to analysis and interpretation. It can be particularly helpful if you have to change track for some reason beyond your control. By going back to the framework you can justify new decisions that you make.
- The questions incorporate big ethical questions that might arise (such as the implications of videoing or photographing children, reporting unpopular findings, ensuring confidentiality), as well as issues around the integrity of your research (such as getting enough data, making efficient use of resources and reporting your findings appropriately).
- Any decisions that you make during this process can be traced back to one of the questions within a particular layer. The decision-making process is therefore recoverable and has a moral basis. Likewise, any decisions that are forced on you as a result of changing circumstances can be checked alongside the framework to ensure the integrity of your research is maintained. For example, you may plan to interview six people for an hour each. It turns out that cover is not available and that you are limited to 20-minute interviews. This can be justified in terms of making use of available resources and not imposing on the participants, but will it generate enough data? By thinking it through in the context of the grid, you should be able to come to a sensible decision about how to proceed. Instead of just settling for what you can get, the framework prompts you to maybe find an alternative source of data.
- Very often in educational research, decisions are made on a reactive basis. The application of this grid encourages you to be proactive in identifying dilemmas before you get into difficulties.

Mary found – as students who use this framework often do – that focusing on the consequences of the research for all the people and the institution involved can be very helpful. Despite the difficulties and dilemmas, it was still clear that this was a worthwhile enterprise with the potential to be of great value in a school where considerable resources had been allocated to promoting a particular approach to learning. Crucially, Mary believed in the philosophy behind the approach; using the framework to interrogate her research plan helped her to articulate her core beliefs, which is very important in research involving people.

Links with the literature from educational research

In educational research, as you immerse yourself in the literature of your chosen area you find, after a while, references to things you have already read and the literature begins to take on some sort of 'shape'. The field of 'ethics', however, is so complex that it is difficult to achieve this in the timescale of a small-scale study. A strength of this framework is that it embraces many of the ideas in the literature in a form that means they can all be considered. Without the framework, the temptation is to adopt one particular approach, and there is a risk of not considering all the angles. Also, most of what is written in this field makes good sense, and there is very little with which one could disagree, but there is a distinct absence of unifying principles, presented in a useful manner (Flinders, 1992; Small, 2001). There is a set of comprehensive guidelines from BERA, but as Homan (1991: 36) argues, 'the notion of an ethical code does not easily fit the conditions which apply in social research'. The grid incorporates BERA's guidelines as part of a comprehensive and systematic analysis of your situation. A popular idea in the field of ethics is the notion of 'situated ethics' (Oliver, 2003). This recognizes that ethical dilemmas and issues will always be specific to a particular context. The framework described could be argued to be embracing the idea of 'situated ethics', but it provides a logical and systematic way of thinking about the particular situation.

At the end of this chapter, there is a bibliography including accounts of ethics that might apply to small-scale research projects. By applying the grid, you will have incorporated many of the ideas presented.

    Key ideas

In small-scale educational research projects conducted in school by practising teachers, it is unlikely that huge ethical dilemmas will arise. However, by applying this framework to your work, any that there are will be identified, and the implications of methodological decisions can be checked. Hence the integrity of your research will be maintained; you will be 'doing the right thing' as well as 'doing things right'.

Reflective questions

1 Negotiating access

   (a)   Do you have formal permission to carry out your investigation?
   (b)   Have the participants agreed to be involved?

2 Ethics

   (c)   Is what you are proposing to do ethical?
   (d)   Have you read the BERA guidelines?

3 Information for participants

   (e)   Have you discussed what you intend to do with your participants?
   (f)   Have you discussed what the outcome of the research will be?
   (g)   Will you provide the participants with a copy of the final report?

4 What information?

   (h)   What hunches and thoughts arise during the research?
   (i)   Is the context or background information important?
   (j)   Is it likely that there is a wide range of views and of practice?

5 Why collect this information?

   (k)   How will the kinds of information identified in (1) above help you answer a particular research question?
   (l)   Do you need to collect data from all the possible sources available?
   (m) Are some more vital than others?

6 When do you need it?

   (n)   Is there an order of priorities for data collection?
   (o)   Is certain information only available at particular times in the school year?
   (p)   Do you need to collect baseline data before you start with your intervention?

7 How do you collect it? Will you need to:

   (q)   observe situations?
   (r)   sit in on discussions?
   (s)   interview those involved?
   (t)   use a questionnaire?

(Continued)

(Continued)

8   Where can you find the information?

(u)   Should you seek this in classrooms, staffrooms, corridors, meetings, filing cabinets, official documents, or through private contact with individuals?

9   From whom?

(v)   Are you clear about who all the participants are?
(w)   Has every possibility been identified?

Further reading

Anderson, G. and Arsenault, N. (1998) *Fundamentals of Educational Research.* London: The Falmer Press.

Bridges, D. (2001) 'The ethics of outsider research', *Journal of Philosophy of Education*, 35(3): 371–87.

Busher, H. and James, N. (2012) 'The ethical framework of research practice', in A.R.J. Briggs, M. Coleman and M. Morrison, (eds) *Research Methods in Educational Leadership and Management* (3rd edn). London: Sage Publications.

Cohen, L., Manion, L. and Morrison, K. (2000) *Research Methods in Education.* London: RoutledgeFalmer.

Denscombe, M. (2003) *The Good Research Guide.* Maidenhead: McGraw-Hill (Open University Press).

Pendlebury, S. and Enslin, P. (2001) 'Representation, identification and trust: Towards an ethics of educational research', *Journal of Philosophy of Education,* 35(3): 361–70.

Pring, R. (2004) *Philosophy of Educational Research.* London: Continuum.

Simons, H. and Usher, R. (eds) (2000) *Situated Ethics in Educational Research.* London: RoutledgeFalmer.

Taskakkori, A. and Teddlie, C. (1998) *Mixed Methodology: Combining Qualitative and Quantitative Approaches.* Thousand Oaks, CA: Sage Publications.

CHAPTER 7

DATA COLLECTION

Elaine Wilson and Alison Fox

Chapter overview

This chapter builds on the ideas about research design introduced in Chapter 5 and will offer advice on the strengths and limitations of each data-collection method to help guide your collection of data. If the methods you propose involve mainly words, then you should also read Chapters 9 and 10 before you start. Alternatively, if you want to collect data involving mainly numbers, then also read Chapters 11 and 12.

Deciding on data-collection methods

Having decided on the focus of your research, the research questions you want to answer, and the overall strategy you want to use, then the next stage is to consider what data you need to collect to help you to answer the research questions.

There are three possible approaches to obtaining evidence about schools and classrooms. Firstly, you can observe students and teachers at work to find out what is going on. Secondly, you could ask students or teachers about what they think is going on, and, thirdly, you could look for traces of other evidence to verify that whatever you were investigating has taken place.

There are no rules which say you must only use one method in an investigation. In classroom-based research, using more than one method will be an advantage, although it will add to the time needed to carry out your research. Indeed, by using only one source, you may miss key ideas, or worse, be lulled into thinking your survey has discovered the 'right' answer about the issue in your classroom. Using more than one source of data will help you take into account other perspectives in your developing understanding of the situation.

Recording events – using a research diary

Writing a research diary is a very effective way of keeping control of the information your research generates. You could also use the contents of your diary as a source of data, although this will be different from the information, observations, records or other data which you collect. The diary contains information about you and what you do, and will provide an accurate record of the process of research. It complements the data yielded by the research methodology.

Some people use a highly structured format using prepared forms. However, this is not essential, provided you can find your way around your own diary. It is very useful to leave space for later comments or additions – in wide margins, on the backs of pages, or in good spaces between entries.

There are no hard and fast rules about style, language and spelling. Keep your diary in the style which you find useful, and which helps you to reflect on what you are doing. Reflect critically on your own diary keeping by doing Activity 7.1.

Activity 7.1   Keeping a research diary

What goes in your diary?
1 A summary of what happens each day you work on the project.
2 Accounts of conversations, discussions, interviews, planning sessions, and so on, with peers, co-researchers, teachers, supervisors and participants.
3 Questions and topics for further study or investigation.
4 Hunches and thoughts.
5 Diagrams, drawings and mind-maps.
6 Observations.
7 Reflections on what you saw.
8 Reflections on re-reading the diary.
9 Plans for future action or research.

Planning the data-collection process

Having decided on your approach and the data you want to collect, it is a good idea to plan each stage carefully before you start. The example in Table 7.1 illustrates how Nicky, a secondary science teacher, went about planning her research design. She asked the question *What are students' attitudes to writing in science lessons?* She refined this question further and decided to try out a range of strategies in her class and look for changes in the students' attitudes. She developed three questions and chose a range of data-collection methods which she believed would help her answer these questions. Her overall research design is shown in Table 7.1.

Table 7.1 Research design of a secondary science MEd student

What are students' attitudes to writing in science lessons?				
Question	**Data source**	**Data source**	**Data source**	**Data source**
RQ1 – What attitudes do students have about science?	Attitude questionnaire (Kind et al., 2007)	Semi-structured interviews (individual and/or group) with pupils		
Sub question 1 – Can writing to an authentic audience other than the teacher improve student *attitude* to science?	Attitude questionnaire, before and after (Kind et al., 2007)	Semi-structured interviews (individual and/or group) with pupils	Analysis of written comments in student learning journals	
RQ2 – What would help them to be better writers?	Analysis of students' written work	Semi-structured interviews (individual and/or group) with pupils	Analysis of written comments in student learning journals	
RQ3 – Can writing to an authentic audience other than the teacher improve students' *learning* of scientific concepts?	Concept map before and at the end for each topic	Semi-structured interviews (individual and/or group) with pupils	Analysis of student written work and comments in student learning journals	Summative assessment results

Nicky carried out a survey of her class first and then selected a sub-sample for follow-up interview using the survey data. This method of merging data is sequential. Nicky also concurrently collected three other sources of qualitative data: the students' written work, concept maps and learning journals. Her final data source was summative assessment of students' work (Figure 7.1).

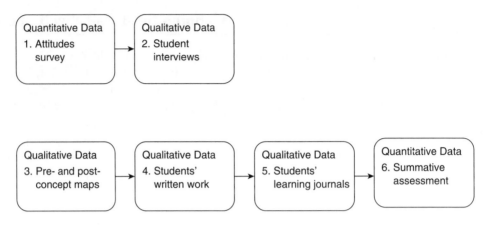

Figure 7.1 Meeting multiple methods

The grids in Figure 7.2 will help you to structure your research design and plan the project timescales.

Title:				
Research question:				
Sub-questions	**Data source**	**Data source**	**Data source**	**Data source**
1.				
2.				
3.				

When do I need to collect the data?			
	Pre-intervention?	**During**	**Post-intervention**
Sub-Q 1			
Sub-Q 2			

An example timescale					
Jan. – Apr.	**Apr. – Jun.**			**Jul. – Aug.**	**Sept.**
Review literature	Essay 1	Methods/pilot study		Writing up	Essay 2
Data collection	Lit. rev. chapter	Data analysis	Method chapter		Thesis

Figure 7.2 Planning data collection

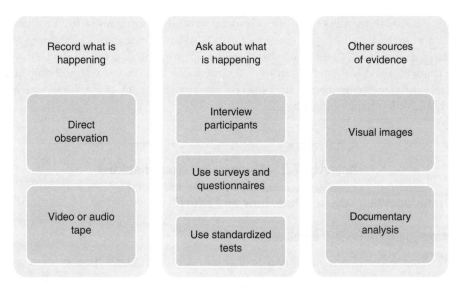

Figure 7.3   Data-collection methods

Reducing threats to the validity and reliability of your data-collection methods

Whichever methods you choose will involve selecting what data you are going to collect. During the process of becoming data, either by being written down, as in an observation transcript or recorded during an interview, some element of selection will have taken place (Figure 7.3). Indeed, focusing on a particular approach means that you have already selected some aspect of reality as important while at the same time ignoring other parts. To some extent, you will have made a conscious decision to ignore some aspects of the classroom dynamic as part of interpreting the research question or choosing a particular methodology. However, it may also be the case that you have done this accidentally, as a result of your own unconscious prejudices, or some known or unknown bias of the methods chosen. There may also be some form of restriction in the research context, such as a timetabling issue which has made it impossible for you to interview a particular pupil, thus affecting your sample strategy, which will also introduce further bias to the process.

Furthermore, having collected the data, you will still need to be vigilant to the fact that selecting the source of data is in itself an interpretative process and that the next stages of making meaning from the data will extend this interpretation process even further, particularly if you intend to transform your own personal experiences into data. So there are many pitfalls along the way which will compromise the reliability and validity of your data-collection process.

The next sections will set out the advantages and disadvantages of the various data-collection methods which you could use in school-based research. The nature of your research question will determine what the most appropriate data is to collect. However, one thing to avoid is the tendency of collecting too much data. It will probably be just you who will have to analyse all the data collected in a finite amount of time. Activity 7.2 will help guide the planning stage.

Activity 7.2   Data-collection checklist

Planning: Who, where, when, how and what?

Have you considered the following?

1 Who or what are you going to include in the data-collection process and why?
2 Do you have a clear plan for where and when you will collect data?
3 Will you collect data in your own classroom or that of a colleague? Have you established what your role will be during the data-collection process? Are you a teacher or researcher or both?
4 Have you identified and set in place measures to help you control your own possible subjectivities?
5 Have you consulted the BERA ethical guidelines? Are you aware of any potential ethical dilemmas?
6 Have you read the relevant sections in this chapter on how to collect each data source?
7 Have you considered how you will minimize threats to the validity of your data-collection methods?
8 Are you sure that the data you intend to collect will help you answer your research question?
9 Do you have a back-up plan in case there are last-minute changes in school?

Preparing and piloting the data-collection tools

10 Can you use an existing standardized test, survey or questionnaire?
11 Have you prepared your interview schedule, if applicable?
12 Have you checked that your audio-visual equipment is working, if you intend to use this approach?
13 Have you tried out your survey or interview questions on a small pilot group?
14 Do you need to modify your data-collection plan in light of your pilot?

Recording what is happening

Observations

Observation is a normal process for teachers. Indeed, teachers are continually monitoring what is going on in classrooms and constantly questioning what is happening. Reactions and responses are often informed by teachers' tacit experiential knowledge which helps to interpret what is going on. This tacit experiential knowledge is constantly being developed, and indeed this may well be why you are embarking on a classroom-based research project. Consequently, if you want to research your own classroom, you will need to be able to stand back and open your mind to other ways of interpreting what is going on in your classroom. In other words, you will need to be systematic in how you collect evidence about what is happening in your classroom.

Evidence collected through observation will rely on your ability to gather data through using all your senses, and to do this you might use checklists, inventories or narrative descriptions as tools to help your analysis.

Classrooms are very complex social settings and there are many things going on at once. You need to have a clear purpose when you come to observe the classroom, otherwise you might end up with a very superficial analysis if you try to record everything. On the other hand, if you limit your focus too much, there is a danger that you only see what you want to see. Remember that when you observe a classroom you are selecting from an ongoing sequence of events, so plan carefully for this opportunity. Activity 7.3 provides a checklist of points to consider before you carry out an observation.

Activity 7.3   Preparing to observe

1   What are you going to observe? Will you focus on a particular aspect of practice? Will this allow you to collect enough data to answer your question?
2   Why are you carrying out the observation? What are the assumptions and expectations on which it is based? Are you sure your biases are not ruling out another interpretation of the situation?
3   When will the observation be carried out, and how long will it take? Will this fit in with the timetabling schedule and other whole school events?

Recording observations

Decide before the observation event what your approach to recording what you observe will be.

Lesson aims: **Year group:**   **Number of students:**

Teacher–student interaction
Key: Mgt = management or admin, Inst = Giving instructions, A, B, C
or D type dialogue, Demo = demonstrating, Explan = explaining,
Quest = questioning

Time	Whole class: Teacher addressing the whole class							Teacher interacting with small groups of students or individuals					What students are doing						How students are grouped		
	Mgt	Inst	A	B	C	D	Demo	Mgt	Inst	Explan	Quest	O	Write	Listen	Talk	Read	Practical	Other	individual	Pair	Group
0–5 mins																					

Figure 7.4 Classroom observation schedule

Classroom observation methods include a wide range of approaches: checklists, inventories, timed interval ratings, holistic ratings, narrative descriptions, logs, questionnaires, rubrics, matrices, models, conceptual grids and open-ended questions.

Another important consideration is to agree what time period you will observe and why. Will you observe an entire lesson? A segment? An entire day?

Figure 7.4 provides an example of a structured observation schedule used to analyse talk in science lessons.

Challenges

Constructing a classroom observation schedule is quite a difficult process, especially if you are going to ask someone else to use your schedule. This is because each observer will approach the classroom with his or her own experiences and biases. As a result, two observers may interpret what is going on differently and may then record different responses to the same lesson.

Moreover, the presence of one or more observers may interrupt the normal class environment which can lead to lessons that do not represent the norm. Table 7.2 summarizes the advantages and disadvantages of observing lessons.

Table 7.2   Advantages and disadvantages of using observation and audio/video recording

	Advantages of this approach	Disadvantages of this approach
Written observations	Immediate account available; observer actually sees what is happening; account can be available for discussion immediately after observation; full view of the classroom or school setting available to the observer at time of observation	Observer must make immediate decisions about what to record, so may be superficial or unreliable account; no chance of 'action replay'; some effects on class behaviour because of observer's presence
Video recording	Both visual and sound record of the lesson which can be replayed several times; no pressure to make instant decisions; focus can be on teacher only or on individual or group of pupils; lesson can be discussed with participants	Loss of information such as room temperature, smells, events out of camera shot; effects on class of presence of camera; time-consuming analysis; one camera provides one perspective
Audio recording	Sound recording can be replayed several times for discussion, analysis, or corroboration of written account; radio microphone can be used to obtain high-quality record of what the teacher says; observer's comments can be recorded simultaneously on twin-track tape; allows lesson to be subsequently transcribed	Loss of important visual cues such as facial expressions, gesture, body language, movement; sound quality can be poor without radio microphone, especially if acoustics are poor; difficult to identify individual children who speak; analysis time substantially increased

Read the thought experiment in Box 7.1, which challenges the notion that observation can reliably assess how well students are learning in classrooms.

Box 7.1   A thought experiment

Consider this example, taken from Fenstermacher and Richardson (2005):

As a way of gaining purchase on the properties of good teaching, consider this thought experiment. Imagine a school classroom with two large one-way glass panels, one on each side of the classroom. You are seated behind one of the glass panels, along with several colleagues who are considered experts in the appraisal of classroom teaching. You join them in observing an eighth grade world history lesson, on the topic of the Roman conquest. On the opposite wall, behind the other one-way glass, an operator sits in an elaborate control room, where she controls all the students, who are actually robots programmed with the capacity for speech, facial gestures, and arm and hand movement. While they look just like typical eighth grade children, these robots have no neural or cognitive capacity of their own. They cannot learn anything, in any usual sense of learn. Neither you nor any of your fellow experts know that the students are robots.

The teacher is a fellow human being, fully certified, including National Board Certification, with 15 years of middle school experience. Like you, she does not know her students are superb replicas of 13- and 14-year-old humans. Her lesson on the Roman conquest lasts for 47 minutes, during which the operator in the control room has the robots smiling, frowning, raising hands with questions, offering answers to questions the teacher asks, and even one case of disciplining one of the 'students' for launching a paper wad using a fat rubber band. The operator does this by having different robots make pre-programmed comments or ask previously programmed questions. The operator chooses from a vast repertoire of available gestures, speech acts and bodily movements, while computers manage the activities of other students who are not being specifically managed by the operator.

At the conclusion of the lesson, you are breathless. What a performance! Your colleagues murmur assent. If they were holding scorecards, they would hold high their 9.9s and 10s. Indeed, if this had been videotaped, it would certainly qualify this teacher for a Teacher of the Year Award. The subject matter was beautifully wrought, pitched right at the capacities of these students, as indicated by their enthusiasm and their responses to the teacher's superbly framed questions. You leave the room renewed, unaware that after the last of your colleagues departs,

(Continued)

Box 7.1   (Continued)

the operator turns off all the robots, who are now in exactly the same state as before the lesson. There are no brain cells to be altered, no synapses to fire. No learning could take place, and no learning did.

The next day you and the other expert pedagogues are informed of the truth, that the students were really robots. What have you to say now about the quality of the teacher's performance? Does it occur to you that the teacher's instruction the day before is now less remarkable and less deserving of praise? If you and your colleagues had indeed given all 10s for the teacher's performance, would you now wish to withdraw these high marks? These questions are intended to prompt consideration of our sense of what makes up good teaching.

There seems little doubt that the judgments rendered by you and your colleagues are likely to be affected by the robot responses selected by the operator. Suppose the operator had the robots respond differently, appearing to be bored, asking impertinent questions, and generally indicating a desire to be anywhere but in that classroom. You and your colleagues are likely to base part of your assessment of the teacher on how the students react to the teacher, providing higher marks to the teacher if the students are fully engaged with her, and lower marks if the students appear to be running strongly against her. We take this circumstance to indicate that our judgments of the worth or merits of teaching are learner sensitive but not learning dependent.

Source: Fenstermacher and Richardson, 2005: 193.

Supporting and supplementing observation

It is good practice to record information about the context in which you undertook your observations, for example you ought to note how many students were involved, what the seating arrangements were, and perhaps also write a chronology of the events that took place during the observation. Making an audio or video recording will capture some of the classroom interaction in a more permanent form.

Making audio recordings

Tape recordings capture the sounds of a situation – although information about the classroom surroundings together with the non-verbal cues and gestures will be lost, the technique does enable you to collect a more complete record than just direct classroom observations. You might want to supplement your classroom observation with a tape recording of certain selected parts of the lesson. This is a relatively straightforward process, although listening to these later and making notes about the recording will take a substantial amount of time. Transcribed classroom dialogue is a really useful data source, but it is probably only necessary for you to transcribe short extracts of the dialogue unless the focus of the research is on classroom dialogue.

Making video recordings

Video recordings are a good way of collecting the dialogue of the lesson as well as many of the details recorded in direct lesson observation. By representing the sequence of events in time, video recordings can make the context and causal relationships more accessible than other methods of data collection. Student behaviour patterns can also be recorded including the relationship between verbal and non-verbal behaviour. Additionally, videotapes are also an excellent way of presenting a situation to others to open up discussion.

However, there are also disadvantages. Although video recordings can provide a relatively holistic record of the lesson, the sequences only show the view seen from the perspective of the camera. In addition, good quality video recordings involve the use of a lot of equipment which can be very distracting in a classroom, although the use of smaller webcams has minimized this problem. The main difficulty lies in using the camera in a static position and using it sufficiently frequently for it to become routine. More seriously, video recordings can be misleading because they give the appearance of being a complete record of events when, in fact, they are highly selective (the camera has been pointed in one direction and there is no indication of periods of time when it has not been recording).

Making good use of video recordings takes a lot of time. A careful analysis concentrating on events that appear to be essential in terms of the research question requires repeated viewing of the tape.

Sometimes a fixed camera is sufficient, positioned on a tripod at the (window) side of the classroom and allowed to run for the whole session without pause. It can be focused on a whole area of the room, on a group of pupils, or on one pupil. Recordings of this kind make rather boring viewing for people not involved, but they provide a more complete record of the session for purposes of analysis or discussion.

See Table 7.2 for a summary of the advantages and disadvantages of using audio/video recording.

Asking people about what is going on

Surveys

Surveying involves gathering information from individuals using a questionnaire. Surveys can be descriptive or explanatory, involve entire populations or samples of populations, capture a moment or map trends, and can be administered in a number of ways. Another advantage is that this approach offers a degree of confidentiality and anonymity to the person taking part in the research.

Using a survey means that you are able to reach a large number of respondents and generate standardized, quantifiable, empirical data in the process. The use of closed questions forces respondents to choose from a range of predetermined responses, which are generally easy to code and analyse.

You can also use open questions which ask respondents to construct answers using their own words. Such survey questions can generate rich and candid data, but this can be difficult to code and analyse.

Although using a survey can generate large amounts of credible data, it is difficult to construct the actual survey. The overall process involves formulating questions, response categories, writing up background information and giving clear instructions. Getting the layout and setting right, as well as achieving the right length and organization are also tricky. It can be difficult getting the questions just right and you must always try them out on a small group before widening your field.

It is best to keep the language simple and ask a critical friend to look out for poorly worded questions and statements that use complex terms and language. Avoid using ambiguous questions and statements with double negatives. Try not to 'lead' the respondent by using loaded, 'ring true' and hard-to-disagree-with statements or questions.

Surveys and questionnaires are usually administered mainly on paper, but data can also be collected online using open-source software such as SurveyMonkey.

Standardized tests

Psychologists and other social scientists have developed a wide range of self-report measuring instruments to assess attributes such as attitudes to learning, or cognitive ability tests used by some schools to measure students on entry.

Technically, such tests provide a scale on which you would assess an individual's performance. You do need specialized training to develop such tests, so it is more sensible for you to use a recognized standardized test to supplement your own data, provided you can obtain details of the scoring system and are able to analyse the data collected (see Chapters 11 and 12). For example, the Self Determination Theory (SDT) website presents a brief overview of SDT and provides resources that address important issues such as human needs, values, intrinsic motivation, development, motivation across cultures, individual differences and psychological well-being (http://www.selfdeterminationtheory.org/).

Table 7.3 summarizes the advantages and disadvantages of using surveys and standardized tests.

Interviews and focus groups

Strictly speaking, an interview is a conversation between two people, and **focus groups** are conducted in small groups. The principles involved in both approaches are the

Table 7.3 Advantages and disadvantages of using surveys and standardized tests

	Advantages of this approach	Disadvantages of this approach
Questionnaire-based surveys	Surveys are relatively easy to administer, on paper or online	The overall usefulness will be determined by the quality of the questions
	Surveys are useful for collecting information from large samples	You need to ensure that a large number of the selected sample will reply
	Many questions can be asked about a given area	Participants may not recall information or tell the truth about a controversial question
		Surveys are inflexible in that they require that the survey remains unchanged throughout the data collection
Tests and scales	Standardization ensures that similar data can be collected from groups and then interpreted comparatively	Tests are difficult to develop and need considerable expertise to write and analyse
	The tests are usually reliable and data is easy to obtain, so observer subjectivity is eliminated	

same, although using focus groups can add further complications to the process, which will be examined later. Both interviews and focus groups are communications that aim to consult teachers and students about their points of view, interpretations and meanings to help understand classroom dynamics. They are most often used to gather detailed, qualitative descriptions, although even when done carefully, you will only be able to establish what the interviewee thinks of his/her perceptions at a particular time.

Establishing trust

In both interviews and focus groups, it will be important to establish trust and build confidence before you start and this can be done by reassuring the interviewees that their views are important. The relationship between you and the person you are interviewing will influence how they understand what is being said and vice versa. If you are interviewing one of your own students, this might be problematic as you and the student will have already developed a relationship, and, with this, various attitudes towards each other. This may range from a completely trusting relationship to one of mistrust, or one of affection to outright animosity. It may be the case that carrying out an interview with a student who you find difficult might actually improve your relationship, if as a result you come to understand them and their behaviour better. However, if the student perceives that you are only interested in reinforcing your negative impressions, then this may make things worse, and the student will assume that you are not interested in their own personal perceptions. In this case, it may be better if you could ask a colleague who does not know the students to do the interviews.

Focus groups

Focus groups are useful for revealing the beliefs, attitudes, experiences and feelings of participants. The interaction between participants as well as what participants have to say can reveal quite a lot about people's views. For example, careful observation of the dynamics of interaction within the group context, can show consensus, disagreement and power differences between the participants. O'Brien (2007) used a group interview method to tap into the dominant, expected and approved views of a group of secondary school students. As this is an innovative method and one which might be useful to classroom teachers interested in consulting pupils, the procedures used are set out in Box 7.2.

Box 7.2

The 96 groups were asked to list, collectively and anonymously, pejorative names that they hear being used at school, while the interviewer left the room for a few minutes. Each group was given a green sheet of paper headed 'Extremely bad names to be called' and a yellow sheet headed 'Names which are bad to be called but not too bad'. The colours served as useful shorthand for referring to evaluations of severity.

Pejorative names were used as a proxy for perceived reasons for being bullied. They were coded by the researcher as targeting group or individual attributes, depending on whether they were racial or sexual epithets or insults that applied mostly to individuals. A pilot study revealed that this 'confidential' group activity was the most effective means of eliciting sensitive information regarding the pejorative names that young people hear being used between peers at school. It also revealed that abstract discussion about the relative severity of pejorative names was possible without the interviewer seeing the lists during the interview.

Discussion was prompted by the following questions:

A What makes extremely bad ('green') names worse than not so bad ('yellow') names? Conversely, what makes not so bad ('yellow') names less severe?
B If you were bullied, would you rather be bullied for your skin colour or for your looks?

The first question prompted general attributions, while the second forced respondents to consider what victims of different forms of bullying might feel, thereby eliciting more focused answers about protective and harming attributions pertaining to group and individual stigmas. 'Looks' and 'skin colour' were chosen because they are not necessarily distinguishable. Respondents were free to select group or individual features for either, thereby revealing their socially constructed reasons for being bullied.

Source: O'Brien (2007).

Activity 7.4   Preparing for an interview

If you are interested in collecting data through interviewing, then consider the following points:

Before the interview

- What do you want to know and why?
- Have you piloted your questions?
- Make sure you are on time.
- Have you set up and checked equipment?
- How will you explain the purpose of the interview to the interviewees?
- How will you make the interviewee feel at ease?
- Have you explained the ethical guidelines?
- Have you asked the interviewee if they are happy for you to tape the interview? If they do not agree, then how will you record responses?

During the interview

A. Procedures

- Remember that this is an interview so you need to listen more than talk.
- Avoid interrupting trains of thought and accept pauses as a natural part of reflection.
- Accept whatever is said.
- Ask for clarification if you are not sure what the respondent means.
- Prompt and probe appropriately, and keep the pace moving.
- Be true to your role.
- Stop the interview when the time is right.
- Don't forget to thank the interviewee for giving up their time.

B. Questions

- How will you ease the interviewee into the interview?
- What strategic questions will you ask?
- Are you using open questions?
- Have you broken your key question into shorter questions to enable the interviewee to give you extended focused responses?
- How will you deal with responses that will take the interview off in another direction?
- Are any of your questions likely to suggest or lead the interviewee to the response you want to hear?

Table 7.4 Advantages and disadvantages of using interviews and focus groups

	Advantages of this approach	**Disadvantages of this approach**
Interviews	Provides rich data that paint a broad picture	Can be difficult to get students or colleagues to participate because of time constraints
	May highlight issues not previously considered	Interviews and large focus groups may intimidate some participants
	Can provide information to supplement quantitative data collected through other methods	The complexities of people and the complexities of communication can create many opportunities for miscommunication and misinterpretation
Focus groups	Small focus groups may increase the comfort level of participants	There is a danger that you may lead participants and encourage them to agree with your own views
	Focus groups are useful for revealing beliefs, attitudes, experiences and feelings of participants	Some participants may dominate the group and their behaviour may lead to a false sense of consensus
	Focus groups can provide an insight into multiple and different views	You may find it difficult to distinguish between individuals in the groups
	They can also provide information about the dynamics of interaction within a group context	It will be difficult to generalize if your group size is small or not representative of the wider population

Recording responses can be done in a number of ways; you may need to trial a couple of recording methods in order to assess what is best for you.

- Note-taking – this can range from highly structured to open and interpretive.
- Audio-recording – audio-recording allows you to preserve raw data for review at a later date.
- Video-taping – video-taping offers the added bonus of being able to record visual cues, but is more intrusive, is prone to more technical difficulties and can generate data that is hard to analyse.

See Table 7.4 for a summary of the advantages and disadvantages of using interviews and focus groups.

Other sources of evidence

Documents

You may want to use grey literature such as government documents and other school-based data and policies. Activity 7.5 provides questions which could be used when analysing documents.

Activity 7.5   Analysing the relationship between content and context of documents

- Who wrote this document? What is known about the author(s)?
- When? What is the background/context?
- Where did the information come from – how was it collected/assembled?
- Who is the intended readership?
- What is it intended to do? Did the author aim to inform, persuade, express a view or preference ...?
- What is being taken for granted? What is *not* being said?
- Is it complete? Has it been altered or edited? Is it an extract? If so, who selected it?
- What connections are being made with other events/arguments/ideas?
- How clearly does it communicate?
- Is the information authentic, reliable and up to date?
- Does it contain any contradictions/incoherences/understatements?
- Does it rely on facts or interpretation?
- How have the author's assumptions about the audience shaped the document?
- How might interpretations of different recipients (e.g. parents/teachers/educators/policy-makers) vary?
- What do readers need to know in order to make sense of the document?
- What values/ideologies or assumptions about the social/political/educational context are implicit in the text? For example, is there a sub-text? What is not seen as problematic?
- What tone does it take? How credible is it and is there a hidden agenda?
- What alternative discourses exist? Are these acknowledged, ignored or resisted?
- What are the potential implications/outcomes?
- Is there any external corroboration? What other forms of data would be useful?

Secondary sources

Secondary sources are existing data that were originally collected for purposes other than your research, such as baseline data about students' performance on entry to the school, achievement data, standardized test scores and school demographic data. See Chapters 11 and 12 for more details.

Visual images

Visual images can be used in two ways – firstly, you may want to record events in the classroom by using photography or, secondly, photographs can be used as prompts in interviews. This second approach of a photo elicitation technique involves using photographs or film as part of the interview – in other words, you ask your research subjects to discuss the meaning of photographs, films or videos. In this case, the images can be taken specifically by the researcher with the idea of using them to elicit information, and then the interviewee's comments or analysis of the visual material is itself recorded, either on audio tape or video for subsequent analysis.

For example, see Cremin et al.'s (2011) paper which uses visual methods to study how pupils and teachers in an 11–16 mixed secondary school in an area of urban disadvantage in the UK experience pupil voice.

Box 7.3   Key points to consider when starting to use visual images

When working with images for the first time, it is important to recognize that:

1 There is no one visual method or perspective that has ascendancy over all other ways of sense making.
2 We don't 'see', we 'perceive', since the former is a biological norm and the latter culturally and psychologically informed.
3 All images are regarded as polysemic (having many possible meanings).
4 Word- and number-based researchers 'skim' imagery, taking it for granted.
5 Visual researchers give imagery a 'close reading' (in-depth scrutiny and treat the visual as problematic).
6 Images can be 'researcher found' (generated by others) or 'researcher generated' (created by the researcher). Both are integral to the visual research process.
7 The visual, as objects and images, exists materially in the world but gains meaning from humans.
8 A photograph does not show how things look. It is an image produced by a mechanical device, at a very specific moment, in a particular context, by a person working within a set of personal parameters.

Diaries and journals

Diaries can provide a good source of data. Your own research data might be useful as a data source, or you might want to ask your research participants to record their own diaries for subsequent analysis. As with interviews, the guidance given for keeping diaries may be completely open-ended or semi-structured through giving broad categories of what to consider, including, or by asking for, regular responses to very specific questions. So it is vital, if the diaries are to be completed by the participant, that you give clear unambiguous instructions to the writer about how, when and why they should enter data. The process of writing the dairy can empower the diarist too, through encouraging reflection and through valuing their ideas. Diaries also encourage the diarist to express opinions and reflect on activities that might otherwise be difficult for a researcher to expose.

The content of the research journals included personal observations, impressions, feelings and analyses, and self-reflection and self-examinations concerning their team teaching performance, team meetings, and so on. The diaries proved useful as a record of the intentions of a teacher for a lesson, which could be used comparatively across the set of teachers.

Diaries do not have to be in a written form. For some students, this would present an insurmountable barrier, as well as also being a very time-consuming process. Visual diaries offer an alternative, either by asking for a set of photographs to be taken or videos to be compiled. While video capture, if by mobile camcorder, has the greatest cost implications, the advantage is that an audio record of thoughts and reflections can be included. Noyes (2004) circumvented the need to hand out a recorder by instead setting up a video diary room in 'big brother' style. Still imagery collected either digitally (whether by mobile phone or digital camera) or using traditional cameras (such as disposables) requires interviews or focus group discussion to explore the meaning associated with them.

However, Noyes's approach does present ethical dilemmas about how images of students can be used in classroom-based research (see Chapter 6).

Visual mapping

Concept mapping and mind mapping are related techniques currently being used in educational and business settings to make explicit the connections between individuals' ideas. In a school context, these could be used to improve the planning of work, note-taking skills, the organization of thinking and the development of concepts, and in preparation and support of assessments. Many of these techniques use computer software packages both to structure data collection and to manipulate the data in analysis.

These techniques can also be used for research rather than instructional purposes. As with the diary methods, these techniques allow access to the perceptions of those under study. In addition, they also allow a respondent-centred method of exposing conceptual understanding.

Other mapping or visual representation techniques involve freehand drawing of what might be termed 'spider diagrams'. It is these methods, although less straightforward to analyse, which allow the researcher to open up the scope of what is under study to the respondents. An open-ended network mapping tool developed by Fox was used to collect data for a project studying the flow of knowledge relating to the development of assessment for learning practices. This allowed members of staff to represent the personal and professional relationships relating to their school and which could act as channels for sharing practice and/or gaining new information and advice. Network mapping can be used to determine the nature and value of interrelationships relating to teachers and perhaps even be considered as a 'map' of their learning opportunities. It was not possible to guess these networks in advance of this task being used. This tool would also translate well to looking at networks of children to consider the range of resources they have to learn from and/or to understand their social milieu. An alternative method of network mapping derived from sociological research, which can be used to examine networks of known extent, is called social network analysis. This is a tool worth considering if this too would be insightful in understanding the structure of a network – for example, how interconnected individuals are one with the other, and who key individuals in a network are, in terms of their personal networks. Questions are asked systematically of all members of the network about how others relate to them and their relationship with named others. Free downloadable software is now available to handle such data – see, for example, http://www.graphic.org/concept.html

To complement the use of imagery, referred to above with respect to diaries, freehand visual representations have also been found to be useful ways of gaining an insight into the perceptions of spaces.

In summary, there are many methods that classroom teachers could use to help answer a clearly identified research question. See Table 7.5.

Table 7.5   Everyday tools for enquiry

Classroom maps	Drawings and photographs
• Look critically at the set-up and decoration of the classroom. Whose work is up on the walls? How is the seating arranged? • Track movement flow – your own, a child's, that of a group. • Track verbal flow – conversation between teachers and students and conversation among students.	• Quick sketch, visual notes. Put both sketches and photographs in the same notebook used to record anecdotal records and time samples. • Student work, a sample of an individual's, small group, or entire class's work collected over time.
Anecdotal records	**Interviews and conversations**
• Always add a date. • Regularly jot down time. • Focus on particulars. • Write down actual quotes. • Don't censor.	• Always note date, time, place and name of the person(s) being interviewed. • Think ahead about your goal for this conversation or interview. What do you want to learn? • Decide ahead about audiotaping and check your equipment. • Don't ask questions that give you yes/no answers. • Be a good listener.

(Continued)

Table 7.5 (Continued)

Surveys	Sociograms
• These are good for large groups or a whole class when you want comparative data. • The types of questions you ask are important. • The time it takes to complete is important.	A sociogram is an analytical tool used to help you portray the social networks in your classroom. They are particularly useful if you're trying to figure out how to change the interactive dynamic of the class. To develop the data for a sociogram, you ask every child in your class the same three questions, for example, (1) If I were to form reading groups of four pupils, who would you like to have in your group? (2) If I were to have four pupils stay for lunch with me, who would you like to have in your group? (3) If you were a new pupil in the class, which three pupils would you suggest I ask to help you learn the ropes? Questions can be asked orally but you need to record students' answers so you have data to draw on as you begin to map their responses.
Time-sampled observations	**Teacher research journals**
See Figure 7.4	Every teacher researcher should keep a research journal. It could have everything—the 10 minutes a day of writing that you are doing about your question, your notes from your anecdotal records, your reflections on those notes, your notes from background reading that you have done on your topic. It could, on the other hand, just be the place you record your thoughts about your research. Whatever, try to set it up so it really is a friendly place for you to write and so that it becomes precious to you. Do not leave it lying around in your classroom. This is where you think on paper. You want to keep it as a special place that you come to for special work on something that is of great importance to you.

Key ideas

There are numerous methods you could use to collect evidence to help answer your research question. These methods are usually identified during the research design stage. Each method has advantages and disadvantages. As a researcher, you need to be aware of what these are and do as much as you can to reduce the limitations imposed by a particular method.

Reflective questions

- Have you considered the ethics of using the data-collection methods suggested in your research design?
- Before you start collecting data, have you cosidered how you will minimize the limitations of the data-collection methods you propose using?

Further reading

Deci, R. and Ryan, R. (2012) 'Self determination theory'. Available at: http://www.self determinationtheory.org/ (accessed April 2012).

Drever, E. (1995) *Using Semi-structured Interviews in Small-scale Research: A Teacher's Guide*. Edinburgh: SCRE.

Fox, A., McCormick, R., Procter, R. and Carmichael, R. (2007) 'The design and use of a mapping tool as a baseline means of identifying an organisation's active networks', *International Journal of Research and Method in Education*, 30(2): 127–147.

Hay, D. and Kinchin, I. (2008) 'Using concept mapping to measure learning quality', *Education and Training*, 50(2): 167–182.

Kinchin, I., Streatfield, D. and Hay, D. (2010) 'Using concept mapping to enhance the research interview', *International Journal of Qualitative Methods*, 9(1): 52–68.

Munn, P. and Drever, E. (1997) *Using Questionnaires in Small-scale Research: A Teacher's Guide*. Edinburgh: SCRE.

Prosser, J. (2006) 'Real Life Methods Working Papers: Researching with visual images', ESRC National Centre for Research Methods NCRM Working Paper Series 6/06. Available at: http://www.ncrm.ac.uk/ (accessed April 2012).

Prosser, J. and Loxley, A. (2008) *Introducing Visual Methods*. National Centre for Research Methods NCRM Review Papers NCRM/010. Available at: http://www.ncrm. ac.uk/ (accessed April 2012).

Simpson, M. and Tuson, J. (1997) *Using Observation in Small-scale Research: A Beginner's Guide*. Edinburgh: SCRE.

Wragg, E. (1994) *An Introduction to Classroom Observation*. Abingdon: Routledge.

CHAPTER 8

HANDLING DATA

Elaine Wilson and Alison Fox

Chapter overview

This chapter will provide help with data reduction and data display. The other two stages between reduction and display, that is data analysis and data synthesis, are covered in Chapters 9, 10, 11 and 12.

The chapter will start with practical advice on how to store data in a systematic way as it is collected. Examples of appropriate presentational devices will also be provided, along with further guidance on how to review qualitative data so that the reader can see clearly how you have been interpreting written and visual data.

Do not underestimate the sheer quantity of data that you will rapidly gather during your research project. It is easy to find that you have collected so much data that you are not certain how to analyse it or write it up. Somehow, gathering data seems more productive than analysing it. Guard against producing excessive unnecessary data as a bulwark against potential failure. Try to analyse your data as you go along as this will also confirm whether

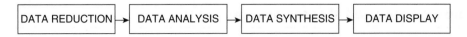

Figure 8.1   The stages of data handling

you are collecting the right sort and quantity of data. It will also help you to check that your original analytical intentions were correct and still appropriate to answer your questions.

Be systematic in making sense of all that you have done so far. Figure 8.2 is taken from Zina O'Leary's book, *Researching Real-world Problems* (2005), and sets out a very clear methodical, organized approach to data handling which clarifies this process into five tasks.

Keeping your eye on the main game

The danger is that you will be overwhelmed by the sheer amount of data that you have collected but don't lose sight of why you are doing the research and what you are trying to find out. Keep comparing the data that was collected earlier in the study with data collected later in the study. Create a visual representation of what you have collected and map out a summary of this. Use diagrams, sketches of things, people and happenings to show different ideas and groupings.

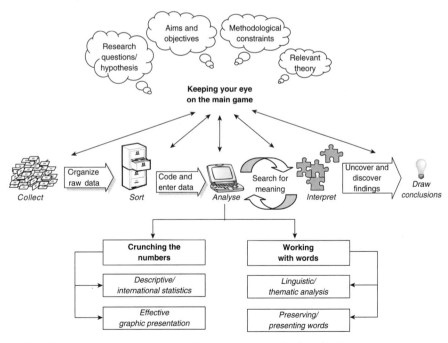

Figure 8.2   The process of data analysis (with permission from O'Leary, 2005)

Setting up an organized storage system

Data will accumulate rapidly once you start the research process so set up a recording and storage system before you start collecting data. The easiest way of doing this is to keep a research diary. Log in your data as you collect it, record information about the context and any anomalies or issues that arose while you were collecting the data.

Organize and group sources into logical categories. Start to select and focus on all the relevant important sources before you start to transform the data using presentational devices.

Activity 8.1   Making data summaries in your research diary

Review your interview schedules, observation notes or other data collected immediately and write a summary. This will provide both easy access to the data later and an overview of what is emerging so far so that you can relate this to your research question.

Use the following questions to prompt you as you write your data summary:

- What is the context in which the data were collected?
- Why were they collected? Why in this particular situation? Why use this method of collection? What are the most important facts in the data? Is anything surprising?
- How is the data linked to your original research question?
- Do the data give rise to any new questions, points of view, suggestions or ideas?
- Do the data suggest what should be done next, in terms of further analysis or action?

The models in Figures 8.3 and 8.4 both appear in Ivens's (2007) paper 'The development of a happiness measure in school children'.

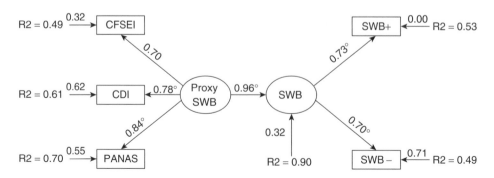

Figure 8.3   Ivens's diagram of his theoretical model

Analysing and interpreting data

Working mainly with numbers

If your data is mainly numerical, then start by reading Chapters 11 and 12 and use this chapter to find ideas on how to display data. You might want to check out http://www.statisticshell.com/html/limbo.html too.

There are various data displays that you could use to present numerical data. Tables, graphs and figures can present certain types of information, including models and sequences of events, more clearly and in less space than the same information would require in sentence form. However, do not use tables, graphs and figures for small amounts of data that could be conveyed clearly and succinctly in a sentence.

Tables

Summarizing your data in a clear table is a straightforward way of making your 'raw' data easily accessible. Try to make your data tables complete but not too complex. Sometimes it is helpful to break a large table into several smaller ones to allow the reader to identify important information easily.

For example, in Table 8.1, O'Brien summarizes information about the size of the data sample, together with information about the gender, age and geographical location of the sample. In Figure 8.4, Ivens (2007) summarizes his correlation data and in Figure 8.5 Hayes et al. (2007) illustrate how the authors use pre- and post-data in tables.

Graphs

Graphs are one of the best ways to display data, but avoid making mistakes in how you use graphs – for example, don't connect discrete points with a continuous line. It is more appropriate to use a bar graph or histograms for discrete points (see below).

Table 8.1 Table used in O'Brien (2007)

	Girls (n = 253)	Boys (n = 218)
Year 7 (n = 159)	47	53
Year 9 (n = 156)	50	50
Year 11 (n = 156)	65	35
	East London (n = 237)	Cambridgeshire (n = 234)
White (n = 311)	36.3	95.7
Black (n = 137)	55.7	2.6
Mixed race (n = 23)	8	1.7

Source: Ethnic groupings, adapted from Kelly's (1988) schema.

Table 2 Study 1, Correlation of SWB with adapted single-item measures

		Terrible – Delighted	Line Positive	Line Negative	Faces
Subject Well-Being (SCHI)	Pearson Correlation	.40**	.39**	.40**	.39**
	Sig. (2-tailed)	<. 001	<. 001	<. 001	<. 001
	N	77	77	77	75

**Correlation is significant at the 0.01 level (2-tailed).

Table 3 Study 1, Correlation of SWB with multiple-item measures

		Self-esteem	Depression	Affect
Subject Well-Being (SCHI)	Pearson Correlation	.49**	-.55**	.71**
Sig. (2-tailed)		<. 001	<. 001	<. 001
N		77	77	77

**Correlation is significant at the 0.01 level (2-tailed).

Figure 8.4   Ivens's (2007) correlation data

Hidi et al. use a graph accurately to illustrate changes in pre- and post-survey data (Figure 8.6).

A box and whisker plot is a way of summarizing a set of data measured on an interval scale. It is often used in exploratory data analysis. It is a type of graph which is used to show the shape of the distribution, its central value and variability. In other words, you can see if there are any unusual observations outside the average range. Ivens (2007) used a box plot to set out the distribution and range of the data collected from his three studies (Figure 8.7).

Bar charts and histograms

Bar charts are pictorial representations of the distribution of values of a variable. You can use bar charts to show distributions of interval or nominal variables. Bar charts of interval variables are also called histograms.

A histogram is a graphical way of presenting a frequency distribution. It is constructed by first selecting a number of 'intervals' to be used. Most computer programs that construct histograms will allow you to select the number of intervals, as well as their width. If you don't tell the computer how many intervals to use, it will make the decision based on the data it has. Chapter 11 shows the type of histograms produced by SPSS.

A graph very similar to a histogram is the bar chart. Bar charts are often used for qualitative or categorical data, although they can be used quite effectively with

Table 1 Pre-intervention teacher questionnaire

		% rated 7 or more
1	On a scale of 1–10, how would you rate your confidence to manage behaviour effectively in your classes?	50
2	Could you rate your confidence to problem-solve situations where pupils' behaviour is particularly challenging in your classes?	38
3	How good are your current opportunities for discussion and planning with colleagues in relation to behaviour issues?	38
4	Do you find it easy to talk to colleagues about behaviour difficulties in school?	63
5	To what extent do you feel your personal behaviour management skills make a difference to pupils' learning in class?	63
6	How satisfied are you with your job overall at present?	38
7	How stressful would you say your job is at present?	56

Table 2 Post-intervention teacher questionnaire

		% rated 7+
1	Please rate the value of the five process steps in the Staff Sharing Scheme as contributing to purposeful discussion around behaviour management.	
	(a) Clarifying problem situations.	72
	(b) Building up an understanding of the problem situation.	83
	(c) Generating a range of possible intervention approaches.	84
	(d) Selecting the best approach.	89
	(e) Setting up ways of measuring whether the intervention plans have actually made a difference.	67
2	Please rate the value of the process overall.	83
3	Please rate the value of the Staff Sharing Scheme in terms of outcomes for the groups as a whole.	67
4	Please rate the value of the Staff Sharing Scheme in terms of outcomes for your own management of behaviour.	69
5	How confident would you feel about facilitating another group of staff using the same/a similar process?	45

Figure 8.5 Hayes et al. (2007) tables of pre- and post-data

quantitative data if the number of unique scores in the data set is not large. A bar chart plots the number of times a particular value or category occurs in a data set, with the height of the bar representing the number of observations with that score or in that

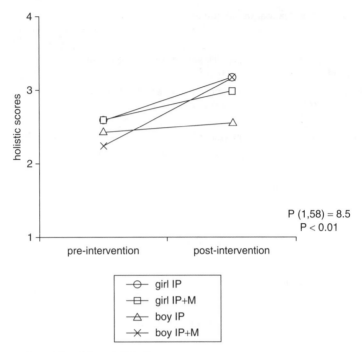

Figure 8.6   Graph used by Hidi et al. (2002)

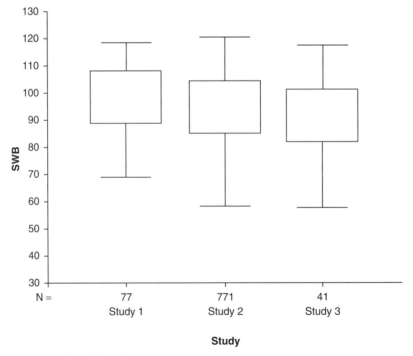

Figure 8.7   Ivens's (2007) box plot

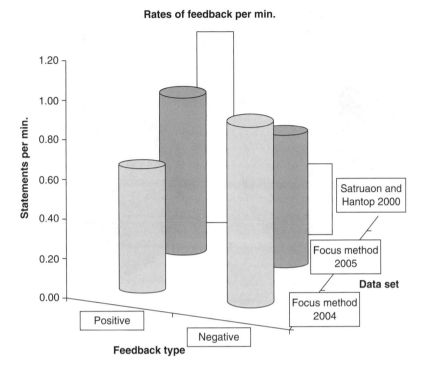

Figure 8.8   Hayes et al. (2007) bar graph

category. The Y-axis could represent any measurement unit: relative frequency, raw count, per cent, or whatever else is appropriate for the situation. For example, the bar chart in Figure 8.8 plots the number of positive and negative feedback statements before and after the reported intervention.

Pie charts

A pie chart is a way of summarizing a set of categorical data. It is a circle which is divided into segments. Each segment represents a particular category. The area of each segment is proportional to the number of cases in that category. For example, O'Brien (2007) summarizes the percentages of types of names evaluated by students as more or less severe (Figure 8.9).

Scatter plots

A scatter plot is a useful summary of a set of two variables, usually drawn before working out a linear correlation coefficient or fitting a regression line (see Chapter 11). Scatter plots provide a good visual picture of the relationship between the two variables, and aid the interpretation of the correlation coefficient or regression model.

Each unit contributes one point to the scatter plot, on which points are plotted but not joined. The resulting pattern indicates the type and strength of the

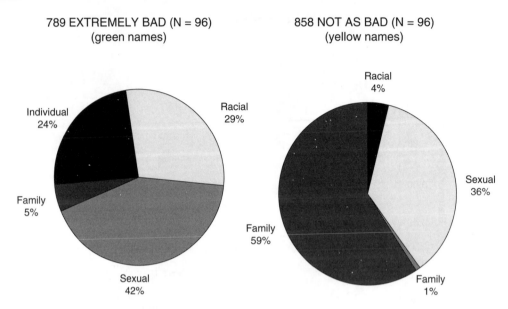

Figure 8.9   Pie chart in O'Brien (2007)

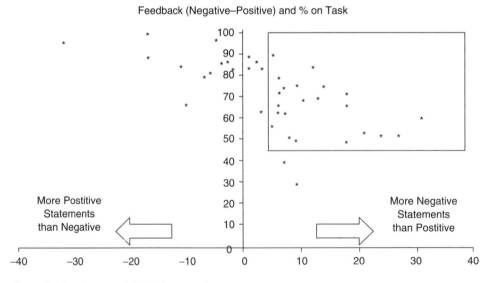

Figure 8.10   Hayes et al. (2007) scatter plot

relationship between the two variables. Hayes et al. (2007) used a scatter plot to show the number of positive and negative comments plotted against on-task behaviour (Figure 8.10).

Working mainly with words

If your data is mainly in the form of words, then you should read about how to analyse qualitative data in Chapters 9 and 10 before you start. The next section will help with ideas to present qualitative data.

The best way of moving from raw qualitative data, such as interview transcripts or journal entries, to meaningful understanding is through becoming immersed in the data. In other words, you need to try to look for themes that run through the data and then interpret the implications of these themes for your research project. These themes can be either discovered or uncovered. Use the constant comparative methods to ana-lyse your data, then read Box 8.1 to find out how Nardi and Steward (2003) analysed their interview transcripts and developed headings and codes, which they used in their second reading of the text (Figure 8.11).

Activity 8.2   Constant comparative method: step-by-step guide

1 Read your notes, diaries, interview transcripts (recordings), notes from obser-vations, etc. and highlight parts that you think are important ideas. Use dif-ferent colours for different kinds of 'important' ideas. So, you *interpret* the text to identify those patterns or themes which underpin what people are saying. This is called *coding*.
2 These are called **temporary constructs**. Make a list of them.
3 Now read through your data again, comparing the data against your list of temporary constructs (this is the constant comparative bit).
4 Now make a grid with the temporary constructs in a column on the left and on the right side note the page numbers where the temporary construct is mentioned in your data. You can make notes and observations on the grid as you do this.
5 Delete any temporary constructs that are not 'earning their keep'.
6 After your second reading make a list of second-order constructs that seem to explain your data. These ideas should help you to summarize impor-tant themes in your data.
(Adapted from Thomas, 2010)

This approach of discovering themes inductively through a **constant comparison** of data and building theory using a **grounded theory** approach to analyse data is explained in greater detail in Chapters 10 and 17.

Box 8.1   Inductive analysis

Data analysis of the interview data

Immediately after each interview, an Interview Protocol, a condensed account of the interview where the interviewees' statements are reproduced from the audio-recording, not with verbatim accuracy but as faithfully and concisely as possible, was produced. The interviews were also fully transcribed and the contents of the audio-tapes were digitized and copied on compact disks. Within a spirit of seeking data-grounded theory, as proposed in Glaser and Strauss (1967), but with due attention to foundational theoretical perspectives, as indicated, for example, by Hammersley (1990), a first level of coding followed according to seven wide categories, as set out in Table I. A second-level coding of the now *Annotated* Interview Protocols led to the production of a Code System (a gradually enriched, eventually 'saturated' version of the preliminary one consisting of 36 T, 29 P, 40 C, 30 M, 14 S, 5 Sc, 2 METH categories, giving a total of 156). Numerous examples of these categories can be seen in the subsequent section of this article. Occurrences of each category in the now 27 *Coded* Interview Protocols were recorded in a massive interviewee-by-category spreadsheet. The frequency of each category is available in the last row of the spreadsheet. By examining the spreadsheet horizontally, we could identify the codes in which each interviewee scored higher and thus form an impression of his/her focal points. By examining the spreadsheet vertically, we could identify the codes that featured higher frequencies across the total body of interviewees. Subsequently, each category was assigned an ordered pair (x, y) as follows: x corresponds to the number of times the category has been identified in the Coded Interview Protocols and y to the number of students who have referred to the category. Further scrutiny based on validation of significance relating to frequency, researcher emphasis, and external theory led to the selection of the Pivotal Categories around which we clustered all the categories, across the Code System, that were tangentially relevant (covered part of the same ground, highlighted a different angle of the same issue, etc.). Out of this clustering, five major characteristics of quiet disaffection emerged. In the following, we introduce each of the characteristics using the corresponding cluster of categories and substantiate using extracts from the interviews. The evidence is supported further with references to the classroom observations, the student profiles and the relevant literature.

Nardi and Steward (2003: 348–9)

Name of category	Abbreviation	Content: Interviewees' statements on:
Conceptual difficulty	C	Difficulties in various mathematical topics and ways of coping
Mathematics	M	Nature and significance of mathematics
Performance	P	Own and others' ability and performance in mathematics
Teaching	T	Mathematics teaching including the role of activities, teaching styles and teacher personality
Social	S	The role of peers, parents and others in mathematical learning
School	Sc	Schooling in general
Methodology	METH	The impact of the researcher's presence in the classroom

Figure 8.11   Nardi and Steward's (2003) coding schedule

Maloney and Plaut had a predetermined theory, and their approach was to deductively uncover data to support this theory. For example, Maloney (2007) analysed video recordings of students' roles in lessons, using a series of codes derived from previous work carried out with teams (Figure 8.12).

Plaut (2006) constructed a conceptual model of confusion (Figure 6.13), which she then used to analyse the stimulated recall interviews with teachers.

Representing interactions

If you have used focus groups, you will need to decide whether to transcribe the complete group discussions or whether to use abridged transcripts in your analysis. Transcripts are useful in that they can provide more than a record of the discussion, and they also allow for a more intimate understanding of the content of the talk, the flow of discussion and the group dynamics. You could also analyse the linguistic elements such as gestures, laughter, sounds of disbelief, gaze, and so on. O'Brien (2007) represents the dynamic nature of the dialogue which took place during the focus group interviews in Figure 8.14.

Table 5   Characteristics of the roles

	Role	Code	Features
Positive roles	Chair	Ch	Asks questions and asks others for contributions Suggests what the group can do
	Discussion Manager	DM	Starts and/or ends discussions Makes final decision with or without consultation Directs the groups; suggests what action to take
	Information Manager	IM	Checks on the tasks to be done or validity of evidence Refers back to the E1 evidence Summarizes evidence
	Promoter of Ideas	PI	Suggests idea – may or may not be acceptable to others Impatient when discussing ideas other than their own Wants to get the decision made
	Influential Contributor	IC	Makes claims with reference to data Responds to others by posing questions or challenging ideas Suggests a possible decision
Negative roles	Non-influential Contributor	NIC	Responds to others' comments with agreement or confirming points made Makes suggestions that are ignored by the others Agrees with the decision that someone else makes
	Non-responsive Contributor	NRC	Has own ideas but puts them forward only when asked May make a different decision to the others Does not attempt to persuade others to change their minds
	Reticent Participant	RP	Makes little contribution May read out E1 evidence but not make any comments Makes few claims
	Distracter	Di	Talks about issues not related to the task Tells long stories that are marginally related to the discussion Displays silly behaviour

Figure 8.12   Maloney's (2007) codes for analysing video recordings of lessons

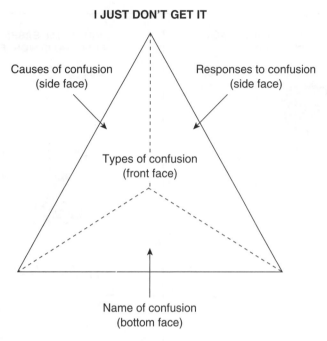

I JUST DON'T GET IT

Causes of confusion
(side face)

Responses to confusion
(side face)

Types of confusion
(front face)

Name of confusion
(bottom face)

Figure 8.13   Plaut's (2006) conceptual model of confusion

Analysing images

Photographs can provide a speedy (when using a digital camera) and clear point of reference for discussion. They can serve as an illustration to accompany transcripts. You can also print out multiple copies for learners to comment on. However, remember that viewers don't always interpret as much or indeed the same things from photographs as they would from written excerpts of conversation.

Issues of representation

Photographs can be interpreted in two ways: firstly, you can focus on the content of any visual representation – for example, who is the person in the photograph? Secondly, you may want to look at who produced the image, and for whom. Why was this photograph taken of this particular person, and then kept by that particular person?

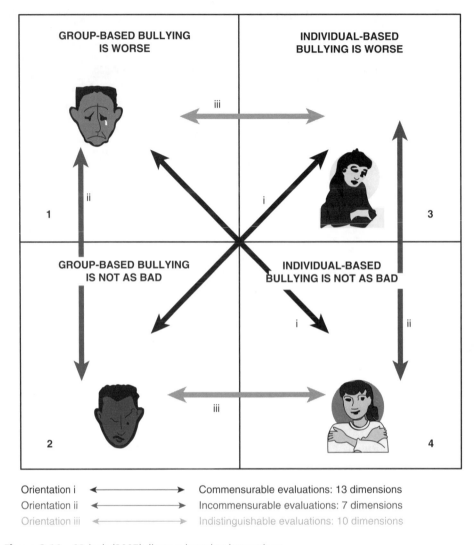

Orientation i   Commensurable evaluations: 13 dimensions
Orientation ii   Incommensurable evaluations: 7 dimensions
Orientation iii   Indistinguishable evaluations: 10 dimensions

Figure 8.14 OBrien's (2007) diagram interview interactions

Concept and network maps

You can carry out a descriptive, first-level analysis of concept maps. This could be followed by an analysis of nodes which might be grouped according to their proximity to other items, such as types of roles.

You can also extract information about the links made between words or themes. The map, and its first analysis, is a really useful basis on which to come back to people and talk about your perceptions of networks, or concept maps, the value and strength of links and how you are using them.

Key ideas

Present your findings in ways that capture the key ideas so that it is easier to see at a glance. Using figures such as diagrams, tables, graphs, charts or maps can be a very useful way to show and emphasize information in your report. They can be used to compile data in an orderly way or to amplify a point and are a useful tool to help your readers understand complex data. Figures that are supportive rather than essential to your explanation can be placed in the appendix section so that the continuity of your writing is not broken up. Avoid including tables and figures without referring to them in the text; make sure that you do discuss the information represented in the diagrams, tables, graphs, charts and maps. Try to produce text and figures that can each stand alone, that is the text should be readable without figures, and vice versa, although a good diagram can really make your point very clearly.

Reflective questions

1 Have you planned a systematic method of recording when and how you collect data?
2 Have you analysed your data as opposed to just describing the data?
3 Have you used appropriate conventions associated with the methodology?
4 Have you helped the readers by using a range of presentational devices to make your ideas more easily accessible?

Further reading

Altrichter, H., Posch, P. and Somekh, B. (2007) *Teachers Investigate their Work: An Introduction to the Methods of Action Research* (2nd edn). London: Routledge.

Field, A. (2009) *Discovering Statistics Using SPSS* (Introducing Statistical Methods series). London: Sage Publications.

http://www.statisticshell.com/html/apf.html# (accessed April 2012).

Huberman, M. and Miles, M. (1994) *Qualitative Data Analysis: An Expanded Sourcebook* (2nd edn). London: Sage Publications.

O'Leary, Z. (2010) *The Essential Guide to Doing Your Research Project*. London: Sage Publications.

CHAPTER 9

RELIABILITY AND VALIDITY IN QUALITATIVE RESEARCH BY TEACHER RESEARCHERS

Michael Evans

Chapter overview

This chapter will define and discuss what *reliability* and *validity* are in the context of school-based qualitative research carried out by teacher researchers. Three types of strategies for checking the internal validity of qualitative studies by teacher researchers will be described and exemplified. How *triangulation* of sources, of methods and of investigators can protect the study against threats to internal validity of findings will also be explained. Finally, how *looking for negative evidence* can be used as a way of confirming particular patterns in the findings by examining contrary evidence will be elaborated on.

Introduction

One of the main anxieties that someone carrying out a small-scale qualitative enquiry can have at any point in the investigation is in relation to the overhanging question: 'so what?' The research in question is only a drop in the ocean of experience, and so what possible significance can the highly individual and localized findings of my experience have for anyone else? Completely different findings can emerge in different contexts, so what use is my study to other people? In part, this anxiety is a reaction to the perceived weightiness of large-scale quantitative research, due to the access it has to a greater volume and breadth of evidence. The more subjects, classrooms, schools and contexts that one can draw on in an enquiry, the more one can seem to be able to make claims that will have a general relevance and applicability, especially if they are supported by statistical measurement. At the same time, worries about the reliability and validity of one's own research are a positive indication of an awareness of the limitations of educational research. What distinguishes an accomplished from a naive researcher is the former's reluctance to rush to make confident claims about findings: incontrovertible certainty is on the whole a rare commodity in educational research. At the very least, a measure of doubt is important in that it keeps us alert and open to new and at times contradictory evidence.

However, for an enquiry to stand as research, a degree of systematicity and validation is required, since, despite my opening remarks, research aims to appeal to a wider community and to represent more than an instance of personal and subjective reflection. Lincoln and Guba (1985) have argued that in the context of 'naturalistic inquiry', the quality of the study can be measured by the concept of 'trustworthiness', and by examining the procedures used as part of the process of persuasion:

> The basic issue in relation to trustworthiness is simple: How can an inquirer persuade his or her audience (including self) that the findings of an inquiry are worth paying attention to, worth taking account of? What arguments can be mounted, what criteria invoked, what questions asked, that would be persuasive on this issue? (1985: 290)

It is this systematicity and wider validation that arguably makes the difference between a research study (which seeks to analyse and interpret its data) and a personal project (which merely describes the data), or between a 'case study' and 'case story' (Bassey, 1999: 62). In order to help with this, the discipline of social science has been developing two sets of concepts and strategies for strengthening the validity and reliability of research, and we shall be examining them in detail in the context of school-based research in the rest of this chapter. But before we proceed, it is worth considering what is meant by the term 'qualitative research'.

What is qualitative research?

Defining what qualitative research is, as opposed to what it is not, presents a challenge, as the term is used to cover a wide range of methodological and epistemological paradigms.

However, in educational research, the focus of such studies is on an in-depth probing of phenomena such as people's beliefs, assumptions, understandings, opinions, actions, interactions or other potential sources of evidence of the processes of learning or teaching. Furthermore, these phenomena are often not taken as given (i.e. they are not seen as pre-existing realities waiting to be uncovered), but as complex, developing, multifaceted, intertextual and largely dependent on the process of interpretation used in the investigation. In this way, one cannot divorce a discussion of qualitative methodology from the epistemological assumptions that underpin it. The epistemological paradigm on which qualitative research is predicated rejects the positivist view of knowledge and instead sees empirical data as being the product of 'multiple constructed realities' (Lincoln and Guba, 1985: 295). This is why it is important to distinguish between qualitative or quantitative research design and qualitative or quantitative research methods since it is quite acceptable for a qualitative study to include the use of 'quantitative instruments' such as questionnaires, or tests, but the ultimate purpose of their use is as a contribution to understanding the particular constructions, beliefs and understandings of the subjects being researched. The range of instruments most frequently used to elicit relevant qualitative data consists of interviews (of which there are several types, serving different purposes), lesson observation notes and recordings, diaries (or other forms of written narrative), as well as information captured through non-verbal means.

Despite this focus on the particular, the 'constructed' and the context-dependent, qualitative research in education also seeks to produce knowledge, hypotheses, theoretical frameworks or case studies which will contribute to the systematic understanding of aspects of the processes of education.

One can infer from my above summary that qualitative research can be grouped under two broad categories: observational and introspective. Observational perspectives within a research design involve investigating phenomena which occur under 'natural' conditions, as, for instance, in the case of a teacher examining aspects of interactional dynamics between pupils working on group tasks in lessons. Unlike the conditions of quasi-experimental research, which usually involve some specially designed set-up, with a control group acting as a comparison, a qualitative approach would be to examine the phenomenon as it naturally occurs in lessons. This is why the term 'qualitative research' is often used interchangeably with the term 'naturalistic research'. The emphasis of introspective research, most commonly based on the use of interviews, is an examination of how individuals or groups make sense of or conceptualize phenomena related to teaching or learning. In this case, the researcher can be dealing with two layers of evidence: the informant's verbalized introspections and the phenomena in question.

Let us look at two hypothetical examples of qualitative studies conducted by classroom practitioners at an early stage of their career: one observational study and one introspective. We should note, of course, that it is often advisable to combine observational and introspective strategies within the same enquiry, as data from both sources can be complementary, but it is nevertheless important for the practitioner researcher to be clear which perspective is the focus of their study.

Example A

John Smith is a PGCE student teacher who specializes in the teaching of geography at secondary school level and who has begun his main professional placement at a mixed comprehensive school. As part of his training, John is required to carry out an in-depth subject studies investigation into some aspect of his school-based experience. The guidelines for the assignment require him to engage in a study that serves three distinct purposes: pedagogical, intellectual and developmental. What this means is that the study should be useful in terms of ultimately contributing to improved teaching in the area selected; it should also explore a legitimate theme which has been discussed by others within the subject and/or educational literature; and the experience of the research should be integral to the developmental training and not just an artificial add-on. How can a qualitative study serve these purposes? Following a discussion with his faculty tutor and school mentor, John decides to conduct an enquiry into teachers' and Y7 pupils' perceptions of the Key Stage 2/3 transition with regard to the teaching and learning of geography.

Over a period of a few weeks, John carries out individual interviews with the head of department and two other teachers of geography at his school. He also interviews five Y7 pupils individually and a focus group of six other Y7 pupils. He also teaches a Y7 geography class and keeps an ongoing record of relevant data emerging from this.

Example B

Jane Collins is in her second year of teaching at a specialist language college, teaching French and Spanish to children across the 11–18 age range. She has registered on a Masters course aimed at teacher researchers at her local university and needs to design an empirical study based on some aspect of her current practice. Again, the rationale for the choice of topic is that it should be an appropriate intellectual investigation of an issue raised in the relevant literature, and contribute to an informed development of some aspects of the teacher's professional work. So the choice of topic will normally be linked to a problem or issue which the teacher has encountered within their own classroom teaching or other sphere of work within their school. Jane has found in her experience of language teaching that target language interaction takes place predominantly in teacher–whole class mode. Group or pair work interaction has proved difficult to fit into her normal work scheme schedule, but there have been signs that the pupils would be eager to interact amongst themselves in the target language, given the right conditions and support. So with appropriate preparation and task design, Jane introduces opportunities for small group work within her lessons with a Y10 French class over several weeks. What interests her is how the pupils collaborate in learning through the group interaction, the quality of the French produced, and when and why the pupils code switch from French to English and back again. The interactions of each group are recorded and an analysis of the transcripts is based on a separate coding framework for the three areas of focus.

These two examples of qualitative studies may well provide the teachers conducting them with valuable anecdotal information and insights regardless of the quality of the study as an instance of systematic research. However, this value is largely hit-or-miss and will not normally be of much use in contributing to the body of knowledge on the subject. In order to measure the quality of the research, two criteria are available to the educational researcher: reliability and validity. It is worth noting that to some extent these are conceptual labels, each enclosing a variety of different types of measurement, not all of which are applicable in the qualitative context. What follows is a description of those which are applicable in this context, and their value will be illustrated where relevant through reference to the two examples described above.

Reliability

The notion of reliability refers to the rigour, consistency and, above all, trustworthiness of the research. In this sense, reliability is 'a precondition for validity' (Lincoln and Guba, 1985: 292). If a study is unreliable, then it cannot be said to be valid, if by the latter (as we shall see in the next section) we mean the extent to which a study measures what it intends to measure. However, the reverse does not hold: a reliable study can conceivably still be invalid, as in the case of research which is rigorous and trustworthy in its procedures but ends up answering a different set of questions to the ones it claims to do.

Given the importance of the construct, how can we estimate whether a research study is reliable or not? As Denscombe (2010: 213) notes, in qualitative studies, this is commonly done by asking the following question in relation to a particular study: 'If someone else did the research would he or she have got the same results and arrived at the same conclusions?' This operation therefore consists of holding the research as a constant variable and substituting the researcher, so that if the results turn out to be the same, we can eliminate the possibility of unreliability due to researcher bias. More specifically, there are two ways in which such a reliability test can be carried out. If 'someone else' (more usefully described by Nunan (1992: 17) as 'an independent researcher', since if it were a friend or colleague then there might be a transference of the initial bias) carried out a replication study in the same or different context and reached the same conclusion, this would verify the '**external reliability**' of the original study. If the independent researcher re-analysed the data from the original study and reached the same conclusions, this would be an indication of the '**internal reliability**' of the research.

However, while these operations are feasible in the context of quantitative research, they are much more problematic when applied to qualitative studies. While checking internal reliability is feasible as a procedure, it is limited in the context of qualitative research. Confining one's judgement exclusively to the evidence of re-analysis is to focus solely on the data produced and to ignore everything that led to the output. As we have seen, process and product are intricately linked in qualitative research, and an assessment of the latter cannot be made without also taking account of the former. Establishing external reliability is, on the other hand, totally problematic. It is obvious that the chances of a qualitative study ever being repeated in the same context using the same informants and procedures by an independent researcher are remote or even, some would say, impossible, since the context-dependent conditions of qualitative research are constantly subject to change: time passes, situations change, pupils are exposed to new learning and experiences, and so on. An exact repetition, which logically is what is needed for verification, thus becomes impossible. Replication based in a different context with different pupils would introduce even more new, extraneous factors, potentially influencing the findings.

A further problem relates to the fact that qualitative research (particularly in the case of an ethnographic study carried out by a teacher researcher) needs to acknowledge the role of the researcher in the research: this role is not merely an instrumental or procedural one but constitutes an integral part of the findings themselves, as interaction between the researcher and the researched is seen 'as an explicit part of knowledge production' (Flick, 2002: 6). In the case of action research by teachers, it is also quite likely that the responses and behaviour of pupils (or for that matter colleagues) being researched will consciously or subconsciously be influenced by the fact that the person interviewing or observing them is their own teacher (or colleague).

So replicability as a criterion for measuring the reliability of a qualitative study is here usually confined to the realm of the virtual or the hypothetical. The importance of the criterion therefore shifts to the strategies and processes that the researcher puts in place to allow such a hypothetical replication of his or her study.

In John's case, there are three main ways in which he can be explicit about his processes so that others can (in theory) do a repeat performance.

Firstly, it is important to situate the study within the context of an existing wider, intellectual and professional debate. John needs to provide a clear account of the aims and objectives of his research. These should not merely be listed, but the rationale behind them should be presented and linked to prior discussion in the literature. The latter point is important for the purpose of reliability because it allows the researcher to connect with ideas, arguments, theories and the research of others, and uses aspects of this shared resource and shared understanding as a basis or starting point for the individual study. In so doing, it allows for scrutiny of the aims and objectives, at least, on a more generalized and 'objective' scale. This connection could be made in different ways, including, for instance, by alluding to the literature on relevant educational policy-making such as Ofsted's (2003) view that secondary schools fail to ensure that their 'pupils build on what they learned at primary school'. In addition, John's aims and objectives can link to prior analyses of pupils' perceptions of learning geography at KS2 and KS3.

Secondly, the reliability of a study depends on the degree of transparency research rationale and decisions guiding the selection of the research sample. John needs to be explicit about how his research was undertaken. This information would refer to the selection of the pupil sample as well as to the educational profiles of the people involved. The rationale for the sample selection needs to be given: why were the pupils chosen from one Y7 class? Did the group include pupils who had gone to different primary schools? Why was this important as opposed to selecting pupils with the same primary school history? What was the basis for choosing to interview those teachers in particular?

Finally, reliability depends on the accessibility of data collection and analysis procedures. These will involve keeping transcripts of interviews and records of lesson observation and other fieldwork notes. Questions used at interview need to be justified in relation to the specific study aims. This is important, even though in qualitative studies, especially when interviewing children, one is likely to use semi-structured interviews which are flexible and allow individual interviewees the scope to follow their own thread of thinking rather than being constrained by closed, structured questions.

Validity

Validity too is an umbrella term which encompasses a variety of different qualities that have been applied to educational research. As with the concept of reliability, a study's validity is often identified through reference to the following binary contrast: **external validity** and **internal validity**.

External validity has been defined as the extent to which the research design succeeds in allowing one to 'generalize beyond the subjects under investigation to a wider population' (Nunan, 1992: 17). In other words, external validity is an indication of the generalizability or 'transferability' (Miles and Huberman, 1994: 279) of the study's findings. In quantitative studies, researchers use randomized samples from a given population in order to strengthen the generalizability claims of their findings. However, given that qualitative research is essentially context-bound and ethnographic, external validity is generally viewed as inappropriate since it contradicts the epistemological and methodological perspectives in this approach. However, Lincoln and Guba (1985: 301) suggest that 'thick description' should be provided 'to enable someone interested in making a transfer to reach a conclusion about whether transfer can be contemplated as a possibility'. The term 'thick description', popularized by the anthropologist Clifford Geertz who borrowed it from the philosopher Gilbert Ryle, refers to the close analytical account and interpretation of the 'structures of signification' (Geertz, 1973: 9) inherent in events and social behaviour.

Internal validity, on the other hand, is highly applicable to the qualitative context, and it is very important for the researcher to consider since in its most fundamental form, it refers to the extent to which a study 'actually investigates what it purports to investigate' (Nunan, 1992: 14). In other words, this quality refers to the 'authenticity' or 'credibility' of the findings (Miles and Huberman, 1994: 278). Checking internal validity involves different strategies, as we shall see, but the key element is that of evidence of a persuasive connection between the conclusions made in the outcome of the study, and the procedures and methodology used in collecting and analysing the data. Maxwell (2005) usefully warns the researcher against the automatic use of strategies to offset threats to the study's validity. Masters students sometimes describe an inventory of strategies they have used, quoting authorities from the literature but without reference to the specific threats within their own study, as if this automatically endorses the internal validity of the research. 'Validity threats are made implausible by evidence not methods' (Maxwell, 2005: 105), and therefore it is important to identify the potential areas under threat in the proposed study first, and then to implement appropriate strategies to counter them. The methodology chapter in the report (or thesis) should discuss that connection explicitly, and should be honest about the extent to which the strategy is successful in reducing the particular threat.

What follows is a selection of strategies which are particularly applicable in the context of school-based teacher research, and illustrated through reference to the study described earlier in Example B.

Long-term involvement

This is one strategy where the teacher researcher is at an advantage over the external researcher. The purpose of this strategy is to overcome weaknesses, errors of judgement and patchy knowledge of the field due to the researcher's status as an outsider, and therefore it will enhance the credibility of the study's findings. However, when teachers are researching aspects of their own practice at their own school, an ethnographic 'feel' for the context in which the data is generated, the contextual background of the research, can be more easily achieved.

Why is it necessary?

Lincoln and Guba identify two aspects of long-term involvement (1985: 301). The first they call 'prolonged engagement' which serves the purpose of making the researcher 'more open to the multiple influences of the phenomenon being studied'. In the case of Jane Collins's study (Example B), the researcher could rightly claim that she has a good knowledge of the pupils' attitude and performance in French since she is teaching them over the academic year, and may have taught some at least in her previous first year at the school. She also has access to information relating to the pupils' personalities, behaviour and general academic performance through other colleagues and extra-curricular contact. This first-hand contact, developed over time, will help to build trust between Jane and her pupil-subjects, and will allow her to understand the 'culture' of the school and how to interpret it. It is unlikely that the validity of her research will be threatened by insufficient knowledge in this area.

The second aspect of long-term involvement which is identified by Lincoln and Guba is what they call 'persistent observation' and this does require proactive planning by Jane. The authors argue that this strategy serves the purpose of identifying 'those characteristics and elements in the situation that are most relevant to the problem' being investigated.

How can the threat be reduced in Jane's study?

Jane's study involves the analysis of small group interaction on pupils' target language use. The purpose is to see how this kind of learning situation, to which the pupils are not accustomed, generates their use of spoken French. Insufficient opportunities for pupils to engage in such tasks will not lead to valid findings: two or three lessons over the term could produce results which may be invalid because insufficient time has been allowed for the pupils to overcome their lack of familiarity with the learning task and situation. Pupils who are reluctant to speak French in whole-class situations may need time to adapt to group interaction. As well as its importance in allowing her pupils to adapt to their new learning situation, the strategy of 'long-term engagement' will help Jane to develop a clearer research focus through her preliminary observation of the interactions. She can do this through a pilot phase which serves the purpose of identifying what features of the pupils' interaction seem to be the most salient, what the obstacles are to her investigation and where the promising kinds of evidence in terms of her research aims seem to arise. In this way, the specific focus of Jane's observation and of her eventual analysis emerge from the research itself.

Triangulation

This is a widely endorsed strategy for strengthening the internal validity of qualitative studies in social science. It is based on the principle of confirming findings through the use of multiple perspectives. The key aspect of the strategy is threats to the validity of the conclusions, caused by the particular biases of any one source, method or agent of research, and which will be lessened by employing a variety of type.

Why is it necessary?

Writers have argued that there is a need for several types of **triangulation** in relation to qualitative research, but I shall focus on three modes which can have a bearing on the type of research design discussed in this chapter: triangulation of sources, of methods and of investigators. Triangulation of different sources can mean simply the inclusion of multiple informants (i.e. interviewees or subjects under observation). However, by including different categories of informants (e.g. teachers and pupils, secondary- and primary-based informants, pupils of different gender or ability or from different classrooms), the converging perspectives will arguably make the findings more powerful. Triangulation of methods involves the use of different data-collection instruments with the same subjects. This has the merit of counterbalancing the threats inherent to any one method. For instance, the likelihood of the 'Hawthorne effect' (changes in participants' behaviour during the course of a study may be related only to the special social situation and social treatment received) occurring is arguably stronger in the case of individual interviews than in the case of question-naires, particularly if the interviewer is known to the interviewee. Questionnaires, however, have their own and different weaknesses, such as less freedom for the interviewee to develop their own thoughts and a reliance on the written form of expression. Finally, triangulation of investigators refers to the use of more than one person in collecting or analysing the data. One can argue that triangulation as a research device is particularly valuable in the case of introspective research, though as we shall see in our examples, it is also a useful strategy in strengthening the cred-ibility of observational studies.

Some commentators (e.g. Silverman, 2010: 371) argue that the use of triangulation is inappropriate in qualitative research as it contravenes the ethnographic perspective in which the context of each source of evidence, of each method used and of each inves-tigator's approach is of intrinsic value. Comparing results from different angles of enquiry, therefore, cannot be used to strengthen a common finding. However, a less extreme view would be that it is possible to maintain the primacy of the researcher's main source and methods of research as well as of his or her own interpretation of the results, while also drawing on multiple sources of evidence and analysis in support of the validity of that main focus.

How can the threat be reduced in both studies?

As an example of introspective research, John's study would benefit from all three kinds of triangulation. In particular, the type of study envisaged here calls out for the need for triangulation of sources. By interviewing teachers and pupils, including, if possible, teachers from the feeder primary school, John would be able to gather together the views of a range of people on the issue of the effects of a KS2/3 transfer on the learning of geography based on triangulation of sources of information. If the conclusions relied exclusively on evidence from the pupils, we would feel less confident about them, since, taken alone, the pupil interview data may be skewed by the '**Hawthorne effect**' or by a partial recall of geography learning in the primary school.

Despite the observational focus of Jane's study, the internal validity of the findings would be strengthened in particular by the use of triangulation of methods. In order to make general claims about how her pupils collaborate in small-group interaction and what forms of target language use this generates, she needs to have some evidence that the pupils' performance is not entirely dependent on the nature of the group task or on the dynamics of particular peer interrelations. In order to do this, Jane can usefully think about different methods of eliciting group target language use by asking them to engage in different types of language tasks over her data-collection period. These could, for instance, include role plays, debates, problem-solving tasks or description tasks. It would be important to include a variety of task types since hidden pupil preferences may be determined by the type of language needed in the different tasks (for instance, knowledge of particular vocabulary topics), or by the possibility of different kinds of interaction (e.g. argument, collaboration) appealing to different types of personality.

Jane's interest in probing the reasons why her pupils perform linguistically in particular ways could lead to conclusions whose validity may be under threat unless she took suitable measures to strengthen her case. In order to offset exclusive reliance on her own explanation of the data, Jane could carry out individual pupil interviews as another form of methods triangulation in her study. This would be especially useful in investigating the reasons why individuals code switch at particular points in the group dialogue. Though Jane may be able to interpret some possible reasons by looking for patterns of switching in the transcripts, her analysis would benefit from asking some of the pupils to come up with their own explanations. She might also be able to use the interviews as an opportunity to test out some of her own interpretations of the code-switching patterns on the pupils themselves to see whether they confirmed her own views. Of course, even if the pupils rejected some of her conclusions, this would not necessarily invalidate them, since the impulse might be operating at a subconscious level. However, having this discussion with the pupils in itself would strengthen her study by providing a thicker layering of interpreted data, and by demonstrating more of an awareness of the complexities of the research process.

As far as triangulation of investigators is concerned, both John and Jane would gain some benefit from asking a colleague to examine a sample of their data relating to a particular aspect of their research, in order to see if the kind of interpretations they themselves are making of the data are reiterated in their colleagues' responses.

Looking for negative evidence

Why is it necessary?

This is a way of confirming one's findings by revising hypotheses in the light of **negative evidence** in the data. Miles and Huberman (1994: 263) describe this tactic as part of a set of strategies for looking at 'unpatterns' that 'test a conclusion about a "pattern" by saying what it is *not* like'. Other similar strategies they list are 'checking the meaning of outliers', 'using extreme cases' and 'following up surprises'. Perhaps more explicitly than the previous two strategies I have examined in this chapter, looking for negative evidence focuses on the link between the empirical evidence collected and the theories, hypotheses or conclusions which the researcher draws once the analytical process is throwing up some insights.

How can the threat be reduced in Jane's study?

Looking for negative evidence is one way of guarding against one's natural tendency to be over-enthusiastic about a particular interpretation or pattern of findings. Qualitative research is not about proving a point or seeking confirmation of theories, but often the excitement of discovering one or more instances in the data which support a particular interpretation of the phenomenon under scrutiny can lead the researcher to fix too quickly and too unequivocally on a particular interpretation of the data. For instance, Jane might discover that pupils are more ready to use the target language if it is in a repeat situation (i.e. where they have already encountered a need to use the expression in a similar communicative situation in a previous task). Without resorting to a quantitative count of the number of times target language use appears in a repeat situation, which would not be a very useful approach in a qualitative study, Jane could also look at cases where pupils did use French in new communicative situations or failed to do so in repeat situations. Whether this results in her revising her conclusions or not, simply by demonstrating to us (and to herself) that she has looked at negative evidence will give us and her more confidence in the hypotheses she does make and the conclusions she ultimately draws.

Conclusion: thinking about reliability and validity in relation to your own project

As the examples discussed in this chapter have demonstrated, these two concepts are important issues to consider at different stages of your research design. At the back of your mind, you should think about how your research findings and plan will look to other practitioners in educational research. At the planning stage, think about where the weaknesses are likely to be in data collection and analysis. How effectively do they relate to your research questions and objectives? It is always useful to discuss your plan with a colleague or a supervisor before you commit to it. Look for examples in the literature to see how other people have designed similar studies. Having identified the potential weaknesses, then you can start planning strategies such as those described above which you can tailor to deal with particular threats to the reliability and validity of your research.

Remember that there is a fundamental difference between qualitative and quantitative research: the former does not seek to reach hard factual conclusions based on some form of measurement; its aim is to generate hypotheses and arguments, or to explore themes supported by trustworthy evidence from the data. Be explicit (and self-critical where relevant) about how you tried to ensure that that evidence and your analysis are trustworthy.

Activity 9.1   How does pupils' use of ICT in lessons support their learning?

Imagine that you want to investigate this question in relation to the context of your subject teaching. Consider the following questions which you would need to address in the design of a qualitative study focusing on your own classroom experiences with one or more groups at your school.

- What sort of pupil use of ICT would you want to examine and why?
- Which aspects of their learning would you want to begin by looking at?
- What sort of evidence would you want to gather relating to the pupils' use of technology?
- What other forms of data collection would you carry out?
- List the procedures and types of information that would be needed for others to carry out a replication study.
- What would be the likely threats to the internal validity of your study?
- What strategies would you use to guard against these threats?

  ## Key ideas

This chapter has sought to identify the main benefits of thinking about the *reliability* and *validity* of research carried out by teacher researchers. I have argued that the two notions are important measures for use in the assessment of both observational and introspective qualitative research. Reliability refers to the degree of rigour, consistency and trustworthiness of a study. This measurement is traditionally conceived in relation to the agent of the research. If an independent researcher carried out the same study, would they arrive at the same findings (*internal reliability*)? If an independent researcher carried out the same research elsewhere, would they reach the same conclusions (*external reliability*)? Validity was described as the degree to which a study measures what it claims to measure. *External validity* refers to the generalizability of the findings. This was seen to be inappropriate in real terms within the epistemological framework of qualitative research. However, it can be useful if seen as a tool for hypothetical validation. *Internal validity*, on the other

(Continued)

(Continued)

hand, was described as an important quality which focused on the connection between a study's findings and the data-collection and analysis procedures used to reach them. Three types of strategies for checking the internal validity of qualitative studies by teacher researchers were described and exemplified. *Long-term involvement* provides the researcher with sufficient time to develop a familiarity and understanding of the subjects, the data and research process which result in a strengthening of the validity of the findings. *Triangulation* of sources, of methods and of investigators protect the study against threats to internal validity of findings due to exposure to the biases inherent in any one source, method or individual researcher. *Looking for negative evidence* is a way of confirming particular patterns in the findings by examining contrary evidence and therefore being able to say what the patterns are not like.

Reflective questions

1   Have you been scrupulously honest about the procedures and limitations of your study? Qualitative research is as much about the process as about the outcomes of the research. Questions about reliability and validity are a good way of critically reporting on the process.
2   Have you considered the threats to reliability and validity issues before you start, as well as reviewing these after you have completed your data collection?
3   Make a list of the strategies you used to strengthen the reliability and validity of your study. First identify the potential threats, then talk about the strategies you devised to offset the threats.
4   Have you got the appropriate number of research objectives for the study? Be realistic within the time and resource constraints you're working under.

Further reading

Denzin, N. and Lincoln, Y. (2011) *The SAGE Handbook of Qualitative Research* (4th edn). London: Sage.

Saldana, J. (2009) *The Coding Manual for Qualitative Researchers*. London: Sage.

Silverman, D. (2010) *Interpreting Qualitative Data* (3rd edn). London: Sage.

CHAPTER 10

ANALYSING QUALITATIVE DATA

Michael Evans

Chapter overview

This chapter will introduce some of the key features of the process of analysing qualitative data using examples to illustrate some of the practical tools and strategies commonly used which may be of particular relevance to the teacher researcher.

The analytical steps involved will be explained and a definition of what is meant by coding will be provided, drawing on actual examples from PGCE and Masters students' work. The benefits of computer-aided qualitative analysis will be discussed, and how **displays** and **matrices** can be useful tools to use on qualitative data.

The form of qualitative data

Most qualitative data in empirical research first appear in their raw form as oral (non-textual) data. Interviews or classroom interaction are perhaps the most common forms of oral data which are of interest to the educational researcher. In order to analyse these data, it is necessary to be able to reflect on them repeatedly and at length; to be able to fragment and manipulate them in the search for underlying patterns and meanings. For this reason, it is useful to convert the oral data into textual form through the process of transcription. However, it becomes immediately apparent that this process is usually fraught with problems related to the risk of distorting the original version. For instance, non-verbal signs (such as gestures, facial expression and pauses) which accompany verbal discourse can have an important bearing on the meanings expressed in the interaction. Efforts should be made to systematically capture such paralinguistic messages and to note them in the transcript. There are numerous differences in the systems used by researchers and it is important for you to use only those markers which are relevant to what you are looking for in your data. For instance, an extract of a transcript that focuses on pupil discourse, where the nuances of language and expression are central to the study, will look different to the transcript of an interview where the focus of interest is in the content of the informant's responses rather than on the form of their expression. So it is unnecessary, unrealistic and unwise to try to capture everything in a transcript. It *is* necessary, though, for you to think about what you do need to note and then to be systematic in the notation. The key to the coding system you are using should always be included in the report, usually in an appendix. The following is an example:

Box 10.1   Example of a transcription system (adapted from Ellis and Barkhuizen, 2005: 29)

1 T = teacher; R = researcher; subjects are designated by their (fictional) initials, or P for pupil.
2 Each line is numbered for ease of reference (useful with long extracts).
3 Pauses are indicated in brackets:
    (.) indicates a pause of a second or shorter;
    (.3.) indicates the length of a pause beyond one second.
4 XXX is used to indicate speech that could not be deciphered.
5 ... indicates an incomplete utterance.
6 Words are underlined to show overlapping speech between two speakers.
7 Words are italicized to show a very heavily stressed word.
8 A limited amount of contextual information is given in brackets.

The blurred line between data collection and analysis

Analysing qualitative data can be an exciting phase in the research process since it relies on a creative engagement by the researcher in the production, application and interpretation of ideas. To refer to it as a 'phase' is perhaps to misrepresent its nature, since in qualitative research data collection and analysis are not always separate; analysis does not always follow collection – it can sometimes precede it. It is also likely to occur at different points of the research rather than just in one block. The two are not isolated activities but interact with one another in the common pursuit of investigating the research question. This interaction between data collection and analysis is evident on different levels. At the level of research strategy, different collection and analysis activities feed off each other. For instance, in action research, the results of an analysis of one set of data will inform subsequent data collection activities. Huberman and Miles (1998) describe the process in more cyclical terms, seeing analysis as containing three interlinking sub-processes – data reduction, data display and conclusion drawing/verification: 'These processes occur *before* data collection, during study design and planning; *during* data collection as interim and early analyses are carried out; and *after* data collection as final products are approached and completed' (1998: 180). The interactive nature of their model is captured in Figure 10.1.

This interaction between data collection and data analysis is also apparent at a more local level. A semi-structured interview, for instance, allows the interviewer scope to free the interview to develop in certain directions in response to comments made by the

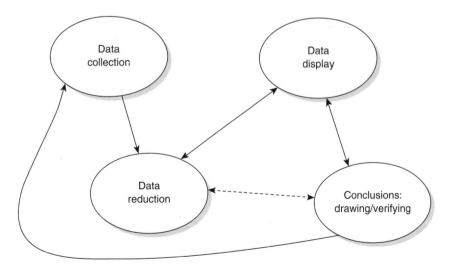

Figure 10.1   Components of data analysis: an interactive model (Huberman and Miles, 1998: 181)

interviewee. The following extract, for example, is from a focus group interview with Y9 pupils as part of a study I carried out on the impact of school exchange visits on pupils' proficiency in French. It illustrates how my questioning was influenced by an implicit ongoing analysis of the responses I elicited.

Transcript extract: focus group interview with Y9 pupils

1   R: Did you have a lot in common with them?

2   P1: Well, no (.) it's just that ... I don't know, it just seemed that We didn't (.) we didn't have

3   a lot in common. It was just that I got to know him quite quickly and I mean that we can

4   speak together easily.

5   R: Was it you who made the effort or him or both equally?

6   P1: Well, he wasn't very good at English so ... I mean, he tried to be friends, if you see

7   what I mean. But he didn't speak that much so he just like showed me around in his room

8   and his house and stuff like that. So that helped.

9   R: Some of you put in your questionnaire that you got on well ... you liked the family, or

10 the adults, but you didn't have that much in common with your partner. Was that anybody

11 from this group?

12 P2: Yes.

13 R: What did you mean by that? I'm a bit surprised by that.

14 P2: Well, the mum was really friendly to me and it was odd but because I was sharing

15 their house with Tamsin, mine seemed to offload me on to Tamsin and her French

16 exchange so I didn't really get to know my partner but I got to know the mum and

17 Tamsin's exchange, so it didn't really work that well.

18 R: And did they speak to you in French, the parents?

19 P2: Um, yes, because she didn't know any English.

20 R: And did that pose a problem?

21 P2: No.

22 R: What about the rest of you? Did you communicate in French?

23 P3: No, my parents were all like really really strong in English so we spoke in English the

24 whole time.

25 R: Did you find that a bit annoying?

26 P3: No, it was really easy!

27 R: Because that made you feel more at home?

28 P3: Yeah.

29 P4: Yeah, my one's mum got all her university English work out to show me!

30 R: Did you feel that you could say to them, 'Well, can we practise the French?' at all? I

31 know it's difficult to do that.

32 P4: No, because you've got your French person.

33 R: Right, your partner, yes. What were the sorts of situations which were difficult for you

34 in terms of language? I mean, where you had to speak in French and you thought, you

35 know, 'I don't know what to say'? Were there any particular situations where you wished

36 you could speak French?

37 P4: They had like lots of (.) kind of sayings which when they're translated into English

38 they don't like mean the same thing in English. So even if you've like translated with a

39 dictionary, it still doesn't mean anything to you.

40 P2: I would say the English. You can't explain to them like when they want to do

41 something and you don't want to do it, you can't say it politely! Because you can't say

42 'I'm sorry, I really just don't want to do this'. You have to say 'No'.

43   P5: I had loads of arguments with mine actually.

44   R: Really? With your partner?

45   P5: Yes.

46   R: What sort of thing?

47   P5: I got told to stop being rude!

48   R: Rude? Who by? By him?

49   P5: The mum.

50   R: By his mum? Right! What were the arguments about?

51   P5: About going places, because mine didn't want to go anywhere and it was my birthday

52   party and they wouldn't let me go.

53   R: Oh, right.

54   P6: I had to translate for her! Hers got really angry at *me* for saying what *she* was saying!

(Laughter)

As this extract shows, the interviewer is constantly making decisions about what to follow up from the interviewee's responses; and these decisions are made on the basis of what one might call '**online analysis**', made however fleetingly and instinctively by the interviewer during the flow of the interview. For instance, Pupil 3's comments (lines 23–24) that her partner's parents spoke in English to her all the time interested me because this could potentially reveal something about how the pupil saw the relationship between language learning and personal communication. My first hypothesis-suggesting question (that the parents' use of English was 'annoying') was rejected by the pupil. But my second hypothesis-question (that communicating in English had a comforting effect) proved more acceptable and seemed to have the agreement of at least one other pupil in the group. One could therefore argue that for a brief moment what was happening here was a form of '**collaborative analysis**'.

One might object at this point that we are here precariously treading the delicate line between informants' and researcher's constructions of the meanings surrounding events and experiences being researched. However, as noted earlier, qualitative research paradigms to a certain extent legitimize researcher input in the process of data elicitation, provided this input is explicitly acknowledged and critiqued. In the case of young pupil informants, the strategy is arguably particularly needed in order to draw out their analytical thinking.

Deductive and inductive orientations in qualitative analysis

There are two competing tensions when embarking on qualitative analysis which are best seen as two ends of a continuum. On the one hand, qualitative researchers have an overarching idea of what it is they want to investigate in the data and some notion at least of the different areas in which this sought-after information can be grouped. This 'deductive' approach seeks to generate and examine findings in relation to pre-established themes which may not be exhaustive or totally defined at the outset, but which nevertheless provide overall direction to the development of the analysis. At the other end of the spectrum, the inductive approach, adopted, for instance, by grounded theorists, takes an entirely open-minded approach to the data and uses themes which emerge from the data themselves as tools for the analysis. In reality, educational researchers dealing with qualitative material usually employ a mixture of the two approaches, but, as Huberman and Miles point out, the different emphases appeal to different types of studies:

> There is merit in both 'loose', inductively oriented designs, and 'tight', more deductively approached ones. The former work well when the terrain is unfamiliar and/or excessively complex, a single case is involved, and the intent is exploratory and descriptive. Tighter designs are indicated when the researcher has good prior acquaintance with the setting, has a good bank of applicable, well delineated concepts, and takes a more explanatory and/or confirmatory stance involving multiple, comparable cases. (1998: 185)

In either of the two orientations, the systematic character of the analysis is largely dependent on the use of a coding system to organize and structure the examination of the material. Coding is the process by which a text is examined thematically according to certain categories (codes) which are either predetermined or emergent from the data. The categories serve the purpose of reducing the total mass of data elicited in order to focus on what they tell us about the particular themes we are interested in. The process also allows the researcher to identify in the data evidence links to the different categories, to closely organize and inspect that evidence, and to use the process to inform and develop the themes indexed by the categories.

Coding framework

One of the first steps in this process is the development of a coding framework which can be applied systematically to the analysis of qualitative data. The framework should in the first instance remain fluid and develop on the basis of preliminary readings of some of the transcripts or at least of the pilot data. The following example is of a coding framework which I drew up in a study of pupils' code-switching between English and French in an online bulletin board project between pupils in England and in francophone countries. The framework was applied to the analysis of interviews I carried out with some of the English pupils involved in the project (Evans, 2009).

The codes, listed in the left-hand column (Table 10.1), refer to topics which I wanted to identify and for which I wanted to collate evidence from the pupil interviews. The right-hand column provides a brief description of what each code represents. This description is useful for supporting the validity claims of your findings and therefore it is advisable to include it in your methodology chapters in your dissertation or report. The descriptions are also useful to you as a researcher in that they help you to crystallize in your mind exactly what it is that you are targeting with each code. In the above example, I grouped the codes according to different dimensions of language use identified in the sociolinguistics literature. The types of concepts referred to by my codes in this framework are fairly descriptive or factual, in that they sought to locate references to these topics either directly or indirectly in the pupils' interview responses, with minimal levels of researcher interpretation at this stage.

Table 10.1   A coding framework for the analysis of interview data

Ideational dimension	
Code choice	Reasons for using French or English in posts
Codeswitch	Explanation of code switching and code mixing
Content	Choice of topic in post
Word choice	Meaning-related explanations for the choice of a particular word
Opinion	Opinion-related influence on the content of post
Interpersonal dimension	
Borrow	Copying text from native speaker posts
Interact	Perceptions of interactions with other members of the group
Read	Comments on the experience of reading other people's posts
Tu/vous	Rationalization of choice between the two forms of address in posts
Metalinguistic dimension	
Know	Reference to what they know
Learn	Reference to learning goals, outcomes and experience
Schoollang	Reference to the nature of their school language learning
SayWrite	Describing the online communicative process

Different types of coding

The second point to bear in mind is that researchers have identified the need for different kinds of coding and decisions. Although different writers define several distinct types of categories in the coding of qualitative data, it is best to focus initially on two main types: **open coding** and **thematic coding**. I shall from now on, in line with the literature, refer to categories as 'codes', defined as the names or labels that refer to concepts (synonymous with 'theme' in common parlance). The denotation of 'concept' is not trivial, however, since even at its most basic, descriptive level, coding is a process of translating raw data into conceptual references. Let us look at the example provided by Strauss and Corbin (1998: 106–9) illustrating their coding of part of an interview with a young adult talking about teenage drug use. The following extract is taken from the beginning of the transcript presented by the authors, and the labels in square brackets are the codes the researchers applied to the text:

Interviewer: Tell me about teens and drug use.

Respondent: I think teens use drugs as a release from their parents ["**rebellious act**"]. Well, I don't know. I can only talk for myself. For me, it was an experience [**experience**] [in-vivo code]. You hear a lot about drugs ["**drug talk**"]. You hear they are bad for you ["**negative connotation**" to the "drug talk"]. There is a lot of them around ["**available supply**"]. You just get into them because they're accessible ["**easy access**"] and because it's kind of a new thing ["**novel experience**"]. It's cool! You know, it's something that is bad for you, taboo, a "no" ["**negative connotation**"]. Everyone is against it ["**adult negative stance**"]. If you are a teenager, the first thing you are going to do is try them ["**challenge the adult negative stance**"].

One can see that the codes attached by the researchers to this passage are doing more than just labelling: they are lifting the specific points made by the interviewee to a more generalized, conceptual plane. The code 'rebellious act' is an idea which has certain 'properties' and 'dimensions' which differentiate it from other related concepts, such as 'mindless act' or 'self-destructive act', and is applicable in other contexts and in relation to other people. The 'property' in this case might be that the act is directed against authority figures, and the 'dimensions' of this property might be 'parents', 'teachers', 'society in general'. Even at this initial stage of the analysis where the researchers are essentially attempting to identify and itemize the content of the data, the process involves a degree of conceptual interpretation. The above is an example of 'open coding' which Strauss and Corbin define as 'the analytic process through which concepts are identified and their properties and dimensions are discovered in data' (1998: 101).

The act of open coding has the effect of fracturing the transcript into different fragments which are labelled according to extensive lists of codes. Sometimes the same fragment can have several different codes attached to it. This process therefore results in a reduction of the material, which in ethnographic studies especially can be dauntingly voluminous. These fragments can then be examined in groups, thus enabling the researcher to focus on the concepts and the related evidence from the data. The danger of such an analytical strategy is that a textual fragment (and therefore the evidence) becomes detached from its original context and might lead ultimately to a distorted or inaccurate reading. To guard against this, the analyst must attempt to preserve as far as possible a balance between the aims of categorization and contextualization.

Another feature of the process of open coding, which is illustrated by the Strauss and Corbin quote above, is the use of 'in-vivo codes'. These are words or phrases which are borrowed from the data and used as an open code. In this example, 'experience' is an in-vivo code since its use as a code is prompted by the interviewee's use of the word as part of their own explanation of their drug consumption. In-vivo codes are particularly useful in inductive analysis orientations as they help to ensure that analysis and resulting interpretations remain close to the original material and reduce the risk of extraneous ideas influencing the interpretation of the data.

Thematic coding (also labelled 'pattern coding' by Miles and Huberman (1994: 57–8)) is a form of analytical coding which involves the search for thematic patterns in the coded data, often at a higher level of abstraction than open codes. Grounded theorists like Strauss and Corbin, for whom the ultimate purpose of qualitative analysis is the construction of theory, refer to the process as 'axial coding'. As Robson has noted (2002: 494), the process is 'about linking together the categories developed through the process of open coding'. As such, it can be described as a process of analysis which is at a level which is further removed from the textual origination of the data. The focus now is on the codes themselves and their theoretical connotations. In this way, a broader theoretical argument surrounding the emergent themes begins to develop. For instance, in the example of the study referred to above, once I had gathered the relevant quotations from my data in relation to 'code choice', 'code switching' and 'word choice', I was able to examine them in relation to the three concepts and to compare, for instance, the pupils' explanations of their decisions in relation to the three phenomena. This allowed me to see whether different types of considerations were at play in the pupils' minds and therefore to develop an argument about the pupils' communicative priorities and the constraints on these.

The practice of coding: by hand or by computer

The first step in open coding is to go through the transcript and, line by line, label those bits of it that correspond to the codes which you have previously identified or new ones which emerge as you proceed. If you are doing this by hand, then the codes should be written in the margin with some form of highlighting of the selected text. Working on a word processor, the codes can be entered in brackets within the text, usually immediately after the relevant segment.

One of my former Masters students gives the following vivid and honest account of how, having started off by entering her data onto a computer software analysis program (namely, NVivo) and begun the process of coding the data, she eventually abandoned the medium in favour of the less technologically sophisticated but time-honoured tradition of pen and paper:

> Confident that the programme would help me formulate an assertion about gender and motivation, I started to form trees or families of nodes with different attribute values. It did not take me long to realize that my data was being transformed into a computer version that had very little in common with the original group interviews. So I stopped the process, printed all the units of analysis from the open coding and displayed them on a wall.

The benefit of doing the analysis manually is, as this student found, that you maintain a sense of overall control and viewing of the data globally. For some researchers, the physical ability to cut up the different quotations and to sort them according to the different code headings and to view the groupings simultaneously can provide a valuable perspective to stimulate emergent interpretations and findings. This retention of an overall view of the data is part of what helps the researcher to hold on to the original version of the events rather than, as the student above observed, transforming it into a computer version. On the other hand, there are drawbacks to the manual approach. Firstly, it is only feasible to do this with relatively small amounts of data. For studies involving several interviews with several informants or large amounts of transcripts of classroom data, the scissors-and-glue approach could quickly break down. Even with a small quantity of data, the ability to manage the data manually is very restricted: for instance, you will often want to mark the same piece of text with two or more codes. This is not easily done on paper.

Programs such as NVivo or Atlas.ti are quite costly and it may not be economic for a teacher to invest in one for personal use. However, if you are enrolled at a local university for your study, then it would normally be possible for you to make use of that facility.

It is important to recognize from the outset that computer-aided qualitative data analysis software (or CAQDAS) does not analyse the data for you: the programs are simply support platforms which facilitate the storage and management of the qualitative data and phases of analysis. You still have to do the analysis and interpretation yourself. So what are the main ways in which a program such as NVivo can be of use to a hard-pressed practitioner researcher?

- **Software**: Programs such as Nvivo and Atlas.ti were developed specifically as tools for supporting the analysis of data collected in social research. They are therefore designed to incorporate a wide range of data (textual, visual or aural) which can all be subjected to the same sets of codes. This means that it is possible to link bits of visual data or taped interviews to particular open codes and therefore you can have access to an original piece of source material as well as a transcript version. More usually, the database will consist of textual data. Provided the sources are saved as txt, rtf or Microsoft Word documents, they can be uploaded and saved on to the software program and all the coding is done directly on screen. Your bank of data can include informal documents such as notes and memos, as well as formal transcripts of interviews, lesson observations and so on.
- **Coding**: I have already mentioned some of the benefits of the computer-based coding of data, such as allowing the researcher to apply several codes to the same fragment of text, to combine different media in the same coding framework, and the general ease with which one can code (and 'uncode') a transcript. Another major facility is the ability to retrieve and print out all the quotes for particular codes, thus allowing the researcher to focus exclusively on those bits of the text that have been identified as relating to a particular theme or issue. The screen which displays the quotes will also have a hyperlink to the original source document from which each quote is taken, thus allowing the researcher to return easily and at will to the original context of the reference in order to guard against distortion through an overreliance on decontextualized fragments. NVivo also allows the user to incorporate their preliminary thoughts as they code by using the 'annotations' tool. This is a useful facility since it means that you can quickly jot down your thoughts, queries and

interpretations of a particular instance of coding and attach it to the coded piece of text. Your fleeting preliminary thoughts are thus captured and easily retrieved whenever you call up the transcript on the program.

- **Displays**: These allow you to present a visual configuration of aspects of your study. This can have different objectives, including the following: to explore the interrelationship between different concepts or themes in the data; to configure the relationship between different contextual factors influencing the phenomena being investigated. A display in qualitative research can serve different purposes: it can be used as a preliminary template for organizing the analysis, or as part of a final, summative presentation of the researcher's findings. Another useful purpose to which displays can be put is that of supporting research-in-progress. By structuring and restructuring your displays as you progress through your analysis, you can explore your research questions and experiment with your conclusions visually and in a focused way. NVivo refers to displays as 'models'. These are 'dynamic' in that by linking them to specific items in the source data (e.g. transcripts, notes, etc.), you can call up the evidence and examine or present its relationship to a theoretical, conceptual or other framework. In longitudinal research, a series of changing displays provides a 'snapshots' record of the development of your analysis over time, and can thus make a useful component of the reflexive dimension in ethnographic research.

- **Matrices**: Like figures and diagrams, a matrix is a particular format of an analytical display. Miles and Huberman define a matrix as 'essentially the "crossing" of two lists, set up as rows and columns' (1994: 93). The authors list the following benefits to the researcher of producing matrices during the course of the research:

> It requires you to think about your research questions and what portions of your data are needed to answer them; it requires you to make full analyses, ignoring no relevant information; and it focuses and organizes your information coherently. These advantages are repeated when you include displays in a final report; the reader can re-create your intellectual journey with some confidence. (Miles and Huberman, 1994: 239)

The structure of a matrix is based on a comparison of two variables set out in rows and columns. For instance, the rows variable could be a set of codes focusing on a particular theme, and the columns variable might be a particular grouping of the informants.

Table10.2   Example of variable-by-variable matrix: types of learning, by gender

	Male interviewees	Female interviewees
How others learn	0	1
Learning new topics	0	1
Learning a new language	1	2
Learning from others	1	1
Learning about culture	3	2
Improving writing	2	1
Language learning	2	1

Matrices also lend themselves well to case study formats, so that the coded data might be given for individuals or other units of analysis, rather than, as in the example shown in Table 10.2, groupings made on the basis of an independent variable such as gender. Table 10.2 shows part of a matrix I drew up using NVivo for my online pupil interaction study mentioned earlier in this chapter. The organization of the data here allows me to look at gender differences in the coded responses to the themes listed: in particular, the matrix supported my analysis of the pupils' comments on how using the bulletin board led to different types of learning. The benefit of a matrix produced by a software program such as NVivo is that one can access the selected quotations by clicking on the number in the cells. In manually produced matrices, the cells might contain statements (instead of the numbers seen here) representing main themes expressed in the interviews. In this way, the researcher is forced to 'flesh out' the cell items by producing interim verbal summaries of the main points arising.

Activity 10.1

- Re-read the transcript extract in this chapter and code it according to the following open codes:

  o communicating in English
  o communicating in French
  o positive relationships
  o negative relationships
  o linguistic difficulties

- What other concepts emerge from the extract and how would you code them?
- What in-vivo code might a researcher find in this extract?

Key ideas

In this chapter, I have introduced some of the key features of the process of analysing qualitative data. I have also provided examples to illustrate some of the practical tools and strategies commonly used and which may be of particular relevance to the teacher researcher. I have indicated that from the outset, when conducting an interview, the researcher can be engaging in a form of *online analysis* (sometimes collaboratively with the interviewee) of the themes and issues at the centre of the study. The next step is to convert the raw data into the form of a transcript, guided by the

(Continued)

(Continued)

systematic application of a *transcription system*. Transcripts need to be subsequently coded through the application of a *coding framework* which can be generated between a mixture of inductive and deductive approaches. The frameworks should include a brief description of each code listed and should be justified in the methodology section of the report. A *code* is a label that refers to a particular concept that the research is investigating. *Open coding* fractures the transcript into fragments which relate to the different concepts. *Thematic coding* results in higher level, theoretical analysis based on linkage between different open codes. The benefits of computer-aided qualitative analysis are that it facilitates the storage, management and interrogation of the data. *Displays* and *matrices* are useful tools to use on qualitative data for two main reasons: they provide a framework for structuring the analysis; and, if used repeatedly over an extended period of research, they provide a reflexive record of the progression of the analysis over time. When produced through the medium of a computer program, displays and matrices are hyperlinked to the original coded transcripts.

Reflective questions

1 What devices will you use to record your data and how will you make the data accessible for analysis?
2 Try to stand back and make the familiar unfamiliar. Let the transcript speak to you; don't just focus on pre-established questions and issues.
3 Remember that qualitative analysis software does not do the analysing for you. You have to do that. The computer programme allows you to organize your data with ease so you can group and focus more clearly on specific bits of the data.
4 Remember that qualitative research is not concerned with objective certainties. Frame your sentences with appropriate caution, e.g. 'It would seem that ...'.

Further reading

Saldana, J. (2009) *The Coding Manual for Qualitative Researchers*. London: Sage.
Silverman, D. (2010) *Interpreting Qualitative Data* (3rd edn). London: Sage.

CHAPTER 11

TAKING A QUANTITATIVE APPROACH

Mark Winterbottom

Chapter overview

A quantitative approach means using measurements and numbers to help formulate and test ideas. It usually involves summarizing numerical data and/or using them to look for differences and associations between sets of numbers. In this chapter, I'll look at approaches to collecting and interpreting quantitative data. In the next chapter, you'll learn more about using statistics to analyse them.

If you have a natural science background, you may feel at home here, but bear in mind the complexity of human behaviour – don't ignore the depth of data available through the qualitative approaches outlined elsewhere in this book – achieving a fully natural scientific approach in a school context is almost impossible. Read this chapter together with Chapter 12. Never collect a set of data before thinking about how to analyse it!

Before I get going, let's look at some fundamental words and ideas, which can help you to talk about, read about, evaluate and plan quantitative approaches. I'll then introduce you to two approaches for planning your own research, and look at some ways in which school performance data is used ... and misused!

Ideas and definitions

Variables

A quantitative approach usually means measuring a property of something or someone. That property is called a variable. Variables are called variables because they are entities that can vary. You can collect quantitative data about individuals by designing questionnaires or tests. Alternatively, you can simply record data by observing the subjects 'from afar'; it all depends on the data you want. However, do bear in mind that the act of collecting data can sometimes change the data you get! Some examples of variables include:

- the number of students 'on roll'
- the test result
- the proportion of students gaining five GCSEs at A–C
- the tier (e.g. primary, secondary, etc.)
- the school governance system.

Variables described using numbers are quantitative (e.g. the proportion of students gaining five GCSEs at A–C). Those described by categories are *qualitative* or categorical (e.g. the tier – primary, secondary, etc.). Although this chapter is about a quantitative approach, we usually look at qualitative variables as well.

Quantitative variables fall into two types. Continuous variables can take any value in a given range (e.g. 3.2, 4.798), whereas discrete variables have clear steps between their possible values (for example, you can't get 100.324 pupils at a school!).

Another way to think about variables is the *scale*, or level of measurement that we use. The scale itself determines whether they'll be qualitative/quantitative or continuous/discrete.

- Nominal scales are for qualitative variables to categorize observations. The value assigned to a group is just a label, and implies nothing about quantity. *Sex* would be a variable measured with a nominal scale: we could use '1' for boys and '2' for girls.
- Ordinal scales assess rank or order and yield discrete variables. Imagine you rank the pupils in your class according to test score; the best student has a rank of 1, etc. Rather than just being labels (as above), a '1' is better than a '2'. This type of scale gives an effective summary, but the exact value of the differences between each person's scores is unclear, and not necessarily identical.
- Interval and ratio scales provide discrete or continuous data where there are equal intervals between the units of measurement (for example, a minute is the same length however you measure it!). In a ratio scale, a zero means zero – there are no children or they got no answers right. In an interval scale, the zero is relative – e.g. zero may describe a baseline motivation level.

Validity and reliability

Some variables are direct measures of what we're interested in – recording a pupil's sex is a direct measure of their sex. Others are more indirect measures. For example, test scores are an indirect measure of pupils' learning. It is important that such measures provide a genuine measure of the underlying construct. Such validity is important when collecting your own data, and when interpreting other people's data and conclusions.

It is also important to consider reliability – the consistency and repeatability of data collected over time, across different samples, and across different measures of the same underlying construct. Box 11.1 suggests some ways to assess reliability using one pilot group, or using two groups that are closely matched for variables relevant to your study.

Box 11.1   Assessing reliability

- Use one questionnaire with one group on different occasions and see if their answers are significantly correlated (see Chapter 12). (Be aware that they may remember their responses though!)
- Use two different questionnaires (but whose questions examine the same ideas) on different occasions with the same group, and look at the consistency between responses to matched questions.
- Use one questionnaire with both groups, and check that their responses are not significantly different.
- Use two questionnaires (whose questions examine the same ideas) on different occasions with both groups and check that responses to matched questions are not significantly different.

Samples and populations

When collecting quantitative data, distinguishing between your sample and your population is important. A sample is a sub-group of the population. Collecting data about a sample that is representative of a wider population lets you draw conclusions about the population. We often use samples because measuring all the individuals in the population is impractical.

To ensure your sample is representative, it's essential to understand who your population is – this is something it is easy to overlook. For example, if you want a study which is generalizable to the population of all the 14-year-old students in the country, then you would randomly choose your sample from all the 14-year-olds in the country – this is so-called probability sampling. You can see four types of probability sampling in Box 11.2.

Box 11.2   Probability sampling

- **Random sampling**: Here there is an equal chance that each member of the population is included. Including one individual in the sample has no influence on whether another individual is included.
- **Systematic sampling**: Sometimes practicalities may make it preferable to sample individuals in some sort of order – say every fourth subject in a line. To do so, you should randomize the list of individuals and choose your starting point randomly.
- **Stratified sampling**: You may suspect that other variables (e.g. sex) could affect your results. To try to eliminate the effect, you would randomly choose half your subjects from the boys and half your subjects from the girls.
- **Stage sampling**: You can stratify your sampling at a number of levels. For example, if you thought that the year group and tutor could affect your data, you would randomly choose year group, then within each, randomly choose tutor groups, and then within each again, randomly choose the pupils to study.

However, your own research is likely to happen within your own school and often in your own classroom – this is so-called convenience sampling, a type of non-probability sampling (see Box 11.3). The children in your class are not representative of all the 14-year-old children across the country, and you cannot therefore make generalizations. Your pupils' characteristics may be dependent on upbringing, socio-economic group, location, year group, your idiosyncrasies as a teacher, and many other variables. Hence, when conducting research in your own classroom, your class is the population – there isn't a wider group to which you can generalize your findings.

Box 11.3   Non-probability sampling

- **Convenience sampling**: You use individuals to whom you have easy access. You cannot generalize your conclusions to a wider population.
- **Quota sampling**: You may suspect a particular variable (e.g. sex) could affect your results. To eliminate any influence, randomly choose your subjects from boys and girls, but in proportion to the number of boys and girls in the group of pupils you are interested in (e.g. the population of pupils in Cambridgeshire). Your findings are only generalizable to this limited population of pupils.

(Continued)

> ## Box 11.3   (Continued)
>
> - **Dimensional sampling**: If you suspect that a number of variables will influence the variable you are interested in, you can deliberately choose individuals who are subject to every combination of those variables.
> - **Purposive sampling**: You choose which individuals will be in your sample based on how representative you think they are of the group you want to study. It is unwise to generalize beyond your sample as your choices are unlikely to be fully objective.

If you have a natural science background, you may feel this makes your research rather pointless – after all, if it's got no wider application, what's the point in doing it? There are two answers: (1) researching your own practice in your own classroom contributes strongly to your ongoing professional development; and (2) providing you make the context of your research clear when you write it up (you, the nature of the class, the lesson content, the whole school context, etc.), anyone reading your study would be able to decide the extent to which your findings may apply to them (so-called user generalizability).

Finally, although you probably won't need to generalize to wider populations in your own research, you will read large-scale studies that do just that. Even if individuals have been sampled randomly, instinct probably tells you that a study based on two individuals is less generalizable than one based on two hundred – but why is that?

Well, if you take lots of different samples from the same population, it's unlikely that each will have the same mean (what most people would call the average) or standard deviation (how much the data is spread out around the mean) for the variable you're measuring. However, if you use a bigger sample, the mean will be closer to the population mean; hence, the bigger the sample, the better. If you do adopt a quantitative approach, a sample size of 30 or more would be good.

Quantitative approaches to research

So how do you actually generate some data? There are two key approaches: experimental (measuring the effect of some sort of intervention) and non-experimental (looking at what's there and trying to make sense of how different variables may affect each other). You'll learn how to analyse your data in the next chapter.

Experimental

This approach looks at the effect of one variable on another, by making a change in one of the variables (the independent variable) and seeing how the other variable changes (the dependent variable), while keeping all other variables constant (controlling them). An experimental approach is broadly underpinned by the stages shown in Box 11.4.

Box 11.4   Planning an experiment

1   Identify what you're trying to find out, and work out what you think will happen. Predict how you are expecting the independent variable (the treatment) to affect the dependent variable (the response).
2   A variable like 'pupils' learning' cannot be measured directly, and you'll have to use a 'proxy' or indirect measure of it, such as 'test score results'; remember to justify your choice of 'proxy' as a valid indicator of the variable you're interested in.
3   Decide who your population is, and then randomly choose a sample of individuals from the population.
4   If your experimental 'treatment' is something like 'receives new teaching approach' or 'doesn't receive new teaching approach', then randomly allocate your pupils to each group. Even if your experiment involves a more quantitative independent variable, such as the length of time spent working on computers during a lesson, randomly allocating pupils evenly across levels (one hour, two hours, etc.) is still essential.
5   Make sure that the levels of treatment are realistic within the context (usually a classroom). For example, looking at how eight hours of computer access affect pupils' learning is unrealistic in a single lesson. Also ensure that the range of treatments you provide will enable you to see trends and differences. Comparing 60 minutes of computer access with 61 minutes won't yield any startling conclusions.
6   Identify potentially confounding variables (variables that could affect your findings, such as variable C in Figure 11.2), and develop strategies to control them (keep their levels constant between individuals receiving the different levels of treatment), or eliminate them (e.g. removing a teaching assistant from the room).
7   Pilot your methods with a different sample to iron out any difficulties.
8   After the experiment, measure the dependent variable for each individual and use a statistical test to make a conclusion. Don't leave it until now though to consider which statistical tests you intend to use – it is all too common to realize that the data you've collected is not compatible with any statistical test.
9   Be careful to state the extent to which you can generalize your conclusion across a wider population.

An experimental model is a good basis for scientific research in a laboratory, but employing this approach in a classroom, with the multiplicity of variables in existence, and the constraints of school timetabling, is not always easy.

Let's imagine you're researching the effect of a six-week motivational training programme with a group of Year 9 students. Rather than being constrained by the groups already set up, you've randomly selected a group of students and you're teaching them at lunchtime. You use a questionnaire to assess their motivation beforehand. You use the same questionnaire after the six-week programme and find an increase in motivational levels. To your delight, you conclude that the training programme has had a positive impact!

Or do you? Are you certain that you've controlled all other variables that may affect your results? You may have begun your programme at the start of term, and then measured motivation again at the end of term; perhaps you could expect children to be more motivated as the end of term draws near! In fact, all sorts of other variables could be responsible for your findings. Hence, thinking about and collecting additional data to examine such confounding variables is essential to working out what's really going on. If you do want to use just one group, you may find your work sits better as one cycle of an action research approach, particularly if you were unable to sample children randomly.

Using a control group

However, if we stick with an experimental approach, how can we get rid of the effect of these extra variables? The easiest way is to use more than one group whose members have been chosen randomly. One group gets the training programme and one group doesn't.

Because you've chosen your groups randomly, any systematic effect of the other variables should be spread across the groups, and will 'confound' your results to the same extent. You therefore look at the effect of the training programme by comparing the increase in motivation for the 'trained' group against the increase for the 'untrained' group. Even though both groups may have greater motivation at the end of term, any additional effect of the training programme should be clearer.

It's still not necessarily simple though.

- Just doing something with your experimental group (even if you gave them a free lunch for six weeks) may affect their motivation. Hence, leaving your control group with no intervention at all would not be appropriate – you'll have to consider what an appropriate control treatment would be.
- You need to be careful of the effects of other variables 'creeping in'. For example, if you taught one group on Monday lunchtime and the other on Tuesday lunchtime, you're introducing another variable which could bias your outcomes.
- Variables can interact in unpredictable ways. For example, being given a pre-test may actually influence the results of the post-test (children may think about their

responses between the two tests and want to 'put the right thing'), particularly if the tests are very similar. Comparing your results with two further groups (one control and one experimental) which do not experience the pre-test would help to clarify the extent of this problem.

Identifying these problems, and collecting some supplementary data to explore them, will add weight to your study when you write it up.

Quasi-experiments

So what happens if you cannot choose groups randomly, you cannot control variables, etc.? Well, you have to do the best you can. A 'quasi-experiment' is probably as good as you're going to get.

This approach still uses an experimental and control group, but rather than being able to randomly choose the members of each, you should choose existing groups (to which you have access) which are most similar on as many relevant variables as possible. This means that if you're looking at motivation levels, you really want two groups that have very similar motivation levels in the first place, and a similar range of other variables that could be important, such as prior attainment and socio-economic factors.

Rather than just looking at the overall differences between the two groups, comparing the effect of the experiment between pairs of pupils from the experimental and control group, matched as closely as possible on such relevant variables, is even better.

Non-experimental

In this approach, you don't do your own experiment; you can't control any variables. You just look at what's already happened and try to understand it. This means that you take the variable showing an effect (the dependent variable) and try to find the variable(s) (the independent variable(s)) which could have a causative relationship with it.

This approach is very common in education, and is also useful when ethics preclude an experimental approach. For example, it would not be ethical to run an experiment deliberately subjecting pupils to something detrimental to their learning, but studying the outcomes of such a situation (which already exists) would be perfectly ethical. Two examples may help make things clear.

At a particular school, the governors suddenly realized that the proportion of pupils gaining five GCSEs at A–C ('5 A–C') has been dropping over the past 15 years. At their meeting, they came up with a number of variables which could be responsible. They find that as the number of teachers at the school went down each year, so did '5 A–C' (we can say that '5 A–C' correlates significantly with the number of teachers at the school – you'll learn more about correlations in Chapter 12). One of them suggests an explanation – the presence of fewer teachers leads to less variety of ideas for teaching and learning, and hence the drop in attainment.

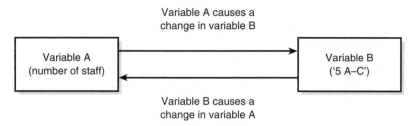

Figure 11.1 Making sense of a correlation between two variables

But was the change in teacher numbers the cause of the change in '5 A–C'? Look at Figure 11.1. Actually, it may be the other way around (reverse causation). For example, the '5 A–C' may have dropped one year, and encouraged parents who are interested in academic success to send their children elsewhere. With fewer pupils, the numbers on roll go down and the same number of teachers is no longer required.

Let's look at a different example, which tries to explain observed differences between two groups. The head teacher at school A knows that different tutor groups have different levels of truancy. He uses a statistical test to confirm that tutor groups led by women have less truancy than those led by men. Is he justified in concluding that female form tutors are better?

Not necessarily. At this school, the extent of truancy happens to vary with age (older children truant more), the Year 9 tutor team is composed mainly of women and the Year 11 tutor team is composed mainly of men. Hence, we've a third variable – year group – which affects both truancy levels and the sex of the tutor (Figure 11.2), creating a plausibly causal, but in fact artifactual, relationship between a tutor's sex and truancy levels.

So it is important to realize that finding a relationship does not mean that it is a causal relationship, and that causation could happen in either direction. In fact, sometimes a relationship may be pure coincidence – there is a proven relationship between stork population size and human birth rate!

To some extent, you can control the effect of potentially confounding variables by how you choose your sample, and by what you measure. For example, the head teacher above could do the following:

- Randomly choose, and compare, equal numbers of male- and female-led tutor groups from each year group. This does reduce the sample size, but removes the effect of age.
- Compare multiple pairs of tutor groups, matched as closely as possible by the children's socio-economic status and other potentially relevant variables, with the only difference being the tutors' sex.
- Decide which variables are likely to affect truancy levels, and measure them at the same time as collecting the rest of the data. Some clever statistics (beyond the scope of this book) can remove the effect of the extra variables, and 'uncover' any effect of the tutor's sex.

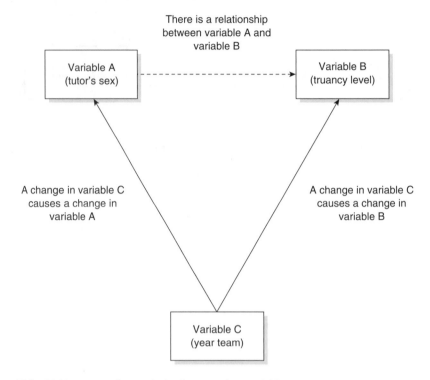

Figure 11.2   Making sense of a correlation between three variables

Even with these strategies, it is still difficult to know you've accounted for all potentially confounding variables. As such, your interpretation of the data is vulnerable to your own biases, and it is often possible to come up with contradictory explanations for the same set of data. You should discuss such explanations when you write up your research, pointing out the limitations of your derived ideas. Using other sources of data to shed more light on such alternatives would also be sensible. In an ideal world, explanations and hypotheses would be tested by experiment at a later date, but that's often not possible. The benefits and potential pitfalls of the non-experimental approach are summarized in Box 11.5 and Box 11.6.

Box 11.5   Benefits of a non-experimental approach

1 It is the 'next best thing' where an experimental approach is impossible.
2 It is good for initial exploration of a data set and for generating hypotheses, which can be experimentally tested later.
3 It avoids using an artificial intervention, examining only 'natural' variation in the data.

Box 11.6   Pitfalls of a non-experimental approach

1 It is difficult to control variables or get truly random samples.
2 It is difficult to identify all the variables (including the one(s) which actually has a causative effect) that are potentially relevant to an observed phenomenon.
3 Cause and effect are not always obvious; it is easy to assume one variable causes another if it fits in with your prior ideas.

Looking at other people's data

Looking at data with a healthily sceptical eye is always a good idea! In the rest of the chapter, I'll help you to examine the story of pupil and school performance data.

League tables

When league tables were first introduced in 1992, exam results were used to decide if a school was effective – on the assumption that better results mean better schooling. Ofsted based their assessment of school performance on raw exam results, and teachers were (and are) expected to use pupils' attainment data to support their own promotion applications. So what's the problem?

Many commentators have criticized 'exam results' as not being a valid measure of school effectiveness, and suggested that they should not be used to compare schools. Think about the following questions.

- Why do 'exam results' only give a limited picture of school 'effectiveness'?
- What other variables could affect exam results, which are unrelated to the school itself?
- Suggest reasons why it is not valid to reward secondary science teachers on the basis of their classes' exam results.

Hopefully, you've realized that there's an enormous number of variables which could affect exam results. Research suggests that 76 per cent of variation in GCSE scores is determined by pupils' prior attainment (which itself is related to their own prior education and socio-economic characteristics). This means that the influence of a secondary school on GCSE scores is pretty limited, and the best way for schools to improve their league table position is to select pupils according to prior attainment!

Value-added

In 2004, the Department for Education and Skills published a *value-added* measure; it was billed as a more valid measure of the 'value' that a school 'adds', taking into account prior attainment. The aim was to help parents make valid comparisons between schools. For primary schools, data were reported in relation to a figure of 100.

Activity 11.1

Explain why this ought to be a more valid measure of school effectiveness, and what you think it still lacks.

Let's look at how they worked out value-added between Key Stage 2 and Key Stage 3, using SATs results as a measure of attainment in each case, but comparing pupils with similar levels of prior attainment. Here's a simplified explanation of it:

- All the pupils in the country who performed very similarly (e.g. within half a level) at Key Stage 2 are put in order of numerical result for their Key Stage 3 results.
- For each set of pupils, the median result (the middle one) is found, and every pupil is given a value-added score relative to that result. If someone does better than the median pupil, they get a positive score. If someone does worse, they get a negative score.
- Hence, for schools with a low-attaining intake, it should be easier to see the 'value' they are 'adding', even if their Key Stage 3 results are much lower than, for example, another school which selects on prior attainment.

To assess the whole school's performance, you average the results of all the pupils in the school and add the result to 100. Hence, a score of 100 reflects 'average' value-added, 98 reflects 'below average' value-added and 102 reflects 'above average' value-added.

Activity 11.2

A local journalist is looking at the value-added scores for the schools in her county. She realizes that half of the schools have value-added scores below 100 and publishes the story with the following headline: 'Scandal! Letting down our children – half of Smedshire's schools are below average'. What is wrong with this headline?

But how do you interpret these scores? If the average (mean) value-added score for a school is a long way below the mean value (100) for all the schools, then you may be pretty confident that there's a problem. If it's really way above the mean, then you know something is going right. But how far apart do schools' scores need to be to know that they are really significantly different?

Statisticians work this out by calculating something called confidence limits above and below the mean for each school. This is often not quoted in the media, but without it, you can't interpret league tables properly.

- You can only say that two schools really have significantly different value-added scores if the confidence intervals (between the upper and lower limit) do not overlap.
- You can only say that a school is above the national average if the school mean is above the national mean, and if the school confidence interval does not include the national mean.

Activity 11.3

Look at Figure 11.3. For each school, it shows the mean and confidence intervals. Which two of the following is it possible to say with 95 per cent confidence?

- School A is significantly better than school B.
- School D is significantly worse than school B.
- School C is significantly better than the national average.
- There is a significant difference between school A and school C.

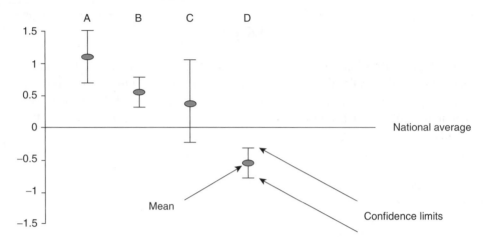

Figure 11.3 Understanding confidence limits 1

However, it gets even more complicated. The way in which confidence limits are calculated means that:

- if you calculate the mean and confidence interval for a small school with few pupils, the limits are likely to be relatively far apart
- if you calculate the mean and confidence interval for a school with a lot of pupils, the limits are likely to be relatively close together.

These differences make it difficult to validly compare schools of different sizes, and even more difficult when comparing particular subjects or classes with even fewer pupils.

Activity 11.4

Look at Figure 11.4. It shows mean and confidence intervals for three schools. School A has 2000 pupils, school B has 500 pupils, and school C has 2000 pupils. Which of the following can you say with 95 per cent confidence?

- School A is significantly below the national average.
- School B is significantly above the national average.
- School C is significantly above the national average.
- There is no significant difference between school A and school B.
- There is no significant difference between school B and school C.
- There is no significant difference between school A and school C.

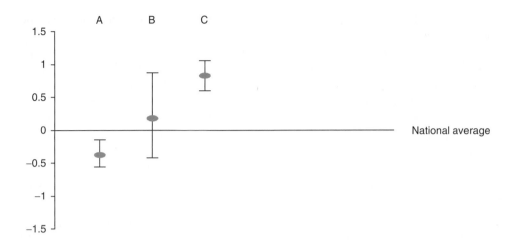

Figure 11.4   Understanding confidence limits 2

Contextual value-added

Using value-added scores still assumes that all changes in pupil performance are determined by what happens in the school. But what about the other variables that could affect performance? Is it possible to tease apart their effects from the effects of the school?

Initial attempts to do this adjusted for the number of pupils on free school meals as an index of socio-economic status. Then in 2006 the government developed a more complicated statistical model. They tried to identify relevant variables, and remove the effect of each, one by one, using clever statistics called multi-level modelling, to provide a way of predicting 'expected' attainment for each pupil. The deviation from that 'expected' attainment then provides a *contextual value-added* score (CVA). The variables included in calculating the model can change year on year, but commonly have included most of the following:

- pupil prior attainment
- gender
- Special Educational Needs
- first language
- measures of pupil mobility
- age
- an indicator of whether the pupil is 'in care'
- ethnicity
- free school meals
- Income Deprivation Affecting Children Index (IDACI)
- the average and range of prior attainment within the school (KS2–3, KS2–4 and KS3–4 only).

This sounds like the 'holy grail' for assessing school effectiveness, but there are some problems with this model in particular. The way in which the CVA model handles missing data could generate bias, and some variables may also interact to affect CVA in non-linear ways (e.g. income deprivation may affect the attainment of younger pupils more than that of older pupils). Having pointed these things out, CVA is just one of a number of value-added measures which have emerged commercially since 1991, including Fischer Family Trust scores, and models derived by the Centre for Educational Management (CEM) at the University of Durham (examples include MIDYIS, Yellis and ALIS). There are differences in the population data used to derive these models, and again in some of the variables included, but each is based on a CVA-type approach.

The data provided by these kinds of models have been used as part of accountability procedures (e.g. via Ofsted), to direct school improvement planning (e.g. for schools, teachers or pupils), and by parents when choosing a school for their child. You'll probably recognize many of the names given above. Indeed, Ofsted compelled schools to show evidence that they use CVA data in school improvement, providing it to schools via an online platform called RAISE online, and CVA data have been published for access by parents. However, using the same data, and hence the same model, for each of these purposes can be problematic, and the variables to be included in such models may need to differ, depending on the use each model is put to.

For example, if CVA is to be a predictor of future attainment (as it is for students in many of the CEM models), then every factor should be included in the model to make such a prediction as accurate as possible. On the other hand, if CVA is to be used as a focus for school improvement, then it is more sensible to include only those variables which the school actually has control over. Likewise, if CVA is to be used for accountability, then all stakeholders should be able to understand the meaning of the indices produced, and hence complex multi-level modelling like this may be inappropriate.

Given the above, the apparent precision and 'authority' of value-added data like CVA or Fischer Family Trust scores can mislead parents, teachers and children into trusting such data unquestioningly. There are two good examples of when this becomes problematic with respect to how parents interpret CVA data.

1 We've already seen how parents can assume that a greater value-added score implies a better school, without looking at the confidence intervals. However, given that CVA models use data from pupils who have been in the school for, for example, the last seven years, they may not actually provide insights for parents into *future* school effectiveness (after all, if your child is just starting in a school you want to know how it will perform in seven years' time). Instead, they reflect the performance of the school over previous years, and do not take into account any uncertainty associated with predicting school performance into the future. When statisticians introduce such prediction uncertainty into CVA-type models, schools' predicted performance is so similar and it becomes almost impossible to differentiate between schools on the basis of their CVA score.

2   Although a CVA score for a school may provide a measure of school effectiveness, controlled for the range of factors included in the model, when creating a model to help parents choose a school, it is important not to control for school-level variables. This is because a parent wants to know whether a particular school (with all its contextual features) will provide a better education for their child (with his/her own characteristics) than another school. If the school-level factors are associated with achievement, then this is part of the effect the parent is interested in. Hence, using raw CVA data would not be appropriate.

Parents and others instinctively base their judgements on figures they understand, and continuing to publish raw data about school performance is misleading. However, it is important to ensure parents and teachers realize that even value-added measures like CVA still provide a narrow metric of school or teacher effectiveness, and that such data should really be used only as a starting point for conversation, rather than as concrete evidence of school or teacher effectiveness.

 Key ideas

- You can use a quantitative approach to describe and analyse your own data.
- Experimental research involves changing a variable (the independent variable) in order to examine its effect on another variable (the dependent variable), while controlling for any other confounding variables that could affect the dependent variable.
- Non-experimental research involves looking for explanations for phenomena by seeking out potentially causal relationships between variables, while accounting for the effect of other variables.
- An association between variables A and B does not necessarily mean that an increase in A causes an increase in B. It could be the other way around, or both may be affected by a third variable, C.
- Understanding the derivation of data (such as performance data) is essential to make informed conclusions about it.
- Don't be scared of numbers – even if you're not good at maths, it doesn't matter. Think of numbers as a servant to help you understand something.
- Collect data at the highest level of measurement possible.
- Just because two variables are related, it doesn't mean one *causes* a change in the other.

Reflective questions

1 Have you asked your tutor or a critical friend to check your data collection plans before you start – they will often think of confounding variables that you've missed?
2 What are the limitations of your data? Be critical of your methods and conclusions when you write up your research. Everyone's data have limitations – being up front about them is important.
3 Are you sure about your conclusions? Be sceptical about what the data is showing you. Be wary of blindly interpreting the data to fit your prior expectations without considering alternative explanations. Be wary of anyone else doing the same!

Further reading

Brace, N., Kemp, R. and Snelgar, R. (2009) *SPSS for Psychologists* (4th edn). Basingstoke: Palgrave Macmillan.
Cohen, L., Manion, L. and Morrison, K. (2011) *Research Methods in Education* (7th edn). London: RoutledgeFalmer.
Coolican, H. (2009) *Research Methods and Statistics in Psychology* (5th edn). London: Hodder & Stoughton.
Field, A. (2009) *Discovering Statistics Using SPSS* (3rd edn). London: Sage.
Sani, F. and Todman, J. (2008) *Experimental Design and Statistics for Psychology* (2nd edn). Oxford: Blackwell Publishing.

For the Curriculum, Evaluation and Management Centre at the University of Durham (for ALIS, Yellis, etc.), visit: www.cemcentre.org

CHAPTER 12

ANALYSING QUANTITATIVE DATA

Ros McLellan

Chapter overview

This chapter is about how to use some statistical techniques to start to analyse and interpret quantitative data. I am not claiming that you will be an expert by the end of the chapter but I hope you will have the confidence to get started. Those of you who want to pursue this type of approach will need to consult more specialist texts, and some appropriate references are listed at the back of the chapter that you'll need to move on to.

Introduction

Let's start by debunking a myth. You do not have to be brilliant at mathematics to do quantitative analysis. Many people are put off statistics by the complicated-looking equations they see, but computers can do the number crunching for you, and at one level you don't need to understand any of the hieroglyphics you might see in advanced statistical texts. What is important is that you understand some basic concepts and what sorts of analysis are appropriate to apply to answer particular questions. An appropriate analogy is that of driving a car: you need to know to put fuel in (the basic concept of fuel provides the driving force) and how to drive (the right technique for the situation – for instance, not to brake too sharply on a frosty morning), but you don't need to understand the underlying mechanical and electrical engineering principles which make it operate, if you just want to drive it. Similarly, with statistics; you need to know the statistical entities you might calculate and what would be appropriate to the situation in hand, but you don't need to have a detailed understanding of how the computer processes data to calculate these entities. This chapter therefore aims to give you a sense of these basic entities and processes and to introduce you to a particular statistical package, SPSS, which is widely used to do such number crunching.

The other important point I would like to make before we get down to business is that analysis is not something you start thinking about once you have collected all your data. This is a common error made by newcomers to research. If you don't think about analysis before you collect your data, it is quite likely that your data won't be able to answer the questions you wanted to ask. For instance, if you wanted to examine the relationship between ability and motivation, it would not be enough to use ability band/ stream as a measure of ability if you wanted to know whether the motivation of the most able students in the top band/stream was different to those who had just scraped into that band/stream. A finer graded scale or instrument for measuring ability, such as the NFER Cognitive Ability Tests, would need to be used. Hence, you need to think ahead and pre-empt the type of questions you want to ask, in order to plan data collection accordingly. As a rule of thumb, collect data at the highest level of measurement you can sensibly manage because you can create discrete categories from data measured on a continuous scale (such as the ability categories 'low', 'average' and 'high' by deciding cut-off points on an ability scale), while you cannot create a continuous scale from discrete categories.

It should now be clear that it is essential to consider what analysis you want to do during the initial design stages of the research so that appropriate data, as far as possible, are collected in the first place. For this reason, if you have not yet read Chapter 11, I strongly urge you to at least skim through it before going any further.

Now we can turn to the matter in hand: the analysis of quantitative data. Assuming you are planning to use a computer to assist you in this process, the first step is to set up a database using the appropriate software program. In this chapter, I will be referring to the SPSS package, as this is the most widely used program of this type in the social sciences, and most higher education institutions subscribe to it. Once the data is entered, analysis, which has two distinct phases, can be conducted. The first phase is to describe the data that has been gathered, which involves the calculation of descriptive statistics and the graphical presentation of the data. The second phase is to interrogate the data to answer the research questions posed, which entails calculating inferential statistics. The rest of the chapter, therefore, gives an overview of each of these steps. As it is easier to understand such processes if they are discussed with reference to a specific example, data gathered during my PhD research will be used for illustrative purposes. I start therefore with a brief description of my PhD research in order to contextualize the examples given in the rest of the chapter.

The example database

Cognitive Acceleration through Science Education (CASE) is an intervention programme consisting of 30 science activity lessons for students in Years 7 and 8, which aims to promote cognitive development. It is widely used by secondary schools, despite the fact that some students make very limited progress, and it has been suggested that student motivation might account for this, but this has not been investigated. Consequently, my main research question was: 'Do differences in motivation account for the differential gains made by students doing CASE?'. I was also interested in whether there was any difference in the progress made by boys and girls, as the literature suggests that girls are more motivated than boys; and in school generally, girls get better exam results than boys. Employing a longitudinal quasi-experimental design so that I could compare students following the CASE programme with similar students that were not (to allow for normal cognitive development), I followed a cohort (over 1700 students) through the first two years of secondary school in nine schools (five doing the CASE programme and four not). This is probably a lot more students than you might be considering including in your study, as in all likelihood you are studying students in your own school. However, the process of analysis is the same whether your sample size is 1700, one year cohort, or one class.

I assessed the cognitive development and motivation at the start of Y7 (before starting CASE – the pre-test) and at the end of Y8 (after completing the programme – the post-test) so that changes in cognitive development could be measured. I could also see whether any changes in motivation had occurred. Here, we will only focus on some of the data gathered at pre-test. I used a commercially available test to measure cognitive development (a Science Reasoning Task). This is conducted as a series of teacher-led demonstrations, which students then have to answer questions about on an answer sheet. Answers are marked using the mark scheme provided and then the total score is converted to a level of cognitive development (a numerical score which is an interval level measurement).

Motivation can be measured in many ways, according to which theory of motivation you subscribe to. I chose a framework that suggested there were four dimensions to motivation. Each dimension can be assessed using a scale comprising a number of items, which students are asked to respond to. I used a questionnaire that had been used in previous research. There is a common stem for each item – 'I feel successful when' – and students indicate their level of agreement on a five-point Likert scale

Table 12.1   Example items in motivation questionnaire

Scale	Underlying motivation	Example item[1]
Task	To develop competence	... I finally understand a really complicated idea
Ego	To demonstrate competence	... I do better work than other students
Work avoidance	To avoid demonstrating incompetence (passive avoidance)	... I don't have to do any homework
Alienation	To avoid demonstrating incompetence (active disruption)	... I mess around and get away with it

Note: [1]The common stem is 'I feel successful when...'.

(from 'strongly disagree', scoring 1 to 'strongly agree', scoring 5). The overall score for each dimension is the total score of the individual items for each scale. An example item from each of the four scales is shown in Table 12.1, to give a sense of what the four dimensions relate to.

I asked students to give their opinion about science, English, and school in general, as these were different areas I was interested in. Hence, the database contained three answers to each question, and separate total scores for each dimension for the different subject areas.

Now that you have a sense of the data I gathered, we can consider how I set up the SPSS database to do the analysis.

Activity 12.1

Collect data using the motivation questionnaire (see Appendix at the end of the chapter). Use this data to follow the steps in the text to learn how to use SPSS.

Creating a database in SPSS

In this section, I will take you through some of the issues you need to consider when setting up an SPSS database, illustrating these with reference to my own database. If you go to the website, you will find a tutorial that takes you through the process of setting up a database using SPSS, which you will probably find helpful to look at in conjunction with this section. At the end of the section, you will find an activity to allow you to check that you have understood how to set up a database.

Blank databases in SPSS look quite like Excel spreadsheets when you open them initially, however, unlike Excel, there are two ways of looking at the same database: 'data view' and 'variable view'.

'Data view' (the default shown on opening a database) shows you the actual data in your database. Each row represents one 'case'. I collected data from over 1700 students, hence I have over 1700 rows in my database. Cases do not need to be individual people. If, for instance, you have collected data about schools rather than individual students, then the rows would represent each school. The columns represent each variable you have collected data on. In my study, this includes demographic data (such as gender), level of cognitive development score, and answers for each of the questions on the questionnaire. There are also a number of variables I created in the database from existing variables. For instance, there are variables for the total scores for each motivation dimension.

'Variable view' provides information about each of your variables. This is one of the ways SPSS differs from a spreadsheet – because it is a database, it can hold all sorts of useful information about your variables that Excel isn't capable of, and this information is needed for conducting statistical analyses. Before entering data, you set up your variables in variable view. Here, each row relates to one variable and the columns represent specific characteristics of the variable. To avoid later grief, it is well worth defining your variables fully before entering data, as SPSS has default settings which may not be appropriate for all your variables.

Regardless of whatever else you have data for, it is sensible to define your first variable as a unique identifier for each case, so that you have a way of going back to the original data you collected later if you need to. For data protection and ethical reasons, you should create a code rather than type in an identifiable name. I therefore called my first variable 'ID'. You are limited to eight characters for variable names and if you attempt to type in more, SPSS will truncate it. However, you can list a name in full, such as 'unique identifier' under 'label' and when you later do analysis, SPSS will use what is listed under the label rather than the variable name in its output of results.

SPSS will generate default information for the remaining headings. Although most of these are appropriate, you do need to consider 'type', 'values', 'missing' and 'measure'. SPSS has different options for these already stored. For instance, for 'type', you can select from many options, including numerical and string. I decided that the easiest way to give a unique identifier to every student's response would be to give each student a number and to write this number on their questionnaires/cognitive development test sheets. Thus, I selected 'numerical' under 'type' for variable 'ID'. It is possible that you might want to give non-numerical codes, for instance pseudonyms (but note that if you have a large number of cases, this can quickly get confusing so it is often better to stick to numbers). In this case, you would select 'string' as the type, and in both cases, the 'measure' is 'nominal'.

In order to understand how to use 'values' and 'missing', we need to turn to a different variable. I wanted to record some background demographic information, and it is quite likely that you would want to do the same. For instance, I wanted to record whether each student was male or female. Thinking ahead, I knew I wanted to compare boys and girls on a number of dimensions (for instance, scores on the 'task' motivation scale). To do this sort of analysis, you have to create a numerical rather than string variable, so I chose 'numerical' under type and 'nominal' under 'measure'. I used the code 1 to represent boys and 2 to represent girls, and recorded this information under 'values'.

As with variable labels, SPSS shows value labels rather than numerical codes in analyses, which is handy as you don't have to remember whether '1' represents 'boys' or 'girls' (although of course you can look this up at any time in variable view).

It is important to set up missing data values for variables where missing data is very likely to occur. For instance, although students were asked to indicate their gender on the front of their questionnaires, a number did not, and as gender is not always obvious from a name (for instance, Sam can be a girl or a boy), in these cases, it needed to be recorded as missing. Setting up a special numerical code for missing data enables SPSS to recognize cases where data is missing and omit them from specific analyses. You define one or more values to represent missing values under 'missing'. Usually, you would define one value and this can be whatever you like, as long as it is not a value you have already used in your coding (so I couldn't use 1 or 2 for gender), but traditionally researchers tend to use '9' or '99' so that missing data stands out. You can use different values for different variables but I would caution against this, as it will get confusing. You might define more than one missing value to represent different reasons for the data being missing – for instance, 'the student was away on the day of the test' compared to 'the student missed one question on a test', but again keep it simple to start with.

Once you have set up all the variables you want to include, you can then start to enter your data. You do this in 'data view', where you will find that the column headings now refer to the variables you have defined. Entering data is a simple case of typing in the relevant values for each variable for each case. Usually, you would enter all the data on your first case before moving on to your second, but of course you can go back at any time to add in any missing data gathered at a later point in time. So in my database, I started with the first student I had data for, and typed '1001' under 'ID', '2' under 'gender' because she was a girl, and so forth. If you forget any of your codes, you can always check under value labels in variable view. Don't forget to save periodically.

You will probably come across some problems with data entry, for instance students who have ringed two answers on a questionnaire. There are various ways of dealing with this. You can either go back to the student and get them to clarify their response (which is time-consuming); you can code it as a missing response (this is probably the best approach but you may then be losing a lot of data) or you can decide to code new values to allow midpoints on scales (but this can distort later analysis). Whatever approach you choose, make sure you apply it consistently.

Data analysis – generating descriptive statistics

1. Checking the accuracy of data entry

The very first thing you should check is that you have entered your data correctly, as no matter how careful you are, mistakes can be made. This 'cleaning' of the data also starts the process of examining the data. One of the most common errors is entering the wrong code for a particular response, for instance '11' instead of '1' (i.e. the value entered doesn't match a code you've set up), and the quickest way of checking for this is to look at the frequency distribution (or summary of response) for each variable.

In SPSS, descriptive statistics, such as frequency distribution information, are accessed from the 'analyse' drop-down menu. There are various descriptive statistics options but frequency distribution tables are generated using 'frequencies'. By selecting this option, SPSS produces a dialogue box asking you which variables in your database you want frequency information about. You need to select the variable(s) of interest and ask for the relevant information. SPSS then generates the frequency distribution table(s) requested, which is produced in an SPSS output file that appears on the screen. For each variable requested, you will be able to see the different response categories listed in the first column of the table and the number of responses for that category in the second column. A quick glance down the first column will reveal whether there are any illegal responses. Tables 12.2 and 12.3 show frequency distributions for two of my variables, 'gender' and 'task motivation (science)' scale scores.

Table 12.2 Frequency distribution for gender

		Frequency	**Per cent**	**Valid per cent**	**Cumulative per cent**
Valid	Boys	710	41.2	43.0	43.0
	Girls	942	54.7	57.0	100.0
	Total	1652	95.9	100.0	
Missing	9.00	71	4.1		
Total		1723	100.0		

If you don't have any illegal responses, as here, you can move on to other descriptive analyses. If you want to save the frequency distribution data (which you might if you planned to copy and paste the table into a report), you can save the output file in the same way you would save any other file. If you have some rogue responses, you will need to go back to your data to find them. This can be done using 'find' in 'data view' (much as you would find and replace in Word or other packages). By looking at the identifier for the case identified, you can go back to the original data (for instance, the original questionnaire) to amend the response.

2. Producing variable summaries

While the frequency distribution provides information about all the responses for a particular variable, quite often we want to give a more succinct summary, especially for variables measured at an interval level. For instance, knowing that the task motivation (science) scale scores in my study varied from 8 to 30 does not really help paint a picture of the overall response to this scale. If I told you a particular student scored 18, you wouldn't know without looking carefully at Table 12.2 whether this seemed typical or not. We really need to know two things to make judgements about individual scores. Firstly: what is a typical response? For this, we would normally calculate the mean score (obtained by adding up every individual score and dividing the sum by the number of scores included). Secondly: how much variation is there in the responses? If there is a small amount of variation, then most people are recording the same responses. A larger variation implies that scores that markedly differ from the average (lower and higher) are not that unusual. The commonly used measure for this is the standard deviation, which is one measure of the average deviation from the mean score.

Table 12.3   Frequency distribution for task motivation (science)

		Frequency	Per cent	Valid per cent	Cumulative per cent
Valid	8.00	1	.1	.1	.1
	9.00	1	.1	.1	.1
	10.00	3	.2	.2	.4
	11.00	1	.1	.1	.4
	13.00	4	.2	.3	.7
	14.00	6	.3	.4	1.1
	15.00	9	.5	.6	1.8
	16.00	8	.5	.6	2.3
	17.00	14	.8	1.0	3.3
	18.00	31	1.8	2.2	5.5
	19.00	32	1.9	2.2	7.7
	20.00	52	3.0	3.6	11.3
	21.00	66	3.8	4.6	16.0
	22.00	88	5.1	6.2	22.1
	23.00	111	6.4	7.8	29.9
	24.00	131	7.6	9.2	39.1
	25.00	144	8.4	10.1	49.2
	26.00	167	9.7	11.7	60.9
	27.00	159	9.2	11.1	72.0
	28.00	167	9.7	11.7	83.7
	29.00	126	7.3	8.8	92.5
	30.00	107	6.2	7.5	100.0
	Total	1428	82.9	100.0	
Missing system[1]		295	17.1		
Total		1723	100.0		

Note: [1] Missing system responses appear because students had not supplied answers for one or more of the questionnaire items that make up the task motivation (science) scale.

Summary statistics including the mean and standard deviation (usually referred to in textbooks as descriptive statistics) are obtained using the 'descriptives' option of descriptive statistics. Summary statistics for 'gender', 'task motivation (science)' and 'level of cognitive development' are shown in Table 12.4.

Returning to the question of whether 18 is a low score on the task motivation (science) scale, knowing that the mean score for this scale is 25.0 (rounded off) and that the standard deviation is 3.6 suggests that a score of 18 is unusually low, as most people are scoring between 21.4 (3.6 below the mean of 25) and 28.6.

Table 12.4 also illustrates an important point to bear in mind when using a computer program. As gender is a nominal-level variable, it makes no sense to talk about the average or mean gender, as clearly my participants were either boys or girls. Yet SPSS will calculate this value if asked. You always need to ask yourself the question, is what I'm asking the computer to calculate sensible? In simple terms, if you put rubbish in, you will get rubbish out!

Table 12.4 Descriptive statistics for gender, task motivation (science) and level of cognitive development

	N	Minimum	Maximum	Mean	Std deviation
Gender	1652	1.00	2.00	1.5702	.49519
Task motivation (science)	1428	8.00	30.00	24.9965	3.60574
Level of cognitive development	1723	2.00	9.00	6.1977	2.18647

3. Producing graphs

It is often easier to get a sense of how frequency distributions look by plotting graphs rather than looking at tables or summary statistics. For instance, you have seen the frequency distribution table and know that the mean score on the task motivation (science) scale was 25.0, while scores ranged from 8 to 30 and there was a relatively small amount of variation as the standard deviation was 3.6. If you think about these figures carefully, they suggest that scores were bunched up at the higher end of the scale. This can be seen much more clearly by plotting a histogram, which is a graph of the frequency distribution.

In SPSS, graphs can be produced through the 'graph' drop-down menu, which gives you the option of producing a histogram. The histogram for the task motivation (science) scale is shown in Figure 12.1 and, as expected, students' scores are bunched up towards the top of the scale. This scale is about learning things so it is hardly surprising that most students say they are motivated by this, given that they know their answers are going to be scrutinized by someone else.

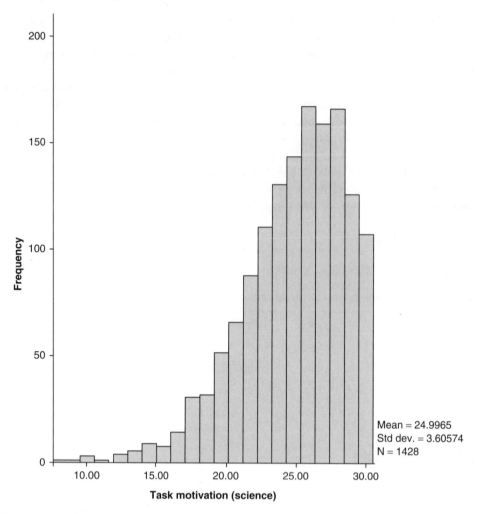

Figure 12.1 Histogram showing the distribution of response to the task motivation (science) scale

A second type of graph that is useful when conducting a descriptive analysis of data, which is also an option from the graph menu, is a scatter diagram. This shows the relationship between two interval-level variables. For instance, I was very interested in knowing whether there was a relationship between students' cognitive development scores and their task motivation scores. I expected students who said they were motivated to try hard to learn new things to develop cognitively. A scatter diagram would help me decide whether I was right about this relationship and this is shown in Figure 12.2.

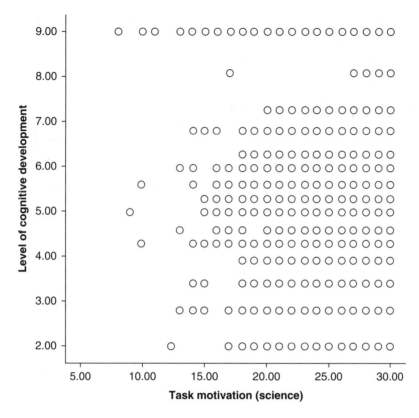

Figure 12.2   Scatter diagram showing the relationship between task motivation (science) and level of cognitive development

Each circle represents one or more students' scores on the variables in question. For instance, the circle at the bottom right of the graph represents students that scored 30 (the maximum value) on the task motivation (science) scale (so are highly motivated to learn new things), but at the same time got the lowest score of 2 on the level of cognitive development test. So, for these students, being very keen to learn new things does not appear to be associated with helping them to develop cognitively. In general, if there was a positive association, which statisticians call a positive correlation, between task motivation and level of cognitive development, the graph would show a series of circles falling around an imaginary line sloping from the bottom left to the top right of the graph (i.e. sloping upwards). Here, we have a general swirl of dots filling most of the graph, suggesting no relationship (or no correlation) between task motivation and level of cognitive development. This is not what I expected. Note that it is also possible to have a negative correlation between two variables. For instance, you would expect a negative correlation between alienation and cognitive development, which would appear as a band of circles following an imaginary line from the top left to the bottom right (i.e. sloping downwards).

Data analysis – inferential statistics

Having explored the data and gained a sense of the relationships between different variables, it is now time to get to the crux of the matter and answer the original research questions. I was interested in the relationship between motivation and level of cognitive development. I predicted that students scoring highly on the task motivation scale (the desire to learn and master new things) would have overall higher scores on the test of cognitive development than students with low scores on the task motivation scale. Similarly, I would expect that students with high scores on the alienation scale (actively disrupting learning) would have overall lower scores on the test of cognitive development than students who have low scores on the alienation scale. I also thought that girls would have higher scores on the task motivation scale and lower scores on the alienation scale than boys, and that girls' level of cognitive development would be higher.

In order to assess whether these hypotheses are correct, we need to run a number of statistical tests. Essentially, I am asking two different types of question:

1   Is there a relationship between two variables (for instance, between task motivation and level of cognitive development)?
2   Is there a difference between two groups on a given variable (for instance, between boys and girls on task motivation)?

Each type of question requires a specific statistical test, and these are outlined below.

1. Tests of correlation

The first type of question relates to relationships or correlations between variables, therefore the appropriate statistical test in this case is a test of correlation. The logic behind this type of test is that we look at the actual relationships found (so we need to calculate a particular entity to assess this) and then make a judgement as to how likely this result would be, if in fact there wasn't a relationship between the variables of interest. In essence, we are judging the likelihood that the results we found were a fluke, i.e. in reality, motivation and cognitive development aren't related in any way; it just happened in this sample of schools that there was some type of relationship. The reason we have to take this approach is because we simply don't know whether there is in fact a relationship or not, and we have to make the best judgement we can based on the data we have on the balance of probabilities. These probabilities can only be calculated by starting from a position that the variables are not related. A slightly different starting point is taken when we are looking at differences between groups, which is described below. However, it is the case that the calculations conducted in any statistical test involve calculating probabilities to enable the person running the test to make a judgement call. This is why the outcomes of the calculations made are referred to as inferential statistics and the tests themselves are often called significance tests.

The entity calculated in a test of correlation to quantify the relationship between the two variables of interest is a correlation coefficient. The statistical test enables me to judge whether this is significant (i.e. the balance of probabilities is that there is a relationship between motivation and cognitive development). At this point, I have several choices of correlation coefficients to calculate, dependent on the measurement level and distribution of my variables. If you intend to use inferential statistics, you will need to read up on this in more detail, as all I am doing here is giving an introduction to this area. Specifically, you can choose to do either a parametric or non-parametric test. The former is generally preferred because it is more powerful and sensitive to your data, however it also makes certain assumptions about your data. For reasons there isn't the space here to explain, my data are acceptable for a parametric test, hence I need to calculate the appropriate correlation coefficient, a Pearson correlation coefficient, and then look at the significance test results. In SPSS, this procedure is conducted in the 'correlate' option of the analyse menu. The results for the test of correlation between level of cognitive development and task motivation (science) scores are shown in Table 12.5.

Table 12.5   Significance test for correlation between task motivation (science) and level of cognitive development

		Level of cognitive development	Task motivation (science)
Level of cognitive development	Pearson correlation	1	−.043
	Sig. (two-tailed)		104
	N	1723	1428
Task motivation (science)	Pearson correlation	−.043	1
	Sig. (two-tailed)	104	
	N	1428	1428

Initially, this may look a little confusing because the same information is repeated in the table. What we are interested in is the relationship between the level of cognitive development and task motivation (science). If you look in the relevant quadrant (top right or bottom left), you can see the correlation coefficient, significance figure and number of students whose data contributed to calculating the statistic (1428). The correlation coefficient -0.043 is practically zero. As correlation coefficients range from -1 (strong negative correlation) through zero (no correlation) to +1 (strong positive correlation), this indicates that there is no relationship between the level of cognitive development and task motivation, which is contrary to initial predictions (but perhaps not that surprising having seen the scatter diagram previously). The significance figure tells you the probability that you would have obtained the correlation coefficient of -0.043 if cognitive development and task motivation were not related in real life beyond my study. Hence, there is a probability of 0.104 (which you can transform into a percentage by multiplying by 100 – so 10.4%) that my correlation coefficient of -0.043 would have arisen by chance when there is no relationship between these two variables. Although a 10% chance might sound quite low to a newcomer to this approach, in fact that is still reasonably likely. Consequently, we conclude that there is no evidence to deviate from the status quo that cognitive development and task motivation are not related. In fact, a rule of thumb is that in this type of test (a two-tailed test – again, I won't say more but you can look this up), you would have to have a probability of less than 2.5% before you would make a judgement call that the two variables might be related. Even then we don't know for sure one way or the other, so you are never able to couch your conclusions in definitive terms.

2. Tests of difference

As with tests of correlation, there are different types of tests of difference available to suit the characteristics of the data you have (relating to the measurement level and distribution of the variable under consideration). If we conduct a parametric test of difference (because the data are appropriate, as noted in the previous section), then we compare the mean score of each group on the variable of interest. So, for instance, if we want to know whether girls and boys differ in their scores on the task motivation scale, we compare the mean scores of girls and boys on this scale. The entity calculated in the comparison process is called the t statistic and the test itself is referred to as a t-test. Here, the assumption underlying the calculations of the t statistic is that there is no difference between the two groups under consideration (i.e. boys and girls).

In SPSS, t-tests are accessed via the 'compare means' option in the analyse menu. Although we are conducting a parametric test, there are different ways of comparing means, and this is reflected in the choice in the 'compare means' procedure. Because we are comparing two different groups (boys and girls) on a particular variable (task motivation), this is an independent samples test. This is in contrast to a situation where you might be comparing the same people on two different variables (for instance, in my study, I compared students' scores on each of the motivation scales at the start and end of the two-year study to see whether they had changed), which would require the use of a repeated measures test. You also need to specify which groups you are comparing (under 'define groups'), which you do by inserting the codes you created for the groups you want to compare (in my case, 1 and 2, representing boys and girls respectively). The reason you need to specify groups is because it may be that you have more than two groups for a particular variable in the database (for instance, I might want to compare task motivation scores from two of my nine schools). The results of the test are shown in Table 12.6.

Table 12.6   Significance test for the difference between boys and girls on the task motivation (science) scale

Group statistics					
	Gender	**N**	**Mean**	**Std deviation**	**Std error mean**
Task motivation (science)	Boys	625	25.0224	3.65273	.14611
	Girls	803	24.9763	3.57090	.12601

Independent samples test									
		Levene's Test for Equality of Variances		**t-test for equality of means**					**95% confidence interval of the difference**
		F.	**Sig.**	**t**	**df**	**Sig. (two-tailed)**	**Mean difference**	**Std error difference**	**Lower**	**Upper**
Task motivation	Equal variances assumed	.101	.750	.239	1426	.811	.04606	.19240	−.33136	.42348
	Equal variances not assumed			.239	1326.515	.811	.04606	.19294	−.33245	.42457

The top part of the table shows descriptive statistics, which is handy because we hadn't found out in advance what the mean scores for boys and girls are on the task motivation scale (although normally in this sort of analysis you would start by looking at the descriptive statistics before conducting statistical tests). As might be expected, the mean scores for boys and girls are not exactly the same. In fact, boys (with a mean score of 25.02) overall record slightly higher scores than girls (with a mean score of 24.98), which is not what was expected. To see whether these small differences are statistically different, we need to look at the lower part of the table.

Although there is a lot of information given, for the purpose of this introduction, you only need to focus on two figures: the *t* value and the second 'sig.' (significance) value. There are two variants for each and the one that is appropriate to interpret again depends on the characteristics of the data (in this case, whether the amount of variation in the girls' scores is as great as that in the boys', which for these data is a fair assumption – again, you would need to read up more on this). Hence, assuming equal variances, we need to focus on the top figure in each case. The calculated *t* value is 0.239. Unlike the correlation coefficient, this in itself doesn't tell you much about the difference between boys' and girls' scores, except to say that the larger this value, the bigger the difference between the groups. The significance value (0.811), however, tells us how likely it is that we would have got a *t* value of 0.239 if there was no difference between boys and girls. Therefore, in this case, the probability of getting a *t* value of 0.239 if there was no difference between boys and girls is 81.1%, i.e. very likely. Using the same benchmark as before (i.e. we would have to have a probability of less than 2.5% for a two-tailed test), there is clearly no evidence to depart from the status quo of no difference. So our conclusion would be that there is insufficient evidence from these data to suggest that boys and girls differ in their task motivation.

Concluding comments

The purpose of this chapter has been to introduce some statistical techniques, and to show you how to use a widely available statistical program to do this. Inevitably, this has been a real rattle through some quite complicated ideas, and some details have been glossed over. However, hopefully, you feel you've grasped some of the basics and have the confidence to follow these ideas up by consulting one or more of the texts listed under Further reading. If so, the chapter has served its purpose.

 Key ideas

- Don't be scared of statistical analysis – even if maths was a mystery at school, you *can* do this – anyone can – you just need to know some basics.
- Note that use of a specialist program, such as SPSS, means you do not need to be a specialist at number crunching, however you still need to understand what is going on to ensure you conduct the most appropriate analysis to answer your research questions.

(Continued)

(Continued)

- Spend time setting up your database properly by allocating an identifier and relevant demographic variables and defining characteristics of your variables, and allocating values for missing data; and always deal with ambiguous data consistently.
- Always clean your data before starting on statistical analysis to ensure any input errors are removed.
- Start your analysis by examining the frequency distributions through producing frequency distribution tables and, where appropriate, histograms. Look at the relationships between variables measured on scales by plotting scatter diagrams.
- Calculate descriptive statistics to summarize and describe the frequency distributions. Only then, use inferential statistics to test whether: there is a relationship between two variables, or there is a difference between two groups on a particular variable.
- Test relationships between variables using a test of correlation, by calculating a correlation coefficient.
- Test differences between groups on a variable using a test of difference, by calculating a *t* value.
- Remember that you can only conclude that you have evidence to reject the default position (of no relationship/no difference) if your significance figure is less than 2.5% for a two-tailed test.

Reflective questions

1 How will you analyse the data? Think about analysis and plan this before you collect the data so you can be sure that the data you gather can answer the questions you want to ask.
2 Which discrete categories (such as low, average and high) will you choose for a variable such as ability, from data that has been assessed on a continuous scale (such as scores on NFER Cognitive Ability Tests)? Remember you can't do the reverse. So, if in doubt, collect data at the highest level of measurement possible.
3 Don't forget that *you* tell the computer program what to do. It just follows your instructions. So if you put rubbish in, you'll get rubbish out!

Further reading

Brace, N., Kemp, R. and Snelgar, R. (2009) *SPSS for Psychologists* (4th edn). Basingstoke: Palgrave Macmillan.

Cohen, L., Manion, L. and Morrison, K. (2011) *Research Methods in Education* (7th edn). London: RoutledgeFalmer.

Coolican, H. (2009) *Research Methods and Statistics in Psychology* (5th edn). London: Hodder & Stoughton.

Field, A. (2009) *Discovering Statistics Using SPSS* (3rd edn). London: Sage (Introducing Statistical Methods series). See also http://www.statisticshell.com/html/dsus.html and accompanying student video clips at http://www.sagepub.com/field3e/SPSS studentmovies.htm (accessed April 2012).

Howitt, D. and Cramer, D. (2007) *Introduction to Statistics in Psychology* (3rd edn). Harlow: Pearson Education.

Muijs, D. (2010) *Doing Quantitative Research in Education With SPSS*. London: Sage.

Sani, F. and Todman, J. (2008) *Experimental Design and Statistics for Psychology* (2nd edn). Oxford: Blackwell Publishing.

Appendix: motivation questionnaire

Name: ....Ros McLellan.................   Date of Birth: ...25/07/96.......................
School: ...KTS.........................   Science Teacher: ..class 1...............................
Date: ......13/09/07....................   Boy or Girl: ...girl...

I am going to ask you some questions about your experience of school. There are no right or wrong answers. Please answer all the questions as honestly as you can. Your teachers will not see your answers.

For each question decide whether you: 1 – strongly disagree, 2 – disagree, 3 – neither agree nor disagree, 4 – agree, or 5 – strongly agree.

For each question cross the answer that is closest to what you think.

For example:

Baked beans taste good   1   X   3   4   5

This person doesn't really like the taste of baked beans. That is why 2 is crossed, which is disagree.

Another example:

Tottenham Hotspur are great   1   2   3   4   X

This person is a big Spurs fan. 5 is crossed, which is strongly agree.

First of all I want you to think about WHEN you feel you've had a really SUCCESSFUL day at school.

Please answer the following questions and remember:

1 – strongly disagree, 2 – disagree, 3 – neither agree nor disagree,
4 – agree, 5 – strongly agree.

1) I feel successful when I don't have to work hard

In school generally	In science	In English
1 X 3 4 5	1 X 3 4 5	1 2 X 4 5

2) I feel successful when I learn something interesting

In school generally	In science	In English
1 2 3 4 X	1 2 3 X 5	1 2 X 4 5

3) I feel successful when I show people that I'm clever

In school generally	In science	In English
1 X 3 4 5	1 2 X 4 5	1 2 X 4 5

(Continued)

(Continued)

Remember:

1 – strongly disagree, 2 – disagree,
3 – neither agree nor disagree, 4 – agree, 5 – strongly agree.

4) I feel successful when I do almost no work and get away with it

In school generally	In science	In English
X 2 3 4 5	X 2 3 4 5	X 2 3 4 5

5) I feel successful when people don't think I'm thick

In school generally	In science	In English
1 2 3 X 5	1 2 3 X 5	1 2 3 X 5

6) I feel successful when I solve a tricky problem by working hard

In school generally	In science	In English
1 2 3 X 5	1 2 3 X 5	1 2 3 X 5

7) I feel successful when I'm the only one who can answer the teacher's questions

In school generally	In science	In English
1 2 3 X 5	1 2 3 X 5	1 2 3 4 X

8) I feel successful when I don't have to do any homework

In school generally	In science	In English
1 X 3 4 5	1 2 X 4 5	1 2 X 4 5

9) I feel successful when I do well without trying

In school generally	In science	In English
1 X 3 4 5	1 X 3 4 5	1 X 3 4 5

10) I feel successful when a lesson makes me think about things

In school generally	In science	In English
1 2 3 X 5	1 2 3 X 5	1 2 3 X 5

(Continued)

(Continued)

Remember:

1 – strongly disagree, 2 – disagree,
3 – neither agree nor disagree, 4 – agree, 5 – strongly agree.

11) I feel successful when I tell a teacher a fib and get away with it

In school generally	In science	In English
X 2 3 4 5	X 2 3 4 5	X 2 3 4 5

12) I feel successful when I don't have any difficult tests

In school generally	In science	In English
1 X 3 4 5	1 X 3 4 5	1 X 3 4 5

13) I feel successful when I do better work than other pupils

In school generally	In science	In English
1 2 X 4 5	1 2 X 4 5	1 2 X 4 5

14) I feel successful when I don't do anything stupid in class

In school generally	In science	In English
1 2 X 4 5	1 2 X 4 5	1 X 3 4 5

15) I feel successful when I work hard all day

In school generally	In science	In English
1 2 3 4 X	1 2 3 4 X	1 2 3 4 X

16) I feel successful when I mess around and get away with it

In school generally	In science	In English
1 X 3 4 5	1 X 3 4 5	1 2 3 X 5

17) I feel successful when I get higher marks than other pupils

In school generally	In science	In English
1 2 3 4 X	1 2 3 4 X	1 2 3 4 X

(Continued)

(Continued)

Remember:

1 – strongly disagree, 2 – disagree,
3 – neither agree nor disagree, 4 – agree, 5 – strongly agree.

18) I feel successful when teachers don't ask me any hard questions

In school generally	In science	In English
1 2 X 4 5	1 2 X 4 5	1 2 X 4 5

19) I feel successful when I get good marks on a test without studying

In school generally	In science	In English
1 X 3 4 5	1 X 3 4 5	1 X 3 4 5

20) I feel successful when I finally understand a really complicated idea

In school generally	In science	In English
1 2 3 4 X	1 2 3 4 X	1 2 3 4 X

21) I feel successful when other pupils get things wrong and I don't

In school generally	In science	In English
1 X 3 4 5	1 X 3 4 5	1 X 3 4 5

CHAPTER 13

WRITING ABOUT YOUR RESEARCH

Elaine Wilson

Chapter overview

Writing research reports and dissertations is a daunting process for the novice researcher, and this can cause extreme anxiety which can lead to writer's block. There are number of ways of reducing the complexity of the task and, more importantly, of minimizing the stress on yourself when you start to write in earnest. This chapter will provide advice on strategies and structures to help you write about research projects. The intended audience here is novice researchers about to write an extended essay for a postgraduate certificate course and Masters students who need to write a fairly lengthy thesis.

Getting started

Essay and thesis writing is a difficult task, so the temptation will be to put off starting to write and to get side-tracked by deflecting activities such as sharpening your pencils and ordering your desk! Discipline yourself to write something each time you sit down. Don't be too much of a perfectionist at the early stages and don't discard your early ideas, even if they are far from final draft material. Also, don't worry about handing in draft work to your supervisor – nobody produces perfect work at the first attempt, and that is what your supervisor is there to help you with. Don't be put off either, if there are a lot of corrections when you get your draft back – keep in mind that your draft work is not being evaluated; only the final product will receive a grade.

Planning is crucial

Set yourself targets and discuss a reasonable schedule for producing chapters, and, ultimately, finishing your thesis, with your supervisor. Draw up a schedule that is broken down into chapters, with indicators of when certain chapters are due, and take these dates seriously. Successfully completing each section will also boost your confidence.

Be disciplined and write as you go along

Set aside some time each week to write a little, and don't put off writing tricky sections – write down your ideas, even if this is in the form of rough notes. Leave enough time to step away and think about your ideas. You will have a fresh perspective on things when you return.

Organize your draft sections using electronic folders

Make a folder for your whole thesis or essay, a subfolder for each section or chapter, an additional folder for your references, and a final folder just for general notes. As you proceed with writing your thesis, include notes and reminders in each folder as well as your general notes folder. Try putting notes and text in different colours. Don't forget to save your work and make back-up copies of each change.

Know what you want to write

Plan time for reading, because if you start to write too soon, you won't have anything to say so you will tend to 'freeze' at the sight of a blank screen. Above all, do not suffer in silence or put the process off – ask your tutor for help!

Activity 13.1   Generating ideas

To stimulate writing try one of the following:

1 Imagine that you are being interviewed by someone. What questions would the other person ask you about your work? What would they want to find out about your project? Why did you do it? When did you do it? Where did you do it? How did you do it? What did you find out, and so what?

(Continued)

Activity 13.1   (Continued)

Or

2 Map out and organize your ideas visually to explore relationships between the processes.

Then write freely or brainstorm ideas and don't worry about revising or proof-reading at this stage.

Composing your essay or thesis

Planning the structure of the work

Composing your essay or thesis involves making major decisions about what you need to include and how to organize the work. This is probably the most difficult part of the writing process. The next paragraph written by Peter Lipton, the late Professor of History and Philosophy of Science at the University of Cambridge, sums up this process of essay writing succinctly:

> An essay is not a list of sentences: it has *structure*. The structure should be obvious to the reader. Write informative introductions and conclusions. The introduction should not only introduce the topic, it should introduce your argument. That means that you should tell the reader what you are going to prove and how you are going to prove it. Unless the introduction gives the reader a clear *map* of the essay, she is likely to get lost. Be direct and specific. Replace sentences like 'Throughout the centuries, the greatest minds have pondered the intractable problem of free will' with 'In this essay, I will show that free will is impossible'. The conclusion of the essay should tell the reader what has been accomplished and why the struggle was worthwhile. It should remind the reader how the different moves in the body of the essay fit together to form a coherent argument. (Lipton, 2007)

This is really good advice, and if you follow it you will produce a good essay or thesis.

Structuring your work

Before you start, organize your essay in the form of an outline to help you to visualize the flow of ideas and ensure coherence throughout the work (see Figure 13.1).

Although you will probably be asked early on to submit an essay or thesis title, it is highly likely that you will refine this and even rewrite the title after you have finished writing up your project. A title ought to provide a succinct summary of the whole essay or thesis.

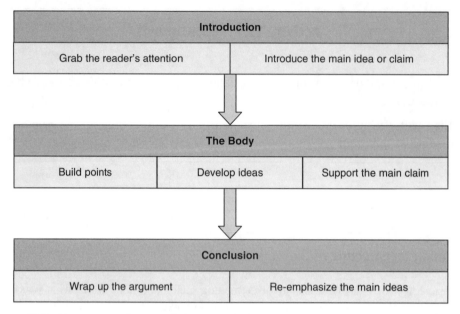

Figure 13.1   The structure of an extended essay or thesis

Box 13.1

Examples of PGCE essay titles:

- Does the use of active teaching approaches to encourage independent learning increase students' understanding in Year 12 chemistry lessons?
- How effective are the use of analogies in teaching electricity to a Year 11 class in an 11–18 mixed comprehensive school?

Examples of thesis titles:

- Developing the role of written feedback in promoting students' engagement in early secondary mathematics: An action research study.
- 'Ebbing the tide' of teaching to the test in secondary science classrooms.

Some unusual academic paper titles:

- McIntyre, D., Pedder, D. and Rudduck, J. (2005) 'Pupil voice: comfortable and uncomfortable learnings for teachers', *Research Papers in Education*, 20(2): 149–68.
- Younger, M. and Warrington, M. (2006) 'Would Harry and Hermione have done better in single-sex classes? A review of single-sex teaching in coeducational secondary schools in the United Kingdom', *American Educational Research Journal*, 43(4): 579–620.

The Introduction

The introduction is a statement of purpose which will contribute to answering a central question expressed in general terms. This might also include, firstly, a summary of the more specific aims of your research and, secondly, a justification of the significance of the substantive topic you have chosen and why this is important for your practice. Explain your own value position in relation to this topic that has shaped the focus of your enquiry. Then you should clarify what the broad issues or problems are, linked to the specific aims of your research, and include a brief description of the context of your enquiry. Table 13.1 illustrates how Martin (2007) introduced her work.

Table 13.1   Introduction

A *justification* of the significance of the substantive topic	In accordance with national and local priorities, the school prioritizes raising achievement in literacy.
A statement of the broad issues	The Big Book approach was already an established reading strategy in the early stages, up to Primary 3 (aged 7). As a class teacher, my intention was to investigate the potential of interactive talking books and an interactive whiteboard as a teaching and learning resource, to develop writing with Primary 6 children.
A *description* of the context of your enquiry	This research was carried out in the school where I teach, as part of the new Scottish qualification of MSc. in Chartered Teacher Studies, for which students are required to plan, implement and evaluate small-scale research and development work that has professional relevance to the student and to the school.
An *outline* of the rest of the study	Through this medium, I wanted to find out how helping children to interact with and reflect on the writing of professional authors might motivate them, develop their understanding and influence their own writing.

Source: Martin (2007).

The main body of the work

The main body of the work is likely to include the following sections:

A review of the literature

The literature review sets out what is already known in your area of study (see Chapter 3), and should start by signposting what will be covered. Firstly, you should set out a critical and focused review of the literature, guided by review questions relating to your substantive and theoretical issues or problems in turn. Start with your substantive knowledge area and then the theoretical ideas informing your study. Secondly, include a brief summary of your position concerning your ideas about the substantive and theoretical issues or problems in the light of your review. Finally, end this section with an indication of how the research design you plan to use will take forward your work in relation to the substantive and theoretical areas and your research questions (see Table 13.2).

Table 13.2 Literature review section

A critical and focused review of the literature guided by review questions	Martin's review considered literature about: • The Big Book approach • Whole-class interactive teaching • Interactive whiteboards
A brief summary of your position concerning your substantive and theoretical issues or problems in the light of your review	The conclusion made is that there is a strong relationship between the ways in which ICT has been used and the resulting attainment outcomes. This suggests that the crucial component in the use of ICT within education is the teachers and their pedagogical approaches.
An indication of how the research design will take forward your work in relation to the substantive and theoretical areas and your research questions	For the reasons set out above, in order to improve children's writing, I therefore decided to explore the use of interactive electronic Big Books that have graphics and sound to support the text. In addition, an interactive whiteboard would allow children to make use of writing tools such as highlighter pens, and speech and thought bubbles while composing, using the touch screen facility.

Source: Martin (2007).

Details of your research design

This section will set out your research questions and the theoretical framework you are using to help you understand and analyse the substantive topic relating to the central question. If you are writing a thesis, this section will be substantial and will also include a brief critical and focused review of the literature relating to your methodological issues or problems, indicating how other researchers have approached them and have investigated similar substantive topics. Finally, include a brief summary of your position about your methodological approach and any issues which arise in the light of what you have read and found out so far.

Your methodology and methods

In the methodology section, justify the methodological approach you have taken and explain the methods of data collection you are using and your justification for using them (see Chapters 9–17).

Table 13.3 shows Martin's research methods section from her paper in Literacy (2007). This section is an abridged version of Martin's final thesis which would also have included a summary description of her data collection instruments, indicating how her research questions are addressed and her rationale for the instruments chosen. In her thesis, she will also have presented a summary of her pilot data collection stage and included details of how data were analysed. The thesis would also have included an extended ethics section, outlining how Martin ensured that her research followed all the necessary school and research ethical guidelines. Finally, Martin would also have discussed the strengths and limitations of her design and told us how she had overcome threats to the reliability and internal and external validity of her methods (see Chapter 9).

Table 13.3   Research methods section

As a class teacher investigating my own classroom, I felt an action research model was most appropriate as this would allow me to reformulate ideas in response to my findings, and feed these back into teaching in a continuous process. It would also allow me to include qualitative as well as quantitative approaches.

Research questions	Data collected
1. To what extent has using interactive whiteboard technology (IWB) to support whole-class teaching of reading and writing improved children's writing?	A random sample of six boys and four girls (every third child on the class register) provided samples of character description and persuasive argument before and after the project, producing four pieces per pupil. (It is recognized that this was a very small sample and no generalizations can be made from the results.) It was agreed beforehand that two colleagues would assess the writing pieces. However, because of constraints of time and workload, four colleagues were eventually involved. 'Taking a Closer Look at Learning to Write' (SCRE, 1995) was used as the assessment tool and the writing samples (with pupils' names and dates removed) were graded on a scale of one to six, where one represented limited understanding, and six represented sound understanding.
2. To what extent has using interactive whiteboard technology (IWB) to support whole-class teaching of reading and writing improved children's writing?	The second question set out to monitor the effect of interactive whiteboard technology on the learning of two boys in class labelled pupil X and pupil Y, both with additional support needs. I created a scaled observation schedule that measured aspects of behaviour before and during the project, and in each of four writing sessions. My support assistant observed one boy and various colleagues shared in observations of the other, leaving me free to teach the rest of the class. To address issues of reliability, an inter-observer agreement (Simpson and Tuson, 2003) was drawn up and discussed with colleagues beforehand.
3. What benefits/disadvantages for the teaching and learning of writing are offered by using IWB?	The third question looked at the advantages and disadvantages of using the technology in teaching and learning. Two questionnaires were designed to assess children's understanding about their learning and their views on using the technology in writing lessons. As the project developed I took the decision to investigate patterns in pupil behaviour during interactive whiteboard lessons and a further observation schedule was designed and administered by my support assistant.

Table 13.4 is Dorion's (2009) research design, extracted data from his paper written after the publication of his PhD thesis. This is not an appropriate table for a research paper, but for an extended thesis such a table would help the reader to see clearly what data collection methods you have used in your design.

Table 13.4   Dorion's (2009) research design

Research question:
What are the characteristics of the drama activities employed in some secondary science lessons?

Sub-questions	Data source	Data source	Data source	Data source
1. What types of drama are used?	Teacher interviews			
2. What objectives initiate the use of drama?	Teacher interviews	Student interviews	Lesson observation	
3. What characteristics of these activities are perceived to enable achievement of the teaching objectives?	Teacher interviews Stimulated video recall	Student interviews	Video	Lesson observation

Dorion (2009) uses a table (Figure 13.2) in his paper to collate his field studies and this is another possible way of presenting this information in your thesis.

Table 3. Fieldwork stages

	Stage 1	Stage 2	Stage 3	Stage 4
Method	Teacher pre-observation interview (45 min)	Lesson observation (1 hr 20 min–1 hr 40 min)	Teacher post-observation interview (45 min)	Student post-observation interview (20 min)
Structure	Semi-structured	Open-ended and unstructured	Focused and semi-structured	Semi-structured
Rationale	Provides context for student learning and knowledge	Interpretive; highlights important moments during the intervention; triangulation with teacher and student perceptions	Utilises experiential knowledge of the teachers; narrow focus on case activity; triangulation	Triangulation with teacher interviews, and observations
Specific resources	Show cards	Video	Stimulated recall with video for teachers	Show cards

Figure 13.2   Table from Dorion's 2009 paper

Your presentation of the findings

This findings section will set out a summary of all the findings broken down into topics relating to the research questions. It is a good idea to support this in the form of tables, matrices, diagrams and quotations from participants and informants, where appropriate, and end the section with a concluding summary of key findings and emerging issues which you have identified.

Your discussion of the findings

The purpose of the discussion section is to explain the meaning of the results you have obtained. Although the discussion comes at the end of your thesis or essay, constantly keep in mind why your study is important and how your study relates to previous studies while you are doing the research. Your final discussion should include the following five points:

State the major findings of the study
The discussion should begin with a statement of the major findings of the study which will be the very first paragraph in the discussion in the form of a direct statement. Don't include data or reference to the study design at this stage.

Explain the meaning of the findings and why the findings are important
By this stage in the research process, you will be so close to the design and data collection process that the meaning of the results and their importance will seem obvious to you. However, your reader might not be so familiar with all that is in your head, so you need to explain everything really clearly and not assume that the reader can interpret the tables and data for themselves.

Relate your findings to other similar studies
The discussion section should relate your study findings to those of other studies. You can tell the reader about the prompts and questions raised by previous studies which motivated you to do your study. These other studies may support your findings and this will serve to strengthen the importance of your work.

Consider alternative explanations for the findings
The purpose of research is to *discover* and not to *prove*. It is easy to fall into the trap of designing the study to prove your strongly held bias rather than to challenge and test this out by looking at the evidence. Consequently, when you write the discussion section, carefully consider all possible explanations for the study results, rather than just those that fit your biases.

Make suggestions for further research
Although a study may answer important questions, other questions related to the subject may remain unanswered. Moreover, some unanswered questions may become more focused because of your study. You should make suggestions for further study in the discussion section too.

Table 13.5 shows how Pedder (2006) has done all of this very succinctly in the discussion from his paper about class size.

Table 13.5 Structure of the discussion section

State the study's major findings	The secondary school study developed no evidence of simple one-way relationships between class size and optimum conditions for all kinds of teaching and learning. This is a key finding.
Explain the meaning and importance of the findings	Different teachers recognized increased opportunities for promoting and supporting learning in large as well as in small classes; they also recognized constraints in small as well as in large classes. Politicians therefore need to be receptive to the possibility that benefits to pupils' learning arise in large as well as in small classes and thus need to promote frameworks within which schools can adopt more flexible approaches to allocating pupils to learning groups of different size for different teaching and learning purposes.
Relate the findings to those of similar studies	The American large-scale class size reduction experiments mentioned at the beginning of this article appear to be motivated by a concern with political and economic decision-making at government level more than with decision-making at school or classroom level.
Consider alternative explanations of the findings	At a glance it might seem, therefore, that the focus on class size as an isolated variable is not only understandable but also justifiable. However, research approaches that combine, within the same design, observation of patterns of classroom behaviour with fine-grained analysis of practitioners' perspectives stand the best chance of developing evidence that is relevant to, and useful for, thinking and decision-making at the global policy level. The challenge is for politicians to face up to the complexities involved and to be open to more flexible approaches to the organization of teaching and learning in schools.
Make suggestions for further research	McIntyre argues for flexible reform that includes increased non-contact time for teachers and pupils and more flexible arrangements for conducting face-to-face contact between teachers and pupils individually as well as in classes and groups of different size on a fitness for purpose basis. Should politicians and policy makers begin to construe the development of class size policy within this kind of inclusive framework of change, then it may be possible to gain the potential benefits from small classes but also the benefits from large classes without a net increase in expenditure in the long run.

Source: Pedder (2006).

Activity 13.2

Use the checklist below to assess your own discussion section:

1 Have you included all the points set out in the discussion of findings section (see Table 13.5)?
2 Are you confident that your interpretation of the results does not go beyond what is supported by the data and that you are not being speculative?
3 Are there any tangential points included which run the risk of diluting and confounding your message?

Conclusion and recommendations

Finally, Table 13.6. illustrates what a good conclusion should look like. Pedder (2006) has included: *recommendations* for different audiences – in this case, policy makers;

suggestions for further research; an evaluation of his research design, including flagging up his uncertainty about answers to research questions; and a final clear take-away message. Wyse (2006) has provided guidance on the approximate length and word count for each section, and this is included in Table 13.7.

Table 13.6 Conclusion

Recommendations for different audiences – in this case, policy makers	Politicians can be helped in their decision-making by research that uses multiple methods of inquiry into effects of class size variation in both primary and secondary school contexts.
Suggestions for further research	Further research is needed to help us develop much better understanding of the kinds of strategies and knowledge teachers can adapt for effectively promoting high quality learning opportunities for all pupils in different contexts of class size variation. Such research should aim to generate useful insights into how, in large and small classes, learning for a range of different purposes can best be promoted. Class size research needs to attend to the contexts within which class size variation occurs by investigating the different ways class size interacts with other key variables. Teachers bring different strengths and expertise to the classroom. They teach different subjects and work in contexts of varying levels of resourcing and space. The pupils they teach come to class with different personalities, and behavioural and ability characteristics. Taking all these facets of classroom life into account, it is unsurprising if we find teachers maximizing opportunities for pupils to learn in classes of different size in different ways. We need further research to find out how teachers manage to do this in classes of different size in different primary and secondary school contexts.
Evaluation of research design and degree of certainty about answers to research questions	Blatchford and colleagues have made important headway through their CSPAR study in developing research that investigates the impact of class size as one among many important factors influencing classroom processes. Greater sophistication of qualitative design is still needed, though, if we are to adequately understand and represent the kinds of teacher and pupil expertise involved in promoting and maximizing opportunities for high quality learning in different large and small class contexts. Here, class size research can learn a great deal from a growing tradition of classroom-based research that is making exciting progress in gaining access to pupils' perspectives and experiences of classroom learning as a means to improving what we know about effective classroom processes (e.g. Cooper & McIntyre, 1996; Pollard, 1996; Rudduck et al., 1996; Pollard & Triggs, 2000; Rudduck & Flutter, 2000, 2004). By contrast, class size research has neglected pupils' voices as key sources of insight.
Final take-away message	Embracing their perspectives, as well as their teachers', provides the best opportunity for improving our theoretical and practical understandings of class size effects on classroom teaching and learning processes and outcomes.

Source: Pedder (2006).

Now that you have got all your ideas down on paper, it is a good idea to leave the draft for a few days before you come back to revise it. Writing is a process of progressive refining so don't underestimate the time it takes. Visit the library and look at examples of previous students' work in readiness for the next reviewing stage.

Table 13.7   Recommended lengths for different sections of a 6000-word research report and a 20,000-word thesis

	Number of words		
	Percentage of the overall report	6000-word essay	20,000-word thesis
Abstract	2.5	150	500
Literature review	30	1800	6,000
Methodology	17.5	1050	3,500
Results	30	1800	6,000
Discussion/Conclusion	20	1200	4,000

Source: Adapted from Wyse (2006).

Reviewing what you have done

Reviewing your work involves revising the essay at the ideas level. It is literally seeing the argument of the paper through revising the organization to make the essay coherent and clear.

Peter Lipton explained this reviewing stage very eloquently as:

> Think[ing] of your essay as composed of a series of descriptive and argumentative moves. Each major move deserves a paragraph. Generally speaking, a paragraph should start with a transition sentence or a topic sentence. A transition sentence indicates how the paragraph follows from the previous one; a topic sentence says what the paragraph is about. Both types of sentences are really miniature *maps*. In the middle of a paragraph you may want to give another map, explaining how the move you are making here is connected to others you have made or will make. The order of your paragraphs is crucial. The reader should have a clear sense of *development* and *progress* as she reads. Later paragraphs should build on what has come before, and the readers should have a feeling of steady forward motion. To achieve this effect you must make sure your sentences hang together. Think about glue. You can get glue from maps, from transition sentences and words, and especially from the logic of your argument. (Lipton, 2007)

The structure of an argument

An academic essay is about persuasion, and the structure of your argument plays a vital role in this. To persuade a reader, you must explain why you are undertaking your research, provide a context, and then explain your evidence, so don't just list findings without a discernible logic.

Constructing an argument

Don't assume that the reader is as familiar as you are with the subject. Are your points really clear? Try them out on a non-expert – in other words, you need to make the familiar unfamiliar. Put yourself in the reader's position so that you can convince them that your argument is sound.

Have a clear point to argue

Start by making some sort of claim. By that I mean you will need to agree or disagree with the statement in the title you have chosen, then use evidence to support your argument. In other words, you need to stake out a position and use evidence to argue your case.

Begin by asking yourself, 'What is my point?' If your essay does not have a main point, then you cannot argue for anything. Having a point will help you to avoid your essay being simply a list of findings.

It is likely that the person who is assessing your essay knows a lot more than you do about the subject matter. So don't simply provide them with material they already know; instead demonstrate to them that you understand the issues fully. In your essay, you can do this by engaging critically with the material you have read and applying it to your own school situation.

Back up your point with evidence

You must back up your point with evidence by demonstrating that you can collect reliable and valid data to test out your ideas, and that your claims are warranted by the evidence you are presenting. The strength of your evidence, and how you use it, can make or break your argument. Be consistent with your evidence but make sure that within each section you are providing the reader with evidence appropriate to each claim. Getting the structure of your essay tidy and ordered will be important because you can't convince a confused reader.

Include a counter argument

Be up front about the limitations of your research design and the possible threats to the validity of your claims, and point out what you have done to minimize these threats. You can test out counter arguments by asking your tutor or peers to challenge your claims.

Revising your work

Revising the organization

Start by revising the organization and check for clarity and coherence. If your writing is ungrammatical or difficult to follow, it will be awkward to read. This may be because you are not using your own words and are relying on too many phrases and quotations. Even if you are using somebody else's ideas, try to use your own words to paraphrase them. And acknowledge this by adding a reference. Try reading your work aloud to see if it flows.

Proofreading your work

Leave enough time to sort out the mechanics of writing, that is, checking spelling, punctuation, sentence structure and referencing. You have spent a long time on the organization, so don't skimp on the time spent on this stage, as a poorly presented study will detract from the overall work. Finally, use the checklist in Activity 13.3 before you submit your work.

Activity 13.3 Questions to ask yourself regarding the presentation of your study

Coherence

- Is the main argument clearly stated and logical?
- Are there clear headings and sub-headings so that the reader can follow your thinking throughout the essay or thesis?
- Is the content connected within and among sections of your essay?
- Is the work coherent?
- Does the abstract provide an overall representation of your thesis?

Clarity of information

- Have you used a range of presentational devices, such as tables, figures and graphs?
- Have you ensured that you have explained all the technical language, with new terms and contextual features introduced?

Clarity of data

- Have you presented data in an understandable layout and explained findings clearly to support your argument?

Format

- Does the format of your manuscript conform to the style recommended in your course handbook or used by the journal (e.g. Harvard, APA)?
- Have you avoided using sexist language?
- Have you used appropriate terminology which will help your work flow and be up to date (e.g. participants rather than subjects)?
- Have you explained abbreviations or acronyms, demystified jargon and avoided the overuse of metaphors?
- Have you used the correct mechanics (e.g. grammar, punctuation)?

Turning your thesis into a paper

It may be the case that during the process of writing your thesis the thought of ever writing again will fill you with dread. This will pass! Your work is important and you ought to consider how to disseminate it more widely. Publishing your work in a teachers' professional or academic journal is a good way of getting your ideas into the public domain.

There are, obviously, fundamental differences in the content, format and length of a journal manuscript or article compared to a dissertation. A dissertation is typically a lengthy, elaborate work that runs to more than 100 pages and over 20,000 words. The typical journal article is 15–25 double-spaced pages (4000–7000 words) in length. The important thing to remember is that a paper is not a summary of the dissertation. So the biggest challenge will be to select and prune the necessary sections into a coherent paper. The danger is that you will try to report everything that you have written about in your thesis. The best approach is to pick one dimension or outcome to focus on.

Start by selecting an appropriate journal for your work. Read about the scope and goals of the journal. The typical types of papers that can be generated from a dissertation and their corresponding chapters are: (a) critical reviews of the literature; (b) methodological innovations; (c) specific findings or results; (d) implications for policy, practice and/or research; and (e) insider experience conducting research. Then read other papers from the journal to get an understanding of what the editors expect.

Collaborating with your university tutor is a good starting point as it is likely that they will have experience of submitting (and re-submitting!) papers to the sort of journals your work would suit. You tutor may co-author the work with you. For example, Jonathan worked with Mark, his university tutor to write a paper for the journal *Educational Studies* and that is why Mark's name is also included – see Box 13.2. which shows the title and abstract from their paper.

Box 13.2

Galbraith, J. & Winterbottom, M. (2011) Peer-tutoring: what's in it for the tutor?, *Educational Studies*, 37(3): 321–32.

Peer-tutoring: what's in it for the tutor? Abstract.

Drawing on role theory and socio-constructivist ideas about learning, this study explores how peer-tutoring can support tutors' learning. The sample comprised

(Continued)

Box 13.2   (Continued)

ten 16–17-year-old biology tutors, working with 21 14–15-year-old students from a science class over eight weeks. Data were collected through an online wiki, tutor interviews, paired tutor discussions and video recordings. Tutors' perceptions of their role motivated them to learn the material, and their learning was supported by discussion and explanation, revisiting fundamentals, making links between conceptual areas, testing and clarifying their understanding, and reorganizing and building ideas, rehearsing them, and working through them repeatedly, to secure their understanding. When tutors employed long answer questions, there was evidence of reflection on their learning and links made between conceptual areas.

When preparing to tutor, tutors could focus on key points and engage with basic ideas from alternative perspectives. Mental rehearsal of peer-tutoring episodes helped them appreciate weaknesses in their own subject knowledge.

 ## Key ideas

Writing is difficult and most people find it hard to start. Don't procrastinate but develop a strategy to get started and overcome the 'blank page syndrome'. It is easier to write in small batches, so start by writing about your work as you go along. In fact, keep a notebook with you at all times to jot down your ideas. If you write in regular short bursts, it will fit around the demands of your work and won't seem so onerous. One point which this author seems to forget before every writing project is that it is best to avoid writing frantically just before a deadline. There are at least three stages to every writing project: getting the ideas down on paper; restricting and redrafting; and finally the proofreading and presentational stages. Leave plenty of time for the last stages. The work put into the research process leading up to the submission of your thesis or essay is considerable, so don't risk diminishing your work though lack of something as straightforward as adequate proofreading.

Reflective questions

1 Do you understand the criteria which will be used to judge your work?
2 Are all the points you have made relevant to the unfolding argument?
3 Have you substantiated all the claims you are making?
4 Is there adequate depth to the points, and do you show the importance of the idea?
5 Is there adequate breadth to your research so that you are able to discuss your ideas in the wider context?
6 Is the essay or thesis written in plain concise English and have you used your own words?
7 Have you used the recommended referencing system and have you checked that you have included all the references?
8 Finally, have you been able to 'bribe' a friend or partner to do a final proofread of your work for you? By the end you are too close to the work to notice small spelling and punctuation errors.
9 Don't lose sight of the big picture – this is an important formative process that you have been through and once you have finished you will come to appreciate how helpful this 'gluing' of your ideas to paper has been in developing your own understanding.

Further reading

BERA (2000) 'Good practice in educational research writing'. Available at: http://www.bera.ac.uk/system files/goodpr1.pdf/ (accessed August 2012).

Bowen, G. (2010) 'From qualitative dissertation to quality articles: seven lessons learned', *The Qualitative Report* 15(4): 864–79. Available at: http://www.nova.edu/ssss/QR/QR15-4/bowen.pdf (accessed April 2012).

Oliver, P. (2008) *Writing Your Thesis* (2nd edn). London: Sage.

Section 3
METHODOLOGIES

This section will provide further details about the key methodological approaches that school-based practitioners are most likely to use. Chapter 14 introduces the historic roots of action research and the philosophy underpinning it. Chapter 15 sets out how to do action research in classrooms using published examples and how to evaluate the validity and reliability of action research. Chapter 16 focuses on the case study approach, and explains the strengths and limitations of this approach. The final chapter is an introduction to grounded theory which explains the value and difficulties of this form of education enquiry.

CHAPTER 14

WHAT IS EDUCATIONAL ACTION RESEARCH?

Elaine Wilson

Chapter overview

This chapter will clarify what we mean by practitioner educational action research. The first section will set action research in an historical context, then the philosophical roots will be discussed, and finally the debates about the differences between educational research and research in education will be rehearsed.

Origins of action research

The creation of the process of action research is often attributed to Kurt Lewin, and whilst he appears to have been the first to publish work using the term, he may have earlier encountered the method in Germany from work performed in Vienna in 1913 (Altrichter et al., 2007). Indeed Buckingham's book *Research for Teachers*, published in 1926, cited in Altrichter et al., advocates a recognizable action research process.

Furthermore, Rogers's (2002) account of John Dewey's notions of reflection, for instance, shows that it is very similar, and it might even be possible to suggest that the ancient Greek empiricists used an action research cycle.

Nonetheless, Lewin was the first to describe action research as 'proceeding in a spiral of steps, each of which is composed of planning, action and the evaluation of the result of action' (Kemmis and McTaggart, 1990: 8). Lewin argued that in order to 'understand and change certain social practices, social scientists have to include practitioners from the real social world in all phases of inquiry' (McKernan, 1991: 10).

Action research as a form of practitioner enquiry

Practitioner educational research is a conceptual and linguistic umbrella for an array of research approaches (Cochran-Smith and Lytle, 2009), such as ethnographic research and case studies. In the wider literature there are various approaches to practitioner inquiry reported, each with a different emphasis and intention, as well as different historical and epistemological traditions. However, there are also a number of features which are common to all traditions. For example, all forms of practitioner inquiry involve someone carrying out a practice which has involved training and which demands constant updating of practice knowledge. For example, when a teacher or medical practitioner simultaneously takes on the role of researcher they become practitioner enquirers. The important premise is that such practitioners, who work inside a particular practice context, have significant knowledge and perspectives about that situation that an outsider would not have. This inside knowledge means that the practitioner researcher has a deep understanding of the interactions and dynamics within the practice context. Conversely, there are also drawbacks – because the practitioner is so close to the context then this familiarity can prevent or limit objective thinking.

Practitioner enquiry also builds on the premise that the relationship between knowledge and practice is complex and non-linear, and that the knowledge needed to improve practice is influenced by the contexts and relations of power that structure the daily work of the specific practice.

Kemmis and McTaggart (2005) describe a number of broad types of practitioner action research in a range of settings and organizations. However, this chapter will be restricted to school-based research contexts, and to educational action research in particular. Here we are defining school-based research as collaboration among school-based teachers and other educators and university-based colleagues, although others involved in education, such as parents and other members of the wider school community may also be involved.

What do we mean by education?

Education is the social process by 'which a new generation is initiated into the language, rituals, roles, relationships and routines which its members have to learn in order to become a member of the society' (Carr and Kemmis, 2009: 75). It follows that if education is about initiating young people to become members of society then the social practices of teaching must fulfill this role. However, it can also be argued that those occupying such social roles must also be willing to respond to the changes taking place in the immediate society and wider world context.

Consequently, the process of education has two dissonant functions: first to reproduce existing patterns of social life, and second to overcome the natural conservative tendency of education systems which might hinder transformation of practice, so that future generations are also equipped to participate in a rapidly changing social world. It is because of this tension that debate about education is overtly political. Indeed the inherent, often contradictory, beliefs and values held by all the relevant disparate groups involved in education colours debate about what is a 'good' society and therefore what is 'good' teaching. Therefore, the kind of education prevailing in a society at a particular time is a product of previous political policies and the resultant relationship between education and society, which has been modified and transformed over time.

Educational action as praxis

If we accept that education is not value free, and indeed that the purposes and process of education are highly contested, it follows then that educational action is not a neutral action either. Carr and Kemmis argue that educational action is more appropriately understood as a form of human practice or *praxis,* a term derived from Aristotelian philosophy. More precisely, praxis is defined as 'ethically informed (social) practices, in which, and through which, some understanding of the individual good and the good society are given practical expression' (Carr and Kemmis, 2009: 77). Therefore, to act educationally is to act on the basis of an ethical code. Furthermore, the social roles or disposition of the teacher is to act in accordance with a tacit understanding of what constitutes a good society or good teaching. Such social practice undertaken by ethically informed teachers is termed *phronesis,* which has also come to be known as practical wisdom. This practical wisdom cannot be learned in theory and then applied in practice because the context is 'imbued with historically bequeathed traditions, educational thought and action' (Carr and Kemmis, 2009: 78). These tacit features of a practice context mean that practical wisdom can only be 'acquired by practitioners who, in seeking to achieve the standards of excellence inherent in their practice, develop the capacity to make wise and prudent judgements about what, in a particular situation, would constitute an appropriate expression of the good' (Carr and Kemmis, 2009: 79).

In summary, educational action is therefore a form of praxis, that is, political action aimed at realizing the view of the good society to which the educational practitioner is tacitly committed.

What is school-based educational action research?

School-based educational action research is the process whereby practitioners deliberate on and respond to school-based problems. This form of research is not so much 'in' and 'about' education as 'for' education. Consequently, it is the role of the teacher to engage in the process of self-reflective enquiry so that they will understand and improve their own practice. The efforts of the participants of educational action research are geared towards changing the curriculum, challenging existing school practices and working for social change by engaging in a continuous process of problem posing, data gathering, analysis and action.

Kemmis goes further suggesting that:

> Action research changes people's practices, their understandings of their practices, and the conditions under which they practice. It changes people's patterns of 'saying', 'doing' and 'relating' to form new patterns – new ways of life. It is a meta-practice: a practice that changes other practices. It transforms the sayings, doings and relatings that compose those other practices. (Kemmis, 2007: 1)

In other words, transforming practice means transforming what we do; transforming understanding means transforming what we think; and transforming the conditions changes how we relate to each other (Figure 14.1).

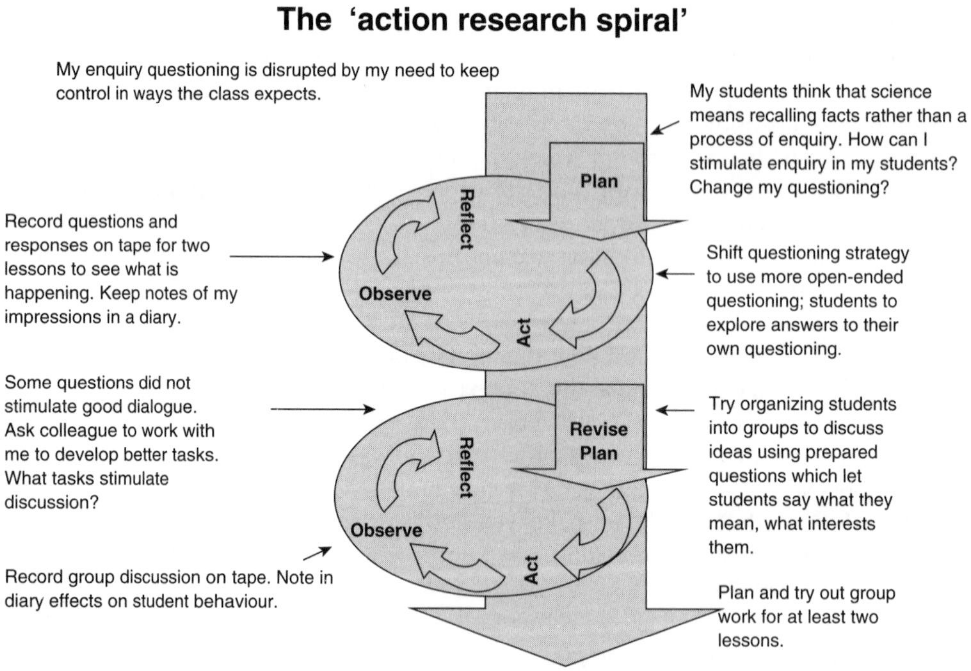

The 'action research spiral'

Figure 14.1   An example of a Lewin spiral used by a teacher researcher

Source: Based on Kemmis and McTaggart (1988).

The purposes of action research

There are also differences in the general purposes of action research. In the 1980s Carr and Kemmis used a theory of knowledge based on constitutive interest (Habermas, 1987) to distinguish three kinds of action research. These were: *technical* action research, guided by an interest in improving control over outcomes; *practical* action research, guided by an interest in educating or enlightening practitioners so they can act more wisely and prudently; and *critical* action research, guided by an interest in emancipating people and groups from irrationality, injustice and harm or suffering.

Twenty years on Carr and Kemmis (1986) have refined these to become 'personal', 'professional' and 'political' purposes – although each proponent of action research places a different emphasis on their purpose, rather than these being discrete typologies. So, for example, Whitehead's 'living theory' approach to action research (Whitehead and McNiff, 2006) places more emphasis on the personal dimension than professional and political purpose. However, Whitehead would argue these other two purposes are also important.

See Table 14.1 for a summary of the traditions of action research.

Table 14.1 Action-research traditions: principles and purposes

Approach	Key proponents	Principles	Purposes
Practitioners conducting research about their own practice to better understand and improve practice	Lewin, Corey, Zeichner, Noffkee (USA); Stenhouse, Elliott, Rudduck, Somekh (UK)	Changing practice is educative and linked to practitioner personal growth	*Professional:* To test out ideas To change and improve practice and evaluate these changes To enable professional growth of the practitioner
	Living theories through self-study and auto ethnography. Whitehead (UK); McNiff (Ireland)		*Personal:* To examine personal values and beliefs, and to uncover hidden dispositions to guide actions and choices
Collective self-enquiry undertaken by participants in social situations which contribute to greater equity and democracy in schools and society	*Critical Emancipatory.* Carr and Kemmis (Australia); Freire (S. America); Elliott (UK)	Undertaking action research is an emancipatory process	*Political:* To close the gaps between problems and theoretical ideas

The field and domains of action research

There are a number of key researchers who have made significant contributions to the field of action research. In the UK Lawrence Stenhouse was the first researcher to advocate this approach and he worked with teachers to help them take an active role in teacher research. Elliott and Rudduck carried this work on and their seminal work promoted action research projects which have made significant changes to classroom practice through mobilizing teachers. These projects include Jean Rudduck's 'Consulting Pupils about Teaching and Learning'.

Carr and Kemmis continue to promote emancipatory notions of action research, and Whitehead and McNiff publish living theories. Both approaches purport to be about closing the gaps between problems and theoretical ideas through examining personal values and beliefs and uncovering hidden dispositions to guide actions and choices.

Schön's long-established reflective practitioner idea proposes that action research is also about building knowledge to support professional practice.

It may be action but is it research?

There are ongoing debates in the literature too about whether action research can justifiably be called research.

Elliott (2009) defends action research and differentiates between *research on education* and *educational research*. He defines research *on* education as the type of research professional researchers do, mainly in university departments. That is, the sort of ethical inquiry aimed at realizing educational 'good'. Therefore, research *on* education is about constructing knowledge about teaching and learning whilst being detached from the context being researched.

On the other hand, educational research is carried out by a practitioner, in their own situation, to make their practice more worthwhile, and involves ethically committed action.

In other words, each category of research has different ways of working and different purposes. Research *on* education is undertaken by professional researchers, some of whom are interested in making the study of method the actual object of study. Other research programmes have large teams of professional researchers and graduate assistants. Their work is often funded by charities or grant-awarding bodies to investigate a topical aspect of education. These teams of researchers collect large amounts of data and try to make causal links between their findings and the object of their study. Their aim is often to produce theories from which policy can be determined, or to develop a greater understanding of a particular phenomenon.

Elliott argues that *educational research* has a different but equally valid purpose. This purpose is not primarily about producing generalizable theory, but is about creating new knowledge about interactions and dynamics of actual classrooms and school situations. This form of research is highly relevant to the practitioner and school. Indeed, it could be argued that such forms of research may even have more impact on the classroom, albeit only on a small, local scale.

Educational research in the form of action research can improve the common-sense **conceptualization** of practice, and help practitioners to formulate a theory of classroom action to improve their own situation; whereas *research on education* conceptualizes classrooms from a 'scientific' research perspective.

It could be argued that an important reason for undertaking research on education is to change educational practice so that practitioners will conform to how education theorists believe that practitioners should practice. It may also be the case that researchers in education produce theories that are formed by professional researchers' ways of doing research. These researchers pay little or no regard for how these theories can actually be incorporated into practitioners' everyday ways of working. Furthermore, much of the research published by professional researchers is usually difficult to get at for classroom practitioners, unless they actually embark on their own practitioner-based research. This dissonance has fuelled the critics of action research who argue that educational research theories produced by teacher researchers are not as valid or reliable as research in education theories (Hammersley, 2004). This may be the case, but this view overlooks the importance to the individual classroom teachers or school in generating classroom-specific research knowledge.

Critics also fail to acknowledge that action research gives practitioners intellectual and moral control over their own practice. The self-transformation process of talking about, doing and relating to colleagues about the research process gives meaning to the practice. However, the corollary is that if school-based participants want their research to be taken seriously then they too must use recognized research techniques rigorously to inform both their actions and data collection methods. The research techniques used should meet the criteria common to other kinds of academic research, that is they must withstand peer review of procedures, be original, significant, and the data must be valid and any claims made must be warranted by the data collected.

Nonetheless, there are significant differences between everyday classroom practice, teachers researching their own practice to make changes, and professional researchers researching classrooms (Table 14.2).

The key differences are that knowledge gained in routine practice tends to remain with the individual practitioner rather than become disseminated through publication, as in the case of the professional researchers. The outcomes of the action research undertaken by teacher practitioners tend to be towards the less valued practitioner end of these continua. However, if excellent teaching is about making explicit the deliberative process of knowledge in action (Chapter 1) and if it is true that when a teacher intervenes in routine practice they are venturing into the unknown, then it follows that being equipped with extensive research and practice knowledge will assist teachers in making expert judgements about what is likely to improve the situation most effectively.

Secondly, action researchers invariably use pragmatic data collection methods, whereas methodology is usually paramount in research in education. In action research, methodology is often subservient to practice. That is, a teacher researcher will not be prevented from making changes to practice because there is no measure or adequate baseline data set. Rather, the teacher will make judgements on the best evidence that is available. This is perceived as a serious flaw in action research by the critics (Hammersley, 2004).

Table 14.2   Action research as educational research

	Routine classroom practice	Action research *as* educational research	Research *in* education
Role	Practice is an habitual process using tacit knowledge which may or may not have been derived from previous educational research or research in education	Teacher action in both practice and research	Externally funded researcher studying practice
	Teacher reacts to the situations in the classroom	Teacher is proactive with regard to change but action is based upon understanding achieved through the analysis of research findings	Researchers use pre-determined strict methodological protocol
	Routine practice is the sole responsibility of the practitioner	Teacher participating in action research in their own classroom but also drawing on external expertise through collaborative ways of working	Research is usually carried out in teams as outsiders looking in at practice
Processes	Routine practice is naturalistic in that it is not researched	Interventionist research through changing some aspect of existing practice so there is inside manipulation of the classroom	Research can be either experimental or a deep study of what is happening from the perspective of an outsider
	Routine practice does not normally allow for much examination of procedures, values and effectiveness	Action research is an improvement process which starts with an identified problem	Research on education proceeds with a given agenda and is generally commissioned by external funding agencies
	Ongoing routine practice is generally only experienced by the participants	Action research is deliberative thoughtful practice	Practice is the object of study
Purpose	The main criterion for routine practice is that it works well	Action research is about finding out about why things don't work and trying to improve them	Constructing conceptual systems to explain and construct theory
	Knowledge gained in routine practice tends to remain with the individual practitioner	Knowledge gained in action research ought to be shared within the school or be disseminated through networking and teaching organizations	Knowledge published for the benefit of other researchers in education

Consequently, action research, as a practical improvement process, is sometimes considered to be *atheoretical*. Whilst it is true that traditional disciplinary theory is not a major priority for teachers (Chapter 1), it is nevertheless important to draw on ontological, epistemological and methodological understanding of classroom situations when engaged in school-based research if an intervention is to be truly transformative (Chapter 5). Elliott (1991) claims that although it is academic theorists that ultimately provide the methods and resources for reflection, the development of practice within an action research process takes place through the problematization and application of expert researchers' 'ready-made' theory. In other words, the teacher researcher comes to 'personally own others' theories' (Somekh, 2005: 260). These other theories are usually encountered when school teachers work in partnership with university academics.

Professional learning

Professional learning is strongly shaped by the context in which a teacher practises. This is usually the classroom, which, in turn, is strongly influenced by the wider school culture and the community and society in which the school is situated. So it is important to situate a teacher's individual classroom within both the specific cultural context in which they are operating and the particular policy context of the time.

Teachers' daily experiences in their practice context shape their understandings, and their understandings shape their experiences, so if learning about practice is to develop then these deep-seated ideas must also be appraised.

Teachers build knowledge about their classrooms through engaging in school-based research. It has been shown that integrated cycles of learning and action promote teacher learning, and that this will improve students' learning experiences. In the UK this

**Teacher inquiry and knowledge-building cycle
to promote valued student outcomes**

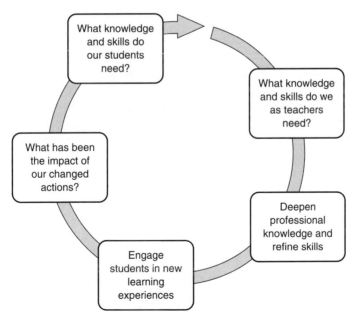

Figure 14.2   Timperley's (2012) teacher enquiry diagram

is illustrated by the work of Frost (2003), Opfer and Pedder (2010), Wilson and Demetriou (2007), and similar work is undertaken in New Zealand (Timperley et al., 2007) and in the USA (Desimone et al., 2002). Timperley helpfully brings these principles together in a cycle of inquiry and knowledge building. The four questions in the boxes are framed from the perspective of teachers and their leaders because it is they who must answer them. However, it is assumed that teachers will receive support to do so: the research evidence indicates that involving external expertise can be crucial for promoting this kind of teacher inquiry and knowledge building. This is what university departments do well.

The next chapter will discuss how to do action research.

Key ideas

Action research is a form of action enquiry that employs recognized research techniques to inform the action taken to improve practice. Action research gives practitioners intellectual and moral control over their practice. Teacher researchers must use research techniques rigorously so that they meet the criteria common to other kinds of academic research, that is their research must withstand peer review of procedures, be original, be significant, and the data must be valid and any claims made must be warranted by the evidence collected.

Reflective questions

1 Can education research be considered to be education research?
2 How does Timperley's framework Using Evidence in the Classroom for Professional Learning at http://www.education.auckland.ac.nz/uoa/helen-timperley compare with the action research process discussed here?

Further reading

Altrichter, H., Feldman, A., Posch, P. and Somekh, B. (2007) *Teachers Investigate Their Work: An Introduction to Action Research Across the Professions* (2nd edn). London: Routledge.

Baumfield, V., Hall, E. and Wall, K. (2008) *Action Research in the Classroom*. London: Sage.

Herr, K. and Anderson, G.L. (2005) *The Action Research Dissertation: A Guide for Students and Faculty*. Thousand Oaks, CA: Sage.

McNiff, J. and Whitehead, J. (2011) *All You Need to Know About Action Research* (2nd edn). London: Sage.

Stenhouse, L. (1985) *Research as a Basis for Teaching: Readings from the Work of Lawrence Stenhouse*. London: Heinemann.

Somekh, B. (2005) *Action Research: A Methodology for Change and Development* (Doing Qualitative Research in Educational Settings series). Maidenhead: McGraw-Hill.

CHAPTER 15

HOW TO DO ACTION RESEARCH

Elaine Wilson

Chapter overview

This chapter will provide a step-by-step guide to carrying out school-based action research. Each stage will be exemplified using an actual published example of a classroom teacher's research to change practice. The researcher's questions and data collection process will be elaborated on to illustrate each stage of the process.

Making the commitment to enquiry

The first step in the process of doing action research is to identify a classroom issue you are concerned about and want to change (see Figure 15.1). The first stage starts with asking questions about things happening in classrooms that others might take for

Figure 15.1   Doing action research

granted. At a very basic level this might be about finding out who is not answering questions in lessons or not handing in homework and why this might be the case. Alternatively the question might be spurred on by reading about 'Learning without Limits' and the transformability potential of setting up a more inclusive classroom environment (Hart et al., 2004). Questions such as these can be uncomfortable to ask. They may produce even more discomforting answers. However, unless and until teachers grapple with the hard questions, it will be impossible to do very much to improve pupils' learning in classrooms. So, in short, action research is a way teachers will learn about themselves as teachers and learn how to become critical thinkers about teaching and learning.

How do teachers do action research?

The next sections will draw on an actual example of action research carried out in a real classroom taken from a paper published in a peer- reviewed journal. The paper is: Tsafos, V. (2009) 'Teacher–student negotiation in an action research project', *Educational Action Research*, 17(2): 197–211. Short sections of the paper will be used to illustrate the research process, which is broken down into stages.

1   Identify the problem you want to solve in your classroom

Box 15.1 shows why and how the author identified the problem.

Box 15.1   A real-world classroom-based problem

'As a teacher I had long diagnosed that students were passive during the herme-neutic analysis of Ancient Greek literature texts ...'. (Tsafos, 2009: 197)

'One of the main problems of teaching Ancient Greek literature is the students' inability to become involved in the process of interpretation; namely, to conquer interpretation strategies that will help them reach valid conclusions. According to the prevailing teaching practice, the teacher should attempt the necessary links, reveal the unique and "noble" meaning of classical texts and offer it to students. Having taught this subject for a series of years and supporting a totally different view than the prevailing one, I decided to proceed with an action research project in order to try out more student-oriented teaching methods. My ultimate goal was to transform students from passive recipients to active readers. The research was organised around the standard multi-cycle action research design: plan–act–observe–reflect.' (Tsafos, 2009: 199)

2   Define the purpose and clarify what form the intervention will take

Box 15.2 sets out the author's rationale and what he proposed to do to rectify the problem.

Box 15.2   Research rationale

'Thus, I decided to conduct an action research project, starting from identifying the needs of the educational practice. I aimed to develop pedagogic strategies that would nurture student involvement in the learning process. As an action researcher, I always considered practice and research to be mutually supportive, and valued the dialogue between theory and practice (Johnson 2003: 370). For this reason, I did not try to predetermine any strategies or curriculum content in detail. On the contrary, in a framework of "praxiology", I wished to invite the students to take part in the selection and organising of the curriculum content, focusing on the learning strategies as well as on a dynamic and reflective pedagogical process (Elliott 1991: 15–16). In this way, it is not educational theory that directs and dominates practice; rather, in an interpretative view of educa-tional theory and practice, "practical deliberation is informed ... by the practical exigencies of situation and it always requires critical appraisal and mediation by the judgment of the actor" (Carr and Kemmis 1986: 93).' (Tsafos, 2009: 198)

3   Action research is about intervening to make changes

Box 15.3a provides details of the classroom context and 15.3b shows how the author planned to stage and carry out the intervention.

Box 15.3 (a)   Action and knowledge: the intervention

'I was the teacher of Modern and Ancient Greek Language and Literature of the third grade of high school (age group 14–15 years) in a pilot High School in Athens. Pilot High Schools are state-run and enjoy an excellent reputation, both regarding knowledge offered and in terms of students gaining access to tertiary education. The term "pilot" is but a name, not designating any experimentation. The students' parents are particularly interested in their children's achievements. This impeded the implementation of a research project, as students were unfamiliar with such processes, while parents could react adversely to the idea of experimentation. However, by choosing action research, I provided students with a more active involvement in the research process.' (Tsafos, 2009: 198)

Box 15.3 (b)   Action and knowledge: general plan

'Based on my teaching experience and on relevant bibliography, I decided to use indexing as a teaching and learning method: The students, divided into teams, undertake to deal with certain topics that are either mentioned explicitly or implied in the text, and to collect data on these topics from all the teaching units, for as long as the process lasts. Such topics could include: women, gods, the political system, hospitality, costumes, and so forth. These are topics on which taught literature expresses an opinion gradually; by continuously dealing with them, students are better able to detect and process some basic ideological parameters of the play.

So the students go through the text with a set of these categories against which they collect information in order to form a general view of the ancient Greek civilisation based on ancient Greek texts, become more familiar with the texts, and practice a way of selecting and evaluating information.' (Tsafos, 2009: 199)

4   Action research involves collecting empirical data in classrooms

Once the question has been decided, the next step is to consider how to answer this and what sort of data to collect (Chapter 5). In this example the author has used a range of data collection methods including interviews, surveys and classroom observation (Box 15.4).

Box 15.4   Participatory and collaborative data collection methods

'In order to collect the data and control the resulting findings intersubjectively, I decided to invite to my classroom, as a *critical friend and observer, the teacher of another classroom of the same grade*, with whom I enjoyed good collaboration. We shared a common code, being fully aware of our differences. Thus, the research material was collected from three sources, to ensure triangulation:

(a) Class teacher:

(i)   Research journal and field notes, written after classroom interventions or discussions with the critical friend and the students.

(ii) Recording of selected intervention extracts.

(b) Students:

(i)   Semi-structured interview by the teacher/action-researcher and the critical friend at the end of the process/research project.

(ii) Questionnaires after classroom interventions, including the questions:

  • What kind of difficulties did you encounter while processing the indexing topics?
  • How would you characterize the process? (Indifferent, boring, interesting, other.)
  • What are your suggestions for its improvement?
  • Student papers on the indexing topics.

(c) Critical friend:

(i)   Observation of the activity and field notes on the process. (Tsafos, 2009: 200)

The action research cycle

Tsafos uses a Boomer et al. (1992) variant of the Kemmis and McTaggart (1988) cyclical diagram Plan → Act → Observe → Reflect → Evaluate to explain the active research process (Box 15.5).

Box 15.5   Cyclical process

'To be more specific, their *(the students)* active involvement in the research was not triggered by their research interest, but by their desire to negotiate the curriculum, as they felt it concerned them personally. Of course, according to Boomer, the stages of a curriculum process, where negotiation has a predominant role, show great similarities with the steps of an action research cycle:
  Planning → Negotiating → Teaching and learning → Performing → Evaluating (Boomer et al. 1992: 35).' (Tsafos, 2009: 207)

You can read how the author analyses and discusses his findings in the full paper:
Vassilis Tsafos (2009) 'Teacher–student negotiation in an action research project', *Educational Action Research*, 17(2): 197–211.

A further example of a teacher doing action research

Figure 15.2 shows an example to illustrate the stages involved in another action research process. In this example, a secondary science teacher carried out action research in her classroom.

The research was initiated by a secondary science teacher who was unhappy with how science teaching was done in her school. She believed that the dominant styles narrowed the curriculum and reduced science to a series of facts. She wanted to improve her teaching by integrating a new approach called 'How science works'. As a curriculum project this was appropriate but as a research focus it was much too general so the teacher first narrowed her focus to that of helping her students to structure an argument.

The next stage involved further reconnaissance in the classroom to establish exactly what was currently being done by her colleagues to help students understand the different ways of thinking about complex controversial issues in the science curriculum. The teacher also asked a colleague to observe her approach and she consulted the students in her class. At this stage, the teacher also found it useful to broaden her thinking about

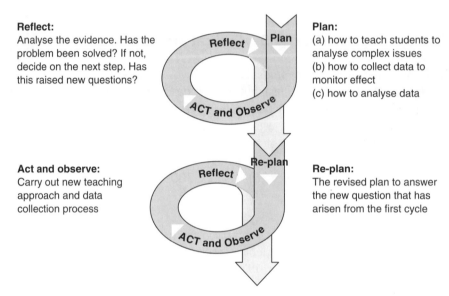

Research question:
'Will my students be able
to structure an argument
better if I teach them explicitly
how to analyse the issues?'

Reflect:
Analyse the evidence. Has the
problem been solved? If not,
decide on the next step. Has
this raised new questions?

Plan:
(a) how to teach students to
analyse complex issues
(b) how to collect data to
monitor effect
(c) how to analyse data

Act and observe:
Carry out new teaching
approach and data
collection process

Re-plan:
The revised plan to answer
the new question that has
arisen from the first cycle

Reflect   Plan

ACT and Observe

Re-plan

Reflect

ACT and Observe

Figure 15.2   Action-research cycles

teaching controversial issues through reading published accounts in the literature and by discussing this with other colleagues beyond the science department. As a result, the teacher refined her area of interest to argumentation in science lessons and decided that the students' problem may be aggravated by not knowing how to analyse the issues surrounding the complex contexts she was teaching. The literature search and discussion with colleagues outside her immediate environment had been crucial in helping her to restate the original problem.

Planning the action research

Having narrowed her focus, the teacher arrived at a manageable research question for her pilot intervention. This was: 'Will my students be able to structure an argument better if I teach them explicitly how to analyse the issues?' The next stage involved not only planning how she would change her practice to help the students analyse complex issues, but also how she would analyse the data collected.

Acting out and observing the intervention

The teacher subdivided her research question into two parts. She looked first for evidence of the students' ability to analyse issues, and secondly at how her students were constructing arguments. The data collected included audio recordings of small-group dialogue, lesson observation notes carried out by a colleague and, following the intervention, the use of a diagnostic probe to find out about students' views of the concepts and the teaching approach. The teacher also analysed the students' written work and interviewed a small representative sample of students (see Table 15.1).

Table 15.1 Action-research data collection plan

Research Question	Will my students be able to structure an argument better if I teach them explicitly how to analyse the issues?			
Sub-question	Data source	Data source	Data source	Data source
1. Can students analyse complex issues?	Audio recording of small-group dialogue	Diagnostic probe	Semi-structured interviews with students	Colleagues' observation notes
2. Can students structure an argument?	Students' written work	Diagnostic probe	Semi-structured interviews with students	

Reflecting and re-planning

Subsequent analysis of the data and reflection on the issues arising from the intervention prompted the teacher to modify her approach and to undertake a second revised action-research cycle with the same data-collection methods. To be transformative, action research needs to be carried out over a sustained period of enquiry and involve reframing the problem in light of new sets of questions. It is this ongoing reframing of the problem that leads to the transformative *action* that characterizes action research.

Going further than simply reflecting in action

In the example given in Figure 15.2, the teacher's aim was to be more reflective and to develop a deeper understanding of this practice. The teacher researched her own classroom through close observation and reflection as well as undertaking informed action. This intervention did not involve the teacher in taking undue risks or making dramatic changes.

Other forms of action research are associated with social transformation through research efforts. Such situations may require that teachers or other researchers make high-risk changes that are driven by a deep commitment to equality, human well-being, deeper understanding and respect for others. In these circumstances, classroom-based action researchers need to have a strong personal interest in the proposed action and also have the authority to act for themselves in the research setting. Consequently, action research involving social changes will mean taking calculated risks and making prudent practical judgements about how to act in specific, often unique, classroom situations. For other action researchers, the primary goal will be to generate knowledge or theoretical frameworks that other practitioners can draw on and adapt to improve practice within their own context.

Accordingly, because of these broad aims, action research has struggled to establish itself as a serious form of academic research. Many questions continue to be raised, such as: do practitioners draw on theoretical foundations when investigating and reflecting on their practices and, if so, how? Do practitioners generate new knowledge as a result of their action research? If so, what type of knowledge is this? Can this knowledge be considered valid? These questions will be considered in the next section.

Challenging your interpretations

You will always bring a number of assumptions to any process, so you need to be clear about your own values and challenge your existing ideas. It is difficult to reflect on your assumptions until you are aware of them, and even more difficult to engage in discourse about something you have not identified. This is why it is essential for you to work with a critical friend or group of people, and to constantly ask yourself, 'What is happening in my class?' 'What is important here?' and 'How can I understand what is happening?'

The general questions below can help structure ideas and lead to enquiring, testing out and reflecting upon practical, personal or political issues within educational situations:

1   What assumptions underlie this teacher's interpretation of the data?
2   Is there another perspective or way of interpreting this situation?
3   What further questions does this analysis raise?
4   What sort of strategies would you suggest that this teacher might use to try to transform the situation?

Activity 15.1

Read the following extract of a classroom teacher's analysis of data she collected from the first cycle of an action-research process and then discuss the questions that follow this with your peers or your critical friend.

'The picture that emerges from our various data sources is complex. By certain standards, our class could be considered an accepting and inclusive environment for all children.

Every student received compliments from his or her peers, most children felt that they were liked by their classmates, and all children were eventually selected as someone's "favourite" friend. However, upon closer investigation, a disturbing fact emerges: the children who look and sound different are not as popular as their classmates. In fact, they form their own, separate social grouping. This may be due to several factors.

First, the majority of our students with special needs suffer from expressive and receptive language delays, which may impede their ability to engage in conversation, share stories, and play with their schoolmates. Children of average development became more linguistically adept across the year, and despite explicit social instruction, the special education students were not acquiring verbal skills at the same rate, and therefore did not learn to be able to negotiate challenging social situations. As a result, they often relied on less language-based play, such as fantasy games, or less rule-oriented physical games such as swinging on the monkey bars in the playground.

Second, because they do not live in the immediate neighbourhood, and because of their parents' busy work schedules, our children with special needs had difficulty participating in out-of-school activities, and missed out on key opportunities for shared social experiences and non-academic interactions. As one parent reached out to these children and made efforts to integrate them into her son's after-school life, they brightened up, and seemed to feel ever more accepted and excited by the prospect of a play date. It was astounding what a play date could do for these children's self-esteem, engagement in the community, and social status.

Finally, when in school, the Inclusion students spent much of their time together, away from the classroom. Jennifer and I tried to schedule group activities when we knew we would have our full enrolment, but students' individual schedules were complex and often unpredictable, and it was impossible to keep

(Continued)

> ## Activity 15.1   (Continued)
>
> all students involved in every activity. In giving them special support, the instruction itself was setting them apart from the mainstream.
>
> In some sense, a caste system has been set up in my classroom. While the children in the class have been open-minded, flexible, and accepting towards one another, some obstacles seem to be insurmountable in creating a truly "inclusive" classroom.' (Zindler, 2003)

Assessing the quality of action research

Action research, particularly classroom-based teacher work, is not universally accepted as a public knowledge-generating process, and this might go some way to explaining why there are few published examples of teachers' own work (Chapter 14). Nevertheless, experts in educational research are beginning to argue that existing criteria for judging practitioner research are inadequate. John Elliott, a well-respected and active proponent of practitioner research, argues that simply using existing tests of theoretical and methodological robustness as the only way of judging practitioner research fails to recognize the value such work has for classroom teachers and the importance such work has for building capacity among teachers as potential agents of educationally worthwhile change (see Chapter 14).

Elliott (2006) has recently published criteria drawing on his own experiences of teacher research to help make such judgements. These are discussed in the next section.

Ensuring that your own work is rigorous and valid

After completing your action-research project it will be important to disseminate your findings to the wider world through the publication of a thesis or at a conference. To this end it will be important that you address how well you have met the aims of your research project.

For most classroom-focused action-research projects, the aim is to bring about a change in your classroom practice so that you and your students grow as a result of your intervention. In the process, you will generate new knowledge which is relevant to your own classroom. This knowledge will have been validated through the systematic collection of evidence by using appropriate methods. In other words, it will be possible to judge the process, outcome, and catalytic and democratic validity of your own work (see Table 15.2).

Table 15.2   Linking action-research goals with quality criteria

Goals of action research	Quality/validity criteria
1. The generation of new knowledge	Process validity
2. The achievement of action-oriented outcomes	Outcome validity
3. The education of both researcher and participants	Catalytic validity
4. Results that are relevant to the local setting	Democratic validity
5. A sound and appropriate research methodology	Process validity

Source: Herr and Anderson (2005).

Table 15.3   Assessing the validity of action research based on Elliott 2006

Process Validity
Are appropriate methods used to answer the question?
(a) Does the research focus on a problem that is of practical concern to the teachers involved?
(b) Does the research involve gathering data from the different points of view, for example, the teacher, an observer, and students (triangulation)?
(c) Does the research enable the teacher researcher to call their existing stock of professional knowledge (tacit theories) into question, and to test it against evidence gathered in their practical situation?
(d) Does the research extend teachers' understanding of their situation in a way that opens up new possibilities for action?

Democratic Validity
Are the researchers and researched engaged and included in the inquiry?
Is the research a rigorous conversational process in which the teacher opens up his/her practice to the rational scrutiny of students and peers, 'in-voices' their views of the action situation, and in the process demonstrates a disposition to subordinate his/her own prejudices to the search for an overlapping and un-coerced consensus?

Catalytic Validity
Is the research transformative?
(a) Is the research a deliberative and self-reflexive process in which the teacher calls into question both his/her teaching strategies (means) and the aims (ends) to which they are directed, and then modifies each by reflecting on the other?
(b) Is the research a process in which the teacher displays:

- integrity in the pursuit of his/her educational aims and values
- curiosity about other people's interpretations of the action situation
- objectivity and honesty about his/her own motives and reasons for action
- open-mindedness towards the views of others and respect for their freedom of thought and action?

Outcome Validity
Has the process led to a resolution and/or a reframing of the problem?
(a) Does the research enlarge the teacher's sphere of personal agency in the practical situation through the realization of his/her educational aims in a sustainable form?
(b) Does the research enable a teacher to generate a description of the complexities of the case in sufficient detail to be of universal significance to other teachers?

Finally, you will find that being able to work collaboratively with colleagues or having a critical friend who can catalyse the process of critical thinking will support you during the action-research process and ensure that you are always reflexive about the process. It is also important to have the support of your department and the autonomy to explore the complexity of your classroom and to take risks to make changes to your practice.

You must remember that your classroom is unique and that the dynamics will change daily, so try to avoid being despondent when things do not follow your plan exactly. However, you need to persevere with your idea and modify your approach in light of your increased understanding. Above all, recognize and value your own skill as a classroom practitioner, especially when you first start to learn about the methods of education research. If possible, seek out expert help from a more experienced researcher or undertake formal research-methods training. Finally, and probably most importantly, set aside sufficient dedicated time to think, reflect and talk so that you can really engage fully with this professionally liberating process.

Action research will not provide all the answers to our questions about how students learn or what educators can do to improve practice. But action research happens at the place where these questions arise; it happens where the real action is taking place; and it allows for immediate action.

Key ideas

Action research is an educative process carried out in social situations that usually involves posing and solving problems resulting in a change intervention. This cyclic process of improvement and involvement is common to the research traditions discussed: technical, positivist/post-positivist, interpretive and also to critical inquiry.

Reflective questions

1 What key issue have you identified that you want to change?
2 Have you used the very latest research knowledge to inform what you do in your intervention?
3 Have you read Chapters 5 and 6?

Further reading

Altrichter, H., Feldman, A., Posch, P. and Somekh, B. (2007) *Teachers Investigate Their Work: An Introduction to Action Research across the Professions* (2nd edn). London: Routledge.

Baumfield, V., Hall, E. and Wall, K. (2008) *Action Research in the Classroom*. London: Sage.

Herr, K. and Anderson, G.L. (2005) *The Action Research Dissertation: A Guide for Students and Faculty*. Thousand Oaks, CA: Sage.

McNiff, J. and Whitehead, J. (2011) *All You Need To Know About Action Research* (2nd edn). London: Sage.

Somekh, B. (2005) *Action Research: A Methodology for Change and Development*. Maidenhead: McGraw-Hill.

Stenhouse, L. (1985) *Research as a Basis for Teaching: Readings from the Work of Lawrence Stenhouse*. London: Heinemann.

CHAPTER 16

THE CASE STUDY

Helen Demetriou

Chapter overview

This chapter will define the case study approach to research as well as addressing the origins, criticisms and limitations of such studies. The section 'Designing a case study' will look at the different methodological approaches to the case study and the various types of case study will then be explored. This is followed by a section that focuses on the techniques and procedures that may be used when conducting case study research. Finally, the flexibility and effectiveness of case studies in educational research is illustrated through six separate research studies.

The case study is a versatile, qualitative approach to research which enables the researcher to understand a complex issue or object and brings with it a familiarity to the case that no other research approach is able to do.

It is an attractive research method because it has 'face-value credibility', which means that it can provide evidence or illustrations with which readers can readily identify.

The case study approach is now more popular than ever, mostly because it is seen as a convenient and meaningful technique that captures a time-framed picture of an individual or another focus of enquiry.

This chapter will focus on the case study. Its aim is to enlighten and entice you to play detective and thereby use this powerful approach to research. This will be illustrated with examples of research that incorporate the case study in their design, followed by two case-study-related activities that aim to consolidate your knowledge of this important area of research.

Let's begin by looking more closely at what a case study is, and learning a bit about its history, criticisms and design.

What is a case study?

Some definitions

Fry, Ketteridge and Marshall (1999) described case studies as complex examples that give an insight into the context of a problem as well as illustrating the main point.

Lamnek (2005: 20) defined the case study as '… a research approach, situated between concrete data taking techniques and methodologic paradigms'.

Yin (2008: 23) defined the case study as a research strategy with an empirical enquiry that investigates a contemporary phenomenon within its real-life context, when the boundaries between phenomenon and context are not clearly evident, and in which multiple sources of evidence are used.

Case study research is a traditional, systematic approach to looking at events, collecting data, analysing information and reporting the results, with the end goal of describing the case under investigation as fully and accurately as possible. It is a research strategy that investigates a phenomenon within its real-life context. Rather than using large samples and following a rigid protocol to examine a limited number of variables, case study methods involve an in-depth, longitudinal examination of a single instance or event – the case. This approach gives you, the researcher, a sharpened understanding of why the instance happened as it did, and what might require greater scrutiny in future research. This approach to research is purely qualitative as only a few instances are normally studied, thereby limiting the use of multivariate statistics. However, case study research can include single and multiple case studies and quantitative evidence, thereby relying on multiple sources of evidence. Case studies should not be confused therefore with qualitative research as they can be based on any mix of quantitative and qualitative evidence. This is often considered to be a strength of case study research, as it has the capability of uncovering causal paths and mechanisms and interaction effects. It can be used either on its own or alongside other methods. Recent years have seen the case study being used increasingly as the sole means of investigation, although it is more often recommended as part of a multi-method approach of triangulation, in which the same dependent variable is investigated using multiple procedures. The flexibility of the case study approach therefore is that it can involve single and multiple case studies, can include quantitative evidence, relies on multiple sources of evidence and benefits from the prior development of theoretical propositions.

A short history of the case study

As a distinct approach to research, use of the case study originated only in the early 20th century. Dictionary definitions trace the phrase *case study* back as far as 1934, after the establishment of the concept of a *case history* in medicine, and the earliest examples are to be found in the fields of Law and Medicine. Despite being used for many years across a variety of disciplines, the case study research method has not always been at the forefront of research. In the early to middle part of the 20th century, case studies were sometimes used to visualize whole organizations or communities; to describe phenomena, for example findings about mental health in the longitudinal case studies conducted by Vaillant (2002), or to describe individuals, for example as the basis of a developmental model in Levinson's (1978) examination of male adults. The preference for quantitative methods resulted in the decline of the case study. However, in the 1960s, researchers were becoming concerned about the limitations of quantitative methods and, as a result, there was a renewed interest in case studies. Glaser and Strauss (1967) developed the concept of 'grounded theory' and this, along with some well-regarded studies, accelerated the renewed use of the methodology. This trend of continuous, albeit somewhat infrequent, usage continued through most of the 1980s, and more recently, the popularity and frequency of case studies have increased.

Criticisms of the case study

Despite the many advantages of the case study procedure, it has had a somewhat bumpy ride from its critics. However, as you will see, the various negative comments targeted at the case study approach are often turned on their head and viewed as advantageous and necessary for this particular approach to research. Moreover, where limitations to the approach exist, researchers have attempted to remedy these.

The case study has been criticized for limitations in validity and construct validity in particular, the result of which is potential subjectivity by the researcher. Yin (2008) proposed three remedies to counteract this: using multiple sources of evidence; establishing a chain of evidence; and having a draft case study report reviewed by key informants. Internal validity is a concern only in causal (explanatory) cases. This is usually a problem of inferences in case studies, and can be dealt with using pattern-matching. External validity deals with knowing whether the results are generalizable beyond the immediate case. This criticism of case study methodology is that its dependence on a single case limits its generalizability. Unlike random sample surveys, case studies are not representative of entire populations, although they do not claim to be. Critics of the case study method believe that the study of a small number of cases is limited when aiming to establish reliability or generality of findings. Others feel that the intense exposure to the study of the case biases the findings. Some dismiss case study research as useful only as an exploratory tool. Giddens (1984) considered case methodology 'microscopic' because it 'lacked a sufficient number' of cases. However, provided the researcher refrains from over-generalization, case study research is not methodologically invalid simply because selected cases cannot be presumed to be representative of entire populations. Therefore, whereas statistical analysis involves the generalization to a population based on a sample that is representative of that population, in case studies, one is generalizing to a theory based on cases selected to represent dimensions of that theory.

In support of case studies, Hamel (1993) and Yin (2008) have argued that the relative size of the sample – whether two, 10 or 100 cases – does not transform a multiple case into a macroscopic study. The goal of the study should establish the parameters, and then should be applied to all research. In this way, even a single case could be considered acceptable, provided it meets the established objective. A subsequent researcher using case methods will naturally be studying a different case, and therefore may come to different conclusions. Similarly, in experimental and quasi-experimental research, the subjects will differ, meaning relationships may differ. What makes research replicable in either case study or experimental research is not the units of analysis but whether the research has been theory-driven. If the case researcher has developed and tested a model of hypothesized relationships, then a future case researcher can replicate the initial case study simply by selecting cases on the basis of the same theories, then testing the theories through pattern-matching.

Designing a case study

Different methodological approaches to the case study

The approach that you take with your case study can take one of three forms. As proposed by Yin (2008) case studies can be *exploratory*, *explanatory* or *descriptive*.

In *exploratory* case studies, fieldwork and data collection may be undertaken before you define your research questions and hypotheses, although the framework of the study must be created at the outset. Pilot projects are very useful in determining the final protocols that will be used and this will enable you to drop or add survey questions based on the outcome of the pilot study.

Explanatory cases are suitable for doing causal studies. In very complex and multi-variate cases, the analysis can make use of pattern-matching techniques. Yin and Moore

(1988) conducted a study to examine the reason why some research findings get into practical use. They used a funded research project as the unit of analysis, where the topic was constant but the project varied. The utilization outcomes were explained by three rival theories: a knowledge-driven theory, a problem-solving theory and a social-interaction theory.

Descriptive cases require a descriptive theory as a starting point. Pyecha (1988) used this methodology to study special education, using a pattern-matching procedure. Several states were studied and the data about each state's activities were compared with idealized theoretic patterns. This type of study therefore advocates the formation of hypotheses of cause–effect relationships. Hence, the descriptive theory must cover the depth and scope of the case under study.

Types of case study

A general approach to designing case studies was propounded by Jensen and Rodgers (2001) who classified case studies as follows:

- **Snapshot case studies** – the detailed, objective study of one research entity at one point in time. It includes hypothesis-testing by comparing patterns across sub-entities.
- **Longitudinal case studies** – the quantitative and/or qualitative study of one research entity at multiple time points.
- **Pre-post case studies** – the study of one research entity at two time points separated by a critical event. A critical event is one that – on the basis of a theory under study – would be expected to impact case observations significantly.
- **Patchwork case studies** – a set of multiple case studies of the same research entity, using snapshot, longitudinal and/or pre-post designs. This multi-design approach is intended to provide a more holistic view of the dynamics of the research subject.
- **Comparative case studies** – a set of multiple case studies of multiple research entities for the purpose of cross-unit comparison. Both qualitative and quantitative comparisons are generally made.

Conducting case study research: tips for the case study researcher

In order to organize and conduct case study research successfully, you should employ the following techniques and procedures:

1 Determine and define the research questions.
2 Select the cases and determine the data-gathering and analysis techniques.
3 Prepare to collect the data.

4   Collect data in the field.
5   Evaluate and analyse the data.
6   Prepare the report.

Step 1. Determine and define the research questions

The first step in case study research is to establish a firm research focus to which you as the researcher can refer over the course of study of a complex phenomenon or object. You should have one or more hypotheses and establish the focus of the study by forming questions about the situation or problem to be studied and determining a purpose for the study. The research object in a case study is often a programme, an entity, a person or a group of people. Each object is likely to be intricately connected to political, social, historical and personal issues, providing wide-ranging possibilities for questions and adding complexity to the case study. You should investigate the object of the case study in depth, using a variety of data-gathering methods to produce evidence that leads to understanding of the case and addresses the research questions.

Step 2. Select the cases and determine the data-gathering and analysis techniques

During the design phase of case study research, you should determine what approaches to use in selecting single or multiple real-life cases to examine in depth and which instruments and data-gathering approaches to use. When using multiple cases, each case is treated as a single case. Each case's conclusions can then be used as information contributing to the whole study, but each case remains a single case. Exemplary case studies carefully select cases and critically examine the choices available from among many research tools available in order to increase the validity of the study. Careful discrimination at the point of selection also helps to form boundaries around the case.

You must determine whether to study cases which are unique in some way or cases which are considered typical, and may also select cases to represent a variety of geographic regions, a variety of size parameters or other parameters. A useful step in the selection process is to repeatedly refer back to the purpose of the study, in order to focus attention on where to look for cases and evidence that will satisfy the purpose of the study and answer the research questions posed. Selecting multiple or single cases is a key element, but a case study can include more than one unit of embedded analysis. A key strength of the case study method involves using multiple sources and techniques in the data-gathering process. You should determine in advance what evidence to gather and what analysis techniques to use with the data to answer the research questions. Data gathered are normally qualitative, but may also be quantitative. Tools to collect data can include surveys, interviews, documentation review, observation, and even the collection of physical artefacts and archival records.

Throughout the design phase, ensure that the study is well constructed in order to achieve construct validity, internal validity, external validity and reliability. Construct validity requires you to use the correct measures for the concepts being studied. Internal validity (especially important with explanatory or causal studies) demonstrates that certain conditions lead to other conditions and requires the use of multiple pieces of evidence from multiple sources to uncover convergent lines of enquiry. External validity reflects whether or not findings are generalizable beyond the immediate case or cases; the more variations in places, people and procedures a case study can withstand and still yield the same findings, the more external validity. Reliability refers to the stability, accuracy and precision of measurement. If your case study design is robust, then the procedures used will be well documented and can be repeated with the same results.

Step 3. Prepare to collect the data

Because case study research generates a large amount of data from multiple sources, the systematic organization of the data is important to prevent you from becoming overwhelmed by the amount of data and to prevent you from losing sight of the original research purpose and questions. Advance preparation assists in handling large amounts of data in a documented and systematic fashion. Researchers prepare databases to assist with categorizing, sorting, storing and retrieving data for analysis.

Exemplary case studies prepare good training programmes for investigators, establish clear protocols and procedures in advance of investigator field work, and conduct a pilot study in advance of moving into the field in order to remove obvious barriers and problems. You need to be able to ask effective questions, be a good listener – listening carefully to the exact words during an interview, and be able to interpret the answers fully. You should review documents looking for facts, but also read between the lines and pursue collaborative evidence elsewhere when that seems appropriate. You need to understand the purpose of the study and grasp the issues and must be open to contrary findings, as well as being aware that you are going into the world of real human beings who may be threatened or unsure of what the case study will bring.

Step 4. Collect data in the field

You must collect and store multiple sources of evidence comprehensively and systematically, in formats that can be referenced and classified so that converging lines of enquiry and patterns can be uncovered. You should carefully observe the object of the case study and identify causal factors associated with the observed phenomenon. Renegotiation of arrangements with the objects of the study or the addition of questions to interviews may be necessary as the study progresses. Case study research is flexible, but when changes are made, they are documented systematically.

Effective case studies use field notes and databases to categorize and reference data in order to be readily available for subsequent reinterpretation. Field notes record feelings and intuitions, pose questions and document the work in progress. They record testimonies, stories and illustrations that can be used in later reports. They may warn of impending bias because of the detailed exposure of the client to special attention, or give an early signal that a pattern is emerging. They assist in determining whether or not the inquiry needs to be reformulated or redefined based on what is being observed. Field notes should be kept separate from the data being collected and stored for analysis. Maintaining the relationship between the issue and the evidence is mandatory. You may enter some data into a database and physically store other data, but you should document, classify and cross-reference all evidence so that it can be efficiently recalled for sorting and examination over the course of the study.

Step 5. Evaluate and analyse the data

You can examine raw data using many interpretations in order to find links between the research object and the outcomes with reference to the original research questions. Throughout the evaluation and analysis process, you should remain open to new opportunities and insights. The case study method, with its use of multiple data-collection methods and analysis techniques, provides researchers with opportunities to triangulate data in order to strengthen the research findings and conclusions.

A good case study will deliberately sort the data in many different ways to expose or create new insights, and will deliberately look for conflicting data to disconfirm the analysis. You should categorize, tabulate and recombine data to address the initial propositions or purpose of the study, and conduct cross-checks of facts and discrepancies in accounts. Focused, short, repeat interviews may be necessary to gather additional data, to verify key observations or check a fact.

Specific techniques include placing information into arrays, creating matrices of categories, creating flow charts or other displays, and tabulating the frequency of events. You should use the quantitative data that have been collected to corroborate and support the qualitative data, which is most useful for understanding the rationale or theory underlying relationships. Another technique is to use multiple investigators to gain the advantage provided when a variety of perspectives and insights examine the data and the patterns. When the multiple observations converge, confidence in the findings increases.

Pattern-matching compares an empirical pattern with a predicted one. Internal validity is enhanced when the patterns coincide. If the case study is an explanatory one, the patterns may be related to the dependent or independent variables. If it is a descriptive study, the predicted pattern must be defined prior to data collection. Yin (2008) recommended using rival explanations as pattern-matching when there are independent variables involved. This requires the development of rival theoretical propositions, but the overall concern remains the degree to which a pattern matches the predicted one.

Step 6. Prepare the report

A good case study reports the data in a way that transforms a complex issue into one that can be easily understood, allowing the reader to question and examine the study and reach an understanding independent of the researcher. Case studies present data in very publicly accessible ways and may lead the reader to apply the experience in his or her own real-life situation. You should pay particular attention to displaying sufficient evidence to gain the reader's confidence that all avenues have been explored, clearly communicating the boundaries of the case, and giving special attention to conflicting propositions.

Techniques for composing the report can include handling each case as a separate chapter or treating the case as a chronological recounting. Alternatively, you could relate the findings from the case study as a story. During the report preparation process, you should critically examine the document, looking for ways to perfect the report, and rewrite and make revisions accordingly.

The use of case studies in education

One of the areas in which case studies have been gaining popularity is education, and in particular educational evaluation and instructional use in order to develop critical thinking, skills and knowledge (Stake, 1995). Teaching and learning styles are, by their very nature, changing, and in recent years there has been a noticeable move from lecture-based activities towards more student-centred activities. Students can learn more effectively when actively involved in the learning process, and the case study approach is one way in which such active learning strategies can be implemented. Such student-centred activities are typically based on topics that demonstrate theoretical concepts in an applied setting. This definition of a case study covers the variety of different teaching structures we use, ranging from short, individual case studies to longer, group-based activities.

In order to illustrate the implementation of case studies in the field of education, there follow some examples of research that have incorporated this methodology.

Example 1

A critical evaluation of visual teaching and learning methods with special reference to animation and modelling for their conceptual and motivational value in teaching environmental chemistry (research completed for a Masters degree in Education)

The study examined the use and effectiveness of animation and modelling for both their conceptual and motivational value in the teaching of environmental chemistry.

To investigate the role of animation in facilitating students' learning and improving motivation in science, a mixed-gender, high-ability, Year 9 set was chosen as the study group. Flash animation was used to teach the concept of acid rain formation and stop–start animation was used to teach the concept of global warming. Students' views on the usefulness of using animation to promote learning and motivation were obtained by talking to the students individually during lessons. Students also completed a questionnaire, which requested information about the students' favourite subjects and their views of science. In addition, students were asked about their feelings on the animations over the course of the sequence of the lessons. Although there is no measurable indication that animations increased students' learning in science, the majority of the students did report that they felt the animations helped them understand and remember the dynamic concepts. It must therefore not be disregarded as a possible teaching tool for aiding the understanding of concepts in science.

Example 2

Gifted and Talented: Policy and implementation in schools (research completed for a Masters degree in Education)

A study was conducted into the provision made for Gifted and Talented (G&T) pupils at a whole school and departmental level at two high-achieving mixed comprehensive schools. Data were collected via G&T documentation provided by schools, observation of lessons, and via interviews with G&T coordinators, science teachers and G&T pupils. The interview with the GATCO was used in conjunction with the schools' documentation (policy, advice to parents, etc.) to identify how the school had interpreted and implemented the national G&T initiative. The data collected in this project suggest that in order to maintain the motivation and enthusiasm of G&T pupils in our schools, we neither have to differentiate the work for them in every lesson nor overload them with extra work. Rather, by ensuring that they are challenged and stimulated in some areas of their school life (be these curriculum-related extension activities, sport, in-school responsibilities, or other extra-curricular activities), G&T pupils can be provided with a healthy balance between challenge and success.

Example 3

What effect does group work have on the learning and motivation of a Year 7 science class? (research completed for a Masters degree in Education)

This research was conducted as a result of the wider demand for effective groupwork, both from an academic perspective – the report 'Beyond 2000' stated that 'young people need some understanding of the social processes internal to science' (Millar and Osborne, 1998: 20) – and from a national outlook – it has been posited that schools needed to '… use more flexible and successful approaches to the grouping of pupils …' (DfEE, 1997: 39). A sequence of Year 7 lessons on forces was taught, each containing a groupwork task. To address the motivation strand, pre- and post-groupwork motivation questionnaires were given. To assess the students' learning, their levelled test results were compared to a previous test on cells, a topic that was taught with no groupwork. During the teaching period, there were weekly discussions with a small group of students to probe their thoughts on the groupwork. It was found that students responded positively to the work initially and overall there were favourable impacts on learning. With time, social factors began to dominate the effective functioning of the groups and the progression slowed. Motivation styles altered as a result of the sequence, with polarized responses. The use of groupwork is advocated, but with an emphasis on careful planning and preparation of the students' social skills in order that they gain fully from collaboration.

Example 4

'The transfer of pupils from primary to secondary school: a case study of a foundation subject – physical education', by Susan Capel, Paula Zwozdiak-Myers and Julia Lawrence, Research in Education (2007)

Results of research to date (e.g. Galton et al., 1999; Schagen and Kerr, 1999) suggest that, although continuity and progression are promoted in National Curriculum documents in England, they are not promoted consistently by schools during the transfer from primary to secondary school. Fourteen secondary school PE heads of department (10 male and four female) in five local education authorities (LEAs) were selected for this research. These 14 heads of department had been identified as being involved in a range of activities to support the transfer of pupils from primary to secondary school in relation to physical education in an earlier part of this study. Interviews were semi-structured and lasted between 40 minutes and one hour. To ensure a consistency of approach, one researcher interviewed all 14 heads of department. This interviewer had taught physical education in secondary schools in England. The interview comprised questions about the perceived importance of the transfer of pupils from primary to secondary schools in physical education; the activities undertaken to support the transfer of pupils from primary to secondary school in physical education and reasons for these; and the factors constraining support for transfer and potential ways to develop and maintain this support. Follow-up questions were asked specific to responses from each head of department. The interviews were recorded on audio-cassette tape and then transcribed. The transcripts were then read in full by two people and the responses were coded. The results of this small-scale qualitative study showed that these 14 heads of department identified that transfer from primary to secondary school was important in physical education. However, results suggested that this was not consistently translated into practice. This was demonstrated by the majority of these heads of department reporting that they had neither formalized nor written their practice into departmental policy. Rather, transfer seemed to be something that they were trying to do, but rather informally.

Example 5

'From "consulting pupils" to "pupils as researchers": a situated case narrative', by Pat Thomson and Helen Gunter, British Educational Research Journal (2006)

Schools in England are now being encouraged to 'personalize' the curriculum and to consult students about teaching and learning. This article reports on an evaluation of one secondary school which is working hard to increase student subject choice, introduce integrated curriculum in the middle years and improve teaching and learning, while maintaining a commitment to inclusive and equitable comprehensive education. The authors worked with a small group of students as consultants to develop a 'student's-eye' set of evaluative categories in a school-wide student survey. They also conducted teacher, student and governor interviews, lesson and meeting observations, and student 'mind-mapping' exercises. The research has highlighted the importance of the processes that the authors used to work jointly with the student research team, and how they moved from pupils-as-consultants to pupils-as-researchers, a potentially more transformative/disruptive practice. Also queried is the notion of 'authentic student voice' as discursive and heterogeneous.

Example 6

'Can research homework provide a vehicle for assessment for learning in science lessons?', by Louise Newby and Mark Winterbottom, Educational Review (2011)

Many English schools have a homework policy which prescribes how much homework should be set for each pupil each week, irrespective of whether it can be made meaningful. Research recommends Assessment for Learning (AfL) as supportive of students' learning, but teachers can find it difficult to incorporate AfL techniques into their practice. This study explores how research homework, undertaken over several weeks, may provide a vehicle for integration of AfL techniques into science lessons at a 13–18 upper school.

Prior to completing homework, students were provided with formative feedback, and given the opportunity to self- and peer-assess their work against assessment criteria. The work was evaluated to examine how students changed their work in response. Students also completed a short questionnaire, which provided a basis for focus group interviews. Findings suggest that research homework, operating alongside AfL techniques, can support students' learning, and that research home-work can support implementation of AfL.

Activity 16.1

1 Categorize each research study above into the different types of case study as outlined in this chapter, and thoroughly examine each project for the ways in which the research was conducted.
2 Devise your own case study, using a topic for exploration that interests you and employing the optimal case study procedure for it.

 ## Key ideas

Case study research is a traditional approach to the study of topics and its goal is to describe the case under investigation as fully and accurately as possible. Researchers have used the case study research method for many years across a variety of disciplines.

Rather than using large samples and following a rigid protocol to examine a limited number of variables, case study methods involve an in-depth, longitudinal examination of a single instance or event – the case. Case studies therefore empha-size detailed contextual analysis of a limited number of events or conditions and their relationships.

Case study research excels at bringing us to an understanding of a complex issue or object and can extend experience or add strength to what is already known through previous research. It can be exploratory, explanatory or descriptive in nature. A typical protocol for a case study is to: determine and define the research questions; select the cases and determine the data-gathering and analysis techniques; prepare to collect the data; collect data in the field; evaluate and analyse the data; and prepare the report.

A frequent criticism of case study methodology is that its dependence on a single case limits its generalizability. Unlike random sample surveys, case studies are not representative of entire populations, although they do not claim to be.

Case studies have been increasingly used in education. In particular, education has embraced the case method for educational evaluation and instructional use in order to develop critical thinking, skills and knowledge.

Reflective questions

1 How have you defined the case boundary?
2 What are the strengths of a case study approach?

Further reading

Eisenhardt, K.M. (1989) 'Building theories from case study research', *The Academy of Management Review*, 14: 532–50.

Flyvbjerg, B. (2006) 'Five misunderstandings about case study research', *Qualitative Inquiry*, 12: 219–45.

Ragin, C.C. and Becker, H.S. (1992) *What is a Case? Exploring the Foundations of Social Inquiry*. Cambridge: Cambridge University Press.

Scherff, L. (2008) 'Disavowed: the stories of two novice teachers', *Teaching and Teacher Education*, 24: 1317–32.

Scholz, R.W. and Tietje, O. (2002) *Embedded Case Study Methods: Integrating Quantitative and Qualitative Knowledge*. Thousand Oaks, CA: Sage.

Singleton, R.A. and Straits, B.C. (2004) *Approaches to Social Research* (3rd edn). Oxford: Oxford University Press.

CHAPTER 17

BUILDING THEORY FROM DATA: GROUNDED THEORY

Keith S. Taber

Chapter overview

This chapter discusses the value and difficulties of an approach to educational enquiry called '**grounded theory**' (GT). It considers the purpose and advantages of this approach, but also why GT is *seldom a sensible option for any student needing to complete a project in a short timescale*. Despite this, there are aspects of the GT approach that can be useful in studies that do not adopt the approach wholesale. It is also important to understand the GT approach when critically evaluating other studies, as many research reports claim to report GT or to use methods drawn from the GT approach.

What is 'grounded' theory?

Grounded theory is an approach to building up theories about educational or other social phenomena. When the complete set of processes is applied, it is a very demanding way of doing research. However, it does offer a system that is designed to develop rigorous theory in contexts where little reliable theory already exists.

> Grounded theory methodology … is a specific, highly developed, rigorous set of procedures for producing formal, substantive theory of social phenomena … Experience with data generates insights, hypotheses, and generative questions that are pursued through further data generation. As tentative answers to questions are developed and concepts are constructed, these constructions are verified through further data collection. (Schwandt, 2001: 110)

GT has been applied to understanding a range of educational phenomena. It is also name-checked in many studies where it may be less clear that the full set of procedures is being applied. As Juliet Corbin has noted:

> a lot of people claim to be doing Grounded Theory studies. But whether or not they are building theory is quite another matter … There is … a lot of work being done all over the world … that claims to be theory that bears no resemblance to theory, Grounded Theory or otherwise. (Quoted in Cisneros-Puebla, 2004: 52)

In practice, then, in education, there are probably many more studies 'informed by' GT than actually reporting fully grounded educational theories.

Examples of educational studies drawing upon GT

In this chapter, three educational studies drawing upon GT will be used as examples.

Example 1: Learning to play the violin

Calissendorff (2006: 84) reports a study into 5-year-olds learning to play the violin, where she used a GT approach to data analysis. She reports her aim as 'to acquire a deeper understanding of how small children learn an instrument in the presence of their parents'. She observed six young children when they attended their music lessons, visited the children's homes, and interviewed parents and the violin teacher.

Example 2: Learning advanced chemistry

In my own doctoral research, I was concerned with why (my) 16–18-year-old students studying chemistry found the topic of chemical bonding so difficult. I wanted to understand their developing thinking about the topic, to see if I could identify any 'learning impediments' that explained why students commonly misunderstood the topic. This study was primarily based around sequences of interviews with about a dozen students.

Example 3: The overrepresentation of minorities referred to special education provision

Harry, Sturges and Klingner (2005: 3) report a study of 'the referral and placement of Black (various ethnicities, such as African-American and Haitian) and Hispanic (various ethnicities, such as Cuban and Nicaraguan) students in special education programmes in a large urban school district' in the USA. The project had three identifiable stages of field research, in a sample of 12 schools that varied in (a) terms of patterns of ethnicities of the students, and (b) rates of referring students for special educational needs provision.

Data and theory

As the name suggests, the outcomes of GT studies are considered to be 'theory'. This means that GT attempts to go beyond the description of events to produce models that can explain what is going on.

> Theory: A set of well-developed concepts related through statements of relationship, which together constitute an integrated framework that can be used to explain or predict phenomena. (Strauss and Corbin, 1998: 15)

Ultimately, 'grounded theorists' look to produce models that are general – that have widespread value beyond the specific research contexts visited in the study. The 'grounded' part of the name refers to the claim that the theories of GT are 'grounded' in the data – that is, they derive from an analysis of empirical evidence collected in the research. Now, we might expect that in educational studies, all research findings should derive from an analysis of data (rather than perhaps guesswork or some magical divination process). Therefore, this reference to grounding theory in data is claiming more than simply that GT is the outcome of empirical research.

The key point is that not just the findings, but also the concepts used in a GT, are said to derive from the analysis of the data, rather than being drawn from previous literature. In a GT context, a concept is 'a pattern that is carefully discovered' by a process defined as 'constant comparing of theoretically sampled data until conceptual saturation' is reached (Glaser, 2002: 4). This particular meaning (explained below) provides the basis of both the strength and some of the challenges of GT research.

Confirmatory versus exploratory studies

There are different ways of characterizing types of research, but one common distinction is between those studies that are intended to be open-ended and those that are testing a pre-specified question (Taber, 2007: 36–42). **Confirmatory studies** set out with an existing hypothesis to be tested (even if it is not always described as a hypothesis). In these studies, existing theory would seem to potentially apply in a new context, and the research tests out the ideas in this context.

For example, the government may produce the guidance that an effective lesson is commonly divided into three parts. (Whether we should consider such a bland statement as 'theory' in any meaningful sense is questionable – but it is an idea most teachers will have been exposed to!) However, no one has ever undertaken any research to evaluate the effectiveness of this lesson structure in your particular Y9 class, in the school where you are teaching. Rather than just accept and adopt this recommendation, you could decide to read up on the reasoning behind it, and then set out to test whether it is a useful approach in your own lessons with this class.

There are lots of well-developed and argued ideas in the educational literature that might lead you to ask 'does that apply here?' or 'will that work here?'

- Should you increase the wait time between asking a question and selecting a respondent?
- Is it useful to identify profiles of learning styles for the students in this class?
- Does organizing students in mixed-ability teams for group work support the weakest and stretch the highest achievers?

The advantage of this type of approach for a student is that there is suitable literature to provide the background reading, and so support the conceptualization of the project (Taber, 2007: 57–61), and – as there is a single, clear, principle research question – there is a firm basis for designing the study.

However, such approaches are also limiting, as they rely upon the available ideas in the literature. They can provide the basis of a very useful exercise in educational enquiry for a student looking for a project. However, they may not always be as useful for a practitioner with a genuine issue deriving from their teaching practice. If you are concerned about the behaviour, or achievement, or engagement of your class, then you will find plenty of suggestions in the research literature for why there might be problems and how you might address them. However, it is always possible that in your particular class there is a specific factor that is fundamental to the problem you have identified, but which may not relate to the findings from previous research. This is where more exploratory ('discovery') approaches are useful. In an exploratory approach, the researcher has identified an issue or context that is worth researching, but does not have a pre-formed hypothesis. The research question is more 'what is going on here?' rather than 'is this an example of X?'; or 'what might be a good way forward here?', rather than, 'will Y work in this context?'.

So, in reporting their study, Harry et al. (2005: 3) take the 'disproportionate placement of minorities in special education' as well established, but explain that 'what continues to be missing from this body of research is an understanding of the motives and pressures that drive decision-making in this area; in other words, the "hows" and "whys" of the process'. GT is the ultimate approach to exploratory research, as it takes the open-ended nature of the study very seriously.

Activity 17.1

Which of the following questions are more suitable starting points for (a) confirmatory studies, and (b) **exploratory (discovery)** research? Try to explain your reasoning:

1 Does setting homework increase test scores?
2 What metacognitive knowledge and skills do students use when studying in my GCSE class?
3 Is this textbook suitable for my class?
4 Do students find groupwork helpful in my classes?
5 Can peer assessment increase student metacognition?
6 Would 'brain-gym' be a useful way of beginning my lessons with less motivated groups?
7 How does the setting of homework influence student perceptions of the subject?
8 What types of starters will be most useful in engaging my students?
9 What kind of interactions occur during group activities in my class?
10 Is the reading age of this text too high for Year 9 students?

(Hint: can you readily rewrite the question as a specific hypothesis to be tested?)

Characteristics of grounded theory

GT studies are characterized by a number of features, which include:

- a delayed literature review
- an **emergent design**
- flexible and responsive ('**theoretical**') sampling
- an iterative approach to analysis ('constant comparison')
- an open timeline for the research ('**theoretical saturation**').

Each of these features is important in a full GT study, in order to lead to theory that can be considered to be a valid model. However, as will become clear, these features also make a full GT approach potentially inappropriate for any student (or other researcher) who needs to produce a project report or thesis within a limited time-span!

Activity 17.2

Consider the expectations on a practitioner researcher when charged with a research project by the department/school, or setting out on research to support a higher-degree dissertation. Why might it be difficult to persuade a head of department/head teacher/university supervisor that a GT approach should be adopted?

What are grounded theory 'methods'?

GT is not an approach that defines a specific set of methods that must be used (Glaser, 1978, 2002; Glaser and Holton, 2004). GT studies tend to produce data sets that are largely (but not always exclusively) qualitative, but may involve various types of interviews, observations, questionnaires and so forth. So it is not the data-collection techniques that define a GT study, but rather the way they are selected and organized 'for collecting and analysing qualitative data to construct theories "grounded" in the data themselves' (Charmaz, 2012: 4).

Induction: the context of discovery

To understand the logic of a GT approach, we need to consider 'the problem of **induction**' (discussed in Chapter 18). In a confirmatory approach, we start our research with existing concepts to apply to our data: concepts that have operational definitions. In other words, if we are testing a hypothesis about learning styles, we will have developed a conceptualization of the topic before designing our study (Taber, 2007: 57), and our data-collection instrumentation and analytical frameworks will then be designed around an understanding of what we are taking learning styles to be, and how we will recognize and identify them.

However, a GT study that explored the question of *whether* learners in a class exhibited 'learning styles' would not apply pre-existing definitions of how learning styles can be identified, or start with assumptions about which potential 'styles' might be uncovered. Rather, the GT approach would attempt to build up a model from the data collected, starting from a very open question (e.g. 'do these students have preferred ways of learning, and – if so – can I characterize them?').

Answering such questions means being able to spot the patterns in data, without filtering that data through the biases of our existing knowledge and understanding. Yet, if all our perceptions are 'theory-laden' (we cannot help but see the world through our existing conceptual frameworks), then this is an impossible task! There is no logical solution to this problem, although one idea that has been found useful is to attempt to separate the context of discovery from the **context of justification**.

The context of discovery refers to how we came by an idea. As much of our thinking is subconscious and not open to introspection, we cannot ever be sure how we came up with an idea.

> Grounded theory arrives at relevance, because it allows core problems and processes to emerge. (Glaser, 1978: 5)

When we examine data, and spot a pattern, we can never be sure how much of that pattern derives from us rather than the data. Human brains are exceptionally good at finding patterns that have no basis in the external world: as when children see intruders in the shadows at night, or when a cloud is said to be the shape of a weasel (Hamlet) or of Ireland (Kate Bush).

Post-inductive resonance?

When I was undertaking my own research into student thinking about chemistry, I experienced some 'aha' moments where suddenly I had insight into patterns in my data. After 'immersing' myself in data (listening to interviews, transcribing, reading, coding), I would find I could suddenly interpret what a student was telling me. I moved instantly from recognizing that a student was 'misunderstanding' what they had been taught, to understanding how they understood differently. This process of making sense of how another understands was largely a subconscious process, leading to the abrupt change in my conscious thinking (Koestler, 1982). Although I was grateful for the insights, I was concerned with how I would justify them in my thesis – a report where I had to argue a case for my findings.

However, it was not the process of insight I had to justify. Rather, those insights had to be tested further against data, to see whether they 'resonated' (or 'fitted'). This would mean revisiting the data sets to see if the new interpretations made sense of other comments the student had made in related contexts. The new interpretation was also used during subsequent interviews, where it was possible to check my own interpretation more directly by asking the student whether I had grasped their way of thinking.

As we cannot control the subconscious aspects of pattern recognition, we have to justify our findings not in terms of how we came up with an idea, but rather how we then tested it to ensure it had a good match with the data (Medawar, 1990). This is sometimes referred to as the 'context of justification'. We can have our good ideas in the bath, in dreams, or perhaps even inspired by the patterns we see in tea leaves: what matters is how we rigorously test their relevance to the data.

GT research therefore uses an approach to encourage the 'induction' process (of having the ideas), followed by rigorous testing of those ideas to ensure a good fit with the data – this has been called 'post-inductive resonance' (Taber, 1997).

An overview of the grounded theory approach

Washing the mind clean

The characteristics of GT research are intended to support the induction and testing of ideas that best fit the data that can be collected. As 'it is critical in GT methodology to avoid unduly influencing the pre-conceptualization of the research through extensive reading in the substantive area' (Glaser and Holton, 2004: 46), the literature review is often delayed (rather than being carried out before the research starts). This is to avoid findings from previous related research 'contaminating' the researcher's thinking about their data, so they can 'enter the research setting with as few predetermined ideas as possible' (Glaser, 1978: 2–3). This is said to allow the researcher to retain **theoretical sensitivity** to their data.

In practice, researchers normally bring a wide range of potentially relevant ideas from their previous training, reading and experience – so delaying the literature search is seen as necessary but not sufficient. Researchers are advised to try to 'wash their minds clean' before entering the research context (Measor and Woods, 1991). However, there is a limit to how viable this is, and clearly concepts and ideas from other related research could prove very useful – providing 'points of departure for developing, rather than limiting, our ideas' (Charmaz, 2012: 30). GT experts disagree among themselves on how strict one should be about this point – and on the extent to which it is acceptable to adopt and adapt concepts from previous work when they seem to fit our current context.

Calissendorff (2006: 90) reports that in her study, 'the formation of the core category owed a great deal to [a previously published] learning style model'. Although she drew upon an existing model to organize her findings, she *adapted* the existing idea so that although the final version 'owes a debt' (2006: 92) to the published model, it was modified to give a model 'which is based on factors comprising elements that have proved to be of importance to the children when learning the violin' (2006: 91).

Immersion and emergence

A GT does not have a fixed design, as the researcher has to be able to make decisions about data collection as the research proceeds. In GT, there are no distinct steps of data collection and analysis. Rather, data analysis begins as soon as data is collected, and informs decisions about further data collection. Early ideas deriving from data analysis suggest *who* to talk to next, *what* to observe, *what questions* should be asked, etc. This is called 'theoretical' sampling, as the sampling decisions are guided by the ongoing development of theory. (The term 'theoretical' occurs a lot in GT!)

> Theoretical sampling is the process of data collection for generating theory whereby the analyst jointly collects, codes and analyses the data and decides what data to collect next and where to find them, in order to develop the theory as it emerges. (Glaser and Holton, 2004: 51)

GT analysis uses an iterative process of coding ('the analytic process through which data are fractured, conceptualized, and integrated to form theory', Strauss and Corbin, 1998: 3) with several stages. Initial analysis ('open coding') is, at a very descriptive level, breaking down data (such as interview transcripts) into manageable chunks using '**in vivo**' codes. In other words, if your students describe the use of statistics in biology as 'sums', then that might be a good label to use to identify (code) those segments of an interview transcript. If your colleagues knowingly refer to vocational courses as 'vacational', then that may be a useful descriptive code.

As data is analysed, the researcher attempts to build up a set of codes that collectively 'fit' all the data. As new codes are generated, previously analysed data is re-examined to see whether the new codes could be a better fit than some of the previous codes. This process of 'constant comparison' continues through the research, at all levels of the analysis, 'forcing' 'the analyst into confronting similarities, differences and degrees in consistency of meaning' (Glaser and Holton, 2004: 58).

In her study of children learning to play the violin, Calissendorff (2006: 85) referred to following 'leads'. For her, a lead 'derives from an interesting event, statement or observation' and is 'followed up, and eventually either forms a category of its own, [or] is placed within an existing category or is rejected'. The analyst also tries to build up concepts or constructs that can start to describe the data at more theoretical levels: applying to *groups of codes* or showing how different codes are linked. Gradually, a scheme for making sense of the data is developed. At first, the scheme may seem to have ambiguities or incoherencies and gaps. Where the scheme does not fit the data perfectly, it is considered to need further adjustment – theoretical sampling and constant comparison being employed until 'the code is sharpened to achieve its best fit while further properties are generated until the code is verified and saturated' (Glaser and Holton, 2004: 58).

For example, consider a GT study to explore your students' experiences of homework. Your analysis may have revealed, among other things, that:

(a) there seem to be gender differences among the attitudes to, and preferred forms of, homework; and
(b) some students find internet-based work very motivating.

However, if you realize that the only students who have mentioned the internet in interviews are boys, then that may (though not necessarily) be because the girls tend to be less enthusiastic about such activities. Theoretical sampling would indicate who you should talk to next, and what you should ask them, to find out whether internet-based homework is one of the aspects where there is a gender difference.

Harry et al. (2005) describe their analytical processes in some depth, as they move from open codes, to categories, to themes – which are then further tested before being interrelated and linked into a final theory. One of the consequences of such an approach is that a researcher cannot plan a definitive timeline for the research in advance, as the fieldwork will not be 'finished' until all such issues are resolved and the final model matches all the data without leaving any gaps.

Core variables and theoretical saturation

One aim of a GT analysis is to identify any '**core variable**', 'which appears to account for most of the variation around the concern or problem that is the focus of the study' (Glaser and Holton, 2004: 54), and that can act as the key idea around which to organize the theory.

In my doctoral research, I collected data relating to a wide range of ideas students used to discuss and explain many different examples. However, eventually, I was able to identify one notion (or 'misconception') that all my informants used as a central explanatory principle in chemistry, and which could be seen as a central node for the wider web of ideas (Taber, 1998). This single idea could be linked to a range of learning difficulties in the topic.

The point at which no further data collection is needed (because all new data fit into the model without having to make any more adjustments) is referred to as 'theoretical saturation': 'the point in category development at which no new properties, dimensions, or relationships emerge during analysis' (Strauss and Corbin, 1998: 143).

Only at this point is there a grounded theory suitable for writing up and reporting. For some strict GT adherents, it is only at this point that the formal literature review is undertaken, so that the write-up can offer comparisons with previously published research.

This brief account has not detailed the stages used in a full GT study, but illustrates the iterative nature of the process that allows the researcher to claim a theory that is 'grounded' in the data.

Difficulties of a GT approach in student projects

When a full GT approach is applied to an educational issue, it has considerable potential to offer insight and improve our understanding of that issue. However, the potential problems of using such an emergent and open-ended approach in student projects (with deadlines, and supervisors demanding literature reviews and research designs) should also be clear. A student is often told that before planning their project, they must review the literature to find out what is already known about the topic. This provides the 'conceptualization' used to start planning research, and to ensure their research report (usually written when it is too late to do any more fieldwork) will not appear naive or ill-informed. Yet, 'to undertake an extensive review of literature before the emergence of a core category violates the basic premise of GT – that being, the theory emerges from the data not from extant theory' (Glaser and Holton, 2004: 46).

Similarly, supervisors commonly require students to have produced a research design, with a plan for how their research will be carried out, *before* approving the fieldwork. Yet, in GT, 'beyond the decisions concerning initial collection of data, further collection cannot be planned in advance of the emerging theory' (Glaser and Holton, 2004: 51).

It is not only students who are required to offer designs for their studies – this is usually the case when professional researchers seek sponsorship for studies: the funding body generally expects plans that include details of the sample, and the nature and schedule of data collection to be undertaken. Harry et al. (2005: 12) attempted to 'design' their study to meet funding requirements, but to provide phases of data collection that would allow flexibility for a GT approach. However, they faced considerable difficulties in following the principles of theoretical sampling and constant comparison across the full sample of schools they had told their sponsors they would include, and reflected that 'in retrospect, we conclude that we could have achieved a more refined analysis with a sample half this size'.

Finally, students may have very limited timelines for their research, and will usually be expected to provide their supervisors with a schedule for the research that is clearly viable in the time available. Yet, the GT approach 'requires that the analyst takes whatever amount of quality time that is required to do the discovery' (Glaser and Holton, 2004: 60). Again, this limitation does not only apply to student projects. Harry et al. (2005: 12), reporting on their funded project undertaken by a team of researchers, note that 'the complexity of the data set made it impossible for us to pursue the numerous possible connections between all the data within the three-year timeframe of the study'.

The substantive and the general: testing the theory

The research by Harry and colleagues was undertaken over a sample of schools in a district. They summarized their GT thus:

> A complex set of negative influences contribute to the overrepresentation of minorities in special education. Predominant contributors are the assumption of intrinsic deficit and the requirement for a disability categorization; inequitable opportunity to learn, resulting from poor teacher quality in lower-SES [socio-economic status] schools and higher standards in higher-SES schools; negative biases against families perceived as dysfunctional; external pressure from high-stakes testing; and subjectivity in referral and assessment practices. (Harry et al., 2005: 6)

Although these findings all derive from one sample of schools, in one school district, the careful selection of a diverse range of schools suggests these findings could well have wider application. (Although, of course, any criteria used to form such a sample imply some preconceived ideas about the range of factors that may be significant.)

However, small-scale studies usually need to have a more specific focus, and be concerned with issues or educational problems in a particular context. So although Calissendorff

(2006) was interested in 'young children' learning to play an instrument, her theory is grounded in data from just six children attending particular violin lessons. Her theory is substantially based on that context, and although grounded in data, it cannot be *assumed* to apply elsewhere (Taber, 2007: 111–16).

However, as theory, the outcomes are suitable either for further phases of GT research (Glaser, 1978), for the theoretical sampling of other contexts, or for 'testing' as hypotheses in confirmatory studies (Strauss and Corbin, 1998: 213). My doctoral project was based upon the in-depth study of a modest number of students who studied chemistry in the college where I taught at the time. They each had unique 'conceptual frameworks' for thinking about the subjects, but there were some common ways of thinking among the sample that seemed to be acting as barriers to the intended learning on the course.

It was possible to conjecture that some of these ideas might be common among the wider population of students studying the subject at this level. Survey instruments were designed to test out this idea (confirmatory research), and in this way it was possible to generalize well beyond the original sample (Taber, 2000). Whether this is seen as a further stage of GT, or the use of GT as a starting point for a different type of research is a moot point (the founders of GT, Glaser and Strauss, would probably have taken different views), either way this is an example of how different types of research techniques can play their part in a *programme* of research (see Chapter 18) developing our understanding of an issue.

Activity 17.3

Think about issues that you would like to explore in your classroom context. Identify an issue or problem that you feel would lend itself to GT (issue A), and one where you feel GT would be inappropriate (issue B). Why would GT be more useful in researching one issue than the other? The notion of exploratory vs. confirmatory research may be useful here. Think about the key features of GT discussed in this chapter. How would you go about developing GT to understand and explain issue A in your classroom: how would you operationalize such a study in practice? What might be the challenges that you would have to face?

Borrowing from GT

GT was developed at a time when exploratory qualitative studies were not widely accepted as being 'valid', and Glaser and Strauss (1967) produced an account justifying how such research could lead to a theory for understanding social phenomena that retained 'scientific' rigour. Since GT was 'discovered', the research community has relaxed its view of the nature of scientific research (see Chapter 18), and a range of **interpretive** approaches to enquiry have become widely accepted as the means to generate authentic knowledge. Some commentators have implied that GT is now rather anachronistic (e.g. Thomas and James, 2006).

Despite this, GT continues to be a popular approach – certainly in terms of the extent to which it is 'name-checked' in research studies. A full GT study is a demanding, open-ended form of research that offers potential difficulties to the experienced researcher, and is a brave undertaking indeed for a research novice! However, there is much to learn from the GT approach with its emphasis on developing theory rather than just offering descriptive accounts. In particular, the type of iterative approach to data analysis exemplified by the constant comparison method has been widely borrowed by researchers looking to make sense of complex data sets. Such an approach will at least ensure that findings accurately reflect the full range of data collected. However, when such an approach is used to analyse data *after* it has all been collected (as in a standard research design), there is no opportunity to refine and 'plug' the resulting analytical scheme through theoretical sampling. This makes theoretical saturation unlikely, so that findings cannot be seen as a completed theoretical model. However, perhaps a pragmatist (such as a student with a deadline) must sometimes settle for a model that is a provisional best fit, and can at least be presented as a starting point for further research.

 Key ideas

This chapter has introduced grounded theory (GT), an approach to social research that offers a rigorous set of procedures for developing theory to explain educational (and other social) issues based upon principles of:

- the development of theoretical sensitivity by close and open-minded attention to data sets
- data collection within an emergent design, that employs theoretical sampling
- data analysis that starts from open coding and by the constant comparison method moves to the identification of a core variable
- only being considered complete when further theoretical sampling shows that the theory is saturated.

The demands of GT approaches make it a risky choice for novice researchers. However, an understanding of GT is important when reading accounts of educational research that report GT, and the (more common) studies that claim to draw upon aspects of the GT methodology. GT also offers a model for data analysis in 'discovery' or 'exploratory' studies where previous research does not suggest a suitable analytical framework for interrogating the data.

Reflective question

How much time will you have available to you? Will this be sufficient to enable you to carry out a deep GT study?

Further reading

Charmaz, K. (1995) 'Grounded theory', in J.A. Smith, R. Harrè, R. and L. Van Langenhove (eds), *Rethinking Methods in Psychology.* London: Sage. pp. 27–49.

Charmaz, K.C. (2012) *Constructing Grounded Theory: A Practical Guide through Qualitative Analysis* (2nd edn). London: Sage.

Strauss, A. and Corbin, J. (1998) *Basics of Qualitative Research: Techniques and Procedures for Developing Grounded Theory*. Thousand Oaks, CA: Sage.

Section 4
PARADIGMS

This section will delve deeply into two distinct and important philosophical approaches to understanding the world. Chapter 18 starts with a 'post-positivist', 'scientific' approach, discussing the interaction between empirical evidence and theory. Chapter 19 follows on with a deep discussion of three broad streams of thought – symbolic interactionism, phenomenology and heremeneutics – under the heading of interpretivism.

CHAPTER 18

BEYOND POSITIVISM: 'SCIENTIFIC' RESEARCH INTO EDUCATION

Keith S. Taber

Chapter overview

The focus of this chapter is on 'post-positivism' as a guide for carrying out research in education. The chapter will explore what is meant by post-positivism, and how some forms of educational research may be seen as 'post-positivist' – and so, by extension, a form of 'scientific' research. This is an issue you should take seriously, as those carrying out research in educational contexts, and wishing to have that research acknowledged formally (perhaps by publication, perhaps by a university award), are expected to position themselves in terms of what are sometimes labelled 'paradigmatic' commitments.

What is a paradigm?

The term **paradigm** is often used to describe approaches to *educational* enquiry, although it first came into heavy usage after Kuhn's (1996/1962) seminal work on the nature of *scientific* progress. Kuhn believed that science comprised two types of scientific activity: 'normal' science and 'revolutionary' science. As the name may suggest, 'normal' science is what is going on most of the time. In Kuhn's terms, many scientists will spend their entire careers working within an established paradigm or 'disciplinary matrix'. Kuhn used these terms to describe the mindset and rules (maybe including some unwritten, unspoken and not openly acknowledged) which apply to scientists working within a particular field. The paradigm, or disciplinary matrix:

- forms the theoretical basis of the sub-branch of science
- is accepted by all the workers in the field
- determines what is judged to be the subject of legitimate research in the field
- determines the procedures, rules and standards that apply in the field.

Although Kuhn developed his ideas from looking at the history of scientific ideas, the notion of a paradigm has been adopted in *social science*. Here, however, paradigms seldom have the clear hegemony over a field that Kuhn suggested existed in the 'natural' sciences. For Kuhn, paradigms in science ruled – at least until there was a revolution when a new paradigm would usurp the previous one. An example might be ideas about a geocentric universe being replaced by a heliocentric model. However, revolutions were rare, and normal science was the norm!

In Kuhn's model, different paradigms are potentially 'incommensurable' (as they did not share basic commitments, for example to the definitions of fundamental terms, making meaningful dialogue difficult), so that communities of researchers worked together within a single paradigm. In the social sciences, however, it is quite possible for distinct paradigms to co-exist without dominating their field.

A paradigm may be considered as the 'highest' level at which thinking about research occurs (Taber, 2007: 33). If we think of research as being a kind of business (in the widest sense), then paradigmatic choices are made at the 'executive' level. Paradigmatic commitments are reflected in research design: they constrain the selection of appropriate research *strategy* (methodology), which in turn channels the selection of appropriate *tactics* – the techniques for data collection and data analysis.

However, it is important to realize that this is not simply a matter of practical considerations: the adoption of: a paradigm is *principled*. It relates to fundamental notions about the nature of: (a) what is being researched; and (b) the knowledge that may be produced in the research.

The nature of paradigmatic commitments in educational research

Consideration of the 'philosophy' of research is often broken down into the ontological, the epistemological and the methodological.

Ontology concerns beliefs about the nature of the things we are researching, e.g.:

- What kind of things exist in the world?
- Is there a common reality that we all share?

Epistemology (our theory of knowledge) concerns beliefs about the kind of knowledge it is possible to acquire about those things, e.g.:

- Is it possible to obtain absolute knowledge of the world?
- Can we find out some things which we can be sure are 'true'?

Methodology concerns how we go about acquiring that knowledge.

The first two considerations may seem a little obscure, but actually they are extremely important. A researcher needs to have thought carefully about the ontological and epistemological issues that relate to their research, because the researcher's beliefs here will *influence* research decisions.

Activity 18.1

Consider two examples – how would you go about undertaking school-based research into:

(a) how student ability influences GCSE examination performance?
(b) bullying occurring in a tutor group?

The nature of ability

If we consider how student 'ability' influences GCSE examination performance, then we can readily appreciate why ontological beliefs influence research. Anyone researching 'ability' has to have a view of what 'ability' is (see Chapter 1). For example – is 'ability':

- something that is fixed, or that can be developed?
- a unitary quality, that can be measured on a single scale (e.g. IQ), or is it the overview of a set of largely independent abilities to be measured on a range of scales, *or* is it a multifaceted and complex set of interlinked factors such that it is better described (than measured)?
- something that can be meaningfully considered in isolation, *or* can we only consider a person's ability(ies) in terms of their potential to perform in a particular task context?

We might even question whether individual ability is actually a meaningful construct, or whether it is better understood as what can be achieved in a particular social context, under conditions that offer a suitable balance of support and challenge. For example, consider Vygotsky's (1986/1934) suggestion that finding out about a learner's ZPD (zone of proximal development) is more informative than finding out what they can actually do unaided (zone of actual development; ZAD). The type of entity one believes 'ability' to be determines what it makes sense to attempt to find out about it. If we do not believe that ability is a meaningful construct at all, then we could not research it.

There are many examples of constructs used in education that may not be widely accepted as reflecting the 'same' (or any) thing.

Activity 18.2

Consider the following notions – to what extent can they be clearly defined? Pick three examples and attempt to write a definition of what each term means. If you can, ask a colleague to independently define the same terms. To what extent do you share an 'objective' meaning for these terms?

- bullying
- special needs students
- students with specific learning difficulties
- disillusioned students
- gifted students
- challenging students
- a good lesson
- effective school management
- a supporting Head of Department
- a good classroom atmosphere
- poor attendance
- ... for a member of staff
- a good homework record
- a suitable professional development activity
- lively staffroom banter
- unprofessional behaviour.

An ontological question: what kind of thing is bullying?

Let us consider the first example on the list. Research into bullying could look at a number of aspects of the topic. For example, it might be possible to explore *how much* bullying is going on – but only *if* we can agree on:

- a *definition* of what is (and is not) counted as bullying
- what indicators would enable us to be confident when we have *identified* an incident.

Alternatively, we might wish to explore *why* bullying occurs. This would assume that bullying was the type of phenomenon that had *causes* (an ontological assumption), and that such causes could be clearly identified (an epistemological assumption).

If we did not believe that bullying had causes, then there would be no sense in attempting to investigate what the causes might be. If we do believe there are causes of bullying, but do not believe it is possible to establish reliable knowledge about these causes, then there would be no sense in asking *which* methodologies might allow us to discover them.

It could be argued that we have to believe in bullying, as it is the topic of much literature and concern, so clearly must exist in some sense. In the same way, the following entities clearly exist in some sense, as they are commonly referred to, discussed, invoked, etc.:

- fairies
- Superman
- bog-standard comprehensives.

I would suggest that the existence of fairies as something that we can imagine and discuss does not require the existence of fairies in the 'real' world (cf. Popper, 1979). Fairies can populate your imagination even when you do not think they could exist at the bottom of the garden.

However, if some other people give fairies the ontological status of physical beings (i.e. believe that fairies exist as 'real' creatures), then that belief can have effects *regardless* of whether we accept their ontology.

And if this discussion of fairies seems a little obscure, then the same point can be made by substituting fairies with the devil; God; evil; heaven and hell; America as the great Satan; the divine right of kings; destiny; the superiority of the white 'race'; 'naturally' distinct roles for men and women; a fetus as a human being (or not); IQ; giftedness; genius; dyslexia; or many other examples where different people would assign varying ontological status.

We might believe that there is no such thing as bullying per se, but rather that bullying is a construct that has different meanings for different groups. For example, teachers may have an understanding of what bullying is, that leads to the identification of bullies and victims. Those they identify as 'bullies' (or even 'victims') may have very different views of what bullying is, and may exclude themselves from being bullies (or victims). A pupil may consider themselves a victim of bullying, without anyone else considering this to be so. Unless we believe there is a *privileged* view (e.g. that bullying exists, and it is what teachers *believe* it is, regardless of the views of those that then become labelled as bullies or victims), then we are not able to investigate something that has objective existence. This is an ontological issue.

If we take the view that 'bullying' is not a phenomenon that exists in the world as such, but rather a socially constructed notion that allows different observers to construe events in different ways, then we cannot expect research to offer unproblematic answers to questions such as 'how much bullying is going on here?', or 'what are the causes of bullying in this class?'. If 'bullying' does not have an objective meaning, then there is no clear corpus of events about which we might seek objective knowledge.

We might instead ask questions that lead to different *forms* of knowledge: knowledge about the way the notion of 'bullying' is *construed* by different actors in a social context, e.g. teachers and students. Some of these individuals may well construe themselves as bullies or victims (or protectors against bullying), or construe others as bullies or victims (or protectors against bullying), but these labels and the incidents that lead to them will be construed differently by the different actors. It may be sensible to ask what the different actors see as the causes of bullying, or as the causes of incidents that others identify as bullying. However, *knowledge of people's beliefs* about events is a different kind of knowledge to *knowledge about events* themselves.

Why is it important for researchers to take up a position on such issues?

Particular ontological and epistemological commitments underpin any particular study. When reading a study about ability, bullying, classroom atmosphere, effective teaching, student learning, etc., it is important to appreciate the kind of entities the author is writing about: things that can be objectively defined; or cultural entities which are subject to shifts in meaning; or the personal understandings of individuals.

It is also important to appreciate how researchers view the type of knowledge that they are reporting on. An account of bullying in one school class may well offer some tentative explanations of the causes of *that* bullying. If the research was designed to offer a detailed account of one context, it might help us to understand that context, but we cannot consider that the causes of bullying identified may be taken as 'the causes of bullying'. The research may indeed offer insights to other contexts, but a research design that seeks contextualized knowledge of a particular instance cannot be *assumed* to offer general knowledge outside of that research context (Taber, 2007: 111–16).

Educational research paradigms

At an introductory level, we normally think of most educational research studies as fitting within one of two general categories (Taber, 2007: 33), characterized as:

- positivistic, nomothetic and confirmatory; or
- interpretivist, idiographic and discovery.

Positivist is usually taken as a synonym for 'scientific', so that educational research that is considered positivistic is usually considered to be modelled on natural science, and is sometimes simplistically identified with the 'ideal' of 'the randomised controlled experiment or field trial' (Phillips, 2005: 578).

Positivistic or interpretivist?

Research based on the assumption that it is *in principle* possible to find absolute knowledge is seen as positivist. Research that is based on a view that all knowledge is based on interpretation (for which there is no final arbiter) is seen as interpretivist.

Nomothetic or idiographic?

Research which sets out to establish general laws about what is 'normal' is sometimes labelled **nomothetic**. Research that explores the specific nature of individual cases is described as **idiographic**.

Confirmatory or discovery?

Research that tests pre-determined hypotheses is referred to as confirmatory, whereas open-ended enquiry that explores a situation in terms of the categories that are grounded in the data collected are labelled as discovery (see Chapter 17). These two research approaches are often presented as being competing paradigms (Phillips, 2005), as 'an intellectual either/or situation' (Reynolds, 1991: 194), so that 'researchers with different purposes ... tend to see the others as engaged in the same enterprise as themselves, but simply doing it badly' (Hammersley, 1993: xix).

If we accept this notion of education researchers having to choose to work within one or other paradigm, then the choice is something of a stark one – between studies that produce general decontextualized findings, that are usually bound to (and so are dependent upon) the theoretical assumptions the researchers used to design their study, and studies that produce detailed studies of very specific educational contexts, that cannot be assumed to apply to any other context (Taber, 2007).

Phillips (2005: 584) argues that in the USA, government pressure, through the criteria used to fund research, favours research that reflects the positivistic 'gold standard' of the controlled experiment, while 'qualitative case studies, mixed-methods research and ethnographies are beyond the pale'. By such standards, most practitioner research would be considered 'beyond the pale'.

Luckily, some observers (e.g. Carr and Kemmis, 1986: 105) do not think that 'scientific explanation and interpretative understanding are mutually exclusive categories'. Biddle and Anderson (1986) have argued for an integrated, broader notion of how we can come to new knowledge in the social sciences (such as education).

Below it will be suggested that what is a referred to as a 'post-positivist' view can certainly encompass such a broad range of research, by offering a more informed view of how science proceeds (Phillips, 2005). Before we look at this issue, we need to consider two types of 'complications' that make educational research difficult.

Two problems for a positivistic educational science

This post-positivist view is welcome, as in practice very little educational research can meet the 'gold standard' of the controlled experiment that characterizes a positivist paradigm.

Complications of researching educational contexts: the role of the researcher

Positivistic scientific research attempts to be *objective*. This means that, in principle, observers could be interchanged without changing research findings. We should be able to substitute one qualified and skilled researcher for another in carrying out the data collection and analysis without changing the findings of a study. The individual who manipulates the apparatus and the materials is assumed not to interact with them in a way that could be seen as 'personal'.

The way that metals expand on heating, or wires stretch when loaded, or solutes dissolve in solvents, is not dependent upon who heated, stretched or mixed them. New results in natural science are only widely accepted once the work has been replicated by scientists working in other laboratories. A procedure has to be specified closely enough for any competent scientist to demonstrate the same findings.

Social science research, such as educational research, it is argued, is different: it *does* matter who the researcher is. Two different researchers may get very different responses when asking a child why he engages in disruptive behaviour (just as two different teachers may get very different responses). So often in social research, the researcher interacts with the informant(s) in such a way that the data that is constructed is a co-production. A different co-producer will co-produce a different co-production, and so different data will be constructed.

So, if our 'demarcation criteria' for what counts as scientific work is based on whether we could substitute another competent researcher, then much social (including educational) research *cannot* be seen as scientific.

Complications of researching educational contexts: the complexity of the phenomena

A second major complication of educational research concerns the complexity of social phenomena (such as classroom teaching). Science is (sometimes!) able to use a controlled experiment by isolating the various factors that are believed to be the possible causes of or influences on some phenomenon; keeping them constant; and then varying a single factor ('variable') to see what effect that change has. If we get two different outcomes when we have two situations, which are *absolutely identical in all but one respect*, then that difference may be assumed to be responsible for the different outcome. This approach is based on a very important (ontological) assumption: that the world has a kind of regularity in which exactly replicating conditions leads to the same outcomes. This is taken for granted (i.e. is a paradigmatic commitment) in scientific work.

In education, we are seldom able to study phenomena in this way. Even when ethical considerations allow us to manipulate a situation, it is very unlikely we can ever compare perfectly matched cases, or have a single relevant factor that is different between the cases. An additional complication in educational research is memory. Often in the physical sciences we can return a test object to its original conditions to then look at the effect of different conditions. Unhelpfully (for researchers), we cannot assume that a student returns to their initial state after some form of educational experience, even if their test results suggest this is sometimes the case!

Three problems for a positivist natural science

So, educational research does not often match up to the ideal of the experimental model in science. We can seldom undertake educational research that allows us to draw simple conclusions from carefully controlled experiments. However, the assumption that science has a method that leads to absolute (positive) knowledge of the world is now generally considered to be naive and unsupportable (Phillips and Burbules, 2000).

The experimental method is often presented as a way of uncovering true knowledge of the world: by planning our experiments logically, carefully collecting sufficient data, and then applying our rational faculty to empirical evidence to prove (or otherwise) scientific hypotheses. This is a gross simplification and misrepresentation of how science works, that unfortunately has been encouraged by the impoverished image of the nature of science commonly reflected in school science (Taber, 2008).

Here I will consider three particular difficulties with the assumption that science can offer absolute knowledge, each pertinent to considering whether educational research can be classed as 'scientific'.

The problem of induction

The first issue is the '**problem of induction**'. The natural sciences were long considered to be inductive, i.e. to work by 'that process of collecting general truths from the examination of particular facts' (Whewell, 1976/1857: 5). In his history of the 'inductive sciences', Whewell, who is credited with coining the term 'scientist', suggested that this process of forming general rules 'is so far familiar to men's minds that, without here entering into further explanation, its nature will be understood sufficiently to prepare the reader to *recognise* the exemplification of such a process' (Whewell, 1976/1857: 9). Avoiding 'further explanation' might be considered wise, as although science seemed to depend upon generalization, there is no logically watertight argument to show how one could ever be certain of any general statements based on evidence from only some particular examples.

A famous example concerned swans, and the general statement ('truth') that 'all swans are white'. This generalization was based on empirical evidence, i.e. that no one had ever observed a swan that was *not* white! This did not, however, prove that a non-white swan would never be found … indeed, while this example was being discussed in Europe, the black swans in Australia went about their business as yet unobserved by Western scientists. So science may tell us (as a matter of fact) that copper will conduct electricity, that ice will melt at 0°C, that penguins hatch from eggs, or that the sun will rise tomorrow, but the 'problem of induction' was that no one could explain how we could possibly be sure of any of these things simply based on observations of only some of the copper, ice, penguins or tomorrows that have existed and will exist.

Karl Popper (a former school teacher) suggested instead that science works through a process of testing hypotheses, based on the attempt to exclude possibilities by *falsification* (Popper, 1959/1934).

Science does not produce absolute knowledge, but makes progress through the formation of hypotheses that are **falsifiable**, and preferably bold (not just predicting the obvious), and then attempting to prove them wrong. Scientific knowledge is tentative, and open to review as more evidence comes in. So even the experimental method, the 'gold standard' for research, does not automatically offer generalizable objective knowledge.

> The fundamental difference between positivism and postpositivism is this: … postpositivists are united in their adherence to **fallibilism** – the idea that all scientific knowledge is potentially subject to the discovery of error, and thus should be regarded as provisional. (Swann, 2003: 253–4)

The problem of theory-ladenness

This leads to the question of what *justifies* scientists in telling us that copper will conduct electricity, that ice will melt at 0°C, that penguins hatch from eggs, that the sun will rise

tomorrow or that swans are birds with white feathers. The answer is that these generalizations are as dependent upon theory as observation. Samples of copper or ice
behave in certain ways under certain conditions. Theories are developed that are able
to offer explanations or models of how the behaviour depends upon the conditions. It
is these theories, these models of what is going on, that allow scientists to predict what
will happen to *other* samples of copper or ice.

One observation can never of itself lead to a certain prediction. But observations lead
to theories, which lead to predictions that can be used to test the theories. The theories
are not 'proved' by testing (another white swan proves little) but may be falsified this way
(a black swan needs to be explained if we believe that all swans are white). So science is
not about collecting 'facts' or finding 'truth', but developing theories and explanations,
and then identifying related issues and problems worthy of researching to test and refine
the theory.

As Swann points out: 'This conception of science is no less applicable to the study of
human social endeavours, such as education, than it is to the study of natural phenomena' (Swann, 2003: 255). 'Science' then is a body of knowledge, but not a body of facts
or truths – rather, it is a body of conceptual knowledge (based around concepts developed by humans), that is, of theoretical knowledge. It is objective knowledge, but not
absolute: it is always tentative and provisional. Despite that, the methods of science
allow scientists to claim *reliable* knowledge (Ziman, 1991) – knowledge that we can
have confidence in acts as a reliable basis for prediction and action.

Popper offered falsification as the basis of progress in science: that science proceeded by cycles of conjecture and refutation (the '**hypothetico-deductive method**').
But Popper was aware that this was not a simple matter. As scientific knowledge is
theoretical, refutation may sometimes be avoided by simply changing definition. As a
trivial example, if the concept of whiteness is seen as central to the concept of swan,
then it is not possible to have a black swan. In this circumstance, a naturalist exploring
Australia might well see a 'black, swan-like bird', but could not see a black swan. By
definition, the 'black, swan-like bird' would be considered as something other than a
swan. In this case, the black swan was accepted (there were considered to be other
aspects of swanness that are more central than the colour of the plumage). However,
it is said that when Cook first arrived in Australia, the indigenous population did not
'see' the ships approaching shore until they got very close, because they had no past
experience that offered a conceptual framework for making sense of their perceptions. This may be apocryphal, but it offers a nice example of the 'theory-ladenness'
of observations.

There are many examples of this in science, and indeed much of Kuhn's notion of
scientific revolutions was based on an idea that those working within a paradigm take
certain things for granted that make it impossible to interpret results as falsifying key
beliefs. Although Popper believed that scientists should seek to refute ideas, Kuhn
thought that this seldom happened once ideas had become central to a field. When
research leads to findings which suggest a central tenet is false, these are likely to be

explained away. Only a scientific revolutionary is able to recognize an anomaly as such and offer a new way of 'seeing'.

For example, Uranus was 'seen' and recorded as a star many times before Herschel recognized that it does not behave as a star (i.e. anomalous behaviour), and so *discovered* it as a planet (Kuhn, 1996). Interestingly, he actually claimed that Uranus was a comet, but is still considered to be the discoverer of the planet, unlike his predecessors who identified it as a star. A comet is judged like a planet in the features considered *theoretically* significant here, so Herschel was considered close enough!

It may seem that a scientist must be foolish or dishonest to fail to accept clearly falsifying evidence in an experiment. Yet much modern science is based on advanced technology. An anomalous result may mean our idea is wrong, or that the apparatus is faulty or miscalibrated. If careful checking and recalibration of the apparatus do not remove the anomaly, then logically we must adjust our theory. However, we can always choose to believe that the fault lies in the theory behind the instrumentation, rather than some key idea we may be committed to.

When Galileo pointed telescopes towards the sky, he saw objects that the then orthodoxy suggested should not exist. Some of those that he persuaded to look denied seeing those objects. Perhaps they were lying. More likely, Galileo interpreted the fuzzy smudges of light as moons around other planets according to his ontological commitment, and other observers saw no more than distortions due to the imperfect lenses available at the time. According to Kuhn's model, the different observers held incommensurable paradigmatic commitments. Those that could not interpret the patterns within *their ontology* of the cosmos made a *judgement* about the limitations of the telescope for showing clear images of cosmic bodies.

Galileo should not have been too smug, as he also saw Neptune through his telescope – but without 'discovering' it as a planet (Bamford, 1989)!

Activity 18.3

How might the 'theory-laden' nature of observations be used by someone told that 'experiments' on the effect of setting on student learning contradicted their own strong commitment to the effectiveness of set (or mixed-ability) teaching?

The problem of naturalism

Another problem with Popper's model, at least as it was initially understood, was that if 'falsification' is seen as the demarcation criterion for science, then only experimental approaches allow falsification, and so should be admitted as scientific.

> Simply, a scientist uses a universal theory about how the world is, to predict that, under specific conditions, a particular circumstance can be anticipated ... The next step is to devise an experiment by means of which the prediction could potentially be refuted. (Swann, 2003: 257)

Not all science is based on experimental techniques. For example, Darwin proposed that evolution occurred by a process of natural selection. Darwin's theory was largely based on an accumulation of a great deal of observational data. Darwin observed species, geological formations, fossils, etc. However, Darwin did not undertake any controlled experiments to test his idea of natural selection (although he did draw upon the 'experiments' of artificial selection as an analogy for his ideas).

It is not possible to undertake experimental tests in much of geology, cosmology, etc. These sciences build up theories based on the interpretation of observations, not the results of experiments undertaken to find out what would happen if the tectonic plates were a different size, or the earth's crust was thicker, or glaciers retreated at a different rate, or if the earth was closer to the sun or had two moons, or if the conditions in the Big Bang were different. Under a strict view of falsificationism, topics such as these would fall outside science.

However, clearly, we would normally include naturalistic work such as this as science. It is not just 'nature collecting': it is a business of developing models and theories through systematic observations.

> In science, measurements and experimental results, observational or interview data, and mathematical and logical analysis all can be part of the warrant – or case – that supports a theory, hypothesis or judgment. However, warrants are always revocable depending on the findings of subsequent inquiry. (NRC, 2002: 18)

Science does not all involve 'fair testing' and controlled experiments, for 'one well-conducted case study has the potential to cast doubt on existing assumptions' (Swann, 2003: 260). Indeed, some observers would argue that (natural) science has not proceeded by any specific set of methods (Feyerabend, 1987).

A post-positivist notion of 'science' (that can include education)

Taking the problem of induction and the theory-laden nature of observations together leads us to the view that, strictly, 'nothing is proved when predictions are fulfilled, nor even when they are refuted' (Swann, 2003: 260). Not only that, but a strict view of falsification as the key criterion of a science would exclude much that is generally accepted as science.

There are many post-positivist critiques of science, versions of what science is really like, which take the view that science makes progress towards more reliable knowledge, without agreeing on what the characteristics of science actually are.

> [Postpositivists] are united in believing that human knowledge is not based on unchallenge-
> able, rock-solid foundations – it is conjectural. We have grounds, or warrants, for asserting
> the beliefs, or conjectures, that we hold as scientists, often very good grounds, but these
> grounds are not indubitable. Our warrants for accepting these things can be withdrawn in
> the light of further investigation. (Phillips and Burbules, 2000: 26)

If we adopt a post-positivist view of science, then we are not using controlled experimental research as the yardstick for deciding if we are being scientific, but rather asking 'has the overall case made by the investigator been established to a degree that
warrants tentative acceptance of the theoretical or empirical claims that were made?'
(Phillips, 2005: 594). So we do not need to limit 'scientific' research to experimental
research.

Rather, 'methods can only be judged in terms of their appropriateness and effectiveness in addressing a particular research question ...' (NRC, 2002: 3). According to the
US's National Research Council, 'a wide variety of legitimate scientific designs are available for educational research', which 'range from randomized experiments of voucher
programs to in-depth ethnographic case studies of teachers to neurocognitive investigations' (NRC, 2002: 6). Scientific studies are those:

- where the design allows direct, empirical investigation of an important question
- that account for the context in which the study is carried out
- that align with a conceptual framework
- which reflect careful and thorough reasoning
- which disclose results to encourage debate in the scientific community (NRC, 2002: 6).

Such criteria allow us to consider *educational* research to be part of an enterprise
that could be considered *scientific* in terms of producing 'reliable' or 'objective'
knowledge.

> When science is viewed according to the postpositivist model – in which observations are
> theory-laden, facts underdetermine conclusions, values affect choice of problems, and
> communities of researchers must examine methods and conclusions for bias – then the
> perceived gap between social and natural sciences begins to disappear. (Phillips and
> Burbules, 2000: 65–6)

The careful reader may well suspect that this admission of educational research into
the pantheon of the sciences has been bought at a rather heavy cost. The post-positivist
vision of conjectures, grounds, warrants and conceptual frameworks offers the potential for a free-for-all that supports eclectic activity, but at a cost of admitting complete
subjectivism – after all, a free choice of conceptual framework offers considerable flexibility in selecting what counts as data, let alone interpreting any data that are collected.
This does not sound very scientific. One particular post-positivist thinker, Imre Lakatos,
can offer us guidance here.

Post-positivist, scientific research takes place within a research programme

Lakatos (1970) can be seen as offering a view of how science proceeds – through research programmes – that draws upon the kind of description Kuhn put forward, while having a generally Popperian view of the way in which science may make progress by conjectures and refutations. Lakatos argues that science proceeds through the establishment, and development, of what he called 'research programmes'. Several research programmes can co-exist for extended periods, but to remain scientific, a research programme has to be judged **progressive**.

A research programme consists of a 'hard core' of central commitments that are taken for granted and assumed to be true for the purposes of the research. Lakatos suggested that there was a mindset called the 'negative heuristic' that prevented researchers testing the hard-core assumptions. This sounds anti-Popperian, but within a particular programme, research only makes sense if certain commitments are held. Rather, the 'positive' heuristic of the research programme is to develop more detailed knowledge surrounding this hard core (the 'protective belt' of theory). If this terminology makes the ideas seem complicated, then consider Table 18.1 which gives some examples of questions that would be pointless, and questions that could be fruitful, in terms of possible hard-core commitments that could inform feasible research programmes.

According to Lakatos (1970), scientific research programmes were not limited to the natural sciences, but could apply to any field where we are *looking to* develop knowledge that offers models and theories of generality. We can imagine such programmes of research being developed around many different issues, e.g.:

- Is it better to organize teaching in similar ability or mixed-ability settings? Or, if this depends upon context, then what are the contextual factors at work?
- How can ICT be used to enhance student learning? Does this depend upon student age, subject discipline, teaching styles?

As one example of how this perspective can work in education, I have analysed my own main research area – learning in science – in terms of a Lakatosian Research Programme (Taber, 2006). Table 18.2 sets out some of the key tenets of this area of research and some of the questions suggested.

In this example, the general questions set out in Table 18.2 have led to new concepts and conjectures that have allowed research questions to be refined, and have maintained the research programme for several decades (see Taber, 2006). As long as the protective belt of theory is being elaborated and developed by this process (so that new theory offers testable predictions, which are generally not refuted), then the hard core is considered immune from question, and the programme is progressive.

Table 18.1 How scientific research programmes work: how the hard core informs research questions

Research programme	Suggested hard-core commitment (inter alia)	Negative heuristic	Positive heuristic
What is the research about? The particle model of matter	What are the starting points? That all matter is made up of myriad tiny particles	What would there be no point in investigating? Is matter made of tiny particles? Can matter be homogenous and continuous on the smallest scale?	What might it be useful to find out? How small are atoms? Are they all the same? Do they have internal structure?
Defining intelligence	That intellectual ability can be represented by a single measurement	Can intellectual ability be represented by a single value? What are the main factors of intelligence?	Is IQ a good measure of intellectual ability? How can we best design IQ tests?
Increasing girls' participation in physical science courses	Girls' under-representation in physics is due to cultural factors, not biological differences	Are girls by nature less capable of studying physics? Are hormone differences responsible for teenagers' subject preferences?	Why do girls tend to drop physics? Do most girls feel physics is irrelevant to their lives?

Table 18.2 An example of a research programme in education (modified from Taber, 2006)

Hard-core assumptions	Broad general research questions (informing the positive heuristic)
Knowledge is constructed by the learner, not received.	How does knowledge construction (i.e. learning) take place?
Learners come to science learning with existing ideas about many natural phenomena.	What ideas do learners bring to science classes? What is the nature of these ideas?
Each individual has a unique set of ideas.	How much commonality is there between learners' ideas in science?
Knowledge is represented in the brain as a conceptual structure.	How is knowledge organized in the brain?
It is possible to model learners' conceptual structures.	What are the most appropriate models and representations?
The learners' existing ideas have consequences for the learning of science.	How do learners' ideas interact with teaching?
It is possible to teach science more effectively if account is taken of the learner's existing ideas.	How should teachers teach science to take account of learners' ideas?

However, if a research programme only develops by the use of *ad hoc* adjustments to theory, to make theory match findings, then it is seen as degenerating, and no longer part of science. Lakatos (1978) saw fields such as Marxist theory and astrology as being outside of science, *not* because they concerned topics that were not part of the natural sciences, but because they were degenerate programmes, where theory was bland, and open to *ad hoc* adjustment to fit events, rather than leading to specific testable predictions that helped refine the body of theory.

Key ideas

This chapter has been about 'science', but more specifically about a notion of 'science' that can include educational research. I have reviewed the positivist ideal of scientific research, and indicated why its notion of developing knowledge on totally secure foundations has been shown to be unrealistic. Such naive positivist notions of science have given way to post-positivist perspectives that still aspire to 'reliable' objective knowledge, but admit a broad range of methodological approaches, used within programmes of critical enquiry.

The challenge for educational research then is not to be 'scientific' in the sense of limiting ourselves to research designs that are experimental, but rather to ensure that our research is systematic and cumulative, offering theory that supports bold testable conjectures. The interaction between empirical evidence and theory should be seen to make up progressive research programmes, where ideas are refined and developed through the research rather than protected from unfavourable findings.

> At its core, scientific inquiry is the same in all fields. Scientific research, whether in education, physics, anthropology, molecular biology, or economics, is a continual process of rigorous reasoning supported by a dynamic interplay among methods, theories and findings. It builds understandings in the form of models or theories that can be tested. Advances in scientific knowledge are achieved by the self-regulating norms of the scientific community over time, not, as sometimes believed, by the mechanistic application of a particular scientific method ... . (NRC, 2002: 2)

A key message for the novice researcher wishing to undertake 'scientific', school-based enquiry is to pay careful attention to how the research focus is conceptualized (Taber, 2007) to ensure that your research is supported by, and builds upon, a coherent programme of existing educational enquiry.

Reflective questions

1 In a school-based research context, what do you thinks counts as 'scientific'?
2 In what way does the argument depend upon a 'demarcation' of what science is based upon – what might be termed methodological values – rather than upon subject matter or the use of specific methods?

Further reading

Styles, B. (2006) 'Educational research versus scientific research', *Research Intelligence*, 95: 7–9.

Swann, J. (2003) 'How science can contribute to the improvement of educational practice', *Oxford Review of Education*, 29(2): 253–68.

Taber, K.S. (2006) 'Beyond constructivism: the progressive research programme into learning science', *Studies in Science Education*, 42: 125–84.

CHAPTER 19

INTERPRETIVISM: MEETING OUR SELVES IN RESEARCH

Christine Counsell

Chapter overview

This chapter examines some of the major streams of thought that have influenced the interpretivist paradigm – symbolic interactionism, ethnography, phenomenology and hermeneutics. It begins by showing how an interpretivist approach can arise naturally, and become extremely useful, within the context of ordinary planning, teaching and assessment. The chapter shows how a teacher can use interpretivist approaches to start to theorize, in creative and critical ways, about curriculum constructs, approaches to teaching and experiences of learning. In particular, it explores some of the ways in which teacher research can use the teacher's own subjectivity, rather than trying to bracket it out.

Introduction: three teachers

Figure 19.1 is a snapshot of three history teachers' thought processes as they assess an essay written by a Year 8 pupil. Let us assume that the essay is a standard piece of history work for Year 8. The pupil was required to construct a causal argument. This involves creative, independent thought, where pupils must select, connect, arrange and prioritize causes in order to make a coherent causal explanation of their own. Our three teachers are looking for a certain kind of causal reasoning in the pupil's argument.

Each teacher is using empirical data – a pupil's work – to try to reach a warranted and useful judgement about this pupil's understanding and progress. Each teacher is therefore engaged, already, in a form of research.

The teachers start off looking *for* something – a something that might act as evidence towards a judgement that the pupil has reached Level 5 of the National Curriculum Attainment Target. But what happens next?

Activity 19.1

Read Figure 19.1 carefully. Find the key similarities and differences between the approaches adopted by the three teachers.

Amidst our various readings of Figure 19.1, some common themes are likely to emerge. I will now highlight those that are pertinent to this chapter:

Three history teachers assess the quality of a Year 8 pupil's causal reasoning. Each reacts to a particular history essay in a different way. Learning objective: to suggest the relationship between causes (Level 5)		
Teacher A	**Teacher B**	**Teacher C**
Finds two isolated sentences in two different parts of the essay where pupil explicitly makes links between causes. This meets the indication on the mark scheme exactly: 'an explicit link'. And it has happened twice, suggesting the	Finds same two sentences but thinks to herself: 'I'm not sure if these examples show that he's really got it. Strictly speaking, he's done what the mark scheme says, but if I look at that first sentence in the context of the sentence before and	Finds same two sentences and reaches same conclusion as Teacher B, but adds: 'I wonder what this *other* paragraph is telling me though? There's nothing in it at all that directly addresses the mark scheme, but perhaps I'm looking in the wrong places altogether. There is a quality of reasoning in this other paragraph that *may* suggest he's getting closer to causal reasoning than I thought. Perhaps I'm missing crucial signs of learning. But, hang on a minute, what *am* I looking for? As I reflect on this, I seem to be discovering something about my own assumptions about causal reasoning in history. I wonder how pupils are actually interpreting

(Continued)

(Continued)

| pupil's grasp of this aspect of causal reasoning is secure. She notes in the margin: *'two clear examples – Level 5'.* She records this and moves on to the next pupil. | the sentence after, it seems strangely unconnected. I think he's just parking a formula. I think I need to examine the interplay between the bit that addresses the mark scheme and its immediate context.' | the language I use when I'm teaching this in the classroom? I wonder what assumptions my language embodies? I'm going to forget the mark scheme for a bit and look at this pupil's reasoning again. I'm going to try to decide how best to describe it. It may be that there's a lot more to causal reasoning than "suggesting relationships between causes" and I just don't yet have the words to capture it. Trying to capture what this pupil is actually trying to do may be a start.' |

Figure 19.1   Three teachers

Commentary on the three teachers

Teacher A accepts and uses the system of meanings given by the mark scheme. The mark scheme has shown her what to look for. She looks for the language of explicit links between causes. She is being both rigorous and efficient – rigorous in sticking strictly to the manifestation of causal reasoning that the mark scheme specifies ('explicit links'), and thereby ensuring that this piece of work is marked strictly according to the rules applied to all pupils; efficient in that she is using her limited time to go straight to the most readily identifiable manifestation. She rewards only that.

Teacher B does the above, but something disturbs her. Something in the pupil's text seizes her. It prevents her from moving on. She senses a possible gap between the reality she perceives and the concept that the mark scheme has of it. The reality of the pupil's work is teeming with possible meaning, some of which may (she feels) be relevant to the business of causal reasoning: perhaps *more* relevant than the surface manifestation she thought she was looking for. But it is partly concealed.

What is concealing it? The mark scheme? But surely a mark scheme helps us *see*. It defines and classifies. And this mark scheme carries much authority, not merely because it is the department's accepted way of establishing attainment and progress (so it is a matter of professionalism to go along with it), but because it is based on tried and tested ways in which the history education community has traditionally defined causal reasoning for the purposes of assessment. Nevertheless, for all its warranted validity, the mark scheme also conceals.

Of course, Teacher B could just make a quick mental note that there was a problem and recommend changes to the mark scheme at the next department meeting. That may turn out to be productive. But we are interested in what she does much more immediately. Notice two things:

1   As she looks at the work, her looking is characterized by a moving away from the original preconceptions about what she was looking for, and a moving closer to the essence of the thing she was really looking for, that thing which was hidden. She is caught up in a pattern of revealing and concealing that is a natural part of her own reading.

2   Focusing on that natural pattern (a pattern that seems to arise from the very reading process itself), she starts to employ a distinctive interpretive process. This requires a continuous movement between parts and whole, a refusal to rest with either constituent parts or whole, but a determination to read each in the light of the other. She is operating hermeneutically, applying a deliberate approach to the movement between parts and whole that her natural interpretive processes seem to lead her towards. She is now sufficiently conscious of it to name this process that she finds herself adopting: 'I need to examine the interplay between …'.

Teacher C is doing everything that Teacher B is doing. She, too, is led by what is before her. But she is becoming actively thoughtful about this process itself, and rendering it even more explicit than Teacher B.

Teacher C is wondering if she should re-name 'causal reasoning' altogether. It looks as though Teacher C really is going to be in a position to re-write that mark scheme … or to change the language of the National Curriculum, or even the philosophy of history itself. But, for now, the interesting thing is the effect all this is having on her own approach as an assessor, and therefore on her way of being a researcher and her way of being a teacher.

She is starting to think about how this pupil's written reasoning *appears* to her, but without the concepts and tools of NC assessment standing between her and it. This involves a deliberate and difficult attempt to retreat from those concepts.

It is not that the NC tools are necessarily wrong – rather, that a different interpretive process is revealing something more *essential* (i.e. closer to an essence). This has transferred her attention from deciding if Pupil X matches up to a given marker for progress in causal reasoning, to a closer examination of causal reasoning itself. Yet she is still directly using the data provided by Pupil X in order to construct this.

Notice, too, how Teacher C slithers into thinking about language and labelling. She can only think or talk about causal reasoning *through* language and labelling, and yet she is becoming sufficiently self-aware to question the way in which language may have placed limits on her understanding.

Teacher C is now moving constantly back and forth, back and forth, between her existing assumptions and what is appearing to her, between language that conceals and language that reveals, between parts and whole, re-examining each, continuously, in the light of the other. But Teacher C's circular, hermeneutic approach takes her much further than Teacher B. She is:

*   beginning to reject a meaning system bequeathed to her (the given ideas about the properties of causal reasoning)
*   uncovering possibly hidden indicators of how this particular pupil is approaching causal reasoning
*   shining a new light on *herself* as an interpreter, reflecting actively on the possibilities inherent in the interpretation process as it unfolds.

Consider the implications of that third bullet point. Teacher C is now finding out about *herself*, as much as she is finding out about Pupil X's causal reasoning. She has become the object of her own research.

Another way of saying this is to note a shift in the kind of question that Teacher C is now asking. All three teachers are trying to use data to validate a claim that a certain pupil is engaged in a certain kind of causal reasoning. All three teachers know that if they are to defend the view that Pupil X can reason causally, they must ask, in effect, 'How do I know this to be true?' But Teacher C is now asking something else. Not 'How do I know this to be true?' but 'Why do I interpret the truth to be this?'

Teacher C is also noticing a crucial way in which the interpretive process is always moving, dynamic, in a state of flux. It is a circle of movement that she can actively enter and experience more fully and explicitly if she so chooses. She can choose to move into that circle and to learn from it. Indeed, she is already asking – how do things appear to me? What do I need to do to *allow* things to appear to me in their fullness, in their essential features? What is going on when I interpret things and how can I use this to learn more about me, as well as about my object?

Teacher C, even more explicitly than Teacher B, has realized that letting a thing appear as what it is becomes a matter of learning how to allow it to do so.

Of course, if Teacher C carries on like this, she will have a nervous breakdown. She is in danger of spending a whole night on one pupil's work. A more constructive way to make use of this experience might be to begin a research project – one guided by this different way of seeing. If she does this, she will be deciding to work within an interpretive paradigm.

Indeed, all three teachers are at the moment of curiosity cultivation that leads to a fascinating research project. Each could successfully build on the processes they are already using. They are anticipating particular ways of working that the interpretive paradigm offers. By exploring an appropriate methodology, they might find that they can augment what they are learning from and about their own practice. Each is ready to take a walk through the various methodologies that interpretivism has spawned.

As you work through this chapter, keep referring back to our three teachers. I will use them as examples to stimulate your exploration of the different practical possibilities offered by various traditions within interpretivist research. This chapter will present a selection of methodologies – the theoretical position sitting behind a researcher's chosen methods. We will focus on how they arose, what they offer and how they differ.

One word of warning: do not expect the traditions to fit our three teachers neatly. They have not been devised so crudely. Expect surprising convergences. Expect new puzzles. Simply use our three teachers as tools to keep you thinking, and to ground what follows in the practical realities of being an enquiring teacher.

But, first, we need to take a detour by way of the words 'subject' and 'object'.

Re-thinking subjectivity

Off the top of your head, and before reading on, make up a natural, conversational sentence using the word 'subjective'.

I wonder what your sentence sounded like. It is possible that you used the word 'subjective' in a negative way: 'That's a bit subjective, isn't it?' 'We can't rely on that – it's too subjective.'

While there are times when such usage is appropriate, the word's automatic equation with negative, invalid or inadequate judgements is unfortunate, for much of the word's wider meaning is lost.

Subjectivity is the key feature distinguishing people from inanimate objects. Subjectivity is all about meaning. Our words, actions and other creations hold various meanings for each of us. Thoughts, feelings and beliefs influence those meanings. This issue of meaning has important implications for researching the social world.

Consider two ways to wreck a lesson: an earthquake and mounting pupil disruption. In the case of the earthquake, the researcher could identify physical causes leading to the collapse of the classroom in which the lesson took place. In the case of mounting pupil disruption, the causal chain will have to take account of subjective meanings that underlie the pupils' actions. Why were they not engaged in the lesson? How did they become disaffected? What roles did they adopt? The geologist and engineer have no such interest in the subjective perceptions of the earth's crust or the building (Baronov, 2004: 112–13).

In interpretivist research, subjectivism becomes relevant in two ways:

1   The example above reminds us that subjectivity is our object of study. When examining the social world and trying to understand it, we are trying to make sense of human subjectivity or the subjectivities of a group.
2   But we, as researchers, are exercising judgement and making meaning, too. Thus, to a greater or lesser extent, our own subjectivity, as researchers, is also engaged.

In any enquiry, or any ordinary act of assessment or evaluation by a teacher, you, the researcher, are a *subject* enquiring into an *object*. To clarify this, it is worth recalling some basic grammar. Each sentence in Figure 19.2 contains a subject and a direct object. The subject acts, behaves or reacts to the object in some way. The object is passive in this relationship. The subject is 'doing' something to it, whether eating it, contemplating it or hitting it.

Subject and object are used in the same way in research. You, the researcher, are the subject. You are going to have to 'do' something to your object – observe it, count it, listen to it, measure it, engage it in conversation, use it, reflect upon it.

When we hear talk of 'being objective', we are hearing an assumption about the role of *you*, the researcher, the subject. The assumption is that we should minimize what is presumed to be the distorting impact of our subjectivity. According to this assumption, we need to establish that results are untainted by the bias of the observer (the subject). On this line of argument, true understanding results from distancing oneself as one observes. This distancing makes us 'objective' – i.e. object-oriented rather than subject-oriented.

But it is not quite so simple. *You*, the subject, cannot be left out. The object will not research itself. While this holds when researching the physical world too, it creates particular challenges and offers special opportunities when we are researching the social world of human beings and their webs of meaning.

SUBJECT		OBJECT
The dog	*ate*	the cat.
The man	*considered*	the moon.

Figure 19.2   Subject and object in a sentence

Challenge no. 1

What you are researching is, itself, a bundle of subjectivities. You are going to have to make judgements. But what enables you to make those judgements? The answer is: your humanness, the very thing you have in common with your object. If you were not human, you could not make sense out of the meanings made by other humans. So the very thing that supposedly gets in the way – your subjective humanness and its inevitable preconceptions, lenses and biases – is also the very thing that *allows* you to reach across the distance and make meaning out of your object.

Challenge no. 2

If you are researching a situation in which you are intricately involved, if you are researching your own practice, you are not just researching someone else's subjectivity, you are researching your *own* subjectivity. You have actually become your own object.

What does this mean? Should we give up because we cannot be fully objective?

Some would argue that the only solution is to screen out our own subjectivity in order to limit its damage. We could conceptualize our subjectivity as a problem, and then deploy tools and systems to ensure as much objectivity as possible. This is certainly possible as a *quest* (even if total objectivity can never finally be achieved), and for certain forms of enquiry, it may be both desirable and necessary.

But it is not the only way. If we *always* see our own subjectivity as a problem, we lose the essential advantage our subjectivity gives us in Challenge No. 1, and any attempt to rise to Challenge No. 2 becomes impossible. For teachers researching their own practice, to avoid Challenge Nos.1 and 2 is to give up and go home.

So what is the answer? Interpretivist research offers different forms and modes of researching the social world, each of which handles these questions in different ways. One way of thinking about different types of interpretivist research is to talk about *the extent to which and the manner in which* our own subjectivity as researcher is engaged or managed.

So we have choices and possibilities.

Consider Teacher C in Figure 19.1, once again. Her curiosity is leading her somewhere. In her emergent informal enquiry, her own subjectivity is central. It is not something that is getting in the way – it is, itself, both (i) her tool for enquiring, and increasingly, (ii) an object of study in its own right. Increasingly, her focus is as much upon herself, as subject, as it is upon the causal reasoning of Pupil X – her object. She could now decide to pursue an enquiry that makes the most of (i) and (ii) rather than running away from them.

So, has this turned Teacher C away from her original object? No, far from it. What it has done is to create a new kind of *linkage* between Teacher C as the subject and object of her enquiry. Take a closer look at this interesting new linkage:

- She cannot enquire into her *object* without using herself as subject in a very direct way.
- She cannot enquire into herself as *subject* – her processes of seeing, the patterns of revealing and concealing – without using the data that come to her from her object.

This linkage between subject and object is particularly pertinent to teachers researching their own practice. You do not have to be enquiring into or directly using your subjectivity all the time, but you do need to be constructively thoughtful about your role as subject (researcher). Different kinds of project can exploit that linkage in different ways and it is possible to design your research so as to maximize or minimize the emphasis on yourself as enquirer. It is possible to make this work to suit you and the focus of your enquiry. The teacher research projects in Figure 19.3 offer a variety of different ways in which subject (researcher) and object (focus of research) might relate to each other.

As a teacher researcher, the only thing that is impossible to *ignore* is your own subjectivity. At the very least, you will need to reflect upon your own involvement, your starting assumptions, your purposes. You could then make a decision to:

a   heighten that awareness of your subjectivity in order to reduce its effects and be as object-oriented as you possibly can
b   involve your own subjectivity and make it a positive condition for enquiry
c   (more radically) make your own subjectivity the primary object of study.

Teachers B and C are certainly doing (b). Teacher C is perhaps contemplating (c).

Activity 19.2

Now look more systematically at the projects in Figure 19.3. Study the three different arrows in Figure 19.4. For each of the titles in Figure 19.3, choose the arrow that best describes the interplay of subject (researcher) and object.

Before we move on, a caution is necessary. The three positions presented crudely in Figure 19.4 are neither mutually exclusive nor fixed positions. They are just conceptual tools, used here to heighten your awareness of the meaning of the words 'subject' and 'object' and to think about these freshly. They represent a possible continuum, ways of leaning in particular directions. It is important not to fix the researcher in each project in Figure 19.3 as 'being subjective' or 'being objective'. We are just talking about *leanings* in terms of the roles that the subject and object might be playing, and how they dance in relation to each other, in any enquiry.

1. The trouble with critical cultural geography is that the students just don't care. Desire for dialogue: how do we know when they are starting to care? An investigation into three modes of student interaction drawing upon a sequence of six Year 9 geography lessons about 'sense of place'.
2. What am I really assessing in Year 8's work? A reflexive exploration of the features of Year 8 scientific thinking that I seem to be noticing and privileging across a sequence of three classwork and two homework activities.
3. What does motivation in English look like? An investigation of when and how six Year 9 pupils appear to be motivated while reading, telling and creating traditional tales and stories about fenland life in East Anglia.
4. How do groups operate during a shared project in D and T? Developing a model for small group behaviour in a study of how groups of four Year 10 pupils interact, behave and adopt roles towards each other during different stages of design, realization and evaluation.
5. How can we tell what part imitation is playing in Year 5 creative writing? An exploration of ways of determining whether and how four Year 5 pupils are borrowing rhythms, structures and patterns in their creative writing.
6. In what way do students' prior experiences relate to the take-up of GCSE music? A longitudinal study seeking to examine webs of meaning within which decisions to take up or drop music are made, over two years in two schools.
7. How do students experience early secondary school MFL classrooms? A case study seeking to illuminate the experiences, understandings, perspectives and learning behaviours of four Year 7 pupils in the first year of learning Spanish.
8. What do different forms of assessment tell me about Ahmed and Lech as learners of mathematics? A study of how my own processes of understanding were altered by a series of iterative encounters with different forms and styles of Year 6 pupils' work.
9. Reconceptualizing 'revision': can there ever be any such thing as 'going beyond' an examination specification? Examining the relationship between exploring material *outside* the exam specification and strengthening students' ability to perform *within* it. A theory-seeking case study based on action research designed to improve the revision experience of Year 12 studying British politics 1815–1850.

(Continued)

(Continued)

10. Levels and marks, labels and needs – exploring the deficit model in the concept of Special Needs within English. How do the self-image and the school's image of two Year 9 pupils with SEN manifest themselves in these pupils' experiences?
11. Discovering the power of the word: what is the role of the abstract noun in creating mature expression? A case study seeking to uncover how and what four Year 8 and four Year 9 pupils are engaging with during creative encounters with vocabulary in Religious Studies.
12. Can one concept illuminate another? An investigation into the nature and quality of Year 8's thinking about *historical diversity* developed and demonstrated indirectly during a causation enquiry examining the *historical causes* of early Islamic expansion.

Figure 19.3   Sample thesis titles

Thinking about subject and object is a good starting point for thinking about how interpretivist research arose. To do this, we need to examine how the idea of researching the social world, as distinct from the physical world, first became a focus for debate.

Mainly leaning towards an examination of the object

Mainly leaning towards an examination of the subject (that is, you the researcher), but using an object as a tool

Equal emphasis upon and interplay between both

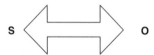

Figure 19.4   Leaning towards subject or object?

The emergence of an interpretivist paradigm

So how did distinctive approaches to social research arise? A little historical background is useful because it shows us just how fluid and contingent was the emergence of the various methodologies. Such background reminds us that methodologies and methods are not gods to be propitiated; they are merely tools for us to select, adapt, blend and challenge. To do this well, we need to be well-informed about their context and purpose.

The idea that researching human, subjective experience might need some special approaches has not always been commonly accepted. The great German philosopher, Kant (1724–1804), saw things rather differently. Setting out to provide a foundation for *all* knowledge, Kant formulated 'categories' that made *all* enquiry possible, such as *contingency*, *plurality* and *cause*. For Kant, these categories were equally applicable to the physical and social sciences.

Eighty years later, the German historian Droysen (1808–1884) challenged Kant by naming two types of knowledge: *erklären* (explanation) and *verstehen* (understanding). Droysen maintained that whereas we seek to explain physical phenomena by means of causes or universal laws, we seek to *understand* social phenomena through interpretation. Other 19th-century thinkers built on this. For example, an explicit contrast emerged between a *nomothetic* approach seeking general causes and an *idiographic* approach seeking to understand unique, individual cases.

The most influential of these thinkers was Dilthey (1833–1911) and the aspect of his thinking we particularly need to note here was the way in which he defined human beings (Baronov, 2004: 117). He said that humans are not just biological creatures; rather, they are beings that make meaningful things. Humans are defined by their subjectivity. Humans make paintings, puddings and parliaments. They make tables, tubas and treaties. The things we create are expressions or *objectifications* of our subjectivity. Therefore, if we study those meaningful things, we can learn about that subjectivity, about the meanings that make us human.

In a direct challenge to Kant, Dilthey came up with his own categories. He believed that there are categories through which we find structure and meaning in social and cultural experience. His main categories were *purpose*, *meaning* and *value*. By using such categories to study the things human beings make, the researcher can identify patterns that shape how humans experience and make sense of the world.

Dilthey's basic premise was that physical phenomena – an earthquake or a chemical reaction – have no hidden, meaningful qualities. Human action, on the other hand, is bursting with meaning. Making sense of that human action requires a special kind of understanding, and this is where interpretation comes in.

Research into the physical world involves investigation through observation. Such a process – observing, recording, describing or counting – involves our ordinary understanding. Research into the social world, when it involves observing or measuring human action, also requires this ordinary understanding. But such social research also requires another type of understanding – one that 'allows insight into the hidden meaning behind human action' (Baronov, 2004: 119). This second type of understanding is *verstehen*.

A pupil in your classroom is balancing a pencil on his nose. 'Ordinary' understanding is adequate for apprehending the physical action of balancing a pencil on a nose. *Verstehen* is necessary for establishing that your pupil is showing off, deliberately creating a distraction, avoiding work, enjoying a new skill, obeying a bully's command or simply being bored stiff. *Verstehen* thus relies on a type of *interpretation* that ordinary understanding does not require.

Let us think further about this interpretation process. On one level, *verstehen* is an everyday process. We use *verstehen* when we sense a mood, interpret gestures or recognize humour. It can be deployed with little or no explicit reflection. On another level, *verstehen* can be deployed as a data-collection method – a developed, systematic, explicit and self-conscious use of *verstehen*.

Activity 19.3

Study Figure 19.1 again. Where can you discern emerging transitions from *verstehen* used in an 'everyday' way, into the beginnings of a more self-conscious and systematic use of *verstehen*? Be sure to consider all three teachers. The answers are not obvious.

What we understand today as *verstehen* or the interpretivist approach has appeared historically in many forms. I will follow Crotty (1998) in presenting these as three streams of thought: symbolic interactionism (especially its influence on ethnography), phenomenology and hermeneutics.

Symbolic interactionism

Symbolic interactionism stems from the American philosopher and social psychologist George Herbert Mead. Just as with Dilthey, it was a particular view of what a human being is that drove forwards this branch of philosophy. This view has influenced many basic ideas that many educational researchers take for granted today.

For Mead, what is distinctive about human beings is a concept of the 'self'. People are different from animals because they have selves. Crucially, the self is social. What and who we are comes from our being part of a community. The practices found within any culture thus form the roots of personhood. Mead wrote: 'A person is a personality because he belongs to a community' (1934: 162).

Yet the term 'symbolic interactionism' was never actually used by Mead. It was Mead's students, especially Herbert Blumer, who disseminated Mead's ideas and who coined the term 'symbolic interactionism':

- 'Interactionist' refers to people's capacity to put themselves in the place of others. For example, it is by seeing ourselves from the perspective of imaginary others that we are able to reflect upon alternative ways of expressing ourselves, and then to select from among those alternatives. This ability to see ourselves as the object of others' attention allows us to direct our actions through self-reflection. Mead said that this process begins in early childhood. It starts with early imitation and develops through play, role-play and games. By putting themselves in the place of imaginary others, children become reflective about how others think and act.
- 'Symbolic' refers to our sharing of symbols (such as language) with others.

Blumer's core propositions were:

- 'human beings act toward things on the basis of the meanings things have for them'
- 'the meaning of such things … arises out of the social interaction'
- 'these meanings are … modified through an interpretive process' (Blumer, 1969: 2).

For Blumer, meaning is not intrinsic to objects, and neither is it a mere reflection of someone's mind. Blumer argued that the meaning of an object for an individual is derived from that individual's manner of acting towards it. Thus, a readiness to use a desk as storage, as a surface to write on and as a personalized space all give the object the meaning of what we call 'desk'. Each object could have an infinite number of meanings. Baert (1998) illustrates Blumer's thinking on this matter:

> Grouse are not the same to a grouse shooter, as to an animal rights campaigner. Again, they are different objects for a discerning gourmet who chooses them for his or her main course, a bird-watcher or scholarly ornithologist. This tendency to act in a particular way is in its turn constituted, maintained and modified by the ways in which others refer to that object or act towards it. Within the household, for instance, numerous expectations by husband and children obviously reinforce a particular meaning of womanhood. (Baert, 1998: 72–3)

Activity 19.4

(a) Try to adapt Baert's descriptions with education/school/classroom equivalents to 'grouse' and 'womanhood'.

(b) From your reading so far on symbolic interactionism (and before reading on!), what do you *predict* will be the likely implications of Mead and Blumer's work for an approach to research?

Blumer teased out the implications of the symbolic interactionist perspective for research methodology. These implications might be summed up as follows:

1   The meanings held by those being studied must be taken seriously. The researcher needs to see the social world from the perspective of those he or she researches. This leads to an important place within research methods for dialogue. Only through dialogue can one discern the perceptions of others and interpret their meanings and purposes.
2   Social research should examine the processes of adaptation and re-adaptation. Just as Mead stressed a dynamic relationship between self and society, so Blumer stressed the dynamic nature of social life – human beings continuously re-adapt to a constantly changing world. Many subsequent methodological traditions have developed models for examining how this process of adaptation occurs. The classroom and its many sub-groups and sub-cultures are arguably settings of continuous adaptation and re-adaptation.
3   Researchers cannot exclude concepts that are not immediately observable, such as mind, self or reflection. People's actions cannot be explained, or even described, through a simple, behaviourist view of response to stimulus. Instead, the researcher needs to explore how people self-monitor and self-reflect.

Symbolic interactionism meets ethnography

The practice of researching a culture or a group of people, commonly known as ethnography, was born within cultural anthropology. But researchers influenced by symbolic interactionism adopted and adapted ethnography. It is easy to see why. Think about the emphasis of Mead and Blumer on putting oneself in the place of the other. Now consider how this links with the underlying ethic of all that cultural anthropologists do. Crotty neatly sums up that underlying ethic:

> Culture is not to be called into question, it is not to be criticised, least of all by someone from another culture. Instead one should observe it as closely as possible, attempt to take the place of those within the culture, and search out the insider's perspective. Here lies the origin of ethnography. (Crotty, 1998: 76)

Ethnography is thus the child of both cultural anthropology and symbolic interactionism. Martyn Hammersley, in his work on special educational needs, teases out the relevance of symbolic interactionism for ethnography:

> Ethnography is a form of research in which the social setting to be studied, however familiar to the researcher, must be treated as anthropologically strange; and the task is to document the culture – the perspectives and practices – of the people in these settings. The aim is to 'get inside' the way in which each group of people sees the world. (Hammersley, 1985: 152)

In sum, what does symbolic interactionism contend? First, that to research human life and society is a complex endeavour. The 'objects' we research are dynamic objects and necessarily elusive. Human beings employ all kinds of tacit knowledge, most of which can never be directly observable. Second, that human beings define themselves within shared meanings. Third, that human beings anticipate the results of imaginary actions and, through interaction, constantly *alter* those shared meanings. Like all human beings, pupils and teachers are constantly monitoring themselves, masking bits of themselves and placing the accent on other aspects. What they say, do and write, how they listen or blank out – all these things are meant to convey and conceal who they are.

How on earth do researchers attempt to address all this? The answer is: with great creativity. I will now briefly introduce five examples of methodologies influenced by symbolic interactionism: the dramaturgical approach, grounded theory, negotiated-order theory, labelling theory and narrative approaches.

Each of these can be drawn upon by novice teacher researchers. Each could find a natural home within the projects listed in Figure 19.3.

Activity 19.5

As you read the following five examples of interpretivist approaches, keep the list of thesis titles in Figure 19.3 close by. Decide which of these five approaches might have particular value for certain titles.

The dramaturgical approach

Ernest Goffman (1970) analysed 'encounters' between individuals by drawing upon metaphors from theatre. For example, he defined individual activities which serve to influence an 'audience' as a 'performance'. Drawing upon Mead's account of the self and role-taking, Goffman argued that in their encounters, all human beings are continuously attending to their actions while adopting other people's views.

Consider the relevance of this to an analysis of learning and students, classroom and curricula. In all interactions, people dramatize their behaviour in order to show that they are performing well or are in control. Sometimes these goals are incompatible. A pupil who tries to convince a teacher that he or she is absorbed in work or can deploy a certain fact might exert so much energy doing this that he or she masks other important learning taking place. Goffman argues that during their 'performances', people tend to express official values. In an education context, these values might be embodied in school or classroom rules, expectations of a teacher or assessment criteria. Sometimes people deliberately play up one aspect of performance that they believe will please others or will foster their own advancement, and so either knowingly or unknowingly conceal others.

Sometimes, people quite deliberately play down a quality – such as children showing off to other children in order to present themselves as disorganized, ignorant or non-compliant with an adult's wishes. The 'performance' of non-compliance or the pretence of igno-rance is deliberate – the child is trying to show that he or she is in control and cannot be manipulated by the adult (Goffman, 1970).

Picture people interacting in an education situation (whether family, after-school club, classroom, staffroom, subject department, tutorial, seminar). In these settings, we find people behaving in certain ways: they move 'front-stage', their speeches take on par-ticular forms or they retreat 'back-stage'. They seek to influence an audience by way of costumes, speech styles and props. Goffman's dramaturgical approach is a form of inter-actionist research which uncovers rituals and investigates their roles and meanings.

Grounded theory

In *The Discovery of Grounded Theory*, Glaser and Strauss (1967) launched this highly systematic form of ethnographic enquiry. The researcher strives to develop a theory about how people act and respond to a phenomenon. This theory must emerge *only* from the data (mainly interviews and field notes). It is said to be 'grounded' in the data.

In grounded theory, data analysis follows a set format. By segmenting information, the researcher forms initial categories about the phenomenon being studied. Within each category, the investigator finds several properties, or sub-categories, and looks for data to *dimensionalize* by showing extremes on a continuum within that property. The investigator might then assemble the same data in new ways. Grounded theorists often end up producing charts or matrix-like schema, thus creating an abstract 'picture', show-ing how the elements of their theory relate to each other. For example, the chart will specify strategies, identify the *context* and the intervening *conditions*, and so on.

Although this sounds complex, it is a logical, rigorous process from which the novice researcher can gain a great deal. If you experiment with grounded theory, you will not waste your time, even if you never use it again. It will discipline your approach to data. Above all, the rigorous stages in the labelling of items will make you newly thoughtful about coding.

I used grounded theory within my own MEd. I was interested in what actually went on in small groupwork when pupils were framing and then supporting hypotheses. What was really going on in the fluid, ephemeral patterns of talk and silence in a small group discussion? I videoed two small groups working in short, 15-minute bursts. I later interviewed pupils about their experiences of cooperating to solve a problem. I wanted to build a theory – one as grounded as possible in what was taking place in my own classroom – about successful group interaction.

Using the video data, I developed an initial category of 'time spaces' to define the moments when no one spoke. After a series of interviews, I named the *properties* of 'time spaces'. One of these properties was 'waiting'. This property proved fruitful when

I tried to *dimensionalize* it. Using the interview data, I discovered how pupils conceptualized and used 'waiting'. 'Waiting' ranged from 'frustrating waiting' ('we're stuck, no one's asking good questions and we're under pressure – this feels bad') to 'helpful waiting' (a positive, comfortable sense of silence, when everyone in the group knew that everyone else was thinking hard; it was a 'waiting without worrying'). This idea of positive or 'helpful' waiting was closely allied to the idea of trust. When the group was trusting itself, this 'good' waiting was possible. This had a relationship with *causal conditions* for such waiting, and so on. Thus, I was able to build an abstract schema fully grounded in the data.

The rigour of grounded theory (Chapter 17) taught me how to look at my data, and to keep going back to it, again and again. Through *dimensionalizing*, I realized why it mattered that I had not opted for 'silence' or 'inactivity' as my original category. 'Waiting' was rich with meaning, meaning that I found only after an iterative encounter with the data, constantly holding it up against this mirror of 'waiting' to see if it fitted it.

As a classroom teacher novice researcher, I found this experience exhilarating. The rigour of the process taught me to look at my classroom in a new way, and to re-think all sorts of taken-for-granted and intuitive knowledge that I had built up in five years' experience. Above all, it made me critical. I could no longer accept uncritically any superficial guidance on 'how to do groupwork', nor the language in which it was couched.

Negotiated-order theory

In this kind of interactionist enquiry, researchers examine how social arrangements and processes are constantly adapted and re-adapted by those who live and work within them. In community, school, classroom and group settings, people negotiate tasks, roles and responsibilities, sometimes directly and openly, sometimes tacitly or unintentionally. Negotiated-order theorists examine this continuous process of adjustment, uncovering the fluid and responsive nature of roles and relationships.

Labelling theory

All societies have at times labelled certain individuals and groups 'deviant'. Some traditions of social research examine the background or heredity of 'deviants' in order to explore causes and patterns in 'deviant' behaviour. According to labelling theorists such as Becker (1963), however, this kind of study will always tell us very little about 'deviance'. Drawing upon a symbolic interactionism perspective, Becker argues that we should examine the labelling process itself. *Why* does society exclude some people from full membership? *How* does it do this? *Why* does society fear and censure certain behaviours? *How* does this designation of deviant behaviour come about? What processes of adaptation and response lead to this labelling?

Narrative approaches

Narrative can be thought of variously as a methodology, as a method, as data, as a tool for communicating the results of enquiry or a blend of all these.

This field of narrative research is vast and with many antecedents. But I make reference to it under the symbolic interactionism umbrella because this is one influence that has affected it in direct and indirect ways. Also, to think about symbolic interactionism in relation to narrative can help novice researchers to explore its potential. See if you can think this through for yourself, using Activity 19.6.

Activity 19.6

Drawing upon the above examples of symbolic interactionist approaches, why do you think that the construction of a narrative might be helpful in educational research?

In Activity 19.6, I hope you came up with 'plot'. You might also have thought about 'time'. Narrative is a tool for exploring the temporal dimension of the social world. You might also have thought of 'perspective'. You might have mentioned 'meaning'. Narrative makes distinctive contributions to analysis and interpretation.

> A [chronological] map has order and relationships. A story has logic and meaning. ... What makes for convenient generalisation in a chronological map [makes for] uncomfortable co-incidence in a narrative, not because everything must be neat and tidy with a complete and perfect explanation ... but because narrative frameworks work with connections: patterns and colligatory generalisations as well as with time and space. [Narrators] construct meaningful accounts that impute narrative significance to events by means of ... trends and turning points, or intentional and causal explanations. (Shemilt, 2000: 94–5)

Consider the forms that stories of pupils or teachers, of groups or classes, of a school or a professional community, might take. Lieblich et al. (1998) construct life course graphs that treat a narrative holistically. They use these to illustrate patterns of ascent, decline and stability in a narrative. In a progressive narrative, the focus of a story is on advancement, achievement, success. In a regressive narrative, there is deterioration or decline. In a stable narrative, there is neither progression nor decline. To examine phases of a narrative is to employ a practical method by which, for example, the transcript of a biographical interview or a personal diary can be analysed.

But a plot has a narrator. And the narrator changes too. The fact that we change, too, brings us back to subjectivity. A narrative is not something that is found – it is created through interpretation.

Phenomenology

Start by reflecting on this interesting definition of phenomenology: 'Phenomenology is a means of being led by the phenomenon through a way of access genuinely belonging to it' (Palmer, 1969: 128).

That probably sounds a little odd, even a bit mystical. It sounds as though it is almost attributing agency to the *phenomenon* being observed. Is Palmer really saying that the phenomenon leads *us*? Isn't that reversing the subject–object relationship?

Not quite, but it does neatly illuminate the distinctive way in which subject and object are conceptualized for the phenomenologist. This is another reason why it was important to reflect upon subjectivity and objectivity at the start of this chapter.

Phenomenology is such a complex field that one can only gradually move into the circle of its considerations. My aim here is to give a mere taste, to foster a little curiosity about its special value when researching the world of education, especially for the novice teacher researcher.

Let us start with a key thinker and some principles. Our key thinker is Edmund Husserl (1859–1938), and his foundational work is his *Logical Investigations*. Our three principles are: (i) a relationship between subjects and objects; (ii) a method of enquiry with twin goals; and (iii) a suspicion of culture and concepts.

(i) A relationship between subjects and objects

At the heart of Husserl's phenomenology is the relationship between subjects and their objects. Each is necessarily connected to the other. Subjects must have objects because a subject's consciousness must be consciousness of *something*. I cannot just say that I am conscious. I must be conscious of something. Right now, I am conscious of a desk and a keyboard. I am conscious of breathing and typing and the tempting possibility of a cup of coffee. I am conscious of the air temperature and images passing outside the window. These are the objects that fill my consciousness. I, as a subject, must have objects in order to be a thinking subject.

So subjects need objects. But the other way around may seem a little less likely. The computer in front of me or planet Mars are objects. Surely neither needs me sitting here thinking about it in order for it to exist?

But Husserl does not quite mean 'need' in that way. He means that the object cannot be adequately *described* apart from a subject. An *account* of this computer or of Mars is dependent on a human being like me, looking, perceiving, touching, measuring, imagining, remembering. In this sense, an object is always an object for someone. Thus neither subject nor object can be adequately described without each other.

This all starts to make more sense when we move on to methods and purposes.

(ii) A method of enquiry with twin goals

The phenomenologist lifts an object out from its wider context and isolates it for investigation. He or she does this for two related purposes: (a) to identify those features of the object that are peculiar to it, that represent its core essence; and (b) to understand the 'structures used by consciousness' that allow us to constitute the object.

Let us take (a) first. The best way to think of essential features is to think of one thing that has many different manifestations. To take a very simple and obvious example, what is it that makes the concept 'dog' hold together? Although there are many different breeds of dog, the word still holds as an umbrella term. But how? After some enquiry, we would find a set of essential features that characterize all dogs, irrespective of breed. This is why we can tell a dog from a horse.

According to Husserl, once the phenomenon has been reduced to its essential features, we can then return to (b), the quest to understand how the 'structures of consciousness' organize our experience of that phenomenon.

But what did Husserl mean by 'structures of consciousness'?

Pick up your pencil sharpener. It has six sides. Each side presents itself to you under different perspectives – if you hold it directly before you, it presents itself as a square, but if you tilt it away from you slightly, it presents itself at an angle; if you tilt it further, that side looks more like a line. If you tilt it a bit further, it vanishes. Let us call each way the side is presented an 'aspect'. If you look at it a few days later, it is a different viewing. The sides and aspects have not changed, but this will be a different moment of looking in time. You will notice different things and 'see' it differently. We can call that momentary presentation a profile. Our perception is dynamic, not static, and we build up ways of perceiving things through sides, aspects and profiles (Sokolowski, 2000).

And these things are real. Indeed, Husserl's slogan was 'back to the things themselves' – this was a realist project, not a project to get lost in the subjective world of ideas alone. This is a common misconception with phenomenology. It is often mistaken for an idealist project because it focuses on the structures of consciousness, but for Husserl, it was a project to do with establishing the nature of things. It is just that the project is carried out through analysis of how we experience and constitute those things in our consciousness. Phenomenologists study *the act of interpretation* by which an object appears to our consciousness.

Sides, aspects and profiles are only the start. Subjects also make sense of objects in presence and in absence. There is a difference between studying the thing before us (the present object) and holding it in memory or anticipation (the absent object). Phenomenology has its own ways of talking about these memories, anticipations and perceptions. It is a very thorough and pure project of *how* we make meaning out of an object.

My use of the word 'pure' becomes clearer when we move to the third principle.

(iii) A suspicion of culture and concepts

Phenomenology involves concentrated focusing and reflecting upon an object. To do this, phenomenologists argue, we must push out the meanings that we already hold – our preconceptions, presuppositions and assumptions. We must 'bracket' these out, and then, to the best of our ability, let the experience of the phenomenon speak to us at first hand. This is why we find Husserlian phenomenologists talking about 'primordial phenomena' or the 'phenomena in their unmediated manifestation'. Phenomenology is about the direct and immediate experience of objects *before* we start thinking about them and attributing meaning to them.

According to Husserl, phenomenology invites us to: 'set aside all previous habits of thought, see through and break down the mental barriers which these habits have set along the horizons of our thinking ... to learn to see what stands before our eyes' (Husserl, 1931: 43). Put more simply, phenomenology is about taking a fresh look at things, but in a conscious, deliberate, disciplined way. At the same time it privileges intuition. It is an endeavour to secure 'a pristine acquaintance with phenomena unadulterated by preconceptions' (Heron, 1992: 164). Another phenomenologist describes it thus: 'Phenomenology asks us not to take our received notions for granted but ... to call into question our whole culture, our manner of seeing the world' (Wolff, 1984: 192).

You will notice a theme emerging here – it is a sense that a pure perception of the world is somehow sullied or tainted, obscured or distorted by our preconceptions. Our culture – the meanings already given to us – get in the way of seeing.

This is almost the opposite of symbolic interactionism. Crotty (1998) is illuminating here. He presents symbolic interactionism as being 'for' culture, and phenomenology as being 'against' culture. They are two different ways of trying to see what is going on:

> Lying behind this attempt to put our culturally derived meanings in abeyance and renew culture in this radical fashion is a deeply rooted suspicion of culture and the understandings it imposes on us. ... Why be suspicious of culture? Surely we owe it our very humanness. Phenomenologists are happy to acknowledge that debt. They recognise that culture allows us to emerge from our immediate environment and reflect upon it. They agree that it is because of culture – our symbols, our meaning systems – that we know our past and can plan our future. But (culture) ... is also limiting. It sets us free but at the same time sets boundaries. It makes us human but in and through this particular culture, this special system of significant symbols, these meanings. In imposing these meanings, it is excluding others. And we should never lose sight of the fact that the particular set of meanings it imposes has come into being to serve particular interests and will harbour its own forms of oppression, manipulation and other forms of injustice ... Phenomenology is about saying 'No!' to the meaning system bequeathed to us. It is about setting that meaning system aside. (Crotty, 1998: 80–1)

Two implications follow:

- phenomenology is a *radical project* – it is about challenging a system of received meanings
- phenomenology has to be a *first-person project* – 'each of us must explore our *own* experience, not the experience of others: no one can take that step back to the things themselves on our behalf' (Crotty, 1998: 84).

It is because phenomenologists are cautious about culture that they are cautious about concepts. We all rely on concepts – we need to name things in order to define and classify. However, all too easily, our labels and categories displace what they stand for. Instead of pointing us to realities, concepts can obscure those realities that they were meant to illumine (Crotty, 1998: 84). Moreover, a concept, even where appositely applied, can never exhaust the fullness of a phenomenon.

Teachers deal with the inherent abstraction of concepts all the time. Our curricula and assessment schema are full of them. One motivation to engage in research can be to transcend or get behind these concepts that can 'stand in' for reality or mask the richness of the phenomenon.

Activity 19.7

(a) Take another look at Figure 19.4. Which of the three arrows seems best to suit Husserlian phenomenology?
(b) Look again at the three teachers in Figure 19.1. In what ways might Teachers B and C be anticipating aspects of a phenomenological approach?
(c) Think of some concepts that you regularly use in talking about your school organization, your subject curriculum or pupils' learning – for example, 'meeting', 'evidence', 'idea' or 'question'. What kinds of hidden realities might these concepts fail to express?

Our three teachers are finding themselves doing this naturally, but they could choose to do this in a much more deliberate, systematic and sustained way, too. They may find that phenomenology suits them.

Hermeneutics

Hermeneutics is by far the oldest of our three streams of thought. It is hard to say when it 'began'. The word really just means 'finding meaning', or the 'study of finding and conveying meaning', and has traditionally been associated with disciplined ways of inter-preting texts, especially biblical and literary texts. Some just use it as a synonym for interpretation. We see biblical scholars developing systematic approaches to hermeneu-tics around the time of the Reformation, for example when the trend towards translation of the Christian Bible led to a growing interest in managing ordinary people's interpreta-tion of the scriptures. But approaches to interpreting texts go back much further than this.

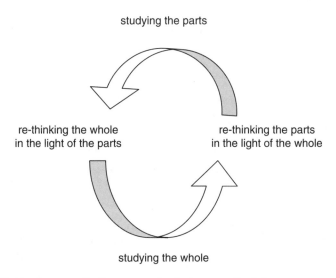

studying the parts

re-thinking the whole
in the light of the parts

re-thinking the parts
in the light of the whole

studying the whole

Figure 19.5 Working hermeneutically: an example of a hermeneutic circle

A key theme of hermeneutics, going back to the Greeks, is that of relating the parts to the whole, as shown in Figure 19.5. This is an example of a 'hermeneutic circle'. Teacher B, in Figure 19.1, is starting to work hermeneutically as she decides to relate parts and wholes in the pupil's text. She may not yet be doing this systematically, but she could certainly develop a method for doing this. There are many other kinds of herme-neutic circle, where different facets of human interpretation could be said to be moving in a cumulative, circular motion.

To complete our story here, we are simply going to look at what happened when hermeneutics met phenomenology in the work of Martin Heidegger (1889–1976). The full picture is extremely complex, so we are just going to touch on: (a) how his ideas relate to and transformed those discussed above; and (b) some implications of all this for how we might use *ourselves* in our own research.

Heidegger's *Being and Time* made a radical break with a central tenet of Western philosophical tradition since Descartes – the principle that the human mind is a mirror.

All positivist scientific enquiry assumes the notion that through observation we can gain an increasingly accurate *reflection* of the world. Heidegger challenged this idea of a mirror. He argued that our minds were designed for creative interpretation of the world, not for objective reflection of it.

If the mind interprets rather than reflects the world, then instead of striving for better and better methods to provide an ever more precise reflection of the world, we should be trying to improve our understanding of how interpretation itself works: 'For centuries the question has been: How do we know this to be true? Now, Heidegger is saying, "Why do we interpret the truth to be this?"' (Baronov, 2004: 123).

Dilthey had thought of the mind as a mirror. For Dilthey, all we are trying to do in social research is find a better way of conveying or representing the world. For Heidegger, this was quite wrong. To understand this, it is helpful (yet again) to go back to how these different thinkers defined human beings:

- Dilthey defined a human being as someone who creates meaningful things. Hermeneutics is a method to understand the meaning behind these things.
- Heidegger defined a human being as someone who interprets or makes sense of meaningful things.

But 'making sense of meaningful things' is just a definition of hermeneutics! Baronov captures the startling radicalism of this position:

> Therefore, Heidegger argues that hermeneutics is not some abstract method but simply a description of human nature, an account of what we do every day. There is no more need to teach a person the techniques of hermeneutics than to teach a fish to swim. (Baronov, 2004: 124)

What are the consequences of this line of thought for researching the social world?

(i) A consequence for the focus of the enquiry

Heidegger is not saying that there is therefore no need for systematic enquiry at all. He *is* arguing for a systematic reflection and analysis. But the focus of reflection is now upon *what it means to be a human, interpreting being*. Heidegger argues that Husserl was wrong to say that the essential structures of consciousness are based on some pre-existing rational, logical order. Instead, consciousness arises from human experience or 'being'. This is why Heidegger chooses to examine something called 'being-in-the-world'. The essential structures of consciousness are generated by a person's *lived experience* and it is that realm of lived experience that we need to study. This quest to find structures within lived experience involves systematic reflection and interpretation.

The focus of enquiry in Heidegger's existential phenomenology is thus rather different from that in Husserl's rationalist phenomenology.

(ii) A consequence for the role of subjectivity

In traditional forms of science, the conventions of enquiry require us to distance ourselves from the phenomena we observe. We must strive to ensure that no bias of any kind creeps into the observation process. Any such bias will weaken the results. Only by minimizing the effects of observer subjectivity, can we hope to approach accuracy. This kind of scientific analysis therefore strives for objectivity – a deliberate minimizing of the role of the observing subject.

But if the human mind only *interprets* the world, then all of this is turned on its head. True understanding can only proceed from full engagement with the phenomena under observation. So, according to Heidegger, *subjective interpretation* is the only road to understanding.

Here is an example of this Heideggerian notion applied to teachers' researching. (I have adapted this from a similar example in the very useful and clear work by Baronov (2004: 124)). Fred is a teacher with long experience of working with pupils who have specific learning difficulties regarding literacy. Freda has never worked with pupils who display such difficulties. They agree to spend a lesson together, working with such pupils. Afterwards, they sit and discuss it. Fred's perspective is biased by the many literacy difficulties that he has worked with and also by his close knowledge of these particular pupils. Freda's perspective is relatively objective; she has no similar prior knowledge to call on, neither of the pupils nor of this type of difficulty. Following our Heideggerian notion, Freda's views will be much less useful in developing shared understanding because she has little basis for subjective interpretation. Understanding emerges from one's subjective biases, not from trying to screen them out.

Thus, while subjectivity was important within Husserl's phenomenology – in that two-way sense explored earlier – with Heidegger, our subjectivity takes on even more importance.

Activity 19.8

Using the commentary on Figure 19.1 on pages 306–7, what themes can you detect in Teachers A, B and C that tie in with (a) Husserlian and (b) Heideggerian ideas about phenomenological enquiry?

Key ideas

Some understanding of three broad streams of thought – symbolic interactionism, phenomenology and hermeneutics – can help us to understand the forms that modern interpretive methodologies have taken. As we examine the ideas behind these methodologies, we can find principles that may guide us in choosing theories and approaches. Crucially, when researching our own practice, we need to be thoughtful about: (a) the complexity of the subjectivities we investigate; and (b) our own subjectivity as researchers – its role and value. These three streams of thought offer different ways of supporting this task.

None of these are positions I would advise you to pick up and rigidly follow. They are simply insights, ways of thinking about the world. At the very least, they will stimulate you to avoid taking certain things for granted ('objectivity is always good' – 'my own biases are a problem'). At best, they offer radical and exciting roads to systematic enquiry that are particularly valuable for teachers wishing to shine a research spotlight on themselves, on their actions towards pupils, and their own ways of thinking, feeling and being as teachers.

In their different ways, both Husserl and Heidegger remind us that we arrive at our investigations full of pre-conceived ideas and meanings – we layer these onto the way we frame our enquiries, the questions we ask, the goals we pursue. We are foolish to ignore this. Equally, we are short-sighted to imagine that it is necessarily a problem. We just have to know how to use it.

> We carry expectations within us and to an extent we make what we meet conform to those expectations. ... A raft of largely undetectable assumptions and preconceptions affects the way we perceive and behave in a place. Our cultural baggage – our memory – is weightless, but impossible to leave behind. (Macfarlane, 2003: 195)

What helps us to see the way can also get in the way. If you try to let your own cultural baggage and preconceptions go, stay humble about how far 'letting go' is actually possible. If, instead (or in addition), you try to make yourself the object of study, be systematic and be realistic about what you may attain. Look to the different intellectual streams of thought for personal inspiration and for insight into the various possible methodologies, but don't try to cling to one of them rigidly. Reflect and experiment, adapt and blend.

Reflective questions

1 Think about the nature and complexity of the phenomenon you want to examine. In particular, consider the different kinds of subjectivities you will be examining. How can the subjective world of other people – whether pupils or teachers – best be understood and represented?
2 When framing your project, consider the role of your own subjectivity. Is this something you want to push to one side as far as possible? If so, how will you do this? If not, how will you use your subjectivity and turn it into a positive condition for enquiry?

Further reading

Clandinin, D.J. and Connelly F.M. (2000) *Narrative Inquiry: Experience and Story in Qualitative Research*. San Franscisco, CA: Jossey Bass.

Creswell, J.W. (2012) *Qualitative Inquiry and Research Design: Choosing Among Five Traditions* (3rd edn). Thousand Oaks, CA: Sage.

Elliott, J. (2005) *Using Narrative in Social Research: Qualitative and Quantitative Approaches*. London: Sage.

Etherington, K. (2004) *Becoming a Reflexive Researcher: Using Our Selves in Research*. London: Jessica Kingsley.

Jasper, D. (2004) *A Short Introduction to Hermeneutics*. Louisville, KY: Westminster John Knox Press.

Moustakas, C. (1994) *Phenomenological Research Methods*. Thousand Oaks, CA: Sage.

CONCLUSION

This book is designed to help practitioners who are working in educational contexts and who want to extend and deepen their understanding of learning environments. We hope that the book will provide a way in to the ideas and methods of the existing extensive research literature. This literature is sometimes difficult to access practically and conceptually. So our book provides an introduction for the novice teacher during Initial Teacher Education as well as the more experienced teacher who wants to think more deeply about their practice and for students embarking on a Masters programme.

We started out by arguing that to research practice is just one dimension of a teacher's complex role, although it is a very important dimension which is often neglected. The plethora of recent studies about teacher 'quality' and 'excellence' are all agreed that knowledge of educational research and other evidence relevant to practices is an important dimension of teaching Knowledge of both how to use research and also how to generate research knowledge is vital to informing future directions and changes to practice in response to the changing world and changing learners. To this end we have provided tools to assist teachers to do just that.

Our first chapter encouraged teachers to be critical about what they do and about what policy makers ask them to do. We encouraged teachers to challenge some of the longstanding 'taken for granted' beliefs which pervade the education system throughout the world. In the first section we provided an introduction to how to access existing education literature together with the tools to sort, store and analyse this literature. We started to think about how to hone an appropriate research question, and how to undertake research with very young children.

In the second section we provided an introduction to the mechanics of carrying out a small-scale research project using the methods of professional researchers. We discussed how to collect data, taking into account the threats to the reliability and validity posed by each data collection method. We introduced modern pragmatic methods of data collection which would serve the classroom practitioner in their quest to better understand their own classrooms.

In the third section we went deeper and explained more precisely about the methodological issues that researchers need to think about in the process of generating their own knowledge about education and teaching in particular.

In the final section we ended with an extended philosophical discussion of the different ways of knowing about the world and the traditions that inform these approaches. These chapters offer a good introduction to these complex ideas and recommend other sources that can extend this understanding further.

Throughout, we have used recent examples of work carried out by our own students as part of their PGCE M-level work, we have included authentic examples our Masters research students' work, and published papers, to illustrate the points made in the book. The most pleasing outcome is that our book has contributed to the success of our own PGCE and Masters courses. Not only have students achieved work of distinction in their Masters degrees, several of them have had work published in peer-reviewed journals, thus disseminating their research more widely. These papers are cited in the text and are the strongest recommendation we could make to potential readers of this second edition.

We hope you enjoy researching your classroom!

Elaine Wilson
Cambridge, April 2012

GLOSSARY

Coding The process of breaking down data by assigning codes that offer interpretation of meaning/significance

Coding framework A structured outline of the codes to be applied to the analysis of data collected

Collaborative analysis The collaboration between interviewer and interviewee in interpreting the issues discussed during an interview

Conceptualization The background understanding of a topic, normally based on a literature review, that provides the rationale for the (need for, approach taken, etc.) current study

Confirmatory studies Research designed to test out well-formed ideas based on claims in previously published literature

Constant comparison A process (in grounded theory studies) of comparing data to codes and codes to data until the set of analytical codes is considered to adequately reflect the full data set

Context of discovery   How an idea came about: the 'creative' or sometimes seren-dipitous aspect of forming a hunch or conjecture

Context of justification   How an idea was tested to show that it is a reliable knowledge claim supported by rigorous data collection and analysis

Core variable   A grounded theory term for a variable identified as being the most significant in constructing theory to explain the research focus

Deductive analysis   The analysis of data according to pre-established themes

Disciplinary matrix   See **Paradigm**

Discourse   The communication of thought and words through written or spoken form

Discovery research   Research designed to explore an issue within a context where there is insufficient guidance from previous research to provide testable hypotheses

Display   A visual configuration that reveals the interrelationship between coded themes or contextual factors behind the data generated in a research study

Emergent design   A term from grounded theory describing how a research design is flexible and evolves in response to ongoing data collection and analysis

Epistemology   The study of the nature of knowledge, and how one can come to knowledge

Exploratory studies   Research undertaken in a poorly understood context where there is an insufficient basis to justify the testing of pre-formed hypotheses

External reliability   In qualitative research, it refers to the accuracy and consistency of the research as measured (hypothetically) by the extent to which another researcher doing the same research would reach similar conclusions

External validity   The extent of the generalizability of the findings beyond the specific context of the study

Fallibilism   A view that all knowledge claims are open to revision and cannot be considered absolutely true

Falsification   The process of testing an idea by setting up studies that could show it to be wrong

Focus group interview   A group interview, where the researcher is primarily interested in interactions within the group and which produces insights and data that can be linked to other forms of data collected in a study, such as individual interviews and questionnaires

Generalization   The process of making general claims about e.g. 'teachers' or 'modern language teachers' or 'teachers of top sets', etc., rather than about 'the specific teachers involved in this study'

Grounded theory   A set of procedures designed to offer a rigorous means of building well-supported theory in exploratory/discovery research

Hawthorne effect   The inclination of respondents to give answers which they think their interviewer would like them to give

Hypotheses   Claims that are specific enough to be tested and can in principle be falsified

Hypothetico-deductive method   A method proceeding by a process of conjecture and refutation (setting up hypotheses, and testing them)

Idiographic research   Studies that focus on the specifics of the individual case, and see the individual as a valid focus of research

Immersion   The process (especially in grounded theory studies) of working closely with a data set to allow hunches/hypotheses to 'emerge' in conscious awareness

Induction   The (logically untenable) process of generalizing from specific cases

Inductive analysis   The analysis of themes in data as they emerge during the process of analysis

Internal reliability   In qualitative research, this refers to the accuracy and consistency of the research as measured by the extent to which the same research conducted again by the same researcher would lead to similar conclusions

Internal validity   This refers to the credibility of a study's findings by examining the extent to which a study investigates what it claims to investigate

Interpretivist research   Research that looks to explore informants' ideas and experiences, and acknowledges the active interpretation of ideas

In-vivo codes   Labels which consist of words or phrases used by one or more of the respondents

Long-term involvement   The strategy of extended fieldwork over time, allowing the researcher to have a feel for the different influences on the phenomenon being studied and to identity the specific elements in the situation that are most relevant to the investigation

Looking for negative evidence   Looking for evidence that contradicts the main findings in your study

Matrix   A display format, with defined rows and columns, that links two sets of variables through the coded data generated by the analysis

Nomothetic research   Studies concerned with establishing general laws

Objective knowledge   A term used for 'scientific' knowledge, i.e. knowledge that is considered independent of the observer

Online analysis   The process whereby an interviewer reflects on responses given to questions during an interview and uses this to generate follow-up questions

Ontology   The study of the nature of the things that exist in the world, e.g. which entities (if any) objectively exist in the world independently of observers

Open codes   Descriptive labels attached to chunks of text when analysing a transcript

Open coding   Coding that uses 'in-vivo' codes based on the data, rather than applying a preconceived analytical framework

Paradigm (or disciplinary matrix)   A term used to describe the norms of a field of study in which certain researchers work, concerning, inter alia, beliefs about the nature of what is being studied, the kind of knowledge that is possible, and suitable procedures for coming to knowledge and reporting it

Positivism   Now usually taken to mean a belief that appropriate ('scientific') procedures can lead to objective knowledge that is not open to revision

Post-positivism   A term applied to the various models of science that see it as encompassing procedures for developing objective knowledge that can be considered reliable, but which are never 'water-tight' and so are open to revision

Problem of induction   The problem that induction is (a) needed to make assured generalizations, but (b) logically non-viable

Progressive research programmes   Programmes of research studies that build upon each other in ways that are considered to make progress within a post-positivist perspective where all scientific methodologies are considered fallible

Semi-structured interview   This includes predetermined questions and topics to be covered, but also allows the interviewer to be flexible and to follow up new ideas and issues that emerge during the interview

Substantive theory   A theory based upon the study of specific contexts (i.e. not a general theory)

Thematic codes   Inferential labels grouping different open codes in relation to interpretation

Theoretical sampling   A process (in grounded theory studies) of using ongoing data analysis to direct decisions about further data collection

Theoretical saturation   The point (especially in grounded theory studies) when further data collection will not provide any additional input to the building of theory

Theoretical sensitivity   The state of mind to be developed in grounded theory studies that allows the analyst to be open to the possible significance of data for suggesting hunches/hypotheses to be tested by constant comparisons and/or theoretical sampling

Theory   A coherent set of propositions that collectively models or explains a phenomenon of interest

Theory-laden observations   The way in which what we see and hear, etc. is always interpreted in terms of our existing conceptual frameworks for making sense of the world

Triangulation   Drawing conclusions on the basis of different sources of information, or of different methods of data collection, or from different investigators in the same study

REFERENCES

Altrichter, H., Posch, P. and Somekh, B. (2007) *Teachers Investigate Their Work* (2nd edn). London: Routledge.

Atkinson, M., Springate, I., Johnson, F. and Halsey, K. (2007) *Inter-school Collaboration: A Literature Review*. Slough: NFER.

Baert, P. (1998) *Social Theory in the Twentieth Century*. Cambridge: Polity Press.

Bamford, G.S. (1989) 'Popper, refutation and "avoidance" of refutation'. PhD thesis, University of Queensland.

Barbour, R. and Schostak, J. (2004) 'Interviewing and focus groups', in B. Somekh and C. Lewin (eds), *Research Methods in the Social Sciences*. London: Sage. pp. 41–8.

Baronov, D. (2004) *Conceptual Foundations of Social Research*. Boulder, CO: Paradigm Publishers.

Bassey, M. (1999) *Case Study Research in Educational Settings*. Buckingham: Open University Press.

Becker, H. (1963) *Outsiders: Studies in the Sociology of Deviance*. New York: Free Press.

BERA (2004). *Revised Ethical Guidelines for Educational Research*. Macclesfield: British Educational Research Association. Available at: http://www.bera.ac.uk/publications/ethical-guidelines.

Biddle, B.J. and Anderson, D.S. (1986) 'Theory, methods, knowledge and research on teaching', in M.C. Wittrock (ed.), *Handbook of Research on Teaching* (3rd edn). New York: Macmillan. pp. 230–52.

Biesta, G.J.J. and Burbles, N. (2003) *Pragmatism and Educational Research*. Lanham, MD: Rowman and Littlefield.

Blaikie, H. (2000) *Designing Social Research: The Logic of Anticipation*. London: Polity Press.

Blumer, H. (1969) *Symbolic Interactionism: Perspective and Method*. Englewood Cliffs, NJ: Prentice Hall.

Boaler, J., Wiliam, D. and Brown, M. (2000) 'Students' experiences of ability grouping: Disaffection, polarisation and the construction of failure', *British Educational Research Journal*, 26(5): 631–48.

Bond, T. (2005) 'Researching education: A question of trust?' Keynote lecture given on the Med course, Faculty of Education, University of Cambridge, 2 March.

Boomer, G., Lester, N., Onore, C. and Cook, J. (eds) (1992) *Negotiating the Curriculum: Educating for the 21st Century*. London: The Falmer Press.

Bourne, J. and Moon, B. (1995) 'A question of ability?', in B. Moon and A. Shelton Mayes (eds), *Teaching and Learning in the Secondary School*. London: Routledge.

Breakwell, G. (2006) 'Interviewing methods', in G. Breakwell, S.M. Hammond, C. Fife-Schaw and J.A. Smith (eds), *Research Methods in Psychology* (3rd edn). London: Sage. pp. 232–53.

Brown, S. and McIntyre, D. (1993) *Making Sense of Teaching*. Buckingham: Open University Press.

Burke, C. and Grosvenor, I. (2003) *The School I'd Like: Children and Young People's Reflections on an Education for the 21st Century*. London: Routledge.

Calissendorff, M. (2006) 'Understanding the learning style of pre-school children learning the violin', *Music Education Research*, 8(1): 83–96.

Capel, S., Zwozdiak-Myers, P. and Lawrence, J. (2007) 'The transfer of pupils from primary to secondary school: A case study of a foundation subject – physical education', *Research in Education*, 77: 14–30.

Carr, W. and Kemmis, S. (1986) *Becoming Critical: Education, Knowledge and Action Research*. Lewes: Falmer.

Carr, W. and Kemmis, S. (2009) 'Educational action research: A critical approach', in Noffke, S. and Somekh, B. (eds), *The Sage Handbook of Educational Action Research*. London: Sage.

Chaplain, R. (2003) *Teaching without Disruption in the Primary School: A Multilevel Model for Managing Pupil Behaviour in Primary Schools* (1st edn). London: Routledge.

Chaplain, R. and Freeman, A. (1994) *Caring Under Pressure*. London: David Fulton.

Charmaz, K.C. (2012) *Constructing Grounded Theory: A Practical Guide through Qualitative Analysis* (2nd edn). London: Sage.

Cisneros-Puebla, C.A. (2004) 'Juliet Corbin: To learn to think conceptually', *Forum: Qualitative Social Research*, 5(3), Article 32. Available at: http://www.qualitative-research.net/index.php/fqs/article/view/550

Clark, A. and Moss, P. (2001) *Listening to Young Children: The Mosaic Approach*. London: National Children's Bureau.

Cochran-Smith, M. and Lytle, S.L. (2009) 'Teacher research as stance', in Noffke, S. and Somekh, B. (eds) *The Sage Handbook of Educational Action Research*. London: Sage.

Cohen, L., Manion, L. and Morrison, K. (2000) *Research Methods in Education* (5th edn). London: RoutledgeFalmer.

Cotton, D.R.E. (2006) 'Teaching controversial environmental issues: Neutrality and balance in the reality of the classroom', *Educational Research*, 48(2): 223–41.

Cremin, H. and Thomas, G. (2005) 'Maintaining underclasses via contrastive judgement: Can inclusive education ever happen?', *British Journal of Educational Studies*, 53(4): 431–46.

Cremin, H., Mason, C. and Busher, H. (2011) 'Problematising pupil voice using visual methods: Findings from a study of engaged and disaffected pupils in an urban secondary school', *British Educational Research Journal*, 37(4): 585–603.

Creswell, J.W. (2009) *Research Design: Qualitative, Quantitative, and Mixed Methods Approaches* (3rd edn). London: Sage.

Creswell, J.W., Clark, V.L.P., Gutmann, M.L. and Hanson, W.E. (2010) 'Advanced mixed methods research designs', in A. Tashakkori and C.B. Teddlie (eds), *SAGE Handbook of Mixed Methods in Social & Behavioral Research* (2nd edn). Thousand Oaks, CA: Sage. pp. 209–40.

Crotty, M. (1998) *The Foundations of Social Research: Meaning and Perspective in the Research Process.* London: Sage.

Denscombe, M. (2010) *The Good Research Guide* (3rd edn). Buckingham: Open University Press.

Desimone, L., Porter, A.C., Garet, M.S., Yoon, K.S. and Birman, B.F. (2002) 'Effects of professional development on teachers' instruction: Results from a three-year longitudinal study', *Educational Evaluation and Policy Analysis*, 24(2): 81–112.

DfEE (1997) *Excellence in Schools*. London: The Stationery Office.

Donohoe, C., Topping, K. and Hannah, E. (2012) 'The impact of an online intervention (Brainology) on the mindset and resiliency of secondary school pupils: A preliminary mixed methods study', *Educational Psychology*, 32(5): 641–55.

Dorion, K. (2009) 'Science through drama: A multiple case exploration of the characteristics of drama activities used in secondary science lessons', *International Journal of Science Education*, 31(16): 2247–70.

Dunkin, M. (1996) 'Types of errors in synthesizing research in education', *Review of Educational Research*, 66(2): 87–97.

Elliott, J. (1991) *Action Research for Educational Change*. Buckingham: Open University Press.

Elliott, J. (2006) *Reflecting Where the Action Is*. London: Routledge.

Elliott, J. (2009) 'Building educational theory through action research', in S. Noffke and B. Somekh (eds), *The Sage Handbook of Educational Action Research*. London: Sage.

Ellis, R. and Barkhuizen, G. (2005) *Analysing Learner Language*. Oxford: Oxford University Press.

Evans, M. (2009) 'Using stimulated recall to investigate pupils' thinking about online bilingual communication: Code-switching and pronominal address in L2 French', *British Educational Research Journal*, 35(3): 469–80.

Fenstermacher, G. and Richardson, V. (2005) 'On making determinations of quality in teaching', *Teachers College Record*, 107(1): 186–213.

Feyerabend, P. (1987) *Farewell to Reason*. London: Verso.

Flick, U. (2002) *An Introduction to Qualitative Research*. London: Sage.

Flinders, D.J. (1992) 'In search of ethical guidance: Constructing a basis for dialogue', *Qualitative Studies in Education*, 5(2): 101–15.

Flutter, J. and Rudduck, J. (2004) *Consulting Pupils: What's In It for Schools?* Abingdon: Routledge.

Frost, D. (2003) 'Teacher leadership: Towards a research agenda', a paper within the symposium Leadership for Learning: the Cambridge Network, at the International Congress for School Effectiveness and Improvement, Sydney, Australia, January. Free download available from the Teacher Leadership website: http://www.leadership forlearning.org.uk/tl-home/

Fry, H., Ketteridge S. and Marshall, S. (1999) *A Handbook for Teaching and Learning in Higher Education*. Glasgow: Kogan Page.

Galton, M., Gray, J. and Rudduck, J. (1999) *The Impact of School Transitions and Transfers on Pupils' Progress and Attainment* (Research Report No. 131). Norwich: DfEE.

Geertz, C. (1973) *The Interpretation of Cultures*. New York: Basic Books.

Giddens, A. (1984) *The Constitution of Society: Outline of the Theory of Structuration*. Cambridge: Polity Press.

Glaser, B.G. (1978) *Theoretical Sensitivity: Advances in the Methodology of Grounded Theory*. Mill Valley, CA: The Sociology Press.

Glaser, B.G. (2002) 'Conceptualization: On theory and theorizing using grounded theory', *International Journal of Qualitative Methods*, 1(2), Article 3. Available at: http://www.ualberta.ca/~iiqm/backissues/1_2Final/pdf/glaser.pdf

Glaser, B.G. and Holton, J. (2004) 'Remodeling grounded theory', *Forum: Qualitative Social Research*, 5(2), Article 4. Available at: http://www.qualitative-research.net/index.php/fqs/article/view/607/1315

Glaser, B.G. and Strauss, A.L. (1967) *The Discovery of Grounded Theory: Strategies for Qualitative Research*. New York: Aldine de Gruyter.

Goffman, E. (1970) *Strategic Interaction*. Oxford: Basil Blackwell.

Habermas, J. (1987) *The Theory of Communicative Action, Volume 2: The Critique of Functionalist Reason*. Oxford: Polity.

Hamel, J. (1993) *Case Study Method*. Newbury Park, CA: Sage.

Hammersley, M. (1985) 'Ethnography: What it is and what it offers', in S. Hegarty and P. Evans (eds), *Research and Evaluation Methods in Special Education*. Philadelphia, PA: NFER-Nelson.

Hammersley, M. (1993) *Controversies in Classroom Research* (2nd edn). Buckingham: Open University Press. pp. x–xxii.

Hammersley, M (2004) 'Action research: A contradiction in terms?', *Oxford Review of Education*, 30(2): 165–81.

Harry, B., Sturges, K.M. and Klingner, J.K. (2005) 'Mapping the process: An exemplar of process and challenge in grounded theory analysis', *Educational Researcher*, 34(2): 3–13.

Hart, S., Dixon, A., Drummond, M. and McIntyre, D. (2004) *Learning Without Limits*. Maidenhead: Open University Press/McGraw-Hill.

Hay, C. (2002) *Political Analysis: A Critical Introduction*. Basingstoke: Palgrave.

Hayes, B., Hindle, S. and Withington, P. (2007) 'Strategies for developing positive behaviour management: Teacher behaviour outcomes and attitudes to the change process', *Educational Psychology in Practice*, 23(2): 161–75.

Heron, J. (1992) *Feeling and Personhood: Psychology in Another Key*. London: Sage.

Herr, K. and Anderson, G.L. (2005) *The Action Research Dissertation: A Guide for Students and Faculty*. Thousand Oaks, CA: Sage.

Hidi, S., Berndorff, D. and Ainley, M. (2002) 'Children's argument writing, interest and self efficacy: An intervention study', *Learning and Instruction*, 12: 429–46.

Homan, R. (1991) *The Ethics of Social Research*. Harlow: Longman.

Huberman, A. and Miles, M.B. (1998) 'Data management and analysis methods', in N. Denzin and Y. Lincoln (eds), *Collecting and Interpreting Qualitative Materials*. Thousand Oaks, CA: Sage.

Husserl, E. (1931) *Ideas: General Introduction to Pure Phenomenology*. London: Allen and Unwin.

Ivens, J. (2007) 'The development of a happiness measure in school children', *Educational Psychology in Practice*, 23(3): 221–39.

Jensen, J. and Rodgers, R. (2001) 'Cumulating the intellectual gold of case study technique', *PAR*, March/April: 235–46.

Johnson, A.R. (2003) http://www.ar-johnson.com/index.html

Kemmis, S. (2007) Opening address for the Spanish Collaborative Action Research Network (CARN) Conference, University of Valladolid, 18–20 October.

Kemmis, S. and McTaggart, R. (eds) (1988) *The Action Research Planner* (3rd edn). Geelong: Deakin University Press.

Kemmis, S. and McTaggart, R. (1990) *The Action Research Planner*. Geelong: Deakin University Press.

Kemmis, S. and McTaggart, R. (2005) 'Participatory action research: Communicative action and the public sphere', in N. Denzin and Y. Lincoln (eds), *Handbook of Qualitative Research* (3rd edn). Thousand Oaks, CA: Sage.

Kuhn, T.S. (1996) *The Structure of Scientific Revolutions* (3rd edn). Chicago, IL: University of Chicago. (First edition published in 1962.)

Kvale, S. (1996) *InterViews: An Introduction to Qualitative Research Interviewing*. London: Sage.

Lakatos, I. (1970) 'Falsification and the methodology of scientific research programmes', in I. Lakatos and A. Musgrove (eds), *Criticism and the Growth of Knowledge*. Cambridge: Cambridge University Press. pp. 91–196.

Lakatos, I. (1978) 'Introduction: Science and pseudoscience', in *The Methodology of Scientific Research Programmes*, Philosophical Papers, Volume 1. Cambridge: Cambridge University Press. pp. 1–7.

Lamnek, S. (2005) *Qualitative Sozialforschung*. Basel: Beltz PVU.

Levinson, D. (1978) *The Seasons of a Man's Life*. New York: Ballantine.

Lewis, A. (1992) 'Group child interviews as a research tool', *British Educational Research Journal*, 18(4): 413–21.

Lieblich, A., Tuval-Maschich, R. and Zilber, T. (1998) *Narrative Research: Reading Analysis and Interpretation*. Thousand Oaks, CA: Sage.

Lincoln, Y.S. and Guba, G. (1985) *Naturalistic Inquiry*. London: Sage.

Lipton, P. (2007) 'Writing philosophy', Department of History & Philosophy of Science, University of Cambridge. Available at: http://www.hps.cam.ac.uk/research/wp.html (accessed April 2012).

MacBeath, J. and McGlynn, A. (2002) *Self-evaluation: What's In It for Schools?* Abingdon: Routledge.

MacBeath, J., Rudduck, J. and Myers, K. (2003) *Consulting Pupils: A Toolkit for Teachers*. Cambridge: Pearson Publishing.

Macfarlane, R. (2003) *Mountains of the Mind: The History of a Fascination*. London: Granta.

Maloney, J.(2007) 'Children's role and use of evidence in science', *British Educational Research Journal*, 33(3): 371–401.

Martin, S. (2007) 'Interactive whiteboards and talking books', *Literacy*, 41(1): 26–34.

Maxwell, J.A. (2005) *Qualitative Research Design: An Interactive Approach*. London: Sage.

McIntyre, D. (2005) 'Bridging the gap between research and practice', *Cambridge Journal of Education*, 35(3): 357–82.

McKernan, J. (1991) *Curriculum Action Research: A Handbook of Methods and Resources for the Reflective Practitioner*. London: Kogan Page.

McMillan, J.H. and Schumacher, S. (2009) *Research in Education: Evidence-Based Inquiry* (7th edn). London: Pearson Education.

Mead, G.H. (1934) *Mind, Self and Society*. Chicago, IL: University of Chicago Press.

Measelle, J.R., Ablow, J.C., Cowan, P.A. and Cowan, C.P. (1998) 'Assessing young children's views of their academic, social, and emotional lives: An evaluation of the self-perception scales of the Berkeley Puppet Interview', *Child Development*, 69(6): 1556–76.

Measor, L. and Woods, P. (1991) 'Breakthrough and blockage in ethnographic research: Contrasting experiences during the Changing Schools project', in G. Walford (ed.), *Doing Educational Research*. London: Routledge. pp. 59–81.

Medawar, P.B. (1990) *The Threat and the Glory*. New York: HarperCollins.

Mercer, N. (2000) *Words and Minds: How We Use Language Together*. London: Routledge.

Miles, M.B. and Huberman, A.M. (1994) *Qualitative Data Analysis*. Thousand Oaks, CA: Sage.

Millar, R. and Osborne, J. (eds) (1998) 'Beyond 2000: Science education for the future'. The report of a seminar series funded by the Nuffield Foundation. Published by King's College London, School of Education.

Nardi, E. and Steward, S. (2003) 'Is mathematics T.I.R.E.D? A profile of quiet disaffection in the secondary mathematics classrooms', *British Educational Research Journal*, 29(3): 345–66.

Newby, L. and Winterbottom, M. (2011) 'Can research homework provide a vehicle for assessment for learning in science lessons?', *Educational Review*, 63(3): 275–90.

Noyes, A. (2004) 'Video diary: A method for exploring learning dispositions', *Cambridge Journal of Education*, 34(2): 193–204.

NRC (National Research Council) (2002) *Scientific Research in Education*. Washington, DC: National Academies Press.

Nunan, D. (1992) *Research Methods in Language Learning*. Cambridge: Cambridge University Press.

O'Brien, C. (2007) 'Peer devaluation in British secondary schools: Young people's comparison of group-based and individual-based bullying', *Educational Research*, 49(3): 297–324.

O'Leary, Z. (2005) *Researching Real-world Problems: A Guide to Methods of Inquiry*. London: Sage.

Office for Standards in Education (Ofsted) (2003) *Ofsted Subject Reports Series 2001/2002: Geography in Secondary Schools*. Available at: http://www.ofsted.gov.uk/resources/annual-report-200102-ofsted-subject-reports-secondary

Oliver, P. (2003) *A Student's Guide to Research Ethics*. Maidenhead: Open University Press/McGraw-Hill.

Oppenheim, A.N. (1992) *Questionnaire Design, Interviewing and Attitude Measurement*. London: Pinter.

Palmer, R.E. (1969) *Hermeneutics*. Evanston, IL: Northwestern University Press.

Pedder, D. (2006) 'Are small classes better? Understanding relationships between class size, classroom processes and pupils' learning', *Oxford Review of Education*, 32(2): 213–34.

Pedder, D. and McIntyre, D. (2006) 'Pupil consultation: The importance of social capital', *Educational Review*, 58(2): 145.

Phillips, D.C. (2005) 'The contested nature of empirical educational research (and why philosophy of education offers little help)', *Journal of Philosophy of Education*, 39(4): 577–97.

Phillips, D.C. and Burbules, N.C. (2000) *Postpostivism and Educational Research*. Oxford: Rowman & Littlefield.

Plaut, S. (2006) 'I just don't get it: students' conceptions of confusion and implications for learning in the high school English classroom', *Curriculum Inquiry*, 36(4): 391–421.

Popper, K.R. (1959) *The Logic of Scientific Discovery*. London: Hutchinson. (Original German edition published in 1934.)

Pring, R. (2000) *Philosophy of Educational Research*. London: Continuum.

Pyecha, J. (1988) *A Case Study of the Application of Noncategorical Special Education in Two States*. Chapel Hill, NC: Research Triangle Institute.

Reynolds, D. (1991) 'Doing educational research in Treliw', in G. Walford (ed.), *Doing Educational Research*. London: Routledge. pp. 193–209.

Robson, C. (2002) *Real World Research: A Resource for Social Scientists and Practitioner-researchers* (2nd edn). Oxford: Blackwell.

Rogers, C. (2002) 'Seeing student learning: Teacher change and the role of reflection', *Harvard Educational Review*, 12(2): 230–9.

Rubin, K.H., Bukowski, W.M. and Laursen, B. (2011) *Handbook of Peer Interactions, Relationships, and Groups*. New York: Guilford Press.

Rudduck, J. (1991) *Innovation and Change: Developing Involvement and Understanding*. Milton Keynes: Open University Press.

Rudduck, J. (2005) 'Pupil voice is here to stay!' Qualifications and Curriculum Agency. Available at: http://www.serviceschoolsmobilitytoolkit.com/resourcedownloads/staffroom/bpv_theneedtoinvolvepupilvoice.pdf

Rudduck, J. and Hopkins, D. (eds) (1985) *Research as a Basis for Teaching: Readings from the Work of Lawrence Stenhouse*. London: Heinemann.

Rudduck, J. and McIntyre, D. (2007) *Improving Learning through Consulting Pupils*. London: Routledge.

Rudduck, J., Chaplain, R. and Wallace, G. (1995) *School Improvement: What Can Pupils Tell Us?* Abingdon: Routledge.

Schagen, S. and Kerr, D. (1999) *Bridging the Gap? The National Curriculum and Progression from Primary to Secondary School.* Slough: NFER.

Schmuck, R.A. and Schmuck, P. (2000) *Group Processes in the Classroom* (8th edn). New York: McGraw-Hill.

Schön, D. (1983) *The Reflective Practitioner: How Professionals Think in Action*. London: Temple Smith.

Schwandt, T.A. (2001) *Dictionary of Qualitative Inquiry* (2nd edn). Thousand Oaks, CA: Sage.

Searle, J. (2007) *Freedom and Neurobiology: Reflections on Free Will, Language, and Political Power*. New York: Columbia Press.

Seedhouse, D. (1998a) *Ethics: The Heart of Healthcare*. Chichester: Wiley.

Seedhouse, D. (1998b) Ethical grid. Available at: http://www.priory.com/images/ethicgrid.jpg (accessed 21 May 2007).

Shemilt, D. (2000) 'The Caliph's Coin: The currency of narrative frameworks in history teaching', in P.N. Stearns, P. Seixas and S. Wineburg (eds), *Knowing, Teaching and Learning History: National and International Perspectives*. New York: New York University Press.

Silverman, D. (2010) *Interpreting Qualitative Data* (3rd edn). London: Sage.

Small, R. (2001) 'Codes are not enough: What philosophy can contribute to the ethics of educational research', *Journal of Philosophy of Education*, 35(3): 387–405.

Smyth, J. and Fasoli, L. (2007) 'Climbing over the rocks in the road to student engagement and learning in a challenging high school in Australia', *Educational Research*, 49(3) 273–95.

Sokolowski, R. (2000) *Introduction to Phenomenology*. Cambridge: Cambridge University Press.

Somekh, B. (2005) *Action Research: A Methodology for Change and Development*. Maidenhead: McGraw-Hill.

Spence, S. (1980) *Social Skills Training with Children and Adolescents: A Counsellor's Manual*. Windsor: NFER-Nelson.

Stake, R.E. (1995) *The Art of Case Study Research*. Thousand Oaks, CA: Sage.

Strauss, A. and Corbin, J. (1998) *Basics of Qualitative Research: Techniques and Procedures for Developing Grounded Theory*. Thousand Oaks, CA: Sage.

Swann, J. (2003) 'How science can contribute to the improvement of educational practice', *Oxford Review of Education*, 29(2): 253–68.

Taber, K.S. (1998) 'An alternative conceptual framework from chemistry education', *International Journal of Science Education*, 20(5): 597–608.

Taber, K.S. (2000) 'Case studies and generalisability – grounded theory and research in science education', *International Journal of Science Education*, 22(5): 469–87.

Taber, K.S. (2006) 'Beyond constructivism: The progressive research programme into learning science', *Studies in Science Education*, 42: 125–84.

Taber, K.S. (2007) *Classroom-based Research and Evidence-based Practice: A Guide for Teachers and Students*. London: Sage.

Taber, K.S. (2008) 'Towards a curricular model of the nature of science', *Science & Education*, 17(2–3): 179–218.

Thomas, G. (2010) *How To Do Your Research Project*. London: Sage.

Thomas, G. and James, D. (2006) 'Reinventing grounded theory: Some questions about theory, ground and discovery', *British Educational Research Journal*, 32(6): 767–95.

Thomson, P. (2008) *Doing Visual Research with Children and Young People*. London: Routledge.

Thomson, P. and Gunter, H. (2006) 'From "consulting pupils" to "pupils as researchers": A situated case narrative', *British Educational Research Journal*, 32: 839–56.

Timperley, H. (2012) *Using Evidence in the Classroom for Professional Learning*. Available at: http://www.education.auckknd.ac.NZ/uoa/helen-timperley. (accessed August 2012).

Timperley, H., Wilson, A., Barrar, H. and Fung, I. (2007) Teacher Professional Learning and Development: Best Evidence Synthesis Iteration. Available at: http://www.education counts.govt.nz/topics/BES

Tsafos, V. (2009) 'Teacher–student negotiation in an action research project', *Educational Action Research*, 17(2): 197–211.

Vaillant, G. (2002) *Aging Well*. Boston: Little, Brown & Co.

Vygotsky, L. (1986) *Thought and Language*. London: MIT Press. (First published in Russian in 1934.)

Wall, K. (2008) 'Understanding metacognition through the use of pupil view templates: Pupil views of Learning to Learn', *Thinking Skills and Creativity*, 3(1): 23–33.

Wall, K. and Higgins, S. (2006) 'Facilitating metacognitive talk: A research and learning tool', *International Journal of Research & Method in Education*, 29(1): 39–53.

Wall, K., Higgins, S. and Packard, E. (2007) *Talking About Learning: Using Templates to Find Out Pupil's Views*. Devon: Southgate.

Whewell, W. (1976) *History of the Inductive Science* (3rd edn). Hildesheim: Georg Olms Verlag. (First published in 1857.)

Whitehead, J. and McNiff, J. (2006) *Action Research Living Theory*. London: Sage. http://www.action research.net/

Wiliam, D. and Bartholomew, H. (2004) 'It's not which school but which set you're in that matters: The influence of ability grouping practices on students' progress in mathematics', *British Educational Research Journal*, 30(2): 279–93.

Wilson, E. and Demetriou, H. (2007) 'New teacher learning: Substantive knowledge and contextual factors', *Curriculum Journal*, 18(3): 213–29. Available at: http://www.tandfonline.com/doi/abs/10.1080/09585170701589710

Wolff, K.H. (1984) 'Surrender-and-catch and phenomenology', *Human Studies*, 7(2): 191–2.

Wyse, D. (2006) *The Good Writing Guide for Education Students* (2nd edn). London: Sage.

Yin, R. (2008) *Case Study Research: Design and Methods* (4th edn). Beverly Hills, CA: Sage.

Yin, R. and Moore, G. (1988) 'Lessons on the utilization of research from nine case experiences in the natural hazards field', *Knowledge, Technology and Policy*, 1(3): 25–44.

Ziman, J. (1991) *Reliable Knowledge: An Exploration of the Grounds for Belief in Science*. Cambridge: Cambridge University Press.

Zindler, R. (2003) *Trouble in Paradise: A study of who is included in an inclusion classroom*. Available at: http://teachersnetwork.org/TNLI/research/achieve/Rachel%20Zindler%20Action%research%revision%20082203.pdf (accessed August 2012).

INDEX

Added to a page number 'f' denotes a figure, 't' denotes a table and 'g' denotes glossary.